IDEA TO SCRIPT

Storytelling for Today's Media

STUART HYDE

San Francisco State University

Boston   New York   San Francisco
Mexico City   Montreal   Toronto   London   Madrid   Munich   Paris
Hong Kong   Singapore   Tokyo   Cape Town   Sydney

Series Editor: *Molly Taylor*
Editorial Assistant: *Michael Kish*
Marketing Manager: *Mandee Eckersley*
Production Editor: *Michelle Limoges*
Editorial Production Service: *Colophon*
Compositor: *Galley Graphics, Ltd.*
Composition and Prepress Buyer: *Linda Cox*
Manufacturing Buyer: *JoAnne Sweeney*
Cover Designer: *Kristen Mose-Libon*

For related titles and support materials, visit our online catalog at www.ablongman.com.

Library of Congress Cataloging-in-Publication Data

Hyde, Stuart Wallace
   Idea to script : storytelling for today's media / Stuart Hyde.
      p.   cm.
   Includes bibliographical references and index.
   ISBN 0-205-34404-6 (alk. paper)
      1. Television authorship.   2. Radio authorship.   I. Title.
PN1992.7 .H93 2003
808.2′25—dc21
                                                    2002026119

Printed in the United States of America

10 9 8 7 6 5 4 3 2 1   VHG 06 05 04 03 02

To My Teachers

CONTENTS

PART TWO

ACKNOWLEDGMENTS

The introduction of *Idea to Script* reads "to my teachers." Throughout the struggle that culminated in this book, I've felt a need to acknowledge my enormous debt to those who helped shape the person I became. Even though their names won't be known to you, I'm sure you'll find their lessons familiar because you most likely have similar obligations to acknowledge.

Kindergarten: Miss Hough, who cast me as a frog in a class play. I had only one line, "ribbit," repeated throughout the play, but she introduced me to the magic of theatre. It was years before I realized that teaching is a performing art.

Junior High School: W. G. Anderson, Speech, who conveyed to his students a reverence for the beauty of language and articulate speech.

High School: Maurice Reetz, Biology, who made me realize that teaching isn't about answering questions–it's about inspiring students to search for answers. Mr. Robert Rees, Drama and Radio Performance, who encouraged me to become a writer. He demonstrated to me that teachers should seek each student's unique potential and encourage its development.

Graduate School: Mr. Dan Mendelowitz, Art History, who taught me that teaching has everything to do with inspiring students and nothing at all to do with issuing grades.

TO TEACH IS TO LEARN TWICE

I didn't invent this expression—I found it in a fortune cookie. I want to acknowledge the vast amount of learning I've received from students; the fortune cookie says it all in six words. Over the years, I have come to understand that unless a person we call a "teacher" makes it a priority to learn from those we call "students," something's wrong in the equation.

Many stories in *Idea to Script* were written by students. These students and hundreds of others over the decades were engaged with me in a reciprocal teaching-learning dialogue. They graciously granted permission to include their writings in this text. Their scripts are identified throughout by an asterisk (*) after their names.

OTHER TEACHERS WHO MADE SIGNIFICANT CONTRIBUTIONS TO *IDEA TO SCRIPT*

This book has immensely benefitted by the contributions of many professional writers, critics, and commentators, most of whom asked for nothing but a copy of the book in return. These contributors are listed in the order in which their writings appear in *Idea to Script*.

Joan Ryan, award-winning columnist for the *San Francisco Chronicle,* and author of *Little Girls in Pretty Boxes: The Making and Breaking of Elite Gymnasts and Figure Skaters*

Eric Poole. The recipient of nearly fifty major awards, including CLIO, Sunny, American Advertising Federation, New York Festival, and London International Festival awards.

Richard Rodriguez. Recipient of a 1997 George Foster Peabody Award for his NewsHour Essays on American life. Other awards include the Frankel Medal from the National Endowment for the Humanities and the International Journalism Award from the World Affairs Council of California.

Bob MacKenzie. Feature reporter for KTVU, Oakland. Bob has received thirteen local Emmys, membership in the Television Academy's Silver Circle, a National Headliners award, and numerous other professional honors.

Wayne Freedman. Feature reporter for KGO-TV, San Francisco. Wayne has been awarded forty-one Emmys, twelve for his scriptwriting.

Bob Davy. Frequent contributor to national radio programs. Bob is the recipient of many awards, including three from Ohio State University, The Preceptor Award from San Francisco State University, as well as awards from The Freedoms Foundation, American Bar Association, the Birmingham Film Festival, and an Emmy from the Academy of Television Arts and Sciences.

Dave Barry. Nationally syndicated columnist for the *Miami Herald.* Humorist Barry was awarded a Pulitzer Prize for his outstanding writing.

Bob Garfield. Longtime commentator/correspondent for NPR's *All Things Considered.* On television, he is the advertising analyst for ABC News. He also co-hosts NPR's *On the Media.*

Arthur Miller, author of *Death of a Salesman, The Crucible, All My Sons, The Misfits, After the Fall,* and *A View From the Bridge,* among other noteworthy dramas.

Robert C. Pritikin, pioneer in effective use of imagery and outrageous originality as an advertising giant for both radio and television.

Sarah Humm, Media Fulfillment Manager of the Advertising Council, who made available a treasury of AdCouncil PSAs.

Chuck Blore, of The Chuck Blore Company, whose creative and humorous commercials add much dimension to *Idea to Script.*

Gerry Sher, longtime Accounts Executive and commercial scriptwriter for KABL Radio, San Francisco.

Nicholas Deluca, award-winning editorial writer for KCBS, San Francisco.

Jan Wahl, documentary and television producer, and Emmy award-winning film critic.

Dave Parker, head of Parker Productions, whose instructional films and video productions focus on such topics as safety ("Hospital Hazards," "Back Injuries," "DUI alcohol-traffic shows," "School Bus Driver Training") and numerous documentaries.

And, Marcia Williamson, who read *Idea to Script* while still a work in progress. Her comments resulted in a more fluent, less pedantic writing style. She made the text more readable, but equally as important, she provided the encouragement that all authors need.

I would also like to thank the following reviewers for their helpful comments: Karen Kremer, University of Wisconsin—Eau Claire; Robert Lochte, Murray St. University; Dr. Bill Dynes, University of Indianapolis; and Alfred Owens, Youngstown State University.

INTRODUCTION

Writing should be fun. If you're fortunate enough to enjoy writing, you know how stimulating it is to start with only a challenge and a desire to succeed, and wind up with a script that makes you proud.

Writing, like other creative activities, begins with a defined goal, requires discipline and creativity, involves struggle, and culminates in intense satisfaction when a quality product has been attained. In this sense, writing isn't that much different from other activities that bring about pride of accomplishment such as rigorously practicing a musical instrument until you get that passage right or solving a troublesome problem at school or work.

Each of these efforts requires creativity, knowledge, skill, and *an organized approach to the challenge at hand.* Creating a script that works should give you a type of catharsis—an emotional lift—that makes your effort extremely gratifying. If you find writing merely painful, with no compensating reward at the end of your labors, or if you struggle excessively with a writing challenge, you most likely lack a systematic approach to conceptualizing and writing scripts. This book can help you develop an organized approach to problem solving, which in turn should result in more consistency in conceiving and writing effective scripts.

This book is not designed to hand you a ready-made system. It doesn't present seven easy steps to success as a writer, and is anything but a fill-in-the-blanks book. Becoming an effective writer isn't that simple. All writers must develop working approaches that suit their needs and their gifts. What this book does offer is many aids for developing a systematic approach and a range of ideas, suggestions, and resources from which you may draw as you develop the process that works best for you.

WHAT THIS BOOK OFFERS YOU

Idea to Script introduces several analytical approaches to the arts, including investigations of human needs and desires and universal themes. Understanding what is commonly called human nature, and recognizing the motifs found in the most moving works that have survived more than three thousand years will help you establish an important center for developing your storytelling abilities. The models taken from these centuries of storytelling are not armatures on which to hang new names, places, and costumes; rather they reflect needs, desires, and fears, and other themes that have captivated audiences as far back into prehistory as we can reach. It's my conviction that stories are likely to succeed when they touch people in those deep, intimate realms we share as human beings. *Stories work best when they touch on deeply rooted human emotions or invoke themes that have fascinated or inspired our species since time immemorial.*

Aldous Huxley, in his essay *Fashions in Love,* tells us

Human nature does not change, or, at any rate, history is too short for any changes to be perceptible. The earliest known specimens of art and literature are still comprehensible. *The*

> *fact that we can understand them all and can recognize in some of them an unsurpassed artistic excellence is proof enough that not only men's* [sic] *feelings and instincts, but also their intellectual and imaginative powers, were in the remotest times precisely what they are now.* In the fine arts it is only the convention, the form, the incidentals that change: the fundamentals of passion, of intellect and imagination remain unaltered.[1] (Italics added)

I would only add that Huxley's comments on the fine arts apply equally to the public arts of all times and places.

THE PUBLIC ARTS

The term *public arts* is used here to mean those arts that are understood, enjoyed, and participated in by great numbers—often the majority—of people in a given culture. The counterpart to public art isn't good art, great art, fine art, or any other term that makes a qualitative judgment. The term that best signifies those arts that are appreciated by a minority of people in a society is *private art.* In the United States today, public arts include most television programs, nearly all radio broadcasts, popular movies, best-selling magazines and novels, comic strips, computer games, popular music, and staged musicals. Private arts include most classical music, opera, classic drama, and most paintings and sculptures found in galleries and museums. To simplify this distinction, it may be said that while public arts can tell magnificent and moving stories, generally they are accessible to all without need for special education or knowledge. A taste for private arts generally is acquired through study and extensive exposure. A more extensive discussion of the public arts in the United States may be found in Chapter 2, "Understanding Your Audience."

THE ELECTRONIC MEDIA

What does the term *electronic media* encompass? It includes radio, television, and cable; audio in nonbroadcast applications, as in audio tours of museums, instructional tapes or CDs to be played on car audio systems, and recordings for the blind. The World Wide Web is another medium of electronic communication where artists—writers, sculptors, and painters—create and share their works on the Internet.

Electronic media additionally refers to telecourses; in-house corporate video; video for single-purpose instruction (as in teaching users how to install computer upgrades); and a wide range of medical applications, including the production of single-subject recordings given to patients for home study. Nonbroadcast video and audio recordings also include employee training tapes in many specializations, such as those directed to bank tellers, seasonal employees in a variety of occupations, law enforcement personnel, airport customs officials, travel consultants, and park rangers, among many others.

Some of the qualities and resources you must have to succeed at this sort of writing are: worthwhile ideas to share with others; a strong desire to communicate them; the ability to reach and move others with your perceptions and values; a sympathy toward and an understanding of people; and a large and functional vocabulary. You also must have an aptitude for visual images and the ability to use language to evoke these images. To take advantage of all these assets, you need, as well, a systematic approach to each writing challenge.

You may not now have all these skills, or you may have them in an underdeveloped manner, but you can consciously work to cultivate them and, in the process, improve your effectiveness as a creative storyteller.

Part I of this book provides much information that should be a part of any serious writer's mental data bank. Great story ideas and the scripts that flow from them don't come from a vivid imagination alone. A knowledge of the stories that have gripped audiences for thousands of years and an awareness of how best to structure stories are fundamental to writing success.

PREPARATION FOR SCRIPTWRITING

Why doesn't this book begin with script assignments? As a university teacher of scriptwriting for many decades, I learned through the trials and errors of generations of students that few were prepared on day one to write in the unfamiliar language and formats of a fundamentally new writing challenge. Peter B. Orlik, in an essay titled "Why Copywriting Should Be the Core Broadcast Writing Course," explains why entering students initially have problems writing effective scripts:

> When they enter our programs, the writing experience of most electronic media students has been print-based. Unfortunately, their secondary school English classes (with an occasional journalism or yearbook course thrown in) have conveyed the syntax and formatic conventions of *writing for the eye rather than for the ear.* Early on then, broadcast educators need to focus their students on the requisites of aural composition—if those students' audio messages and visual soundtracks are to resonate with electronic media audiences.[2] (Italics added)

Electronic media writing differs in important ways from writing for print media. For starters, remember that your scripts will never be seen or read by your audiences. Listeners and viewers hear only the *sounds* of the words you write, and view only the *images* your scripts conjure into being. To be effective, you must write short, clear sentences (aural comprehension demands it), use contractions (to create a conversational style), avoid excessive sibilant and plosive sounds (microphones amplify these, resulting in hissing and popping), and think always of how your words will affect those who'll experience them only as visual images and sounds (video and audio). You should read every draft of your scripts aloud and record and evaluate each one by the sounds you hear on playback.

Additionally, scripts are written in formats that differ in nearly every significant way from those used for essays, short stories, or other writings intended to be read silently by individuals.

If you're typical, you most likely want to start writing scripts at once. Eagerness is a powerful motivator for any creative artist, and nothing written here should in any way dampen your enthusiasm. There's nothing to prevent you from tackling script challenges at once; there also is nothing wrong with jumping ahead of the theoretical considerations that occupy the next several chapters and proceeding directly to your goal: the creation of effective scripts. At the same time, you should understand that your first efforts may be disappointing if you lack a systematic approach to guide you. Part I offers a grounding in such fundamentals of story creation as:

> determining project objectives;
> envisioning the characteristics of those you want to reach;
> choosing appropriate motivational themes;
> structuring your story elements effectively;
> establishing the mood and style of your story;
> listening for ideas that surface from your unconscious mind; and
> channeling your creativity into formats that tell your story most clearly.

Self-taught pianists often begin, not with lessons, but by picking out tunes with two fingers. Obviously, this technique works for some, and plunging immediately into the writing of scripts may well work for you. One thing I can promise you, though: patience and the time taken to equip yourself with multiple tools of analysis, conception, and creation will greatly improve your initial efforts. All writers need self-confidence, and maximizing the likelihood of your success will reinforce your belief in your abilities as a storyteller.

However you choose to begin, I wish you well.

WRITING AS A DISCIPLINE

As a writer, you need a work schedule that causes you to write and write and then write some more! There's no substitute for practice. Becoming a better writer isn't that much different from becoming a better pianist, actor, or graphic artist. Most workers in any medium need talent, motivation, basic skills, good work habits, luck, and a willingness to listen to others. Listening to others doesn't mean mindlessly accepting any and all opinions; you must also possess the will and the ability to weigh suggestions and advice, and to accept them, reject them, or accept them with modifications. Your willingness to revise a script and your determination to hold on to your convictions must be carefully balanced.

Nearly all writers need good teaching (call it coaching or copyediting, if you will), and much information on how to begin, how to practice, and how to organize creative activities into workable, economical procedures. It's no exaggeration to say that your work as a writer likely is destined to become excellent, adequate, or indifferent by the time you begin to pound on your computer's keyboard. The most important steps you can take will be the *conception* or *vision* you form before beginning to write. As you undertake any writing challenge, study it carefully. Make no decisions about the direction to take until you fully understand its requirements. Listen for your inner voice that puts forth ideas, and always relate your responses to the goals of the project.

THE TIME FACTOR

One consideration that writers for the media must take seriously is summed up in the phrase *writing to deadlines.* Writing for the electronic media usually requires quick and appropriate responses to assignments that have urgent deadlines. To succeed with this sort of undertaking, you must develop a conscious approach that reduces to a minimum randomness and wasted effort. When you're writing against deadlines, you can't sit around waiting for inspiration.[3] Inspiration is a cardinal asset for any writer, but you needn't wait until you receive an assignment to start developing an inspirational mode. It should be alive and well and simmering on the back burner at all times; you must have your urgency to communicate in place, a great many ideas stored up—a reservoir of themes and needs to draw upon—and a system for moving forward rapidly when you receive an assignment.

Once you've developed a systematic approach to writing challenges, deadlines actually can work to your advantage because deadlines set parameters for your work. As with any task, it's advantageous to have a time frame within which you can set goals for each step of the process. Having a writing challenge without a deadline can be as unsettling as being on a journey without knowing its duration or time of arrival.[4]

WRITING UNDER RESTRICTIONS

It's not unusual for beginning writers to assume that media writing demands adherence to strict guidelines laid down by those for whom the script is written: assignment editors, supervisors, department heads, advertisers, account executives, and others in positions of authority. While this is at times a valid assumption in limited arenas such as writing commercials, news copy, and station editorials, for the most part it is not.

In Part II, you'll read feature reports by Bob MacKenzie and Wayne Freedman, essays by Richard Rodriguez, commentaries by Dave Barry, reviews by Bob Garfield and Jan Wahl, commercials by Bob Pritikin, Eric Poole, and Chuck Blore, and radio stories by Bob Davy. All of these outstanding scripts were written either without restrictions of any kind, or with only a suggestion as to topic. Award-winning editorials by Nicholas DeLuca had guidelines in the sense that both topics and the station's position on them were determined in consultations between the writer and station executives. Instructional videos by independent writer-producer Dave Parker were written to meet specific objectives, but the *means* of reaching those objectives were determined by writer-producers alone. *In almost every area of scriptwriting your ability to choose your topic and effectively shape your work will be the most valuable assets you bring to your work.*

WRITING AS A REFLECTION OF YOU

Anne Lamott, in her excellent book on creative writing, *Bird by Bird,* begins with these words:

> The very first thing I tell my new students on the first day of a workshop is that good writing is about telling the truth. We are a species that needs and wants to understand who we are. Sheep lice do not seem to share this longing, which is one reason they write so very little. But we do. We have so much we want to say and figure out.[5]

Lamott didn't have the electronic media in mind when she wrote these words so, while you may applaud her honesty and idealism, you may think, "Okay, I can choose what I write about, but how can I tell the truth and reflect my inner core of values when I'm writing stuff like news scripts, commercials, or sitcoms?" Truth to tell, you can't avoid revealing yourself when you conceive and write even the briefest of scripts; your values, your attitudes toward others, your convictions—all are in your words and in the way you put them together. Creative scriptwriters of integrity are able to write worthwhile copy despite time pressures and the realization that what they write is often transitory. Applying Lamott's statement to media writing, here are some examples of both good and questionable writing:

■ *In newswriting.* When reporting a news story about a mugging, one writer wrote, "She was viciously kicked and beaten" while a newswriter at another radio station wrote, "She was stomped on pretty good." Both descriptions were heard on newscasts. The difference from the writer's standpoint is showing respect and concern for the victim rather than using a street expression to amuse or shock. The difference from the listener's viewpoint is empathy rather than entertainment.

■ *In commercials.* Writing from within is the difference between the "Mean Joe Greene" commercial for Coca-Cola and a television commercial for a popular candy bar. In the Coca-Cola commercial, a huge professional football player drags his battered body toward the dressing room after a tough game. He sees a young boy waiting for him with a bottle of Coke, which he offers to the player. After draining the Coke, he gives the boy a souvenir in return—his sweaty, grass-stained game shirt. A moving moment, and a high point of commercial creativity.[6]

In the commercial for a candy bar that's packaged in two pieces, clips are used from the original *Frankenstein* film, the scene in which a little girl gives the monster a flower. We see the monster holding the candy bar. The little girl says something like, "You have to share if you have two of something." This puzzles the monster and, after a moment's hesitation, he wrenches off one of his arms and hands it to the child. Most of us seeing this are aware that in the *Frankenstein* film, the next scene shows the little girl's body floating in the water, the victim of the monster's cruelty. Of course, the candy bar commercial is funny in a sick sort of way, but the writer's values (and those of the people who approved the script) are quite apparent.

As you study this book, and as you conceive and write your scripts, I urge you to keep in mind that your writing isn't just letters forming sentences forming paragraphs on paper; your writing is a reflection of who you are.

Many audiovisual departments in colleges and universities (they use various titles from campus to campus) and some public libraries have archives of memorable commercials on CDs or tape. If you review these recorded samplers you'll see many noteworthy commercials including, perhaps, a series for Taster's Choice instant coffee that tells of a love affair that begins with a borrowed spoonful of instant coffee, and stretches over a number of thirty-second episodes; or those featuring "Joe Isuzu," who spouted lies about the sponsor's automobile, while supers at the bottom of the screen corrected his misinformation. Even a brief drama for a commercial product can reflect creativity, integrity, and sometimes comedy.

AESTHETICS AND ETHICS

Herbert Zettl, in his landmark study, *Sight Sound Motion: Applied Media Aesthetics,* clarifies the relationship between aesthetics and ethics:

> Even when producing a simple commercial, you are essentially manipulating the feelings, emotions, and ultimately the behavior of your recipients. . . . [and] the recipients of your intensified and clarified messages are usually not aware of being manipulated. As a mass communicator who influences millions of unsuspecting people daily, acceptance of such responsibility is a major job requisite. Skill alone is not enough. First and foremost, you must bring to your job a genuine concern and respect for your audience. And you must be prepared to bear the responsibility for your actions.[7]

Humans represent a great variety of possibilities: we are of many sizes, shapes, and ages, colors of hair and skin, degrees of physical dexterity, ranges of intelligence, and numerous personality types. At the same time, we share two overriding, unchanging, and universal attributes:

> First, we all are members of the same species, so we have the same needs, desires, fears, and potentialities.
>
> Second, we all are capable of being manipulated.

Unfortunately, the word *manipulate,* has fallen on evil days. In its purest and original form, it meant "to shape objects by the use of one's hands." *Manus,* the Latin word for hand, is the root of *manacle, manage, manicure, manuscript,* and, of course, *manipulate.* Most dictionaries give manipulate a negative connotation, but I use this ancient and valuable term in a neutral, nonjudgmental way. When applied to human communication, the word *manipulation* is related to *persuasion.* In some instances, manipulation is acceptable; in others, it's only momentarily annoying; while in other applications, manipulation can lead to catastrophic consequences.

Acceptable, and often valuable, manipulation occurs when two people discuss an issue from different perspectives, convictions, or life experiences. Aristotle, in his *Rhetoric,* defined the study of communication as the search for "all available means of persuasion." So, let's say I'm against capital punishment, and you're in favor of it. A typical discussion of this issue would find us marshaling logical and emotional appeals to persuade one another to adopt our point of view. In other words, we use *persuasion* to *manipulate* one another's beliefs. In the process, both participants may very well learn something of value.

Momentary, and only slightly distasteful, manipulation would be that of advertisers who persuade us to buy products we really don't need or products that don't live up to their promises. Children and parents are often manipulated into buying sugar-coated breakfast cereals, or cheaply made, overpriced plastic toys that are far smaller and more fragile than they appear on the television screen. While we may lose some money or a small amount of our child's daily nutritional needs, this manipulation isn't significant in the long run. In time it may even teach us to be skeptical about claims set forth in commercials.

Of far greater importance is manipulation that leads to racial, national, ethnic, religious, or other kinds of bigotry; to mob violence; or to war. As a writer whose ideas will reach and affect large audiences, your opportunity for manipulation is great, and must never be taken for granted. An awareness of your role as a communicator—as a persuader—must be alive in you at all times, along with your sense of obligation to use communications skills for the betterment of individuals and their societies.

HOW TO GET THE MOST FROM THIS BOOK

Computer software manuals often lead off with a brief notice: "Read Me First!" I've always resented being told what I must do before proceeding, just as I bridle when a speaker launches into a topic with "Now, listen up!"[8] I generally skip this Read Me First section until frustration in using the program forces me to come into compliance—and I invariably tune out when told to "listen up!"

So, asking you to read and ponder the words in this part of the introduction isn't a directive; it is, rather, the expression of a sincere desire on my part that you enter our relationship with an understanding of why the book includes the information it does, why I believe it's important to you as a storyteller to learn what's set down here, and why both Parts I and II are equally important; together they provide a sound basis for the conception and writing of effective scripts. Part I stresses theory, while, Part II looks at the application of theory to very practical scriptwriting challenges. *Theory should be thoroughly practical, and practice should be grounded in theory.*

This book mentions a great many plays, films, and television shows to make or underscore important points about scriptwriting. You may not be familiar with all, or perhaps any, of these shows. I urge you to decide for yourself when you need—or want—to know more about the examples, and then look for them in video stores, public libraries, or the audio/visual department of a university. You may also find shows you want to view on cable channels, including American Movie Classics (AMC), Turner Movie Classics, Nickelodeon, Bravo, or on public television stations.

SOME PERSONAL WORDS

Many of the script examples are "regional." Everyone lives somewhere. I happen to live in California, just eight miles north of San Francisco and the Golden Gate Bridge. There's nothing right or wrong about this—it's just a fact. Because of where I live, nearly all of my contacts with professional writers are with those who live and work here, and because of that, some of their scripts are about places or events that reflect the San Francisco Bay Area. Additionally, in my teaching at San Francisco State University, those enrolled in my writing courses also lived in or near San Francisco, and some of their scripts reflect it.

I don't apologize for this. If a script helps you gain insights into writing, then it matters not at all if it's oriented toward life in Chicago, Boston, Houston, or for that matter, Hong Kong. Good scripts are good because they involve us in compelling stories that draw upon universal themes and eternal human concerns and issues.

Throughout Part II you'll find radio and television scripts written by students. Most were written by college juniors, aged roughly from twenty-two to twenty-five, enrolled in their very first course in scriptwriting. These scripts are identified with an asterisk (*) following the author's name. They're included here as they were submitted to me, without my embellishing or rewriting them. During the ten semesters in which these scripts were written, a total of 350 students were enrolled in this writing class. Each student submitted approximately twenty-five scripts, giving nearly nine thousand scripts from which to choose! Obviously, I selected scripts I considered to be among the best of these. It's my hope that the successes of a considerable number of students will convince you that you also possess the ability to conceive and write scripts that are creative, noteworthy, of value to audiences, and marked by integrity and a sense of humor.

You could read these scripts and feel that you can never reach their level of excellence. Or you could take them as evidence that others just like you—beginning writers who once were in your position—succeeded in mastering the craft of scriptwriting, so it's not beyond your grasp. Obviously, I want the student scripts to inspire you and give you hope; otherwise I would not have included them.

If you can tell stories to your friends—anecdotes, jokes, or observations—and hold their attention, you can write effective scripts. This book provides convincing evidence that those who embraced both the theories of Part I, and the practical advice on scriptwriting in Part II, succeeded in becoming effective storytellers for the electronic media. My wish is that you, too, will achieve success as a storyteller for radio and television.

This book is written for you. I created it with the help of hundreds of students over the years as we learned from one another in scriptwriting classes. Its purpose is to help you become an effective and responsible writer for the electronic media. My agenda is to share with you my experiences, ideas, values, and what I've learned about creative writing. I neither expect you to automatically accept and adopt my values, nor to impulsively reject them. Some of what you may gain from this book lies in pondering the positions I take, and examining the values I hold, and using them to help you establish your own.

NOTES

1. Aldous Huxley, *Collected Essays* (New York: Harper & Brothers, 1958), 70.
2. Peter B. Orlik, "Responsive Essay to 'Why Copywriting Should Be the Core Broadcast Writing Course,'" *Feedback* (fall 1999), 38.
3. This comment is not a contradiction of the suggestion that you should use your sleeping mind to help you with your writing challenges. This concept is discussed in Chapter 11, "From Theories to Practice."
4. A personal note: if it weren't for a deadline by my editor, I most likely would still be tinkering with the manuscript of *Idea to Script,* convinced that with just one more revision I'd get it right.
5. Anne Lamott, *Bird by Bird* (New York: Pantheon Press, 1994), 3.
6. This commercial is an acknowledged classic. See Chapter 1 for a more detailed commentary.
7. Herbert L. Zettl, *Sight Sound Motion*, 2nd ed. (Belmont, CA: Wadsworth, 1990), 13.
8. A speaker at a retirement planning forum actually launched a new topic with these words: "Hey, now! Listen Up!" I was out the door in seconds!

CHAPTER ONE

BEGINNINGS AND OVERVIEW

Chapter 1 establishes the major premises of this book and introduces the chapters in Part I. It maintains that scriptwriters must have a grounding in theories that will help them conceive and construct stories emanating from our understanding of human nature. The chapter describes human nature in terms of needs and desires and universal themes; demonstrates using significant themes as the foundation for effective stories; introduces form and catharsis, with indications of how story writers must understand both; and briefly discusses modes in the storytelling arts.

SOME QUESTIONS FOR WRITERS

Why do we laugh? Why do we cry? Why is it funny when someone in a television farce slips on a banana peel? Why do people pay hard-earned money for pornography? Why do we watch game shows? Why do we watch parades, sports events, rodeos, and professional wrestling?

Why do people slow down at the scene of an accident to gawk? Why do we love ghost stories? Why do producers make millions of dollars creating stories that frighten or repel us? Why do romantic love stories thrill us, even though we know that romantic love seldom lasts? Why have people over the centuries paid to see tragedies, searching for stories with unhappy endings, knowing in advance they'd be upset to the point of tears?

Your understanding of the kinds of events and experiences that attract and hold our attention will start you on the way to conceiving and creating scripts that work.

Idea to Script is about audiences and the people who write stories for them. It's about the undercurrents—instincts, wants, needs, desires, passions, and fears—that guide us in choosing our entertainments. Its purpose is to open up for you new ways of understanding the public arts and their popularity, and the human beings who create and consume them. Our public arts include radio, television, and movies, as well as other popular audience events, such as sports contests, rodeos, quiz and game shows, and parades.

You may have seen one of a number of films that tell of a writer, stuck in an unrewarding job, whose dream it is to write the Great American Novel. After futile efforts to break free, the writer finally quits a pedestrian job, finds an isolated spot, and begins to write. Whether by pen, typewriter, or computer, the writer's beginning efforts look like this in a close-up: Title of the Novel; Chapter One.

I'm sure you know it doesn't work that way. It's doubtful that any extended work can successfully be written without countless hours—and in some instances years—of research, observation, mental struggles, and trial and error. In addition and essential to these efforts is a reservoir of knowledge about humans as seekers and consumers of stories, and a vast storehouse of ideas to turn into stories that work.

The chapters in Part I identify and elaborate on the theories that lay the foundation for successful storytelling through scripts. Part II addresses specific applications of theory to practice, including script formatting and the analysis and writing of many program types. You don't have to read all of the first part before you dip into the second; you can go to Part II at any time to see examples of theories put into practice.

At the same time, don't become impatient as you study theory, because a knowledge of the theoretical material provided in Part I will prevent hours of frustration when you begin to write your scripts. You'll actually save time by not being in a hurry!

SCRIPTS AND THEIR INTERPRETERS

Writers for stage, film, television, and radio have something in common with music composers. When composers set down their inked notations on sheets of lined staff paper they've already heard the sounds of the music they're creating: they've heard it while searching for the right sequence of notes and harmonies on their pianos. Scriptwriters, like composers, use the print medium to encode their creations, but unless they envision the sights and sounds of their stories, the words they set in print may not convey their intentions.

Scriptwriters know that their audiences will never see their stories in print. Actors, narrators, designers, and other interpretative artists will complete the link between writer and audience by turning ink on paper into sounds and pictures. As a writer of scripts, your success will depend on your ability to conjure up the sights and sounds of a story, and to encode them with such clarity that your tales will be effectively told by those who will interpret them. Your stories will be enhanced or diminished in performance, so you must encode, along with your messages, guidelines that make clear the interpretation you seek.

Always remember that you're an oral storyteller. Storytelling didn't begin as a written literary art. In the beginning, before there was writing, the great stories were narrated by speakers including Homer, who gave us the *Iliad* and the *Odyssey*; the Mesopotamian tellers of the epics of *Gilgamesh*; the Egyptian reciters of adventure tales such as *The Story of Sinuhue*; Native American storytellers who described the misdeeds of Coyote; the Zulu reciters of the Creation Myth; Chinese narrators of legends of the Queen Mother of the West; Pacific Islanders' legends of Maui, and on, and on, and on. . . .

Eventually someone committed these stories to writing, and most of us have experienced them only as words on paper. Unless, as we read, our minds turn what our eyes see into sights and sounds, some of their power is lost. When you read a story that originated in an oral tradition, always try to hear it as you silently read the words. You'll become ever more sensitized to the sounds and pictures in the stories, which is what you, as a scriptwriter, will be challenged to create. The popularity of book and poetry readings, children's story readings at countless libraries across the land, and the common evening ritual of reading stories to children at bedtime remind us of the power of stories delivered by vocal interpreters.

As you write, think of the sounds of the words and sentences. Try to see the action you're describing. When you feel your script is ready, read it into an audio recorder. By recording and playing it back, you'll hear it as it will be performed. Always review what you've written in such a way as to be able to hear it and, when you listen, try to place yourself in the minds of your intended audience.[1]

CONCEPTUALIZING YOUR STORY

Successful storytelling begins by conceiving a vision. Basically, this means visualizing your projected script in terms of what it's all about. What is its topic? What is its objective (purpose)? If everything goes as planned, what will be the outcomes? Having a clear conception of your intended work before you even begin to write it down is an essential key to success.

Scripts for radio and television are best thought of as blueprints or plans of communication that others will further interpret and present to an audience. The script of a broadcast is a directive to interpreters that sets forth what they're expected to produce. By contrast, a short story is all the reader sees and learns from; all pertinent information *about the story* is *in the story*. Because scriptwriters rely on intermediaries for the production and transmission of their stories, the starting point of any script for the electronic media or film is a conceptualization of the sounds and/or visual images to be conveyed.

Successful storytellers possess an understanding of human nature—a storehouse of knowledge about motivations, hopes, fears, and similar human drives. This knowledge is of key importance in conceptualizing. It helps us decide what stories are worth telling; determines the value of the story to be told; helps us select and develop characters that will connect with an audience; and inspires us to choose conflicts and resolutions that attract, engage, and then satisfy viewers and listeners. This book will help you better understand significant qualities of the human species and provide information about the universal themes found in compelling stories from nearly all cultures and time periods. As a citizen of a multicultural society, this knowledge is vital to your sensitivity and growth as a communicator.

You As a Storyteller

You've been telling stories all your life, and you're probably quite good at it. You may remember anecdotes you've told to small groups of friends that resulted in laughter or cries of "no way!" You may even have found yourself embellishing your stories over time, learning as you went what worked best, what held attention, and what brought about the most rewarding payoff. When you're challenged to turn your ideas into scripts, remember that you already know how to gain attention with spoken words, how to keep listeners engrossed as you weave your story, and how to end it with a flourish. These elements are basic to any good story: a beginning that attracts attention; details, usually told chronologically, that hold attention as expectations grow, and a conclusion that rewards your listeners' investment in time and involvement.

ELEMENTS OF CONCEPTUALIZATION

What areas of study can help you become an even better storyteller than you may be now? Here are the major concepts in brief, each of which is the subject of a chapter following this one.

Human Needs and Desires

As already stated, knowledge of human nature gives us an understanding of how people seek out their experiences with public arts and how they're affected by those experiences. This process is the subject of Chapter 2, but to give you a taste of what that chapter is about, here's a preview. Try to answer the following before proceeding. It will help make what follows more personal and useful.

What are your favorite television shows?
What three—or four or five—movies did you recently enjoy?
What television or film dramas from the past remain vivid in your memory?
What magazines do you regularly read?
What kinds of novels or short stories hold your interest and give you satisfaction?
What storytellers on radio or television attract your interest and satisfy your needs?

These questions are a good starting point for any writer who wants to reach an audience because they link your perceptions and reactions with those of the broader audience and with successful works in the public arts. If you like a particular story, you can be sure others will as well. Your own reactions can teach you much about how audiences are attracted, held, and satisfied. (If you aren't interested in attracting an audience, writing for the public arts may not be for you!)

After identifying the most enjoyable and satisfying experiences you've had as a consumer of stories told by others, the next logical step is to ask yourself, "What was it about each of these stories that grabbed and held my attention?" You may, for example, find that:

Story 1 allowed you to live out a long-held dream (being a hero like Indiana Jones or Xena);

Story 2 posed a mystery that compelled you stay with it until its resolution (*Murder, She Wrote, The Hunt for Red October, The X-Files*);

Story 3 took you back to a past age, evoking nostalgia for a time never personally experienced by you (*The Waltons, Happy Days, That '70's Show*);

Story 4 made you laugh until you ached (*Wayne's World, Fawlty Towers, Monte Python, Animal House*);

Story 5 gave you vicarious experiences in sharing in the suffering of others (*Amistad, Dances With Wolves*); and,

Story 6 gave you a vicarious opportunity to experience romantic love (*Romeo and Juliet, West Side Story*).

What's important here is your recognition that (1) the themes that caught and held your interest undoubtedly did the same for others; and (2) by identifying the public arts you seek and analyzing your own interests, concerns, pleasures, needs, desires, fears, and hates, you can extend your experiences with the arts to others.

Movies, television shows, novels, and other public arts nearly always focus on needs or desires that are common to us all. An examination of what these significant needs and desires are should help you relate them to public arts, as well as to sports events, parades, and religious celebrations. Chapter 3 explores these needs and desires in much detail.

Universal Themes

Throughout this book, myths are considered to be the root of stories that embody universal themes. Chapter 4 relates myths to themes that appear repeatedly in the stories of societies all over the world and in all ages. Many of us think of myths as ancient creations, charming perhaps, but with no counterpart in today's world: the myths of Isis and Osiris in Egypt, Gilgamesh and Enkidu in Mesopotamia, Orpheus and Eurydice in Greece, or Romulus and Remus in Rome. All vaguely interesting, but old and belonging to bygone days. If we believe this, we fail to realize that myths continue to engage us, much as they captivated our ancestors in ancient days.

In 1997, Jane Austen experienced a revival of popularity through the productions on television and film of several of her novels, including *Sense and Sensibility, Pride and Prejudice,* and *Clueless,* based on Austen's *Emma.* It seemed remarkable that novels about the British gentry, written between 1787 and 1814, would captivate an American public in the late twentieth century. Writing in the *San Francisco Chronicle,* Jerry Carroll asked:

> Why can we not seem to get enough of Jane Austen? In the almost exactly 200 years since she sat down to write "Pride and Prejudice," you would think it would begin to lose something. Relevancy, say. Like her five others, the novel [*Pride and Prejudice*] is about the rural English gentry. Not much happened in their society, and it did so slowly.[2]

This love affair with Jane Austen's novels was no surprise to analyst Geoffrey Gorer. In 1941 he commented on the continuing infatuation with the novels of Jane Austen in an article titled, "The Myth in Jane Austen": "The adoration of Miss Austen has at times nearly approached a cult—the sect of 'Janeites'—and I propose to try to uncover the mystery behind the worship." Gorer dismisses traditional explanations of Austen's remarkable hold on people as being inadequate. He then examines four of her most successful novels, *Sense and Sensibility, Price and Prejudice, Mansfield Park,* and *Emma.* After recounting their similarities, he concludes that all four revolve around what he calls "Jane Austen's myth," and continues

This central myth—the girl who hates and despises her mother and marries a father surrogate—is not the exclusive invention of Miss Austen; though, until she wrote, the sexes had been reversed and the subject considered fitter for tragedy than comedy. The most famous example is Sophocles' *Oedipus Rex*. For psychoanalysts, there will be little cause for surprise at the ease with which most of her readers so passionately identify with her heroines.[3]

Of course, there's much more to Jane Austen's success than her myth. Good characterization, dialogue, sequencing of events (plotting), wit, intuitive (perhaps) understanding of human needs, fears, and desires, the role of women as social managers, and so forth. But the insight of Geoffrey Gorer reveals to us a core element of the success of her stories: their timelessness is due to her evoking in us a universal response to a universal theme.

George Lucas drew heavily on universal myths, or themes, in creating the *Star Wars* trilogy. The Indiana Jones films likewise follow well-known myths. The lesson to be derived from this is plain: *humans, being of the same species and having changed little in thousands of years, can be counted on to respond in very similar ways to stories that embody universal themes, especially those of a mythic nature.* Myths of our time include those of the Amazon, exemplified by *Xena* in the 1990s, *Sheena* from 1950s television, and *Wonder Woman* from the 1970s. Male figures include invincible heroes with superhuman strengths such as Batman, Superman, and Spiderman.

Chapter 4 explores how universal themes relate to stories told in films and on television, for example the theme of the perilous journey. Your study of universal themes and their relevance to your scripts will become more obvious as you read the chapter, titled "Universal Themes in the Public Arts," and Appendix B, "Eighty Universal Themes."

Form in the Arts

One of the chief jobs of an artist is to arrange the elements of a work into some sort of order. The elements of a painting are colors, masses, and lines, and these can be arranged to depict whatever an artist wishes to share with us. The elements of a story are incidents, character traits, beliefs (values) held by characters, dialogue, and, in movies and television, music and visual images.

All communications, however randomly put together, have form. Form is the shape or structure of the communication. All sentences—basic units of verbal communication—have structure, which is sometimes effective, sometimes not. Look at these two sentences: (1) "I got into the car, started it, and drove downtown." (2) "Downtown I parked and drove, started the car, and got into it." Both use the same words, but the first is well arranged for our understanding, while the second is not. However, it's important to note that each sentence equally has a structure—a form. In other words, each has 100 percent of its form. How you structure or arrange the incidents of your story determines much of the impact—or lack of it—on your audience.

A ceramic pitcher is a good example of how power can be generated through careful structuring of materials. The material from which the pitcher is made was once a lump of clay. The lump had form, but was of little use to us (except as a paperweight or a missile, perhaps). When the lump was shaped (formed) into a pitcher, it became capable of holding, storing, and pouring water. In other words, when the clay was given a new structure, that is a new form, it was given new powers.

Taken a step further, the ultimate shape and decoration of a pitcher is determined by its intended use. A pitcher may be created for purely utilitarian service, such as storing and later pouring orange juice. And even though mass produced, it may be decorated with colorful scenes to make it more attractive to potential buyers. A distinctly different kind of pouring vessel is that created for religious rituals. While it performs the same function— storing and pouring—it often is made from precious materials rather than clay, inlaid with jewels, and crafted with details symbolic of the rite in which it plays a meaningful role. So this pitcher, used in a religious rite, takes on added power because of its symbolism. Its appearance, which may have artistic merit, has also taken on the power to evoke feelings very different from those brought forth by the orange juice pitcher.

Similarly, it can be said that the way we structure the incidents in a story determines much of the power it's given. A pitcher's form is what we see when we look at it—its shape. A story's form is the order in which we experience incidents as the story moves through time toward its conclusion. Both are structures of communication, one processed through our eyes, the other through our ears.

Communications are classified according to whether they occupy space or time. Physical objects, such as pitchers, paintings, statues, buildings, or natural objects (including human beings) possess *spatial form.* Any communication that can only be revealed over time—a story, a television show, a song, or a joke—possesses temporal form. Of course, a painting takes time to absorb, to see all its details, and to observe how planes and colors interact, yet it can be seen all at once. A television drama obviously takes up space, as does a painting, but it can't be seen all at once. We generally classify works in the arts as *space art* or *time art.* Michelangelo's statue of David is an example of space (spatial) art; Shakespeare's *Hamlet* is an example of time (temporal) art.

A primary concern of Chapter 5, "Form in the Arts," is with *temporal form,* because the media of radio, television, popular music, theatre, film, and written literature are all in the realm of the time arts. Pictorial elements of the public arts are mentioned only as they relate to specific universal themes.

Catharsis

Catharsis, as used in the arts, refers to "a purifying or figurative cleansing or release of the emotions or of tension. . . ."[4] Most scholarly discussions of catharsis center around the emotional impact received from extended stories, such as stage plays, films, and televised dramas, but catharsis on a less dramatic scale can be brought about by a joke or a thirty-second commercial as well. The simplest example is that of any commercial that makes you laugh, laughter being one form of catharsis.

Other examples of catharsis include some of the most honored commercials of all time, including the "Mean Joe Greene" commercial for Coca-Cola, shown during the 1979 Superbowl.[5] The scene of this commercial is the tunnel leading from the field to the locker room. Joe Greene, a huge defensive lineman for the Pittsburgh Steelers, limps through the passageway, his clothing stained with sweat, mud, and grass. In the tunnel a small, shy boy holding a bottle of Coca-Cola waits for him.

The boy calls to Joe Greene, and asks if he needs help. "Naw," says the player, maintaining his stoic persona despite obvious pain. The boy tells his idol that he thinks he's the best player ever, and asks if he'd like his Coke. Greene indicates that he doesn't want it, but the boy persists.

"It's okay. You can have it." Again Greene refuses, but the boy insists, "Really, you can have it." Greene relents, takes the Coke, and downs it in one long swallow.

Music plays and voices sing, "A Coke and a smile, makes me feel good, makes me feel nice." The boy turns to leave, saying, "See ya 'round." The singing continues, "That's the way it should be and I'd like to see the whole world smiling at me."

Joe Greene calls out to the boy. "Hey, kid . . . catch," and tosses him his game jersey, his face smiling at last. "Coca-Cola adds life, have a Coke and a smile," continue the lyrics.

The boy catches the jersey, smiles, and says: "Wow! Thanks Mean Joe!" The screen reads, "Have a Coke and a smile. Coke adds life."

In just sixty seconds a complete story with beginning, middle, and end has been told with great effectiveness. The opening sets up the circumstance, the middle creates tension because of the rejection of the boy's desire to help his hero, and the conclusion brings about a catharsis as the tension disappears through the resolution.

Form and catharsis are inevitably linked, because form—the step-by-step forward movement of your script—is most successful when it ends (culminates) in a moving and meaningful catharsis. Chapter 5, "Form in the Arts," and Chapter 6, "Catharsis" develop these concepts further.

Modes in the Storytelling Arts

Historically speaking, three major storytelling modes evolved in ancient times: *the tragic, the comic,* and *the heroic.* While variations have appeared from time to time, these three basic modes persist in today's public arts.[6] Tragedy can be seen in *West Side Story*; comedy fills the cult classic, Mel Brooks' film *The Producers*; and the heroic, often referred to as the melodramatic, as seen in *Gladiator* and *Titanic* as well as in television series such as *ER, Law and Order,* and *The X-Files.*

Comedies range greatly in vision and execution. Three Stooges sketches, *I Love Lucy,* and *Fawlty Towers* are at one extreme of broad, physical, farce. A step away from such all-out farces is *Romy and Michelle's High School Reunion.* Other comedies are somewhat more restrained, as in these television series *Home Improvement, M*A*S*H*, Seinfeld,* and *The Bob Newhart Show.* At a greater degree of subtlety are films including *The Truth About Cats and Dogs, Shakespeare in Love,* and *When Harry Met Sally.*

Similarly, melodramas range from the least subtle—*Superman* or *Dick Tracy*—to the more sophisticated—*Chariots of Fire* and *The Year of Living Dangerously.*

Modes are defined in terms of form, vision, and purpose. Form, as already noted, is the shape (the outline) of the work; vision is the philosophical outlook of the artist; purpose is the underlying reason for the work's creation.

Tragedy, comedy, and melodrama (the heroic) evolved because of human needs; each mode successfully met the needs of those who experienced them. These forms began as rituals or myths developed in early times because they brought about the release of pent-up emotions. They became standard parts of religious ceremonies and, later, in the public arts, because each story or ritual began by arousing basic human passions, and ended with a purgation of those passions. This much is true, but it's important to qualify these broad statements.

While it's undeniable that noteworthy stories, creatively structured, can create tension and then take its audience from high anxiety to a release of these emotions, it doesn't follow that all—or perhaps *any*—such stories provide a permanent curative remedy. For example, in wartime, melodramas are traditionally produced to show the heroic deeds of outnumbered and desperate warriors. There's no question that audiences experience deep emotion during the last-minute theatrics in which the good guys (our warriors) defeat the bad guys (their warriors), but the consequences of taking an audience through such an experience may be no more than an exercise in wishful thinking and the exhilaration of the moment but a palliative lasting little longer than the closing credits.

Forms and modes in the storytelling arts are the subjects of Chapters 5, 7, 8, 9, and 10. Read and refer to these chapters from time to time because they can guide you in developing a concept (a vision), and seeing it through to a satisfactory resolution—a catharsis.

QUESTIONS

These questions were asked early in this chapter, and now is the time to actually contemplate your answers. Write down your findings and have them available to review when examining an appropriate concept or theme in the chapters of Part I.

1. What are your favorite television shows?

2. What three—or four or five—movies did you recently enjoy?

3. What television or film dramas from the past remain vivid in your memory?

4. What magazines do you regularly read?

5. What kinds of novels or short stories hold your interest and give you satisfaction?

6. What storytellers on radio or television attract your interest and satisfy your needs?

As you connect your media preferences with such topics as the need or desire to share in the suffering of others, the fascination with horror and terror, or the desire to identify with a special group, concepts that at this point may seem theoretical or abstruse will become internalized and very specific to your needs and desires and to other aspects of you as a consumer of the public arts.

NOTES

1. See the more detailed discussion of recording and playing back scripts in Chapter 11, "From Theories to Practice."
2. *San Francisco Chronicle,* 10 January 1996, sec. E, p. 1.
3. Geoffrey Gorer, "The Myth in Jane Austen," in *Art and Psychoanalysis,* ed. William Phillips. (New York: Meridian Books, 1963), 221–22.
4. *The American Heritage Dictionary* (Boston: Houghton Mifflin, 2nd ed., 1985), p. 248.
5. In 2001, a pregame program preceding Superbowl XXXV featured the best-loved and most effective Superbowl commercials of previous years. The "Mean Joe Greene" commercial was chosen as the Best Superbowl Commercial of all time.
6. These categories are useful within limits, but they don't include or adequately explain a hybrid story such as *Abbot and Costello Meet Frankenstein.* Nor do they relate to sensitive dramas that are neither melodrama nor comedy, such as *84 Charing Cross Road* or *Cross Creek.* It's valuable to use categories when they help our understanding, but it's also important to avoid them when they obviously don't apply.

CHAPTER TWO

UNDERSTANDING YOUR AUDIENCE

This chapter describes public arts, contrasting it with private arts. It discusses public arts in the United States, examines the connection between art and ritual, expresses how public arts are used, and looks at schools of criticism.

All scripts are written with listeners and viewers in mind. Some scripts—newscasts, for example—are designed to reach large, diverse groups of people. Other scripts, including commercials for specialized products, target a more closely defined audience. To use an obvious example, a script for denture adhesive appeals to an older audience and a commercial for acne medication focuses on adolescents. When you know the nature of your audience, you should adjust your approach, your vocabulary, and your objectives to that audience.

While target audiences differ in age, gender, economic status, ethnicity, and other characteristics, all of us are essentially the same in many important respects. So, while you write for a specific audience, addressing specific interests, you also must write to reach what is common to us all, such as our need to be informed, our need to experience the beautiful, or our need to have fun, to mention but a few. The key to a script's success lies in providing information that's useful to those who may want your product—your target group—while addressing the need to be attractive to others.

It's important to employ a systematic, analytical approach to each writing assignment before anything other than notes have been set down. In most instances, you shouldn't start a script until you thoroughly understand your challenge, have determined your objectives, and have started making notes. There are exceptions to this advice. At times, the idea for a script will arise in your mind in such a complete state that you're ready to write without further thought or analysis. This has happened to me on occasion, most often when the idea was for a brief comic sketch or a four- or five-page story for children. When the project is one of any complexity and magnitude, though, it's wise to follow a conscious and practical system in which you take a step-by-step analytical approach based on your understanding of humans as viewers and listeners.

PUBLIC AND PRIVATE ARTS

The terms *public* and *private,* when applied to the arts, are imprecise and sometimes arbitrary. They also are neutral in the sense that they refer only to distribution and consumption, and not to quality. The extremes are easy to classify: in 2001, *The West Wing, Survivor, Ally McBeal,* and reruns of *Seinfeld* were public arts; Hugo Wolf's art songs, and collections of poems printed for their authors by small presses in limited editions, were private arts. Other presentations may have the characteristics of public arts in the sense that they'd be attractive and understandable to large numbers if they were widely available, but private in that their creators have decided on limited distribution. (See the discussion of a nonprofit informational production that follows for an example of this.)

Works that fall between public and private are more difficult to classify. While most ballet performances tend to be on the private side, what about *The Nutcracker,* given in hundreds of readily accessible performances each year in all parts of the United States? Clearly, there's a gray area where classification becomes difficult and less useful. Some art communications could be classified as semipublic, but this would begin an endless process of qualifying, classifying, and defining. If the terms *public arts* and *private arts* are to be useful, we must use them in a general way, and must use them with care and with an understanding of the limitations of categorization.

Some conditions for a work to be classified as either public or private art are

- the degree of understanding and acceptance within a society of the symbols used;
- the degree of public access to the communicated message;
- the universality or narrowness of the themes represented in the communication; and
- the culturally acquired motivation to seek out or ignore certain types of communicated messages.

As a writer, you should consciously think about these conditions, and ask yourself these questions:

Will my intended audience understand the symbols I use in my scripts? Symbols in this context means words and the concepts they stand for.

Will the medium I've chosen reach the people I want to affect?

Will the chosen medium be the most economical and practical?

Are the themes and needs universal?

Will my audience be motivated to consider taking the action suggested in my message?

If your answer to these questions is either no or maybe, you may, of course, decide to disregard what you've discovered, and write what you want to write, the way you want to write it. More often, though, you'll try to find ways to turn the no answers into yesses. In any case, raising these questions gives you a realistic picture of where your work stands in relation to a medium and an audience.

Applying these questions to a specific writing challenge may help clarify their usefulness. Chapter 17, "Media in Community Service," offers a description of a campaign on behalf of a nonprofit agency, Amigos de las Americas. Here are responses to the questions posed above for this campaign.

Will my audience understand the symbols I've used? The intended audience is adult and adolescent native speakers of English, as well as those with a limited command of English. This dictates a conversational style, using words that aren't obscure, ambiguous, or unnecessarily technical and suggests the option of creating a second audio track in Spanish.

Does the medium I've chosen reach my target group? The objective is to reach small groups who are open to learning about the Amigos program, so broadcast television is unsuitable. Local cable access programming would reach a smaller audience and would be far less costly than television, but its audience would also be heterogeneous, A slide-tape presentation is the most practical, least expensive, and most flexible medium for making messages audience-specific, so it becomes the medium of choice.

Target audiences will be carefully selected, and presentations will be made to groups of from fifteen to a maximum of fifty. Typically, audiences will be made up of high school parent-teacher-student associations (PTAs), middle and high school classes in world history and social studies, civic betterment groups, and religion-supported youth groups.

The presentation will be made in school classrooms, community meeting rooms, libraries, and similar rooms where the availability of projection equipment is uncertain; this dictates a medium that can be easily transported, set up, and operated with few complications.

As time permits, more than one audio track can be matched to the photos. Because Amigos perform paramedic services throughout Latin America, a Spanish-language audio track would be very productive in attracting Spanish-speaking families whose children are prime candidates to become Amigos volunteers. Fluency in Spanish equips volunteers with an extremely valuable asset.

Is the chosen medium economical and practical? Slide-tape equipment is the least costly and most effective means of telling stories. It offers compelling color photos and recorded sound that may include music. It can be shown by anyone with a single presenter, and no sophisticated knowledge of media equipment is required.

Are the themes and needs I've addressed universal? Appeals stressed in the presentation will include the desire to help others; the satisfaction gained from offering much-needed health programs; the lure of traveling to new places; the experience of living with people of unfamiliar cultures and customs; the opportunity to make friends for the United States; the enhancement of one's people-serving paramedic skills; increasing proficiency with the Spanish language; adding an impressive achievement to resumes, applications to schools, and potential employers; and, not as an afterthought but of considerable importance, the building of self-confidence and self-esteem.

PUBLIC ARTS IN THE UNITED STATES

Contemporary public arts in the United States and much of the Western world includes broadcast material on television and radio, similar programs on cable, popular music recordings, mainstream theatrical films, comic strips, popular newspaper columns, popular novels, children's stories, popular magazines, certain buildings (public architecture), public gardens and parks, fountains, public statues, dances, and the like.

Certain arts that are popular in other nations may also be enjoyed by some in the United States but, because of limited circulation and audience demand, they can't be considered public arts of this society. This includes the Flamenco and Zarzuelas of Spain, Scottish bagpipe music, the Chinese Opera, the Fado of Portugal, Noh drama of Japan, and Irish step dancing.[1]

Public arts are a subcategory of public communication. Newscasts, storm warnings, stock market reports, and other factual data are public communication; soap operas and music on radio are public arts. Commercials, when they're mere listings of items for sale, are regarded as public communication; when commercials use the devices (and symbols) of the arts to make their point, as in a singing or dramatized spot, they're regarded as public arts.

As always, it's misleading to treat these distinctions as though there are no gradations between one and the other. The brilliant film *Shakespeare in Love* was appreciated by a broad audience because it delivered a compelling story of love, adventure, sex, intrigue, and so forth; at the same time, it provided greatly enhanced enjoyment for those with a knowledge of Elizabethan dramatists who appear in the film, including John Webster, author of the bloody and depraved play *The Duchess of Malfi,* and the dissolute Christopher Marlowe, author of *Dr. Faustus,* whose brilliant career was cut short in a drunken brawl.

Clearly related to the public arts and sharing many of the same appeals are competitive sports contests, horse racing, auto racing, and boxing. Also related to public arts are parades, pageants, rodeos, fandangos, festivals, pow-wows, awards ceremonies, dog or cat shows, and inaugurations or inductions into a hall of fame. Many private or semipublic rituals such as weddings, baptisms, bar and bat mitzvahs, wakes, funerals, and similar activities share the appeals and gratifications of public arts and ceremonies. Writers for the public media shouldn't ignore lessons that can be learned by analyzing communications not normally classified as art.

Can a work that doesn't incorporate human needs and universal themes succeed? Probably. Writers with unconventional ways of viewing our world can envision and create within their own parameters, can violate all rules and yet can touch us in unique and unexpected ways. Genius is a gift that evades definition, and it can't be acquired by reading this or that book. We can recognize genius and appreciate it, but we can't order it to be our servant. Before you venture where no writer has gone before, you should work to become effective at telling stories based on what we already know about human nature and what we've learned from several thousand years of human expression in the storytelling arts. Once you've perfected your craft, you may decide to experiment with all sorts of unconventional approaches that violate commonly held views of the right way to do it.

THE ORIGINS OF PUBLIC ART

In the distant past, cave paintings, tribal ceremonies, dances for rain or for success in war or in the hunt, and, much later, religious services of all kinds were among the participatory activities that had paralleled the public arts as they evolved. Jane Ellen Harrison, in her classic study, *Ancient Art and Ritual,* makes clear the relationship between the two terms used in her title:

> Art and ritual . . . have diverged today; but the title of this book is chosen advisedly. Its object is to show that these two divergent developments have a common root, and that neither can be understood without the other. It is at the outset one and the same impulse that sends a [person] to church and to the theatre.[2]

Transferring Harrison's premise to the public arts helps us understand the power inherent in such ancient themes as "death and resurrection" as seen in rituals celebrating the rebirth of Osiris and the risen Christ. The cathartic power of resurrection, although not the details, found its way into such diverse stories as *Sleeping Beauty, Snow White, The Mummy,* and *Frosty the Snowman.* Joseph Campbell relates rituals of cleansing and purgation of sin, such as confession and baptism, to the symbolic rebirth of the penitent.[3] Many stories in our public arts draw on the power of this and other rituals, and a careful analysis of stories that move you may very well lead you to their counterparts in ritual.

HOW PEOPLE USE THE PUBLIC ARTS

People use the public arts in many ways. Every writer should keep this in mind when creating works for a specific audience. What Person A needs at a given time isn't what Person B needs, and may not even be what Person A needed a few days earlier, or will need six hours later.

Television usage differs from person to person and circumstance to circumstance. Housebound people often rely heavily on television to be their window on the world—a world that comes to them through a distorted lens, perhaps, but a world that they can no longer experience directly. Lonely people find it comforting to have sounds and representations of humans in action on their living room television screens. Nurses have reported that hospitalized patients are less bothered by pain when their attention is focused on television shows.

At the same time, very active people with much to do may ignore television for the most part because they have little time for it and less need of it. Most young children watch a great deal of television, sometimes because they're placed before a TV set for parental convenience, and sometimes because they're bored. Some television viewers watch one mix of programs, while others watch an entirely different mix. Television isn't a singular phenomenon. It consists of newscasts, soap operas, MTV, infomercials, documentaries, talk shows, sportscasts, situation comedies, movies, serious dramas, shoot-em-up melodramas, cartoons, game shows, cooking programs, awards ceremonies, inaugurations, parades, political debates, and on and on. It's important to avoid thinking about television as though it were a single offering.

To categorize some viewers as soap-opera-game-show-sit-com-sportscast junkies (as many critics do), is to fail to recognize that most people who experience the public arts don't do so in clearly defined patterns. We choose our entertainments and events on the basis of our needs, our interests, our desires. A further truth is that even the same individual doesn't usually need (and therefore use) the same kind of experience at all times. Today, we need some laughs and decide to watch *The Simpsons* or *South Park*; yesterday, we needed to learn what was going on in our world, so we watched CNN; at yet another time, we have an unconscious need to view a serious drama; at still another time, we need to turn away from one medium (in this example, television), to play solitaire, do a crossword puzzle, read the newspaper, or take a nap.

Our selection of the things we experience isn't unimportant. It's not usually a conscious choice, and it isn't a matter of good or bad. It's a process we go through each day and, if we analyze what we search for, we can learn much about our daily needs and wants—our curiosity, anxieties, fears, desires, and—our boredom! As a writer, to better understand how others use the public arts, you should first know what media experiences your needs and desires lead you to seek out and consume.

Despite the previous statement that we must be careful to avoid thinking about television as though it were a single offering, any high-impact medium—and especially television—affects all of us in certain ways, even when we don't watch it. There's a cumulative, albeit unplanned and unintended, impact of television that can't be avoided. Nor can this impact be measured by the number of times a cartoon character shatters into fragments when running into a wall, or by examining any single program or series.

The ways in which television brings about change are only vaguely understood. Few critics seem aware of the impact television has had in causing enormous upheavals throughout our world. Television brought the civil rights struggle and the speeches of Dr. Martin Luther King, Jr., into America's living rooms, and was a huge factor in bringing about civil rights legislation and long-delayed progress for people of color. The Vietnam War was viewed nightly by American families at dinnertime, and Americans gradually turned against that tragedy as they saw executions of bound prisoners and the burning of grass villages—all while being given the daily body count.

The East European world of communism collapsed from a variety of causes, but the constant availability of Western European television certainly played an important role. The downfall of apartheid in South Africa began when the Caucasian minority finally permitted television in that nation; after its introduction, there was no possibility that the masses of Blacks and so-called Coloreds would continue to accept their poverty and restrictions and remain passive. Television revealed to them the privileges of the White society, and there was no turning back.

The pervasive impact of television isn't all (perhaps not even *chiefly*), positive, however. It's possible that television's unrelenting display of violence on news programs, in documentaries, and in entertainment dramas has helped us become the most deadly nation—in terms of violence toward one another—in the world. One also wonders about the long-term effects of the perverse and denigrating television talk shows that defile our public airwaves. (A moralistic editorial opinion from your author!)

The efforts of many critics of the public arts are hampered by the either-or syndrome. These critics operate with audience stereotypes: a person is either a *highbrow,* drinking chardonnay, enjoying opera, possessing an extensive formal education, supporting public television, and so forth, or a *lowbrow,* guzzling beer, watching televised sports contests in his underwear, embracing Jerry Springer and *Married . . . With Children,* and preferring country music over all other modes. Such stereotypes are nonsensical, and holding to them will only interfere with your ability to reach and move people through your writings. (See Chapter 6 for further discussion of this point.)[4]

ANALYZING THE PUBLIC ARTS

If you write for the electronic media, you should become skilled at analyzing scripts. Analysis is the dissecting of selected examples—good and bad—to see what can be learned from them. In this context, analysis is something done after the fact: that is, a writer (other than yourself) first creates a script and later you dissect it, searching for clues as to why it succeeded or didn't and what made it good, bad, or something in between. The purpose of your analysis isn't to find models to imitate, but rather to clarify for you what you like and don't like, what succeeds with audiences and what doesn't, and how you might have developed the script had you been its creator. A reasoned analysis of your spontaneous reactions to scripts will additionally help you see where you're coming from, what values you hold and what school or schools of thought you represent so that your scripts conform to your artistic and social values.

Developing the ability to analyze others' scripts is beneficial when you face your own writing challenges. When you receive a script assignment, do a prescript analysis. Before making major decisions about your script, ask the same sorts of questions you asked and answered in reviewing the work of others. See Chapter 11, "From Theories to Practice," for specific preanalysis.

SCHOOLS OF CRITICISM

There are many legitimate approaches to analyzing, understanding, and criticizing the arts. Some are listed and briefly discussed here to give you an overview of schools of analysis.

Moralistic criticism undoubtedly was the earliest approach to evaluating the public arts. Plato, who reluctantly decided that the arts must be controlled and, in some instances, banned from his ideal City-State (*The Republic*), is one example of an early moralistic critic. The moralistic approach asks, Is this work of art good or bad for people? The ongoing outcry against excessive violence and explicit sex in our public media, together with demands for censorship, indicate that moralistic criticism is still very much with us in today's America.

Psychological criticism, in one of its important branches, views art in terms of the theories of Sigmund Freud and his followers. It deals with conscious and unconscious motivations of characters in stories as well as audience responses to works of art. A psychoanalytical analysis of the films *Misery, The Prince of Tides,* and *Silence of the Lambs* could help a writer better understand characterization and motivation of agents. Psychological analysis also investigates the theories of Carl Gustav Jung as they relate to myths, fables, and other popular stories.

Sociological analysis focuses on audiences and attempts to understand the effects of public arts, not in terms of individuals (psychological criticism), but as groups of people acting and interacting. Included in sociological analysis are studies of the influence of media on our attitudes and beliefs; content analysis, which seeks to count or measure specific phenomena (for example, the number of incidents of televised violence during a sample time period, roles given to women, ethnic minorities, etc.); and uses and gratifications, which asks, What needs or desires are served by the public arts?

Formalist analysis, also called aesthetic, textual, or ontological criticism, views art as art, and not as an expression of social, religious, ethical, or political ideas. It asks us to free art from a dependence on context, looking at art instead from a variety of viewpoints, including the aesthetics of form, the evocative qualities of the language used, and the effect of a work in its entirety. Roger Fry tells us that in viewing a painting of the crucifixion, a critic looking for that "extremely elusive aesthetic quality which is the one constant quality of all works of art . . . should ignore the literal meaning of the work, and concentrate on the . . . extraordinary power of coordination of many complex masses in a single inevitable whole, by the delicate equilibrium of many directions of line."[5] Like other formalists, Fry believes that form is the determinant of beauty and that form explains the power of art.

The *archetypal approach* is sometime called the totemic, mythological, or ritualistic school of analysis. It owes its origins to several nineteenth-century anthropologists who noted the presence of universal themes in the arts of so-called primitive people of all times and places.

C. G. Jung, mentioned above as a force in psychological criticism, was equally devoted to the study of archetypes, which he identified as mythological images that are the collective legacy of our ancestral life. Archetypal analysis identifies compelling themes that appear predictably in public arts. Later chapters examine the archetypal approach in more depth, because an understanding of archetypal themes in the human psyche is of key importance to conceptualizing effective scripts.

QUESTIONS

1. Name one or more rituals that you have observed or participated in.

2. If your participation in a ritual evoked memorable emotions, what were they? What purpose(s) do you believe the experience served?

3. Identify a film or television program that you feel was effective in bringing about some significant changes in public attitudes, awareness, or practices.

4. What are your stereotypical notions about television viewers?

5. Do these stereotypes apply to you and your viewing habits and preferences?

6. Aside from *Riverdance,* can you think of examples of public arts from other cultures that have been successful in American media?

NOTES

1. A perfect example of how a private art (in the United States, at least) became a public art was the transformation of Irish step dancing into the hugely popular *Riverdance.*
2. Jane Ellen Harrison, *Ancient Art and Ritual* (New York: Henry Holt, 1913), p. 9–10.
3. Joseph Campbell, *The Hero With a Thousand Faces* (New York: MFJ Books, 1949), 251.
4. One Saturday I was at the Oakland Coliseum to see a baseball game, waiting for the gates to open. I was wearing a headset radio and a man asked me what the score was. I hesitated, unwilling to tell him that I was listening to a live broadcast of the Metropolitan Opera. Instead I mumbled something like, "You know these announcers—they never tell us the score." I couldn't tell the truth. Was it because I didn't want to shatter his stereotype about the nature of baseball fans?
5. Roger Fry, quoted in Morris Weitz, *Problems in Aesthetics* (New York: Macmillan, 1959), 174.

CHAPTER THREE

NEEDS AND DESIRES IN THE PUBLIC ARTS

Chapter 3 offers reasons why writers should undertake a systematic study of concerns that human beings share. The popular songs, poems, and stories of cultures in every part of the globe and throughout the ages demonstrate motifs that appear to be eternal and universal. Is it possible that our response to stories that affect us deeply do so because they strike chords that have resonated in our species from our earliest appearance as human beings? These concepts are explored in this chapter, with examples from the public arts offered as evidence.

Movies, television shows, novels, and other popular works focus on common human concerns that derive from our needs, our desires, our fears, hopes, phobias, and other motivating forces. An examination of these significant concerns will help you relate them to public arts and create stories that will attract and move audiences by tapping into the well of the human psyche.

What is a need and what is a desire? The answer is easy if we choose only obvious examples. Our most basic needs as living, sentient beings are for food, liquids, sleep, and shelter. Most of us share a basic desire to be appreciated by others, to be successful in our endeavors, and to know. Between these unquestionable needs and strong desires are an unknown number of urges or aversions that may or may not be actual needs or universal desires. Do we need to love and be loved? Many have lived their lives without experiencing love in either direction. To be admired by others? Some are so secure and self-focused they care nothing about the opinions of others. To vicariously share in the suffering of others? Sociopaths are said to be either asocial or antisocial, and incapable of feeling compassion toward the unfortunate, including their victims.

The process of amassing these apparently important and universal human concerns was one of induction. Stories from many early literate cultures, including Mesopotamia, Egypt, Greece, and China as well as oral tales from preliterate societies preserved by explorers and anthropologists show that certain themes—call them concerns or preoccupations—appear over and over to such an extent that they may be assumed to be eternal and universal.

There are a great many reasons for our pursuit and enjoyment of the public arts. Only by understanding why certain arts are popular, and why and how they work can you hope to create public arts that enlighten, entertain, and inspire others. What follows is an incomplete list, and it will always be incomplete because we cannot establish the criteria to determine what is and what is not a significant need or desire with any certainty. Because it's also impossible in many instances to know whether a specific concern is actually a need or a desire, the list makes no distinction.

HUMAN NEEDS AND DESIRES

to have models of agents and actions

to experience the beautiful

to experience the ugly

to be spiritually cleansed

to identify with a Creator, a Higher Power, a Life Force, or a Supreme Being

to believe that meaningful existence continues after death

to believe that spiritual or moral values are more important than mere physical existence

to believe that spiritual or moral values are more important than material goods

to love and be loved

to have friends

to be independent

to share in the suffering of others

to see authority figures exalted

to see authority figures deflated

to see others make mistakes

to feel superior to societal deviants

to believe in miracles

to see order imposed on the world

to share experiences with others

to identify with a group one considers special

to be recognized and approved of by others

to be physically fit, to achieve physical excellence

to improve oneself

to be attractive to others

to believe in romantic love

to be purged of unpleasant emotions

to have fun—to be amused

to be distracted from the realities of life

to be informed

to have vicarious but controlled emotional experiences

to experience a world of significance, intensity, and larger-than-life-size people

to confront, in a controlled situation, the horrible and the terrible

to explore taboo subjects without guilt

to find outlets for the sex drive in a guilt-free context

to experience hate in a guilt-free arena

to see evil punished and virtue rewarded

to imagine oneself a hero

to see villains in action

to believe in the good old days

Later, it will be seen that these concerns relate to universal themes, and many relate to one or another of the major forms in the storytelling arts.

To Have Models of Agents and Actions.   We learn patterns of behavior from those around us—parents, siblings, friends, teachers—and from stories, including fairy tales, novels, movies, television shows, and comic strips. The public arts have long told us how storytellers (or their sponsors) believed people should and shouldn't behave. The public storytelling arts tell us what actions are, and are not, desirable.

The critic Kenneth Burke believes we can understand a society if we regard its literature as a reflection of its essential beliefs about humankind. Burke tells us to look at five elements in the public literature of a society.[1]

1. *The scene.* This is where and when a story is set. It tells us where and when a society believes important events occur(red). Think about television today. Where and when are the most popular television series set? In the '50s, many were set in the nineteenth-century American West. Burke would tell us that the disappearance of programs such as *Gunsmoke, Bonanza, Wild Wild West,* and *Have Gun, Will Travel,* and their replacement with inner-city locales in such programs as *St. Elsewhere, Hill Street Blues,* and *NYPD Blue* reveals changes in our outlook as a society.

2. *The agent.* This tells us what kinds of people a society thinks are important enough to tell stories about. The agents (characters) in *Beverly Hills 90210, Melrose Place, Rosanne, Beavis and Butthead, The West Wing, the X-Files,* and *The Simpsons* are obviously quite different from those in programs such as *Green Acres, Beverly Hillbillies,* and *Mayberry R.F.D. (The Andy Griffith Show).* What does this change tell us about our society?

3. *The act.* This tells us what kinds of human, superhuman, nonhuman, and Divine actions are seen as consequential. Do the illegal actions of such heroes as Dirty Harry tell us that our attitude toward justice has changed from the days when the motion-picture code required all law breakers to be caught and punished?

4. *The agency.* The agency is the method by which an act is carried out, and how that act is viewed by people who observe or know about it. It reveals to us societal attitudes toward various ways of acting.

5. *The purpose.* This shows the values a society deems necessary for meaningful survival. Not only the storytelling arts, but all public ceremonies, rituals, and similar activities can help us understand human values of a given time and place.

In summarizing these points, Burke says,

> any complete statement about motives will offer some kind of answers to these five questions: what was done (*act*), when or where it was done (*scene*), who did it (*agent*), how he [or she] did it, (*agency*), and why (*purpose*).[2]

To Experience the Beautiful. Beauty is relative. All societies agree that there is such a thing as beauty, although each society has its own criteria for beauty. At the same time, tastes are almost constantly changing, and works that once were found beautiful may later be thought to be uninspiring, or even ugly. For example, the stained glass windows of Notre Dame cathedral in Paris were revered for centuries as spiritually uplifting; in the Baroque era (ca. 1600–1700), the windows were no longer valued as spiritual messages and were removed to let in more light. Obviously, tastes and values had changed.

Each age defines the principles of beauty in its arts. When values change, so do styles in the arts. The new art created as a stylistic period breaks down is seen as ugly or at least incomprehensible by those who want to hold on to earlier traditions of beauty. In time, the new, "ugly" art may be accepted and seen as beautiful. In modern times, popular music has moved from jazz to swing to rock to heavy metal to punk to hip-hop to rap, and so on. Ideas of what is meaningful or beautiful in popular music have changed several times during the past half-century.

To Experience the Ugly. Like beauty, ugliness is a relative term. The human preoccupation with the ugly, whether physical or behavioral, is a mystery to some of us, but there's plenty of evidence to show that most people are fascinated by and somehow drawn to things they find frightening or repugnant. Until recently, people paid to visit so-called "freak shows" at carnivals and circuses. In the arts, many painters, including George Grosz, Paul Cadmus, Hieronymous Bosch, and countless painters of hell scenes have depicted people they believed were both physically and morally ugly.

Perhaps confronting ugliness elevates our self-image. Maybe it gives us a feeling of relief that we're in better shape than the objects of our fascination. Perhaps we simply receive a vicarious thrill from the contemplation of what society considers abnormal. Perhaps, at a deeper level, aversion to those seen as "not normal" is a survival instinct. Times are changing rapidly, and there is more and more acceptance of those who differ physically and mentally from the norm. Eventually, perhaps, this need or desire will disappear. In the meantime, there can be no doubt that both defining a general concept of ugliness and viewing those considered ugly (*The Elephant Man, Mask, Phantom of the Opera*), fulfill some human need or desire.

To Be Spiritually Cleansed.   All people, with the exception of certain sociopaths, have occasional feelings of guilt. Unpurged feelings of guilt can lead to depression, mental breakdowns, and suicide. Many millennia ago, human beings purged feelings of sin and guilt through a variety of ceremonies. Some were magic rituals; some involved the selection and banishment—or murder—of a scapegoat. Confession and forgiveness survive to this day as features of Yom Kippur, also known as the Day of Atonement.

The Christian worship service includes a public confession of sin, read in unison by the congregation, followed by a statement that God has forgiven the penitents. This declaration is followed by a brief hymn of praise to God. This act is designed to bring about spiritual cleansing. Sir James George Frazer, in his classic work, *The Golden Bough,* gives a great many examples of spiritual cleansing. While by no means common, some stories or songs in the public arts bring about a catharsis similar to that caused by religious rites by providing us with opportunities to be purged and cleansed. (For more on this point, see Chapter 5, "Form in the Arts," and Chapter 6, "Catharsis.")

To Identify with a Creator, a Higher Power, a Life Force, or a Supreme Being.   Those of the Hebrew, Christian, and Moslem faiths believe in a single and all-powerful Creator (monotheism), named Yahweh, God, and Allah, respectively. Both the spirituality (reverence) and the morality (ethics) of followers focus on this Supreme Being. Buddhists follow the teachings of Buddha, while most Hindus worship Brahma, the creator god, as well as Shiva, Vishnu, the goddess Devi, and many lesser gods.

Nearly all cultures believe that a force beyond human comprehension is the cause of creation and the source of meaning. Conceptions of God vary, but a belief in a creator or creative force apparently is universal.

Through the ages, public arts worked in harmony with religion to help people experience the creative force and its meaning. In modern American society, religions are present but not predominant. Films centered on the Christian religion include *Shoes of the Fisherman, The Bible, The Robe,* and *Jesus Christ, Superstar.* Television series embodying Christianity are few, but include *Touched by an Angel, Father Brown Mysteries,* and *The Flying Nun.* The Jewish religion is touched on in varying degrees in many films, including the first talkie, *The Jazz Singer,* and in the 1969 film *Goodbye, Columbus.* Many movies about the Nazi era include Jews both in and out of a religious context: *Watch on the Rhine, The Holocaust, The Boys from Brazil, Ship of Fools, Sophie's Choice,* and *Schindler's List.* A rare sympathetic portrayal of the Moslem faith is a feature of the film, *Misunderstood.* Other religions are encountered in films from India, Iran, Taiwan, and China, but these films do not often reach mainstream movie theatres in the United States.

To Believe That Meaningful Existence Continues after Death.   All societies I've studied maintain that the human spirit remains active after physical death. In some, this means a paradise for the good and punishment for the bad. In others, there's a vague belief that the spirits of the dead go to some dark, unknown world. Most religious societies use the concept of an afterlife to establish the belief that one's behavior in this life determines one's fate in the next. Hammurabi's Code, the Golden Rule, and the Ten Commandments are given persuasive force by the notion of a day of reckoning.

Atheistic nations officially condemn religion and the belief in a life after death, but raise their living (and dead) leaders to the status of immortals. The Soviet Union long used Lenin—both his ideas and his embalmed corpse—to inspire its citizens to seek immortality, even though they could not offer pearly gates, wings, or harps. After the collapse of the Soviet Union, a conspicuous religious revival began taking place in the republics that made up that nation. A rational rejection of an afterlife doesn't seem to destroy the unconscious and instinctual feeling that some part of us—some call it our soul—won't be snuffed out by physical death; that in some way and in some form our nonphysical essence will find a new and permanent home.

To Believe That Spiritual or Moral Values Are More Important Than Mere Physical Existence.   Most societies believe that certain values are more important than human life. Many people will kill others, or allow themselves to be killed, to defend moral or spiritual mandates. The soldier who kills and risks his own life on the battlefield demonstrates this. So does anyone who would rather die than be dishonored. History tells many stories of persons who gave up their lives for others or for a principle. Without such a belief, moral dramas and inspiring examples of self-sacrifice wouldn't be possible. The other side of the coin is that such beliefs can support wars and genocidal practices, and, in fact, promote terrorism.

To Believe That Spiritual or Moral Values Are More Important Than Material Goods. Regardless of the greed we may be guilty of in our daily lives, nearly all of us are against the notion that what we get is more important than how we get it. Private and public fictions, as well as codes of conduct, moral preachments, and courses in ethics, have always told us what we want to hear: that it's better to be poor and honest than rich and dishonest.

To Love and Be Loved.   This apparent need is quite personal. It isn't the same as that which motivates us to make friends with others. It's a deeper need, arising from a deeper emotion. It's the basis of the conviction that somewhere there is one special person to whom one can relate in the most intimate, emotional, and enduring of ways. It is the finding of the other half of your being, as Aristophanes describes love in Plato's *Symposium*. If you are, or ever have been, deeply in love, no further comments are necessary!

To Have Friends.   Life without friends would be intolerable. Surely at one time in your life—and more likely at several points—you have been enriched by sharing with friends entertainments, outings, adventures, and ideas. Most teenaged assassins who bring guns to school and use them in mad efforts to exact revenge for real or imagined slights have been categorized as loners. Friendless people lack sympathetic acquaintances to assure them that they matter—that they have value as human beings. Friendships, as depicted in theatre, film, television, and popular novels, are integral parts of most dramas.

To Be Independent.   As contradictory as it may sound, along with a need for the support of friends, we also have a need to feel independent. Because we're complex beings and often have conflicting or contradictory needs, it follows that just as at times we need the support of others (friends or family, usually), at other times we need to assert our independence.

Perhaps you've had the experience of being the lone dissenting voice in a group discussion or have felt a need to go your own way. These are examples of this phenomenon.

To Share in the Suffering of Others.   Immature people of all ages tend to avoid involvement with those who suffer from hunger, disease, or physical or psychological problems. Most of us, however, feel a need to deliberately expose ourselves to the realities of unpleasant situations that affect others so that we can feel a part of them. Perhaps voluntary exposure to emotional pain is undertaken to prove to ourselves and others that we care; more significantly, perhaps it arises from an unconscious feeling that we can ease somebody else's pain by taking some of it upon ourselves, if only symbolically.

Whatever the reasons, when we deliberately court unpleasant feelings by seeking out or just staying with news stories that show the suffering of the people of Afghanistan, those who are starving in North Korea, or those whose homes and lives have been shattered by an earthquake, we vicariously share the suffering of others. And when we deliberately choose to see a movie or television play that we know in advance will sadden us, we show a similar motivation. Although stories of pain and suffering are not common on television, and only a little more so in movies, their mere presence in our public arts indicates that we do, indeed, have an impulse to share in the suffering of others.

To See Authority Figures Exalted.   Most societies have believed in a hierarchical arrangement of their members, extending from the highest or noblest to the lowest. In ancient times and continuing down to the eighteenth century, a person was automatically at the top of the heap if that person was of royal birth or of the priesthood. Early in human evolution, the hero was added to the list of the exalted (Odysseus, Gilgamesh, and King Arthur, for example). Heroes and, later, heroines still inspire us, whether their heroism is demonstrated in war, athletics, the arts, or scholarship. We seem to need heroic figures in our lives. All of us know how far short we fall of our ideals and automatically search for people who seem nearer to perfection than ourselves. We experience pleasure in looking up to such people. Often, we endow them with virtues they don't possess and, later, are unforgiving toward them if their fallibility is revealed.

To See Authority Figures Deflated.   We humans are just contrary enough to want to have it both ways—to both exalt and deflate authority figures. Politicians, actors, college professors, military officers, and others who might tend toward pomposity are especially vulnerable. All of us are at the mercy of "authorities" and, while we tolerate this burden quite well for the most part, we want (or need) to relieve our hostilities from time to time. To do this, we use a disguise, usually hostile wit, which cloaks the hostility we feel and brings about guilt-free laughter.

In societies where it's unsafe to deflate authority figures, it's necessary to go underground with hostile feelings or even to depose or kill the object of one's hostility in order to be purged. Democracies allow free verbal attacks on authorities, but democracies didn't invent the practice. Nearly all ancient cultures had an annual period of license, during which it was safe to ridicule authority figures. (Chapter 8, "The Anatomy of Comedy," examines this further.)

To See Others Make Mistakes.   If we have upward hostility toward most authority figures, we can also see a horizontal hostility toward those who are too much like us at our worst. Everyone makes dumb mistakes from time to time, and we enjoy seeing others make the same kinds of errors. The reciting of our own mistakes in a funny manner is what Freud meant by humor.

To Feel Superior to Societal Deviants.   This completes a three-part set of desires or needs: upward hostile laughter—toward some authority figures; horizontal hostile laughter—toward those who make the same mistakes we make; and downward hostile laughter—toward those we consider beneath us. Freud believed that we feel anxiety or hostility toward those who differ from us because we feel threatened. All societies establish norms—a set of expectations that tell us what persons ought and ought not to be like, and how they ought and ought not to behave. When individuals do not conform to these rules, we see them as a threat to the status quo and so we consider them ignorant, willful, ugly, inferior, or evil.

   If you can imagine a society in which 99 percent of its citizens speak the same language, belong to the same religion, have a common heritage, and also share physical characteristics of skin color, hair color, and so on, you might then imagine how they would feel if they were invaded by a horde of immigrants who were unlike them in nearly every way. As humans, they could be expected to feel some degree of anxiety, if not outright hostility, toward the newcomers. In earlier times, deviants were driven off, killed, or enslaved. Much later, they became objects of hostile wit. Today, in most modern nations and to some degree knowledge has replaced ignorance and sympathy has replaced hostility. Although we still invoke hostile wit against some who differ from us, we laugh less at physical, mental, ethnic, sexual, or religious differences than did our parents or grandparents.

To Believe in Miracles.   Throughout the ages, humankind has consistently reaffirmed its belief in miracles. In recent years, science has attempted to undermine our belief in miracles—at least at the rational level—but our public arts, our prayers, and our unshakable hope for the future seem to indicate that even the most pessimistic person believes that miracles, while they might not occur, *should* occur!

To See Order Imposed on the World.   Some would say that order is an aspect of beauty. But a work of art that some find beautiful may be seemingly without order, as are many paintings by abstract impressionists. And an orderly structure, such as a road, may have nothing to do with beauty. Order seems to be an important element in most things we consider beautiful, but is something that people seem to seek for its own sake, as well. It is unclear whether the need is emotional or aesthetic—perhaps it's both. Why do we straighten pictures that are hanging crookedly?

To Share Experiences with Others.   Sharing experiences with others is one need or desire that's served only sporadically by the electronic media, and in a two-step process. When crowds gather for rock concerts, sports events, or political rallies, its members share experiences simultaneously and communally. Shouts of approval or disapproval affect all present, and as the event moves along there's an almost inevitable buildup of emotions as audience members feed on a growing consensual excitement.

In contrast, most electronic media events are experienced by only a few viewers at any one location. This being so, it would seem that sharing experiences with others via this medium is, in a literal sense, impossible. Yet we can experience momentous events on electronic media that produce in us feelings of communion with others, despite our physical isolation. Some momentous events, such as the terrorist attack on the New York World Trade Center, keep us glued to our television sets, feeling connected in some manner that defies logic, with the millions of others who simultaneously are watching. It isn't until we leave our sets for school, work, or visiting friends that we have the opportunity to actually discuss with others what we've experienced, however. While our communion with others is a delayed one, there's no question that electronic media can bring shocked people from physical isolation to actual contact where sharing feelings can help release pent-up emotions.

Under less dramatic circumstances, even when the audience for a television program numbers in the millions, the dispersal of its audience prevents the development of a unified spirit. Early radio and television producers knew this, and made efforts to compensate for the lack of unity in a scattered audience in two ways: the first was to include a studio audience whose function it was to convey the excitement (or amusement or suspense) of the program to those watching or listening; the second was to add a sound track of audience reactions, usually a track of people laughing. These methods were somewhat successful, but it's clear that radio and television don't make the best uses of their potentials when they try to do something for which they're ill suited.

There are exceptions to this conclusion, to be sure: large numbers of persons gathered in sports bars watching important contests; or spillover audiences sitting in auditoriums to see graduation ceremonies or heated town council meetings. In such circumstances, a group spirit does exist, but these uses of the electronic media are rare and untypical in most Western societies, and they don't invalidate the premise that the electronic media (as used in the United states at least) are not capable of satisfying our need or desire for shared experiences.

To Identify with a Group One Considers Special.   Our need or desire to identify with a group has limitless manifestations, because its essence is a need to belong, to feel accepted by those we admire or respect. Membership in fraternal orders such as the Masons, the Elks, or the Eagles; in civic betterment organizations such as Rotary, the Lions, or Kiwanis; and school fraternities and sororities are examples of benign associations that can, in their best manifestations, build esteem and self-respect.

At the same time, some groups develop around a need or desire to proclaim its members superior to members of other groups. We see it in ethnic clans, high school cliques, and street gangs. This need is also served by extremist organizations—sometimes called cults—such as the Branch Davidians, neo-Nazis, and survivalists.

There's nothing inherently bad about belonging to a group. Group membership is as good or bad as the values it holds and the activities in which it engages. What group(s) do you belong to? Does your belonging make you feel special?

To Be Recognized and Approved of by Others.   We all are social creatures. One characteristic of this reality is that much of what we do and say is intended (though most often unconsciously so) to make others like and respect us. This is most apparent in sports or in war, where people risk their health or even their lives to achieve recognition and approval, but occurs as well in our day-to-day interactions with others.

To Be Physically Fit, to Achieve Physical Excellence.   Physical fitness is part of the need to be attractive to others, but it's more than that. Weight-loss plans, fitness programs, team and individual sports, and vitamin and herbal regimens are all part of our desire to achieve peak performance and physical excellence. A desire for physical excellence began in prehistory because it was only the physically fit who could protect the community from intruders and supply it with food from the hunt. In Greece, the Olympian movement was an expression of the Greek goal of attaining a sound body and a sound mind.

A contrasting view of physical fitness is provided by ascetic members of certain religions—early Christianity, Hinduism, and Buddhism among them. A dedication to spirituality often places physical preoccupations of any kind at a low level of concern.

To Improve Oneself.   Our need to improve takes many forms. On a physical level, it motivates us to work out, to take vitamins and bodybuilding supplements, and to diet when our scale tells us it's time to shed unwanted pounds; on an intellectual level, it causes us to sign up for a class or an entire program of instruction that offers hope for a better job or a more enriched life. This need may cause us to stop taking illegal drugs as well as alcohol or tobacco. To be human is to want to work toward achieving our highest potential. Without this desire and the willingness to sacrifice temporary pleasures, we are less than fully human.

To Be Attractive to Others.   Part of our need to be attractive to others relates to our basic facial and bodily appearance, but this need manifests itself in many other ways. On the physical front, this need determines how we dress, how we wear our hair, and how we use cosmetics or other means—even cosmetic surgery—to enhance our appearance. The basis of our desire to appeal physically to others may well be biological in nature. Through the ages, the human species survived through procreation, so there's no reason to question the importance of physical attraction.

At the same time, as life became increasingly complex and as our ancestors grew in intelligence, attractiveness took on additional meanings. When our focus no longer was dominated by the obligation to produce the next generation, such qualities as a pleasing personality, a gift for stimulating conversation and a sense of humor became part of what we refer to as an attractive person.

To Believe in Romantic Love.   Nearly everyone falls in love, and the feelings that follow are excruciatingly beautiful and painful: the constant preoccupation with thoughts of the loved one; the agony of time spent apart; the palpitations and drumming in the ears when you meet and kiss; the speed with which time passes when you're together; and on and on.

However, human relationships can't remain in this state—people couldn't survive it, and we'd never get anything done! Years of familiarity take the edge off romantic love. And, while the relationship that develops is more permanent, deeper, and ultimately more useful, some of us want to hold on to a naive belief that, somehow or other, romantic love can and should last a lifetime. The incurably immature rush from one love affair to another in search of an inexhaustible fountain of romance. In time, mature people accept a deeper relationship as a reality of life. Such relationships are less exciting, but ultimately more rewarding. All of us, however, seem to enjoy those fictional accounts where romantic love never fades. "They lived happily ever after" is based on anything but human experience, yet we're willing to accept the notion in fiction as though it were the truth. It's conceivable that this romantic view of human relations is damaging to those young persons who believe in it implicitly; sometimes the price we pay for a beautiful fantasy is self-delusion or narcissistic projection.[3]

To Be Purged of Unpleasant Emotions.   Public arts and ceremonies help us maintain a psychological balance by purging a surplus of negative psychological energy. Hostility toward one's boss, toward the system, or toward one's mate or sweetheart—as well as anxieties and fears about economic security, safety, success in school or work—can be relieved (at least temporarily) by the public arts. Both universal themes and the cathartic power of forms, can bring about such relief.

To Have Fun—to Be Amused.   Laughter serves important psychological and even physiological needs. (See Chapter 8 for a discussion of comedy.) What isn't clear, though, is why we're attracted to amusements that aren't, in themselves, funny. The pleasure we receive from watching magicians, jugglers, trained dogs or dolphins, or acrobats is hard to pin down. We may smile, yet there's no joke that causes the smile. We can't perform the feats we applaud, yet we most likely wouldn't want to acquire those skills. We're momentarily distracted from the realities of life, yet we sense more than this negative motivation for our enjoyment. Sword swallowers, acrobats, jugglers, and animal tamers are depicted in some of the earliest drawings and stories that have survived. Perhaps our universal and permanent delight in such performances is merely our astonishment at what highly skilled presenters can achieve.

To Be Distracted from the Realities of Life.   Most of us need periodic opportunities to escape from the problems that plague us. The public arts offer such a refuge, and there are many ways of interpreting this. Some believe that an occasional break from ongoing problems restores our energy and prepares us for a resumption of the battle. Others, including many who condemn the so-called mass media, claim that entertainment becomes addictive and distracts us from the awareness that problems exist that should be identified and engaged. Still other commentators on the public arts believe that the major issues of our time—mass starvation; genocidal wars in Croatia, Cambodia, and Rwanda; the destruction of the ozone layer; and the rape of our planet's resources—are insoluble, and that escapism is a sign of sanity. Some extreme critics believe the public arts are deliberately designed to be irrelevant to prevent the public from being aware of the problems that menace it. As a writer for the electronic media, you should weigh your output against these viewpoints, if only to see where you fit in to the scheme of things.

To Be Informed.   Many public arts furnish us with information. This is obvious in newscasts, documentaries, and how-to shows. But because the public arts pervade our lives, there's information to be gained, too, from variety shows, situation comedies, cop shows, and outdoor adventure shows. If *ER, NYPD Blue,* or *Survivor* provide us with little "useful" information, they're still important to us, because everyone is talking about them; we must watch in order to be informed. In other words, because the public arts are frequent topics of conversation, most of us feel a need to keep up with them to participate in social interchange. (Relate this to the earlier comment that shared experiences aren't usually well served by the electronic media.)

To Have Vicarious But Controlled Emotional Experiences.   Life can be dreary if we seldom experience fear, hate, or other extreme emotions, but most of us really don't want to risk our lives or our health to obtain relief from monotony, so we seek emotional stimulation through the public arts, including films, television and radio broadcasts, festivals and ceremonies, sports events, and circuses. Many psychiatrists believe that vicarious emotional experiences with things we fear help us cope with some of the frightening aspects of real life.

To Experience a World of Significance, Intensity, and Larger-Than-Life-Sized People.   The lives of most of us alternate between periods of excitement and stretches of unremarkable routine. During our down times, we often seek entertainments that stimulate us and provide opportunities to participate vicariously in heroics, life-or-death decisions, or peak experiences. The public arts take us away from the humdrum and expose us to events and agents that are larger than life. For example, in *Rocky, Rambo, Dirty Harry, Xena, Indiana Jones,* and *Thelma and Louise.*

To Confront, in a Controlled Situation, the Horrible and the Terrible.   We associate horror with the destruction of the physical—with mutilation and death. We associate terror with unseen fears provoked by a creaking door or a menacing shadow on the wall. Life is full of horror and terror. Humankind found that the best way to live with horror and terror was to go out and meet it head on. Our early ancestors developed a variety of practices that gave them vicarious experiences with horror and terror in controlled situations. Practices that gave the experience of horror include human and animal sacrifices; public executions; the Roman games; depictions of the martyrdom of saints, reliquaries, mummies; and photos of war dead or accident victims. Practices that provided vicarious terror include shamans' chants; epics; legends; stories of demons; ghost stories; Halloween activities; and movies featuring creatures from outer space, mutants, werewolves, and vampires.

While all societies have developed stories and rituals that deal with horror and terror, the details of what is considered horrible and terrible and the symbols used to depict horror and terror may vary from culture to culture and from time to time.

To Explore Taboo Subjects Without Guilt.   Public arts have, for centuries, explored taboo subjects in a guilt-free way. Despite government disapproval of such acts as rape, debauchery, and murder, scenes showing these acts are common in sculptures and paintings from ancient times onward. A fifth century B.C. Greek sculpture on the temple of the Olympian Zeus shows the "lapith bride" being raped by a centaur; walls of Pompeian homes are decorated with wild pornographic scenes; the beheading of John the Baptist was common in paintings from the early Gothic period on; and murder (Ingres' "The Death of the Marat," eighteenth century), executions (Goya's "The Third of May," early nineteenth century), and orgies (Delecroix's "The Death of Sardanapalus," mid-nineteenth century) prove that depictions of acts officially denounced by church and state always have found their way to eager audiences.

Today, newscasters provide intimate details of the sex lives of famous people, claiming their obligation to "tell all." The serious and objective delivery of these reports belies both the reporter's and the viewer's enjoyment of the story, because of our eternal and universal fascination with forbidden subjects. It also is true that some public arts cause guilt feelings in those who seek them out. For example, some people who partake of pornography on the Internet or elsewhere may receive pleasure at the moment but suffer guilt feelings later.

For years, biblical movies have portrayed nudity, rape, illicit sex, debauchery, and flagellation, yet many of these films are shown on a regular basis to congregations within their very own church buildings! Because they're about religion, they are acceptable for church members to watch. Most stand-up comedians evoke hostile laughter by poking fun at taboo topics such as religion, sexual deviants, or various ethnic groups. The joke disguises the hostility, and makes laughter possible. (See Chapter 8 for a discussion of hostile wit.)

To Find Outlets for the Sex Drive in a Guilt-Free Context. When Freud wrote of tendency wit, he divided it into *hostile wit,* motivated by aggressive tendencies, and *obscene wit,* a form of sexual display. Dirty jokes, comedies about marital infidelity or impotence, double-entendre puns, innuendoes about bodily wastes—these and similar phenomena tend to be funny because they deal with established taboos. Taking part in a sex act or having a bowel movement are not funny to the participant, but sex or scatological talk in a movie or at a dinner party is almost always cast in an amusing light. There are two points to be made here: first, the witticisms are masks that prevent feelings of guilt while avoiding censorship; and second, most people apparently feel that there is something inherently naughty or funny about sex and the elimination of bodily wastes. This attitude is, of course, changing, but it probably will never entirely disappear. Jokes combining romantic love and sex are rare in any culture.

To Experience Hate in a Guilt-Free Arena. Most of us have limited opportunities to express our deepest feelings. If we do occasionally blow up and tell someone off, we typically suffer guilt feelings after we've cooled down. We work for reconciliation, and long for the healing effects of time. We're somewhat freer to express love—at least in private—but even with love, most people are afraid to "let go" and fully experience the emotion.

Of course, we'd be better off if we didn't have these hang-ups, but as long as we do, public arts, ceremonies, and sports will continue to provide outlets for the extreme emotion of hate. We can, without guilt or embarrassment, scream for the destruction of a villainous wrestler; we can thrill to the outrageously illegal behavior of *Butch Cassidy and the Sundance Kid*; we can feel unrestrained glee at the revenge of the three office workers in *Nine to Five* or hatred toward the victims of *Thelma and Louise*. In real life we're expected to understand the behavior of those who annoy us. In fictional events, we can ignore this. We can hate the hateable, without having to hate ourselves for doing do. It's a relief to visit this never-never land occasionally!

To See Evil Punished and Virtue Rewarded.   Despite the prevalence of injustice in the world—or possibly because of it—humankind has consistently wanted to see justice triumph in those fantasies we call the fictive arts.

In comedies and melodramas, the protagonists usually are people with whom we sympathize. Even when heroes break the law, they almost always escape punishment. There are a few exceptions to this: in *Butch Cassidy and the Sundance Kid* the two charming lawbreakers are killed at the film's close. Comedies and melodramas made under Hollywood's code required all lawbreakers to be brought to justice. Professional wrestling matches similarly capitalize on our desire to see evil punished and virtue rewarded. All of this is related to our affinity for the underdog. Fiction often presents us with a struggle between good guys and bad guys, which arouses our fear for the safety and success of the good person(s).

Popeye and Bluto tell a typical story of our love for the underdog. Bluto beats up on Popeye for most of the cartoon, but, at the last minute, Popeye finds and eats his spinach, the tables are turned, and the underdog hero triumphs while the villain is pummeled. Once again we've seen things work out the way they should; once again we've had our faith restored in that elusive commodity called justice. Popeye cartoons give us this scenario in miniature over and over again.

To Imagine Oneself a Hero.   We all daydream, and most of us at one time or another imagine ourselves as heroes.[4] Fictional, sports, and real-life heroes provide us with specific examples of people we'd like to be. Even though we might recoil from real danger, we like to use our imagination to place ourselves in dangerous situations. Although most of us would likely hate the life of a spy, a football star, or a detective, we enjoy pretending, for a time, that we possess the courage, the freedom, and the competencies of such persons. Fantasizing about an exciting life relieves the daily monotony of smog, freeway congestion, parking meters, taxes, sales commissions, or final exams. We want to hold on to our daydreams, even though we're willing to settle for the problems of a more humdrum life.

Heroism is clearly a part of our fantasy world: the risk that accompanies heroic actions is best left at the vicarious level. See you at the movies!

To See Villains in Action.   Villains, more often than not, have been of greater interest to audiences than have been heroes and heroines. The actor who played Herod in medieval cycle plays was paid a higher salary than was the actor who played Christ! Macbeth, Simon Legree, and movie villains played by Margaret Hamilton (the Wicked Witch of the West in *The Wizard of Oz*), Peter Lorre, and Sidney Greenstreet have fascinated millions. Does this mean that we enjoy these villains, or does it mean that we enjoy hating them? Are we pleased at their actions, or at their downfall? Or both?

Is it possible that villains are important because without them we wouldn't have heroes and heroines? Or is the hero important because we must have someone to pit against the villain? My guess is that villains address many needs and desires, but that underlying the whole phenomenon is a kind of vicarious satisfaction in seeing someone who breaks all the rules, codes, and orderly procedures that restrain and inhibit us.

We all were villains, though unconsciously so, when we were little children. We broke things, hit other kids, lied, took things when we wanted them, and had no regret or bad feelings when we refused to kiss Aunt Catherine because she had a mustache. We got away with such behavior for several years, and we really hated the change that took place when we were told (sometimes with a belt) that we could no longer do these things. Perhaps the fictional villain, who continues to act selfishly and amorally in adult life, is secretly admired by those of us who were forced to conform to the demands of society.

To Believe in the Good Old Days.   A. O. Lovejoy, in *A Documentary History of Primitivism and Related Ideas,* documents the fact that the human species has always believed that there was an earlier era when everything was better and people were happier. This vision sees human beings as having forever been in a state of progressive degradation. The concept of a Golden Age is an important feature of many public ceremonies, rituals, and art events; for example, the Renaissance Pleasure Faire, Dickens' Christmas Faire, Disneyland's Main Street USA, and restored sites such as Fort Dearborn, Williamsburg, and the gold rush towns of Columbia and Jamestown.

Cowboy stories in any medium hearken back to the good old days, where no one apparently worked for a living, when there were no taxes, no parking meters or traffic congestion, no water pollution, no wanton depletion of natural resources, and no slums. The chief protagonists of westerns are men without wives, children, mothers-in-law, bosses, or other inhibiting agents. In the good old days, there were no ethnic groups demanding economic and social justice. In this vision of the past, there also were no street people, no juvenile delinquents, no muggers, no graffiti vandals—in fact, no one to remind us that we are a complex, troubled, and multiethnic society constantly struggling to adequately address its many problems.

The true but unwelcome facts of these good old days are quite different from the picture painted in the American public arts. Characteristic of these times were early deaths of children due to common diseases such as smallpox and diphtheria; adult life expectancy of less than forty years; work days of twelve and fourteen hours—for children as well as adults; untold monotony, bigotry, and gross injustice. Also, ethnic minority people were there—they were simply invisible in the public arts, other than when they were used as buffoons or villains. To tell the truth about the American good old days would be to shatter a long-held dream of a Golden Age. Most of us know consciously that there never were any good old days, while others persist in believing that there were. Whatever our beliefs, it's very human to imagine that there was such a time, and most of us like to visit it occasionally in our public arts.

If you try, you should be able to come up with additional needs and desires served by the public arts. As mentioned at the beginning of this chapter, the list isn't complete, and never will be. This is an evolving discipline, and new understandings inevitably will cause additions, subtractions, and modifications of these topics.

There's nothing startlingly new or novel about these findings. Nineteenth-century anthropologists, including Adolf Bastian and James George Frazer, noted the appearance of similar motifs in cultures the world over. A more detailed discussion of their findings may be found in Chapter 4, "Universal Themes in the Public Arts."

QUESTIONS

1. Select five needs or desires identified in this chapter, and answer these questions about each of them:
   - Where and when have I actually experienced these?
   - What can I remember about my feelings on those occasions?
   - Do I believe I was manipulated by any of these encounters?
   - If I was manipulated, was that good, bad, or of no consequence?

2. What sorts of public media (comic books, video games, films, television, novels, and so forth) have I sought out in order to experience

   - horror or terror?
   - romantic love?
   - heroism?
   - the good old days?

3. Have you experienced the suffering of others through the media of radio, television, or newspapers? If so, did you feel any emotions other than pain and sympathy? Did you identify with those who were suffering? Did you feel that, by permitting yourself to suffer vicariously, you somehow or other were giving the victims your support?

NOTES

1. Kenneth Burke, *A Grammar of Motives* (Cleveland, OH: World, 1962).
2. Ibid., xvii.
3. Many scholars maintain that romantic love didn't exist until it was "invented" during the Middle Ages. To support this, they point to arranged marriages and the scarcity of romantic love themes in ancient literature. It certainly is possible that parents so controlled the lives of their children in ancient times that romantic love was nearly impossible to consummate. Yet, if it's true that human nature never changes (as Aldous Huxley maintains in his essay, "Fashions in Love"), it's difficult to believe that it was "invented." What was "invented" during the Middle Ages was a specific type of romantic love—that described in stories of knights and their secret love for unapproachable ladies.
4. The term, *hero,* includes men and women.

CHAPTER FOUR

UNIVERSAL THEMES IN THE PUBLIC ARTS

This chapter establishes the significance of recurring themes that appear in the most successful and powerful stories of all times and cultures, including our own. Appendix B, Eighty Universal Themes, is cited, with a suggestion that you read it now, and review it from time to time, as you develop your ability to conceive stories that will attract and hold audiences.

The predictable recurrence of certain themes in the public arts of all times and places was noted by nineteenth-century ethnographers and anthropologists, who developed several related theories to explain this fact.

One theory states that we're born with these themes buried in our unconscious minds. Adolf Bastian (1826–1905), a German ethnographer, travelled throughout the world in the mid-nineteenth century studying so-called primitive societies. In his extensive travels, Bastian noted that certain themes appeared repeatedly in the folk arts of indigenous people the world over. He termed these the *elementary ideas* (*Elementargedanken*) of humankind. He distinguished these from what he termed *ethnic ideas* (*Völkergedanken*), which he believed were local variations of the universal themes.[1]

Sir James George Frazer (1854–1941), a Scottish anthropologist, later compiled an encyclopedic description and analysis of worldwide folk practices and beliefs, which he published in several volumes under the title *The Golden Bough*. Underlying Frazer's work was his conviction that all humankind represented one species of being, and because this was so, it was inevitable that the same themes would appear spontaneously in cultures that had never been in contact. He concluded that universal themes appear everywhere because humans behave and react in similar ways regardless of where or when they lived.

Later still, Friedrich Nietzsche (1844–1900) picked up the notion that all humans possess an unconscious store of memories that go back beyond the birth of the individual: "In our sleep and in our dreams we pass through the whole thought of earlier humanity." And the distinguished anthropologist Franz Boas (1858–1942) added ". . . there can be no doubt that in the main the mental characteristics of man [*sic*] are the same all over the world."[2]

In offering a related theory to explain the existence of universal themes, the Swiss psychologist Carl Gustav Jung (1875–1961) posited his theory of *archetypes* and the *collective unconscious.* It was Jung's conviction that what we understand as our unconscious is but a part of what lies within our minds. It's an important part, but it isn't the entire reality. We each have a personal unconscious in which are stored memories of past events and feelings—the part that causes us to remember events that have taken place in our lives since birth. We use our conscious mind to connect with memories in our unconscious. Think about an event from your past—a birthday party, a graduation ceremony, or a dispute, for example. Or try to remember an occasion that you haven't thought of for some time; spend a few minutes reviewing events from that experience as your mind continues to bring forth details of that event. These are examples of your conscious mind bringing forth memories that have remained hidden in your unconscious mind.

According to Jung, another force exists within our mind, and this is a collective, rather than personal, unconscious. Jung tells us that *"This collective unconscious does not develop individually, but is inherited. . ."* and adds that, in addition to our immediate, personal, consciousness, ". . . there exists a second psychic system of a collective, universal, and impersonal nature which is identical in all individuals."[3] (italics added)

In other words, our unconscious contains both a personal and a collective component. Our collective layer encompasses memories embedded in our minds before birth. While most of our memories emerge from events personally experienced by us, other memories of events, ideas, fears, and so forth are present without our having actually experienced them. These images, which Jung labelled *archetypes,* are the inheritance all humans share from countless ages of development toward our present state of humanness.

Stanley Edgar Hyman helps us understand why writers of stories should pay special attention to Jung's theories as he makes this unequivocal claim:

> Archetypes are unconscious primordial images, the "psychic residua of numberless experiences of the same type" shared by ancestors going back to primitive times, which are somehow inherited in the structure of the brain. *They are thus basic, age-old patterns of central human experience, and Jung's hypothesis . . . is that these archetypes lie at the root of any poetry (or any other art) possessing special emotional significance.*[4] (italics added)

Joseph Campbell considers the "parallel development of mythological imagery" in *The Masks of God.*[5] He begins by citing the well-known phenomenon of the flight of newly hatched sea turtles to the sea. The female turtles deposit their eggs in the beach sand, safely above the high tide line.

> After eighteen days a multitude of tiny turtles come flipping up through the sand and, like a field of sprinters at the crack of the gun, make for the heavily crashing waves as fast as they can, while gulls drop screaming from overhead to pick them off. . . . There is no question here of learning, trial-and-error; nor are the tiny things afraid of the waves. They know they must hurry, know how to do it, and know precisely where they are going. . . . Students of animal behavior have coined the term "innate releasing mechanism" (IRM) to designate the inherited structure in the nervous system that enables an animal to respond thus to a circumstance never experienced before. . .[6]

Campbell mentions, as well, the fact that

Chicks with their eggshells still adhering to their tails dart for cover when a hawk flies overhead, but not when the bird is a gull or duck, heron or pigeon. Furthermore, if the wooden model of a hawk is drawn over their coop on a wire, they react as though it were alive—unless it be drawn backward, when there is no response.[7]

Linking this to the arts, Campbell conjectures:

The image of the inherited enemy is already sleeping in the nervous system, and along with it the well-proven reaction. Furthermore, even if all the hawks in the world were to vanish, their image would still sleep in the soul of the chick—never to be roused, however, unless by some accident of art; for example a repetition of the clever experiment of the wooden hawk on a wire. With that (for a certain number of generations, at any rate) the obsolete reaction of the flight to cover would recur. . . . "Whence," we might ask, "this abrupt seizure by an image to which there is no counterpart in the chicken's world? Living gulls and ducks, herons and pigeons, leave it cold; but the work of art strikes some very deep chord!"[8]

In citing the instinctual behavior of animals, Campbell raises questions about human instincts and their possible relation to universal themes. He concludes his discussion with these words:

Therefore, though respecting the possibility—perhaps the probability—of such a psychologically inspired parallel development of mythological imagery as that suggested by Adolf Bastian's theory of elementary ideas and C. G. Jung's of the collective unconscious, we cannot attempt to interpret in such terms any of the remarkable correspondences that will everywhere confront us. On the other hand, however, we must ignore as biologically untenable such sociological theorizing as that represented, for example, by the anthropologist Ralph Linton when he wrote that "a society is a group of biologically distinct and self-contained individuals," since, indeed, we are a species and not biologically distinct."[9]

Other scholars, so-called diffusionists, offer an entirely different explanation for the appearance of common themes in the stories and beliefs of peoples the world over. According to diffusionists, the themes found everywhere were spread through the world by early migrant and conquering tribes. One extreme school of diffusionists claims that Egypt was the birthplace of all cultural traits, and that all other cultures were a reflection of that great civilization. A less extreme position is taken by other diffusionists who believe that culture arose in several cultural circles from which it gradually spread.

Diffusionist theories are opposed to those championed by Frazer, Jung, and others cited in this chapter. Whichever theory we prefer, it's important to recognize that none rejects the notion that certain themes are indeed universal. We don't need a deep knowledge of Jungian and Freudian psychology or an encyclopedic knowledge of mythology to employ universal themes in our writing. We can build a table without knowing the chemical constitution of wood, nails, and glue; we likewise don't need to know how these materials were grown or made or where they came from.

One point needs be made, however: the diffusionist theory must be dismissed as a full explanation of universal themes. Almost without doubt, highly specific themes such as the motif of a tree with a serpent at the bottom, and an eagle at the top, are either unique to one society or, if they appear elsewhere, likely were carried from place to place by wanderers. But other themes, such as sibling rivalry, the Oedipal struggle, or death and resurrection certainly did not need an itinerant tribe to spread them from place to place. We would be strange creatures indeed if we took no notice of such basic human preoccupations throughout the millennia, only to be made aware of them by travelers!

HOW CONCERNS BECOME THEMES IN THE PUBLIC ARTS

Human needs, fears, and desires almost inevitably give rise to preoccupations. These concerns may be individual, or widely shared within a society. When a concern is widespread, it appears as a *theme* in the public arts: contagion, famine, and nuclear holocaust have, for example, played roles in stories created when these disasters seemed imminent or were actually ongoing.

Other themes, such as guilt, love, or a desire to become a hero, are independent of group preoccupations; they're present because of our inherited commonality as humans.

To become a story, a theme must be housed within a storytelling *form,* usually comedy, tragedy, or melodrama (the Heroic). The theme of guilt often finds a home within the tragic form; comedy provides an effective form for stories about antisocial behavior; and stories of adventure, heroism, and danger are well-suited to the melodramatic form. At the same time, many universal themes—such as love—can be treated within any of the established forms. In creating a story, it's important to determine at the outset your story's major themes and to select its most appropriate form.

Some needs, fears, and desires are eternal and universal preoccupations, and are found as themes in the public arts of all but the most dehumanized societies; for example, the idea of *imaginary creatures,* such as Cyclops, unicorns, and mermaids. Other preoccupations are less intense, and therefore less universal; for example, the yearning for eternal youth. Some themes have been with us for thousands of years, only to lose their intensity during the present period; for example, infertility. On the other hand, some themes have emerged only recently, as science has given us new causes for concern; for example, the themes of nuclear warfare and of monsters created by radiation-caused mutations.

Contagion, long a major theme in public arts (in literature, *Oedipus Rex, Genesis, The Decameron,* and in film, *The Plague, The Andromeda Strain*), became less prevalent when medical breakthroughs tamed age-old plagues. With the appearance of AIDS, the theme of contagion returned to the public arts. As its true horror became widely known, AIDS became a focus of books, short stories, films, television dramas, stage plays, and as a topic on talk radio and television.

The fear of pestilence remains always within our reservoir of fears. In 2001, following the terrorist attack on the World Trade Center, anthrax spores were sent through the mail to several individuals and businesses. While the identity of the sender was unknown, fear spread throughout the United States as people linked the anthrax mailings to a conspiracy with wider implications: that terrorists had begun an attack using weapons of biological warfare. Day after day, news broadcasts and periodicals saturated the public with information—and misinformation—about anthrax and its dangers. Scientists and governmental medical officers appeared in lengthy and repetitive interviews as eager audiences sought information they considered vital to their survival. As with AIDs, the threat of anthrax demonstrated how close to the surface are our age-old fears of contagion.

Such subthemes, however, are neither universal nor eternal. The theme of *contagion* or *pestilence* is both eternal and universal; specific subthemes, such as the Black Death, polio, influenza, mad cow disease, or AIDS, are neither.[10] There will one day be a vaccine to prevent or cure AIDS. When this happens, the topic of AIDS will appear less often in the public arts, to be replaced (if at all) by another plague—perhaps something along the lines of the Ebola virus that struck central Africa in 1995.

In thinking about universal themes, remember that few works in the storytelling arts display but one theme. It's certainly acceptable to sum up a story (film, television drama, novel) by its predominant theme: in reviewing the film *The Perfect Storm*, for example, it's accurate to say that the film is about a time when three huge hurricanes collided, causing much destruction and the sinking of a boat engaged in swordfishing At the same time, the story invokes many other themes such as courage, fear, sacrifice, love, and death by drowning, which, for the purposes of clarity, we may want to call *collateral themes.*

Graphic and plastic arts are most suited to treating single themes, yet most paintings and statues incorporate more than one theme. A painting of the crucifixion of Christ, for example, may center around the theme of martyrdom, but other themes depicted may be suffering, death, identification with the Deity, rebirth and immortality, and spirituality. Similarly, a story such as that of Cain and Abel features sibling rivalry, but the themes of murder, death, villainy, jealousy, and the punishment of evildoers are also present. Longer stories, including the plays of Shakespeare, embody a greater number of universal themes. In *Romeo and Juliet,* the central theme is forbidden love. Other featured themes are romantic love, parent-child conflict, forbidden love, murder, innocence of youth, heterosexual love, lost love, death, fate, loyal companion, suicide, and unrequited love.

Noted scholar Abraham Maslow based his optimistic psychology on studies of mentally healthy persons, in contrast with earlier studies based on those with serious psychological problems. Out of his investigations came a conviction that human beings have a natural motivation to live mentally healthy lives. He saw human beings as capable of pursuing the highest values and aspirations.[11]

Maslow believed that the biological destiny of the human species is to achieve self-actualization, and in this context he wrote of the human potential. (Maslow eventually came to prefer the term *full-humanness,* because he was dismayed by the tendency of his critics to equate *self* with *selfish.*)

For Maslow, full human potential could only be realized by satisfying a number of *growth needs.* Before being free to work on these needs, however, a human being must satisfy several *deficiency needs.* One does not grow toward self-actualization when one is starving, insecure and frightened, unloved and unloving, or disrespected (both by oneself and others). Given an external environment that includes freedom, justice, orderliness, and challenge, the individual must first satisfy deficiency needs, and then progress to the level of growth needs. Deficiency needs are:

1. physiological needs: air, water, food, shelter, sleep, sex
2. safety and security needs: physical and biological

3. love and belonging needs: to love and be loved, and to be secure in the knowledge that one belongs
4. self-esteem needs and needs for the esteem of others: self-respect, and the knowledge that one is respected by others.

It should come as no surprise that deficiency needs described by Maslow form the basis of eternal human anxieties and fears, and that our most deeply rooted concerns relate to the gratification of these needs. It follows inevitably that deficiency needs relate directly to numerous eternal and universal themes in the public arts. My concept of how this connects is:

a human need;
manifests itself as a fear or a desire;
unsatisfied fears or desires become preoccupations;
preoccupations are reflected as themes in the public arts.

Growth needs, according to Maslow, include truth, goodness, individuality, perfection, justice—to name but a few. Some combinations of themes and forms in the arts can bring about the temporary relief of anxieties through a catharsis, or purging of built-up anxieties and can help us confront important issues in a controlled setting.

Given the age-old precarious state of life on this planet, it's remarkable that the earliest literature we have from Mesopotamia and Egypt reflects not only deficiency needs (that's to be expected) but growth needs as well. Ancient literature shows our ancestors preoccupied with concepts of justice, goodness, and perfection. The Precepts of Ptah-Hotep, set down about 2200 B.C. in Egypt, advises rulers that justice is everlasting, and has not been disturbed since the day its creator brought truth into the world. Around 1780 B.C., the Babylonian ruler Hammurabi engraved his code of justice on an eight-foot stone slab so that all who could read would know what was required of them. Despite such codes of honor and justice, the public arts of most times and places concentrated on the release of anxieties that arise from deficiency needs.

An analysis of human needs and their relation to the public arts can be of great importance to us. First, it can make us aware of the opportunity to help others meet both deficiency and growth needs; second, it makes clear the fact that there's nothing arbitrary about the universal themes in the public arts. On the contrary, eternal and universal themes exist because they delve into aspects of the human condition that fascinate us; they exist because they've helped us maintain psychological stability in a hostile and frightening world; they exist because they help us confront, in a controlled way, our greatest preoccupations; they exist because they reflect human nature as it has existed over the millennia; they exist because they help us move toward self-actualization.

Throughout history, many societies have been repressive and, as a consequence, have used the public arts to preserve the status quo, to facilitate acculturation, or to obscure reality. Such societies are loathe to depict self-actualized qualities such as increased autonomy or more democratic character structure as virtues. These themes are treated in some plays—Shakespeare's *Coriolanus* and Ibsen's *Enemy of the People,* for example—and they've been featured in some films and television programs, including *Roots* and *The Verdict,* but self-actualization themes have not been, in the broader scheme of things, universal over the past several millennia.

Given, however, a just and democratic society, there seems to be no reason why public artists should not more regularly treat themes that can help individuals grow toward higher levels of mental health. Without claiming that the American public is clamoring for programs that will improve mental health, I believe that a significant percentage of any audience will respond to public or private arts that promote growth. If, as Maslow believes, our biological destiny is to achieve self-actualization, no other premise is tenable.

Appendix B, "Eighty Universal Themes," may help you gain a broader understanding of the public arts as reflectors of innate and eternal human concerns and enable you to reach audiences with messages that compel, disturb, challenge, amuse, and enlighten.

QUESTIONS

1. Identify one theme that became a preoccupation and thus appeared in the public arts during your lifetime.

2. Select a favorite story from television, film, or other medium of the public arts and identify as many universal themes as you can detect.

3. Have you had the experience, when enjoying a story in the public arts, that you had a prior association with the theme or the story? Is this the same link that Joseph Campbell describes in his story about the inherited instincts and fears of baby chicks and turtles?

4. Examine the universal themes discussed in Appendix B. Choose several of these and find examples of them in stories from the public media.

5. Think of the most moving story you've experienced in any medium. What role did universal themes play in its effectiveness?

6. Can you think of themes not mentioned in this book that you believe are universal? What are they? Where and when have they appeared as themes in stories?

NOTES

1. Joseph Campbell, *The Masks of God: Primitive Mythology* (New York: The Viking Press, 1959), 32.
2. Ibid., 18–19.
3. C. G. Jung, *The Archetypes and the Collective Unconscious* (Princeton NJ: Princeton University Press, 1959), 43.
4. Stanley Edgar Hyman, "Maud Bodkins and Psychological Criticism," in *Art and Psychoanalysis,* ed. William Phillips (Cleveland, OH: Meridian Books, 1963), 474.
5. Joseph Campbell, *Masks,* 101–02.
6. Ibid., 30.
7. Ibid., 31.
8. Ibid., p. 31.
9. Ibid., 48.
10. In the biblical Book of Revelation, the Four Horsemen of the Apocalypse are usually identified as War, Famine, Death, and Pestilence.
11. Abraham Maslow, *Toward a Psychology of Being* (Princeton, NJ: D. Van Nostrand, 1962). Maslow expands concepts found here in a number of other articles and books.

CHAPTER FIVE

FORM IN THE ARTS

Chapter 5 introduces and discusses *form*—the arrangement of a story's incidents or ideas in a sequence that attracts our attention, retains our interest as it reveals ideas or events that make up the body of the story, and concludes with a resolution that rewards us for our expenditure of time. A successful story of any type is noteworthy for its carefully organized *plot*—another term for a story's *structure*, or form.

THE STORYTELLING ARTS

The components of extended dramas are *incidents, character traits, ideas, dialogue, music,* and, in film, television, and theatre, *visual images.* Dramas written for these media may be analyzed in terms of the six components that Aristotle labelled *plot, character, thought, diction, music,* and *spectacle.*

At the same time, many radio and television scripts don't include all six components. Brief narratives such as essays and commentaries feature ideas and dialogue; thirty-second television commercials may present us with dialogue, music, and visual images; and a radio news story may include only incidents and dialogue.

Despite variations, stories of all kinds and in all media of communication have one element in common, and that is *structure.* Other terms are used for this basic constituent—*plot, form, story*—but whatever term is used, it refers to the *sequence* in which you present your material. Careful structuring of your story's elements is crucial to its impact, and every bit as important as the incidents, characters, and values you choose to include.

TEMPORAL FORM

Stories are told over time—from thirty seconds for a television or radio commercial to two hours for a documentary or drama—so they're given *temporal form* by their creators. An understanding of the nature and the power of temporal form can help you write scripts that attract and hold audience interest while moving a story line step by step to a satisfactory conclusion.

News reports, sitcoms, daytime serials, and documentaries (to name but a few) share one essential characteristic: all are stories. Regardless of a script's length, purpose, mood, or other variables, the primary job of writers for radio, television, or film is to tell stories. And, because stories begin at one particular point in time and end at another, they possess temporal form—in other words, they have a structure that can be revealed only over time. Planning the structure of a script is one of the most important decisions you'll make as a writer. Arranging the sequence of events occurs only after you've established your goals, the mood, the needs to be addressed, and the specific points or incidents that tell the tale.

More than 2,000 years ago, Aristotle, in his *Poetics,* arranged the six parts of a play in order of importance. The first and most important is plot, another term for form or structure. After that comes character (the personality traits of the agents), followed by thought (the ideas embodied in the work), diction (the spoken words), music (all Greek plays were accompanied by choral music) and spectacle (the visual element).

Today, of course, spectacle in many action films and television dramas (*The X-Files, Star Wars*) and comedies (*I Love Lucy, Three Stooges*) has become more important than Aristotle could have imagined. And because of changed and more sophisticated under-standings of human nature, character has replaced plot as the most important element in many modern stories. Despite this, most stories that capture and hold our attention as they work toward their conclusion are characterized by strong, cohesive, plots.

TEMPORAL VERSUS SPATIAL FORM

Drawings and sculptures also have form and structure, and they often tell stories, but they differ from literary or dramatic works in that they exist in *space,* rather than in *time.* Works that occupy space, as do paintings, are grounded in visual or spatial aesthetics. Stories, on the other hand, follow a sequential pattern that takes time to unfold. Stories follow principles of temporal aesthetics.

The reason for studying temporal form is to learn how story materials, when arranged in a carefully chosen sequence, can take an audience through a controlled emotional, logical, and/or aesthetic experience. Random groupings of story elements, like a random grouping of pictorial elements, communicate, of course, but such communication lacks the guidance of an artist (communicator) who consciously shapes and arranges the materials to produce predictable responses in an audience.

To demonstrate the essential difference between the forms of works that occupy space and those that occupy time, here are three ways in which to view a number of photographic images:

First, we may look at a completely unorganized display of photos of a disaster scene, as hung on the wall of a museum. Even without being arranged by an artist, the photos can make a point, and their random arrangement will carry a message about the devastation. The unorganized photos have been given no additional interpretation, as they would have been by an artist who arranged them to tell a story—not the story of each photo, but the story of the disaster as expressed in a sequential viewing of the individual images. As displayed on the wall, the photos exist in space only. We, as visitors to the museum, are free to view them in any order, and even to merely glance at the display, spending but moments noting that an area of a wall is covered with photos, and then moving on. From an artistic standpoint, what's lacking in the random display is *order (sequence), duration,* and *focus.*

Moving to the second arrangement, the photos could be presented one at a time, as in a book, by an artist who wants to take us from long shots of physical destruction to closer and closer views of people in distress. In this example, *order* has been introduced to our experience, so we have objects that occupy *space* (the photos) and the sequencing of the photos that requires us to view them in a particular order, as we see them over *time.* Because we're in control of how we look at the book, we can regulate the pace at which we look at each photo, and can even skip back and forth among the pages, thereby creating our own sequence and, in doing so, override the intentions of the artist.

A third way of experiencing the photos is as a video montage or a slide-tape presentation; this also involves time, but the amount of time viewers are exposed to each photo is determined and controlled by the artist. By arranging the sequence of photos and by varying the length of time each photo is seen, a refined kind of temporal form is imposed. In doing this, an artist presents a new reality—one that has a maximum likelihood of bringing about a more predictable, powerful, and controlled response in viewers than could be achieved by random selection or unguided viewing. This is the power of temporal form.

The way you organize the materials of a script is basic to your success in achieving the goals you've set for it.

CHRONOLOGICAL FORM OF STORIES

When structuring the elements that make up a story, you have many possibilities. The most common structure is chronological, the arranging of the several parts of the story in the sequence in which they occur over time. An ancient fable, told in a condensed version, illustrates chronological organization quite well:

> **THE GRASSHOPPER AND THE ANT**
> It's summer. An ant busily works preparing a home underground, and collects and stores food for the winter months ahead. At the same time, a grasshopper plays and fools around, and thinks only of the pleasures of the moment. Later, when winter comes, the grasshopper dies of exposure and hunger, while the ant stays warm, dry, and well fed in its underground home.

This is a straight chronological organization of the fable's incidents. A variation of the same fable could begin with the suffering of the grasshopper in the present, followed by the core of the story, seen as a flashback, and then a return to the present to witness the death of the grasshopper. This arrangement seems to violate chronology, but, aside from giving us an opening scene that uses a technique called *foreshadowing,* it tells essential incidents of the story in a chronological sequence. This arrangement was followed in the film *Sunset Boulevard,* which opens by showing us the dead body of the protagonist floating in a swimming pool. Near the end of the film—which has been told chiefly in chronological order—we return to the swimming pool and the floating body.

There are other ways of avoiding a strict chronological ordering of events. In his film *The Betrayal,* Harold Pinter tells his story in reverse, moving backward in time; we see the ending at the movie's opening and its beginning as the film ends. Between start and finish, each scene takes us back months or years in time. This was a novel and clever concept; it also was confusing and ultimately undramatic.

Flashbacks were seldom used in stage plays, novels, or narrative poems of the past, but the flashback became an option for filmmakers right from the start, and easily carried over first into radio and then television. A few examples of stories told largely through flashbacks are:

The Autobiography of Miss Jane Pittman tells the story of a 110-year-old former slave whose memories recount Black history from the days of slavery to the Civil Rights movement.

The Prince of Tides centers around repressed memories that are gradually brought into conscious remembrance through the probings of a psychiatrist. The recalled incidents are not revealed in a strictly chronological order.

The television series, *Young Indiana Jones,* began each episode with the elderly Jones recollecting his adventures as a youth, followed by the adventure itself.

In dramas, the simplest chronological structure tells the story from beginning to end without interrupting or leaving the scene of the action; in other words, the story and the time it takes to tell it are identical in duration. Early Greek playwrights followed this form, but it fell out of fashion in later years. *My Dinner with Andre,* a Louis Malle film, is a modern drama that gives us only one extended scene. Nearly all stories seen on television and film depict incidents as they occur over time (as in *My Dinner with Andre*), but they don't tell the story in an uninterrupted pattern. They omit unessential parts of their stories, and change locales as appropriate. Some stories cover only a brief period of time, as in the movie *48 Hours,* while others are revealed over many years, as in *Forrest Gump* and *The World According to Garp.*

Generally speaking, a dramatic story is best told in a chronological sequence with unessential dialogue and unneeded events omitted, and this is the form found in most successful plays of our time. It also is the form followed by hard news stories and commercials that tell a story.

COMPLEX PLOTS

The Grasshopper and the Ant is told chronologically, and has a single storyline. Longer stories on television may tell three or more stories, with incidents interwoven to move viewers from one story to another. Chronological form is retained, but audiences are given multiple storylines, a technique developed early in television's history by daytime serial dramas.

Typically, a continuing serial drama has three stories running at any given time and each receives a share of broadcast minutes in each episode. Over time, as one storyline plays itself to a conclusion (a resolution), another is introduced to sustain (or rekindle) audience interest. Daytime serial dramas depend on hooking viewers through suspenseful conflicts and relationships. Unlike one-time-only dramas, including feature films and television specials, daily dramas succeed only if they bring their audiences back day after day. Customarily, each episode ends with a *cliffhanger,* a term derived from old movie serials. Viewers are left with an unresolved conflict to enhance the likelihood that they will return the next day to learn its outcome.

Parallel and overlapping stories are also told on weekly hour-long dramas. *The West Wing,* to use one popular example, seldom relies on suspense by carrying over storylines from one week to the next. The overarching theme—difficulties that threaten the President's reelection—is a continuing motif, but weekly episodes usually focus on crises or issues that begin and are resolved within that hour. At times, as with the President's undisclosed history of multiple sclerosis, several episodes are devoted to dealing with that particular threat to reelection, but that's an exception to the general rule.

In most episodes, four or more stories are interwoven, some focusing on the President, others on supporting agents or "subcharacters." While the main story focuses on the President, subplots show other agents with various problems, conflicts, aspirations, or character flaws. Often there's a humorous theme whose contrast with the life-and-death issues of the administration makes for poignant and welcome relief.

In one episode of *The West Wing,* "War Crimes," five storylines are played out in the 42 minutes allotted to the drama:

1. President Josiah Bartlet asks his unwilling Vice President to speak out in favor of gun control following a shooting at a Texas church. The personality conflict and lack of respect for one another shared by these executive officers is clearly demonstrated in a tense meeting.
2. Donna, Assistant to the Deputy Chief of Staff, testifies under oath before a congressional committee and lies when she denies that she maintains a diary. Her questioner before the committee is an exlover who knows she's lied.
3. Chief of Staff Leo McGarry debates an old friend and Air Force officer about the United States' future stance regarding war crimes tribunals.
4. White House Press Secretary C. J. tells White House Communications Director Toby Ziegler that a reporter overheard his unfortunate comment that President Bartlet would only win reelection "on the Vice President's coattails."
5. The humorous storyline in this episode revolves around a dispute between Sam, Deputy Communications Officer, and a Congressman who wants to propose legislation that would eliminate the penny.

Each of the storylines is written separately, with an awareness of how many minutes of program time each will receive and where in the program each will enter and exit. As you watch television dramas, you will be able to spot the manner in which interwoven stories are incorporated. Some dramas that may be fruitful for such analyses include *Ally McBeal, Ed, Law and Order, St. Elsewhere,* and *Boston Public.*

Chronological Form of Documentaries

Many documentaries demonstrate a variation of chronological form and follow a pattern similar to *Death of a Porn Queen,* a one-hour program following the life and death of Colleen Applegate, who committed suicide at age twenty-two. This story opens with shots of the house where Colleen Applegate took her life, a still photo of her on her death bed, and a view of her desolate grave. The film asks questions about why and how a young girl from Wisconsin became a star of pornographic films under the name of Shauna Grant, turned to drugs, and eventually killed herself with a rifle. The opening scene is a *tease,* a technique, common in television, to motivate viewers to stay tuned. After the tease, the story roughly follows the events of her life in the order in which they occurred, but abandons chronological order from time to time to pursue various themes, such as details about the porn industry and explorations of the feelings of Colleen's parents and friends. At the conclusion, the documentary takes us back to the scenes that opened this biographical sketch.

LOGICAL OR THEMATIC FORM

Some documentaries, editorials, instructional videos, and feature reports follow a logical or thematic form. Many *National Geographic Specials* present a thematic organization. While chronology may sometimes play a part—as in showing lions mating and producing a cub—most of these stories deal with facts about their subjects in a thematic or logical progression. A special on elephants, for example, may include such topics as how they mate, how they defend against predators, how they feed, how they migrate, what problems they pose for their human neighbors, what problems humans pose for them, and so on.

For an example of a script that typifies logical structuring, read the radio station editorial by Nick DeLuca, *The Washing of Hands,* in Chapter 14, "Narrative Scripts."

COMBINATION OF CHRONOLOGICAL AND THEMATIC FORMS

Ken Burns' monumental documentary series, *The Civil War,* follows a general chronological pattern, from incidents leading up to the war to the surrender at Appomattox and the war's aftermath. But within that framework, it examines specific topics, one at a time, in a thematic manner, as in "medical treatment," "women and the war," "soldier food," and "the North's resistance to the war."

FORM IN DRAMAS

As noted elsewhere, form is the shape or organization of materials in a work of art. In the dramatic arts, form is synonymous with *plot.* Writers invent story incidents and arrange them in a logical step-by-step sequence as they wed content and form. Most dramas begin with a stable situation, soon disrupted by a destabilizing incident, usually unforeseen. Conflicts bring about confrontations between the chief agents. The ways agents speak and act as they struggle with their conflicts establish their character. Words and actions propel the story forward. Outstanding dramas are amalgams of well-chosen stories, intriguing agents, engaging dialogue, incidents of significance, and a structure that takes an audience through an emotional journey, concluding with a resolution that ties things together in a plausible manner while reestablishing stability. While we can look at form and content separately for purposes of analysis, they're not experienced separately by an audience. Form helps give power and beauty to a work of art, although it's not independent of other factors. Form is derived from the intended function of a work of art, and from the vision of the artist.

FORM IN RADIO AND TELEVISION SCRIPTS

Careful structuring of stories is as important to the effectiveness of brief commercials and station promos as it is for conventional dramas and serials. Self-contained television dramas, those that begin and end in a single episode, are given a structure that begins with a premise—an action, a conflict, or other situation that needs resolution—and ends when the major question is resolved. Episodes on continuing series such as *Dharma and Greg, Home Improvement,* or *The West Wing,* are self-contained unless, by exception, two or more episodes are devoted to a longer story than is customary.

Serial dramas—*Guiding Light, The Young and the Restless*—are more complex in their structures than are self-contained dramas. Typically, three different but related stories are ongoing, and each episode cuts from story to story on a formulaic basic. The introduction of new conflicts and the resolution of ongoing difficulties overlap. As one story reaches its resolution, another story is born, so there always are three stories for viewers to follow. In a tradition that reaches back to antiquity, the end of each episode leaves the audience hanging, wondering how the story that closed that episode will be continued or resolved the following day. Centuries ago, professional reciters of lengthy stories such as *Gilgamesh, A Thousand and One Nights,* and the Arthurian legends similarly left their audiences in suspense as they closed the day's portion of the story with a "cliffhanger" ending.

In Part 2 of this book you will find examples of many different types of scripts. Analyzing them will give you models of several genres you may one day want to create. The comic scenes in *Josie,* found in Chapter 16, "Writing Comedy," are arranged in a chronological order, and even though they don't constitute an entire episode, they add up to a story with a beginning, middle, and end.

The essay, "A Matter of Time" in Chapter 14, "Narrative Scripts," has a definite theme. While it doesn't tell a story in the conventional sense, it uses a chronological order to set forth and discuss its theme. "Little League Days," also found in Chapter 14, is told in a strictly chronological order following a brief introduction that establishes the scene and the story's premise.

QUESTIONS

1. Read three narrative scripts from Chapter 14 and outline their structures. What principles of structure (plotting) can you detect (chronological, thematic, combination)?

2. Give an example of a work in the public arts (other than those cited in this chapter) in which the story begins with a foreshadowing of what's to come.

3. Select three radio and three television commercials from Chapter 13. Identify the three parts of each: How do they arouse our interest? How does the copy that follows the opening retain our attention? How does the conclusion connect with the beginning?

4. Give at least two examples of works that have spatial form. Give two examples of works that have temporal form.

CATHARSIS

Chapter 6 introduces and explores the concept and power of *catharsis,* and relates it to the storytelling arts.

Catharsis, or *purgation*, as it often is called, means an emotional release or purifying. A physical impurity such as an infection can be healed by piercing the skin to allow it to drain; in the area of mental processes, catharsis refers to the relieving of tension, anxiety, or other built-up psychic energy by providing an emotive escape valve.

As you'll see from the discussion of catharsis that follows, I'm engaged in an ongoing search for understanding of the cathartic powers of public arts and ceremonies. Why do we need them? How do we choose our events and how do we process them? And, how are we changed by them? Several recent studies in biology and psychology have opened up new prospects of understanding the little-recognized role catharsis plays in promoting our well-being.

The term *catharsis* has somewhat different meanings in various disciplines. The simplest, and most likely the earliest, appearance of the term was in medicine, where Hippocrates used catharsis to describe a purging (or expelling) of unhealthful elements that caused illnesses, as in the example of the infected tissue mentioned earlier. Medical practice, as promoted by Hippocrates, was largely given to *emetics* (agents to promote vomiting); *suppositories* (medicines designed to melt within a body cavity to help expel a toxic substance); *enemas* (the injection of a liquid through the anus for cleansing purposes); *bloodletting* (draining blood through an incision to remove "impurities"); *cupping* (the use of small heated cups, applied to the skin, to draw blood to or through the skin); *fomentations* (poultices, to draw impurities to the surface of the skin); and *ointments, massage,* and *hydrotherapy.* Most of the Hippocrates' healing methods were designed to draw impurities from the human body—in other words, to *cleanse* or *purge* it.

Aristotle, in his *Poetics,* uses catharsis to mean the release of pent-up emotions of pity and fear through the resolution of a tragic drama. It was Aristotle's conviction that tragic dramatists must first arouse these emotions, then purge them, in order for the drama to be successful.

Plato, an older contemporary of Aristotle, knew about the arousing effects of the arts, especially of music and poetry. He warned that the arts, although pleasurable, were dangerous. In his *Republic,* Plato described his concept of the ideal city-state, where he reluctantly banned poets because of what he considered poetry's bad effects. In discussing the rules that would be in force in his ideal community, Plato wrote that poets appealed to the mindless part of the human soul and, in arousing people's passions, destroyed the reasonable part of the soul.

Critic Stanley Edgar Hyman tells us that Plato got it wrong. He agrees with Plato that poetry feeds, or arouses, the emotions, but says that Plato didn't take the next step of *purgation,* which Aristotle did in his *Poetics.* "He [Aristotle] applied his psychology to poetry in *The Poetics,* answering Plato's psychological fallacy in *The Republic,* that poetry *feeds* the passions and is thus socially harmful, with the much sounder psychological theory of catharsis, that poetry arouses the passions of pity and terror in a controllable symbolic form, and then purges them through its operations."[1] In so doing, Hyman writes, Aristotle made a case for the beneficial effects of the tragic catharsis.

In some circumstances in our lives, arousal occurs naturally, as with sex, hunger, or thirst on a physical level, and fear, anxiety, or joy on a psychological plane. At other times, we bring about arousal by choosing to experience an athletic contest or watch a drama; we inject ourselves into a situation that promises to first arouse us and then purge us of the aroused emotions. We aren't forced to go jogging, take in a game at the ballpark, or go to a movie—we choose to do so.

Catharsis explains much that is important about us as human beings. Both physically and mentally, we seek a state of equilibrium. Catharsis, or the purgation of unwanted chemicals, emotions, and so on, is as important to the maintenance of equilibrium as is the acquisition of these chemicals, emotions, and so on, where a deficiency exists.

To be alive is to take in. Physically, this means water, food, and warmth. Emotionally this includes fear, hope, hate, love, pity, or jealousy. We can't be alive and not take in. Some of what we take in raises us to a level of equilibrium, such as food when we're hungry; some of what we take in pushes us above the level of equilibrium, and demands a release in order to return to a state of equilibrium, as with fear. A physically and mentally (emotionally) healthy person is one who, both consciously and unconsciously, constantly moves toward, and at least temporarily achieves, equilibrium.

Except for those rare individuals who want constant stimulation or who try to avoid stimulation altogether, most of us conform to this formula: when we're bored, we seek events or experiences that will excite us; when overly excited, we seek peace and tranquility. In both instances, we're moving away from a deficiency or an excess toward their opposites. A state of equilibrium isn't necessarily dull; it's a state of relaxation that gives our emotions a chance to rest. Prolonged periods of emotional relaxation motivate us to look for some sort of excitement, often through the arts or sports, including active participation.

In the time arts, catharsis is achieved through dramas, including stage plays, movies, and television plays; through stories, as in novels, fables, news reports, and short stories; through songs, most obviously in gospel, patriotic, and "story" songs; and through dance.

What's the connection between the physical catharsis achieved by sweating, defecating, breathing, or crying and the emotional or spiritual catharsis achieved through the arts, ceremonies, and sports? I believe that we needn't separate the physiological, the psychological, and the spiritual into watertight compartments. I further believe that there's a carryover from one human experience to another—as different as those activities may seem at first glance.

Aristotle set into motion more than two thousand years of debate about his concept of catharsis, but most arguments are not helpful to this view of catharsis because they look only for the big, obvious, mind-blowing experience, such as that which blasts us at the end of a great performance of *West Side Story* or the television classic *Brian's Song*. Such a purgative experience is overwhelming, and can affect us in deep and profound ways. At the same time, catharsis of a much less powerful kind occurs so often that we barely notice it. Following are examples of both physiological and psychological catharsis, and thoughts on what purpose(s) each may serve.

PHYSIOLOGICAL CATHARSIS

Crying. Researchers have found that the brain regards any strong emotion—even great joy—as a stress to be regulated. Because stress triggers the secretion of certain chemicals to cause a self-protective reaction in our bodies, the act of crying serves to release those substances from our bodies through the discharge of tears. William Frey, a biochemist, found that emotional tears have a different chemical makeup than irritant tears. When emotional crying takes place the tears remove unwanted chemicals that build up during emotional stress.[2]

Sex. Anyone who has experienced sex knows that among other results, it helps reduce tension and stress. Sex is cathartic in that it allows us to release built-up tensions and frustrations in an enjoyable and harmless manner.

Exercise. Somatic anxiety (rapid heartbeat, excessive perspiration) is reduced or eliminated through physical exercise. Runner's high (or, more broadly, exerciser's high) is a type of catharsis or purging process. This state, achieved when performing physical exercise, allows our minds to break free of everyday constraints of job, family, and society. Achieving this cleanses both mind and body. A drummer who had performed nonstop for about a half hour was asked how he could continue drumming for extended periods; his answer was that it was only difficult for about the first hour—after that, he was in a different state, where time and effort were meaningless abstractions.

Bathing. Aside from the psychological lift of ridding oneself of filth, perspiration, and body odor, what purpose does bathing serve? The Japanese, among many others, use the bath for mental as well as physical catharsis: In the Japanese bathing ritual, the individual first washes away dirt, perspiration, and bacteria, and then enters a deep tub and sits submerged to the chin in hot water. During the time spent there, the bather enters an altered mental state, one in which aches, tension, strong emotions, and all other stressful factors disappear, replaced by a rejuvenating sense of well-being.

PSYCHOLOGICAL CATHARSIS

Sleeping and Dreaming.   Sleep rids us of fatigue, but it also makes dreaming possible. What's the difference between deep sleep, which permits dreaming, and light sleep? According to Dr. Rosalind Cartwright, "Dreams appear to be important for processing emotional information, revising our moods and maintaining a stable sense of self from one day to the next. . . . REM (rapid eye movement) sleep is a very active brain state." She continues:

> **New Findings:** A study conducted at Rush Presbyterian–St. Luke's Medical Center of men and women going through a stressful divorce found that 80 percent of those who were clinically depressed began to dream earlier in their REM sleep and had longer, more active dreams than those who were not depressed.
>
> **Key Finding:** One year later, these people had recovered from their depression without the help of drugs or psychiatric treatment. Those who didn't dream earlier were still depressed. Conclusion: Our dreams act as our own inner therapist, helping us to work through troubling emotional material.[3]

Laughing.   Recent studies show that laughter produces important hormonal changes that help fight disease or prevent illness. Researchers at the Loma Linda Medical School found that laughter significantly reduces stress hormone levels that contribute to high blood pressure. Researchers say that laughter is akin to positive thinking and can have a healing effect. Editor Norman Cousins reported that he cured himself of a life-threatening illness through laughter.[4] Nineteenth-century mechanist psychologists saw laughter as the emptying of an over-full reservoir of psychic energy. Maybe they were closer to the truth than their critics realized.

Daydreams.   Daydreaming is a universal and complex phenomenon, too involved to adequately explore in this textbook. One daydream may find us imagining ourselves a hero, a second about finding a hoard of gold, and a third about gaining revenge on one who's caused us harm. There are many purposes served by these and other variations: They allow us to explore taboo subjects without guilt; permit the discharge of pent-up sexual energies; reduce stress and hostility; provide a safe arena for fantasies of revenge; fight loneliness; provide comfort in times of sorrow; boost self-esteem; inspire works of art; help us solve problems; bring about an entire range of wish fulfillments; and provide a sense of power and autonomy. Psychologist Jerome Singer agrees that daydreams have the power to release tensions, make boredom tolerable, increase creativity, and illuminate solutions to problems.[5]

Meditation and Psychotherapy.   Cognitive anxiety (obsessive thoughts, the tendency to worry too much) is reduced or eliminated through meditation. Both meditation and psychotherapy teach us how to "make space" for obstacles and feelings (such as pain), instead of struggling with them; psychotherapy can help us to work through our problems by examining them and their roots; meditation practices can help us to relax or to let go of our fixations on our problems.

Religious Rites. Religions including Islam, Judaism, and Christianity present regular opportunities for the purgation of feelings of guilt and sin. During the typical Christian worship service the congregation makes a corporate confession of its shortcomings followed by a silent personal confession. After the confessions, there are words of pardon and an assurance of forgiveness.

The confessional of the Catholic Church is an additional means of cleansing: penitents confess their sins to a priest, who prescribes specific tasks, on the completion of which guilt will be removed. In the Jewish tradition, Yom Kippur is a time of confession, reconciliation, and forgiveness—a time of corporate and individual spiritual cleansing and restitution. In Islam, Ramadan is a time for sacrifice, contemplation, thanksgiving, and forgiveness. It serves as both spiritual and physical cleansing.

Other physical and emotional purgations are achieved through less celebrated religious rites, ceremonies, and festivals; from carnival or theme-park rides; or through video games, arcade games, rodeos, spectator sports, bullfights, cockfights, fandangos, pow-wows, fireworks displays, and so forth.

EXPERIENCING CATHARSIS

Reading about catharsis is one thing; actually feeling its effects is another. Without ever having read about catharsis, we've all had cathartic experiences. Few of us analyze our feelings when we're moved to tears by a sad movie or a memorable concert or brought to a state of exhilaration by a bottom-of-the-ninth baseball comeback victory, but these, too, are purgative or cathartic experiences.

Here are two ways to experience the central thrust of this chapter: first, rent a videotaped drama that's structured to first arouse, then purge viewers of high emotion, and watch it alone and without interruption. Out of hundreds of possible choices, I'll mention just two that can be rented or purchased in audiovisual centers: *Brian's Song,* a modern tragedy, and *Chariots of Fire,* a subtle and artistic melodramatic vision.

My second suggestion is to read the following essay. It's a deeply personal and moving account by Joan Ryan about her brother, Bobby, and it's reprinted here with her kind permission. The essay was not written for broadcast, so it should not be seen as a radio script. It's included here not as an example of radio or television scriptwriting, but because it possesses the power to take a reader through a moving experience. Perhaps not everyone who reads this will be moved by it, but to give the essay a fair chance, I ask you to read it only when you're in a position to avoid distractions, when you're in no hurry to finish it, and when you're receptive to its theme—the life and death of Joan Ryan's brother.[6]

A WAY TO LIGHTEN BOBBY'S LOAD—
by Joan Ryan
He grew up with a dent in his head, tumors on his skin and no friends to call his own. And he continued to live a miserable life until it came time to die.

Part One

My brother Bobby never liked Thanksgiving. He didn't eat sweet potatoes, green beans, creamed onions, stuffing or turkey. Maybe he ate mashed potatoes. He'd sit at the table because he had to, a silent glowering presence that only my mother still noticed. The rest of us joked and argued around him, looking his way only when a funny remark finally got the better of him and a giggle suddenly broke from his tight mouth. He chewed with his mouth open so when he laughed bits of potato or bread would shoot out. I tried never to sit opposite him.

Bobby was a year older than I, the second oldest of six children. He was born with a bone missing from his right temple, so his head looked like someone threw a baseball into it. He had neurofibromatosis, so-called Elephant Man's disease. He wasn't disfigured (except for his head) but grew fatty tumors on his skin that had to be removed periodically. Even as a baby, he didn't like to be touched. He struggled in school, though he was clearly brighter than the rest of us. He had a stunning memory, remembering the birthdays of every aunt and cousin in the family and reciting facts about planets, prehistoric eras, World War II battles and Confederate generals until you wanted to scream.

He had no friends except his brothers and sisters, and we only tolerated him. As a preteen, as if classmates needed another reason to torture him, he grew breasts, and my parents' insurance took forever to come through with the money for the operation to remove them. For a year, he walked stooped over so his shirt would hang loosely away from the abominations on his chest. I cried at night sometimes for his misery. I wondered why God wouldn't give him just one wonderful thing, a gift for music, a sense of humor, a friend of his own.

But every day seemed to bring new humiliations, and he often couldn't contain the anger.

If he lost at ping-pong, he might slam the ball at our faces. He once tied my youngest brother up—loosely—and threw him in the pool, prompting my father, when he found out, to summon him from his job down the street as a dishwasher and hold him hard against the living room wall. Veins popped from my father's red neck, dark threats hissed through his teeth. I thought my father might kill him.

Bobby and my father often clashed, and Bobby always professed his dislike for my father. But as he moved through his teen years and early 20s and he had to figure out who he was, he began to become my father. He took on all his mannerisms and even internalized my father's experiences as his own. He parroted my father's conservative views, often word for word. He called bad drivers chowderheads, as my father did. He pointed with his middle finger. He favored old movies and the New York Yankees. He even became a draftsman like my father and worked in the same office for a while, until they drove each other crazy. Bobby once visited my aunt in New York and commented on how he was getting right back into the pace of the city. But Bobby lived in New York only as an infant. It was my father who grew up there.

The first time Bobby came to see me in California, he was nearly 30 years old and had never traveled out of the Eastern time zone. He worried about jet lag. He worried about me picking him up at the airport. He worried about changing planes in Dallas. As he waited for the boarding call in Dallas, he sat in a puddle of soda. Because he was sure the airline would lose his luggage, he had a change of clothes with him. But when he was changing his pants in the bathroom, his wallet slipped out of his pocket. So he showed up in San Francisco with no money or credit cards and soiled pants in his carry-on. It was so Bobby.

Four years ago this week, Bobby decided to have plastic surgery to fix the dent in his head. During a routine blood work-up, doctors found an abnormality, and X-rays showed a tumor in his belly. He figured it was the neurofibromatosis growing a fatty tumor inside this time instead of out. But when the doctor opened him up, he found malignant cancer in Bobby's intestines, stomach and pancreas and two spots on the liver. The doctor took out as much as he could but told my parents there was no hope. No treatment would save him. I flew to Florida. My sister came down from North Carolina. Everyone rallied around him, and he blossomed.

In dying, Bobby came to life. He was weak and thin, but he had never been happier. This was the most exciting thing that had ever happened to him. He was, for the first time, the center of attention, the recipient of cards and flowers and phone calls that had only rarely arrived in his life before. Rather than plunge him into a funk, dying lightened him.

But even in death, Bobby couldn't catch a break.

WHAT BOBBY LEFT BEHIND
Part Two
My brother Bobby had never touched drugs and rarely drank, which surprised the experts my parents periodically consulted throughout his life. A kid with a childhood as unhappy as his—the taunts for his misshapen head, his learning disabilities, his inability to make friends—often turns to drugs as a way of belonging or a way of escape. Bobby never did.

But when he was operated on for terminal cancer four years ago at the age of 33, he took pills for the pain. Then he began washing them down with screwdrivers. He figured he was dying, so what did it matter?

The cancer transformed Bobby in many ways. He laughed more. He allowed us to hug him more often. Though he was weak and in pain, he was happier than we had ever seen him. The family was rallying around him. Co-workers called or sent cards. Dying had put him at the front of the line for the first time in his life. He had always been different, set apart. Now he was different in a way that didn't draw taunts, but sympathy and kindness.

Then the cancer disappeared. When Bobby went for his six-month check-up, the spots on his liver were gone. Blood tests came up clean. The doctors had no explanation. They shrugged. Sometimes it happens.

In the meantime, Bobby had become addicted to his painkillers, and he drank too much. He could no longer keep a job. My parents, who had been caring for him in their home, said it was bad enough watching their child die but they'd be damned if they'd watch him kill himself. They asked the doctors to stop prescribing so much medication. They wrote letters to the pharmacist to stop filling the multiple prescriptions Bobby kept bringing in.

I'd hear from my family about Bobby's scrapes with disaster. When my parents were out one day, a neighbor saw Bobby in front of their house yelling nonsense and pounding on his car. The neighbor called my sister at work, but when she arrived Bobby was gone. She called the police, knowing he was a danger behind the wheel. But the police couldn't go after him until he actually did something harmful. So my sister and parents waited. The next day they got a call from the county mental hospital. Bobby had been found 200 miles away in Cocoa Beach. He had called the police from a McDonald's, saying people were in his car and wouldn't get out. The police sent him to the hospital, where a psychiatrist decided there was nothing wrong with him.

We lived in fear that he would harm himself or someone else. Finally, my parents told him to get help or get out. He promised a hundred times to go to detox but one day he didn't feel well, another day he decided he would kick the habit by himself. My parents had had enough. Bobby found a low-income apartment a few miles away, and it soon smelled of vomit and old food.

He had been so ready to die he no longer could figure out how to live.

My mother tried to get across to him that he had been spared death for a reason, that he had the responsibility to do something with this second life he had been given. Bobby nodded and for a short time he volunteered in an adult literacy program. But I think he saw this second shot at life not as a gift but as a betrayal. He was supposed to die. Dying was interesting and fulfilling in a way life had never been.

In the spring of 1995, Bobby went for his usual six-month check- up. The cancer had returned. My parents cleared out Bobby's apartment and moved him back in with them. As the cancer slowly swallowed him up, my mother sat with him every evening after she returned from work, talking and talking and talking. By summer, he weighed less than 90 pounds. His skin looked like cellophane stretched from bone to bone. My two brothers and sister who live in Florida saw him often during his final months, listening to his dissertations on the designated hitter and affirmative action. I flew in from California early in the summer to see him. Later, in July, my sister in North Carolina finally got away and flew down. Three days after Bobby saw her, the last of his five siblings to make a visit, he died.

In two weeks, the family is gathering in Florida for Thanksgiving, the first time since Bobby's funeral that we will be together. Bobby never liked Thanksgiving. At least he never liked the food. But beneath the glowering at the dinner table, I think he enjoyed the joking and reminiscing about the time my sister and I cut my mother's pearl necklace or the summer vacations to the Jersey shore. He'd laugh in spite of himself and throw in the details the rest of us had forgotten. Then he'd fall silent again, almost militantly keeping himself separate, yet listening to the voices and stories that defined his tribe and his home, the only place he ever really belonged.

More than a year after his death, I still find myself wondering sometimes why Bobby was born. He lived what seemed to be a miserable life, and then he died. Every person leaves the world changed in some way, and I have often tried to figure out what impact Bobby had. I heard a story the other day that made me think of this again.

It was about a Special Olympics race in Seattle. When the gun went off, the mentally handicapped athletes began sprinting down the track. But one boy had fallen at the starting line. One by one, the other athletes noticed and stopped running. They went back to the boy and helped him up. Then they linked arms and walked the length of the track, crossing the finish line together. The crowd cheered for 10 minutes.

Maybe Bobby was like that boy. His stumbling changed us. My brothers and sisters and I knew what it was like to be left behind because we lived it through him. We knew what it was like to be humiliated and left out. When Bobby struggled, we learned to pull our eyes away from the finish line and, in our fumbling way, link arms. If my brothers and sisters and I have one trait in common—and this might be the only one—it is that we are empathetic. We find ourselves being friends to the friendless. This is, I am convinced, a learned behavior.

Bobby drove us crazy with his black-and-white opinions and his endless information about the solar system and the Civil War and baseball. But he was one of us, irreplaceable, running the race alongside as best he could.[7]

QUESTIONS

1. If you've had a cathartic experience when participating in or observing a religious rite, what was the ritual's meaning and what was the nature of your experience?

2. If you've experienced a memorable buildup of apprehension during an athletic contest, following by a release (a purgation or catharsis) of your pent-up emotions, what was the event? Can you describe your feelings about the process?

3. Have you ever cried because of the events occurring in a television or film drama? Describe the experience.

4. Have you ever cried from sheer joy? From the power of a song? From news reports of some person's heroism or triumph?

5. What do you feel was the learning value for Joan Ryan when she set into words the painful experiences of growing up with her afflicted brother? What was the learning value of her story for you?

NOTES

1. Stanley Edgar Hyman, "Maud Bodkins and Psychological Criticism," in *Art and Psychoanalysis,* ed. William Phillips (Cleveland, OH: Meridian Books, 1963), 483.
2. Gregg Levoy, "Tears That Speak," *Psychology Today,* July–August 1988.
3. Dr. Rosalind Cartwright, *Bottom Line* 13, no. 18 (1992), 13.
4. Norman Cousins, *Anatomy of an Illness as Perceived by the Patient: Reflections on Healing and Regeneration* (New York: Norton, 1979).
5. Jerome L. Singer, The Inner World of Daydreaming (New York: Harper and Row, 1975).
6. Joan Ryan, "A Way to Lighten Bobby's Load," *San Francisco Chronicle,* 3 November 1996, p. 10/71. © 1996. Reprinted by permission.

CHAPTER SEVEN

MODES IN THE STORYTELLING ARTS

Chapter 7 traces the origins of epic poetry and staged dramas in Western civilization. Influences from the Far East are not included because they are not seen as direct antecedents to storytelling as it developed in Mesopotamia, Egypt, and Greece. The key modes of the storytelling arts that survived the centuries are identified as *the comic, the tragic,* and *the heroic.* Tragic and comic modes are outgrowths of ancient rituals. The heroic mode developed very early in human evolution. Heroic tales were in circulation before the birth of staged dramas in Europe and the Middle East, and these tales were developed and preserved by professional storytellers who recited myths and legends to tribal members. The heroic mode spawned several distinct genres of stories, including legends, myths, sagas, fables, fairy tales, and one that dominates adventures stories in today's film and television, *melodrama.*

Before there was anything we would recognize as theatre, poets recited epic tales in front of audiences ranging from small dinner gatherings to large open-air assemblies. Stories were crafted from ancient legends and myths born in the dim, preliterate millennia when the only means of preserving them was through the memories of storytellers who learned them as a complete recitation—the words, the inflections, the pauses, and the meter—and who in turn passed them down, generation after generation.

The early epics—such as *Gilgamesh, The Odyssey,* or *Beowolf,* are striking, not only in their power, but also in their lack of consistency of mood and actions. Homer's *Odyssey,* which translator W. H. D. Rouse calls the best story ever written, is typical of ancient, preliterate stories that intermingle heroism, cowardice, tragedy, comedy, fate, human sacrifice, love, the supernatural, death, sex, cannibalism, revenge, monsters, and gods. However dissimilar these elements may seem, they existed alongside one another as compatible in the myths, legends, and epics of antiquity. The nature and form of these adventure stories established the *heroic mode.* When poets created epic stories from myths and legends, their narratives roamed in any direction the fertile imagination of a poet desired. Consistency and conventional logic didn't restrain the free-flowing minds of the inspired fabulists.

But an important change took place in ancient Greece when storytelling evolved into dramatic performances featuring actors and a chorus. From the very first extant tragedy we have, Aeschylus' *The Suppliants,* we can see that artistic freedom did not permit the mixing of modes at will. During Greece's Golden Age, approximately 480–399 B.C., two major modes of storytelling developed in the theatre: tragedy and comedy. Playwrights were expected to write in one mode or the other and to remain consistent within each of these forms. The heroic mode was not at that time a recognized form of drama, remaining instead in the realm of narratives recited by professional storytellers.[1] Elements of the heroic mode alluding to the supernatural, witchcraft, heroism, and incidents from ancient myths were present in both tragedy and comedy, but they did not predominate. Tragic dramas were sharply focused on tragic acts and their consequences, while comedy was concerned with pointing the finger of scorn at people and conventions deemed ridiculous by comic playwrights.

Why did Athenian tragedy and comedy become standardized in subject matter and form, while public storytellers retained the freedom to blend in a single work such dissimilar elements as comedy, terror, horror, heroism, villainy, and anything else that suited the reciter's imagination? The reason lies in their origins. While epic stories such as *The Odyssey* grew out of myth and legend, tragedy and comedy grew out of rituals, ceremonies characterized not only by stories, but by their purgative functions, achieved by first arousing and eventually purging extreme emotions through catharsis. Both form and catharsis began in ritual. Athenian playwrights understood this and selectively employed ritualistic power as they created their dramas. Modern writers can learn much about the inherent potency of the tragic and comic modes by understanding how and why they developed and worked. Although stories in the heroic mode were different in origin and not subject to rules of form, they, too, are capable of producing powerful catharses.

PURPOSE AND VISION IN THE STORYTELLING ARTS

The tragic, comic, and heroic modes are characterized by their purpose, vision, and form. *Purpose* is the intended outcome of the work; *vision* is the underlying social or philosophical outlook of the artist; *form* is the shape (the outline) of the work. The urge to create a particular story may begin with a special purpose, such as to teach the bitter lessons of the American Civil War to an audience far removed in time from that prolonged tragedy. The vision, which would embody the moral and social causes as well as the horrors of the conflict, may also be the motivating force that gives birth to this particular story. The form is the arrangement of the parts in a particular order to achieve the most compelling and stirring response in an audience. Vision and purpose determine the form of a drama.

Purpose

In the storytelling arts, purpose is wedded to both vision and form, because purpose relates to the hoped-for outcome of the effort. In assessing the value of a story, it's important to weigh the work against what we assume to be the purpose of its creator. The purpose can be of many kinds and levels, ranging from serious and monumental to whimsical and transient.

If a story's purpose is to entertain and nothing more, and is successful—even if it doesn't educate or enlighten—then it's achieved one important goal of art. There's nothing wrong with stories that are whimsical, frivolous, or inconsequential. Such films as *Romy and Michelle's High School Reunion, Wayne's World,* and the television series, *Dharma and Greg, Cheers, Friends, Frasier, Seinfeld,* and most daytime serials (soaps) need no apologies; they provide entertainment and satisfy our need for diversion as they tell stories that attract and hold our attention. Successful stories, even when limited in scope, are justified as valid entertainment. We may not remember these stories the next morning, but if they provided laughs, stimulation, or simply diversion after a stressful day, they've served a purpose.

Some stories serve a more serious or even monumental purpose. The television series *Roots* and the film *Schindler's List* are examples. Each began with a desire to explore the events and consequences of two of the greatest evils of all time—the history of slavery in the United States, and the Holocaust. Both had clear purposes and, with great scripts and equally great execution—casting, directing, acting, and visual and aural accompaniments—they were powerful and successful.

Other stories may treat equally monumental issues, be brilliantly conceived and executed, and yet in achieving their goals, are destructive to the nation that spawned them as well as to its victims. In Hitler's Germany and Mussolini's Italy, to use but two examples, artistic vision, form, and purpose became handmaidens to immoral purposes. Nowhere is the perversion of the arts more apparent than in the brilliant documentaries of Leni Riefenstahl: *Triumph of the Will,* about a 1934 Nazi rally in Munich designed to promote the Nazi party and glorify Hitler, and *Olympia,* ostensibly the story of the 1936 Berlin Olympic Games but in actuality a compelling film about Aryan supremacy and the glories of Nazism.

One criterion of purpose is that it serves genuine human needs whether those needs are significant or of passing importance. We turn to the public arts for many reasons, and it's appropriate that the arts satisfy us in a variety of ways. At one time, we need the arts for relaxation; at another, for a purgation of hostile feelings; at yet another time, we need the arts for intellectual, emotional, or aesthetic growth. Which is the most important of these needs? None, for all are essential. We need to relax at times, or we would not be able at other times to exert ourselves.[2]

Vision

The vision one has of a work dictates the form applied to raw materials. The design of a tomato can, for example, is the result of an *economic* vision. That vision sees the can in practical terms that define its purpose: it must be manufactured easily and cheaply; must hold a specific volume of tomatoes; must prevent the product from decaying; and, eventually must be discarded or recycled. The design of the can is independent of the design of the label, which is intended to attract, inform, please, or otherwise impress potential buyers. The vision behind a Greek vase from antiquity was very different from the vision behind a tomato can. The Greeks attached ceremonial or religious significance to such household objects, and the form reflected this—it had to be a beautiful shape, perhaps of a precious metal, or decorated with religious icons or jewels to show respect to the gods.

Turning from examples that exist in space—a tin can or a Greek vase—to the time arts, we can look at the major forms in the storytelling arts in terms of their origins and their characteristics.

FORMS IN THE DRAMATIC ARTS

Most stories, ancient and modern, fall into one of the three forms described here, but many are outside their parameters. Melodrama, born of the heroic mode, shows more variation in form and vision than does comedy or tragedy. We must use these critical categories with caution. We shouldn't ignore them, because they provide useful tools of evaluation; we mustn't, however, lose our flexibility, our objectivity, or an understanding of their limitations because many effective stories in all media have succeeded despite their lack of adherence to traditional forms.

Roots of Modern Dramatic Forms

Tragic, comic, and heroic forms evolved in ancient times to address human needs, fears, desires, and the need to find meaning in life. All were based on primitive understandings of human nature. Tragic and comic forms were derived from rituals and the heroic form followed the narrative tradition of myths and epic tales.

Tragic Form.   The tragic form arose from rituals of spiritual cleansing and death and resurrection. It developed, not for the sake of suffering, but for the transformation of suffering to joy through the tragic catharsis.

Comic Form.   The comic form has its roots in two related phenomena, the annual Period of License observed by most primitive societies, and an age-old aversion to those whose behavior or physical appearance deviated from accepted or established norms. Comic rituals developed to permit occasional release of pent-up feelings of frustration and hostility, by purging these emotions through symbolic acts. Blasphemy, obscenity, disloyalty, ridicule of authority figures, and sexual license were given free reign in early societies under controlled conditions, *and for brief periods of time.* The period of license provided a safety valve for slaves, priests, and others who had to be reverent, loyal, respectful, dutiful, and sexually restricted during the rest of the year.

Additionally, ancient societies abhorred those whose ideas were seen as a threat to the *status quo.* The philosopher Socrates was the butt of a vicious comic thrashing in Aristophanes' play, *The Clouds* (423 B.C.). Years later an Athenian court convicted Socrates of corrupting the youth of Athens, and decreed he must commit suicide. Socrates thus paid the price of one seen as an unacceptable and threatening deviant form the norm. (See the discussion of hostile wit in Chapter 8, "The Anatomy of Comedy.")

Heroic Form.   The heroic form (which we most often experience in melodramas) arose from adventurous stories of good and evil found in myths, legends, and epic tales. It developed to first arouse and then purge feelings of anxiety over the safety of the hero and the society. The hero was the special protector of a community or nation, and his success and the salvation of the society went hand in hand. The heroic form demands a transformation of anxiety to relief and joy through the triumph of the hero over the forces of evil.

Modern Melodramatic Form

The heroic form is the most elastic of the three identified by Aristotle. We recognize one extreme in its descendent, melodrama, in such rousing stories as *Planet of the Apes, Titanic, Twister, The Mummy Returns,* and *The Perfect Storm.* But less overcharged struggles need to be included in this genre as well. A variation of the melodramatic form is a play that may include some lighter moments but that essentially tells a thoughtful story without the requisite catastrophic ending of tragedy or the more extreme dramatic elements of blood-and-thunder melodrama. Examples include the films *Marty, 84 Charing Cross Road, Cross Creek, Forrest Gump, The World According to Garp, Personal Best, The Graduate,* and *Chariots of Fire.* Television programs include *The Waltons, Little House on the Prairie, Party of Five, The West Wing, Touched by an Angel,* and many episodes of *Ally McBeal.*

While this less physical form of melodrama nearly always begins with a conflict and ends with its resolution, it need not end happily (as in comedy) or catastrophically (as in tragedy). Brian's Song ends with the death of Brian Piccolo, but the tragic catharsis is lacking. Similarly, *Forrest Gump* ends at a school bus stop as Forrest sends his son off to school. Forrest has lost his mother, his best friend, and his beloved wife. The conclusion doesn't bring about a surge of joy or despair; it simply completes the adventurous story of a simple man we've come to identify with and to love. *Goodbye, Columbus* ends without a resolution, as Neil walks out of the life of his distraught girlfriend Brenda, while she sits sobbing in a cheap hotel room. These films are examples of a category of the drama that tells an engaging story, yet ends without a resolution. There can be a powerful impact from such a stories, even though the film doesn't tie up the loose ends.

Dramas with No Resolution

In today's storytelling arts, the tragic vision is evident, but the redemptive power of the tragic form is not always present.[3] *West Side Story,* for example, ends with the death of the male protagonist, Tony, while his love, Maria, lives on, distraught over the deaths of her lover and her brother. Throughout the drama, there's violence and senseless hatred, and the ending doesn't bring serenity or a feeling that things will change.

We see the comic vision in televised situation comedies, the late-night shows of Letterman and Leno, *Saturday Night Live, Mad TV,* and on the Comedy Channel, but comic catharsis—occurs only at times. You can recognize comic catharsis at work when a comic deviant such as Archie Bunker of *All in the Family,* Ted Baxter in *The Mary Tyler Moore Show,* Al Bundy in *Married . . . With Children,* or Tim Allen in *Home Improvement* is humbled at the end of the show. From the earliest times it was felt that while it was fun to laugh at comic deviants, they had to receive just punishment at the end of the story. This point is made more explicitly in Chapter 8, "The Anatomy of Comedy."

A story without a culminating purgation isn't necessarily better or worse than one with a purgation—it simply is a matter of artistic or, more often, of ethical choice. Some authors refuse to resolve everything at the end of their stories because plays that tie everything up in neat packages, leaving us contented as they end, may also leave us with little memory of them in a day or two. Stories that arouse in us powerful emotions and then refuse to purge them often force us to continue to think about the issues raised, and even to discuss them with others. When the story revolves around a social injustice or an intolerable human practice, the lack of a happy ending could lead to demands for social change. One example of this is the impact of the 1852 antislavery novel, *Uncle Tom's Cabin.* President Lincoln, on being introduced to its author, Harriet Beecher Stowe, is reported to have said, "So this is the little lady who made the big war!"[4] Of course, *Uncle Tom's Cabin* didn't cause the Civil War, but in focusing on and humanizing individual victims of slavery, it vastly increased awareness of and abhorrence for that brutal institution among Yankees (and many Southerners). Because Stowe's story moved the topic of slavery from an abstract concept to an individualized human level, it accomplished what no orator or newspaper reporter could have done. Although the end of the novel saw some rejoicing over the conversion of a former slaveowner who'd freed his slaves, it would be misleading to say that *Uncle Tom's Cabin* has a happy ending.

Another example is the film *Cabaret,* which presents the story of an American showgirl and a British scholar in prewar Berlin who are caught up in the wild days leading to the Nazi takeover of Germany. Throughout the film, we see the gradual conversion of the German people to Nazism. As the film nears its end, the Nazi seduction of the people is complete. The final scene shows the British scholar (the story's protagonist, despite attention paid to the showgirl and the Kit Kat Club's master of ceremonies) leaving Berlin and Germany the way he entered, by train. No conclusion; no happy ending; no cop-out. We're left with strong and recurring memories of this powerful film.

A well-established theory in the field of mass communication is the *narcotizing dysfunction of the media.* Simply put, it states that presenting a societal problem through television or a similar mass medium with the intent of arousing concern can be counterproductive. The audience, seeing the problem explored, can unconsciously come to the conclusion that something is being done about it. So, as mentioned earlier, some writers avoid the temptation to provide immediate audience gratification, and work instead to achieve the more important goal of raising consciousness.

The major storytelling forms and the rituals and myths from which they arose came into being as an important means of psychological and spiritual cleansing. A catharsis at the end of a ritual was a must. The Egyptian celebration of the Osiris story, which began with mourning over the death of Osiris and ended with his resurrection, would have made no sense at all if that annual event had ended with the people still in mourning for the dead Osiris. Rejoicing over his rebirth was what this festival ultimately was all about. Form in ritual and the storytelling arts developed early in human history, and was practiced and developed by those who most likely had no notion that they were in the process of creating art.

While it's clear that the tragic, comic, and heroic modes arose from magical ceremonies, from religious rites, from periods of sexual license and free expression of hostile feelings toward rulers, as well as myths, legends, and epic tales, it's important to recognize the multitude of changes that took place as ritual gradually gave birth to the arts. While it's important to trace the visions, functions, and forms of the public arts to their earliest appearances, they're not the same thing. We must, however, acknowledge that the major dramatic modes are born of human needs that were and remain very real.

For as long as humans have inhabited this planet, we have had an impulse to tell stories. The creation of stories may, in fact, precede ritual. Stories may have had as much to do with the development of rituals, as the other way around. What's important to understand is that both rituals and storytelling involve presenters (actors or reciters), and receivers (audience) and that very early in human history, our ancestors discovered what worked, what didn't, and how certain themes and their related forms achieved desired effects. These discoveries brought human societies a giant step closer to what we call civilization. The next chapters discuss the comic, heroic, and the tragic in greater detail.

QUESTIONS

1. Look at this list of films and television series. Identify the modes of the stories with which you are familiar: *Party of Five, The Practice, Beverly Hills 90210, Survivor, The Young and the Restless, Friends, Buffy the Vampire Slayer, Xena, Warrior Princess, Dharma and Greg, The X-Files, BayWatch, The West Wing,* and *Ed.*

2. If you've had the experience of seeing—on stage, film, or television—a recognized classic tragedy, such as *Hamlet, Oedipus Rex, Romeo and Juliet,* or a more modern tragedy such as *Death of a Salesman, The Crucible,* or *A Streetcar Named Desire,* how did you react? If you were deeply moved by any of them, can you identify the reasons why these stories of suffering, death, and (in some cases) triumph took you through an ultimately rewarding experience?

NOTES

1. Euripides (485–406 B.C.) the third and youngest of the greatest Greek playwrights, moved from the tragic form to melodrama in several of his plays as he substituted a "happy ending" for stories that were, in every other way, written in the tragic mold.
2. See the discussion of the arts as essential in achieving emotional equilibrium in Chapter 6.
3. For a discussion of tragic vision, form, and function, see Chapter 10, "Tragic Drama Through the Arts."
4. Moira D. Reynolds, *Uncle Tom's Cabin and Mid-Century United States.* (Jefferson, NC: McFarland, 1985), 146.

CHAPTER EIGHT

THE ANATOMY OF COMEDY

*What does laughter mean? . . . The greatest of thinkers, from Aristotle
downwards, have tackled this little problem which has a knack of baffling
every effort, of slipping away and escaping only to bob up again, a pert
challenge flung at philosophic speculation.*[1]

Chapter 8 presents a detailed examination of comedy, with a review of comic theories from Plato
to Freud. The topic is surveyed according to Freud's categories as described in *Wit and Its
Relation to the Unconscious.* The *comic, humor,* and *wit* are discussed with many illustrations.
This chapter is linked to Chapter 16, "Writing Comedy," and both chapters are critical to a
comprehensive understanding of comedy.

Why do we laugh? What causes this strange behavior? More important, what purpose does
it serve? "During a laugh, the throat goes into uncoordinated spasms, sending blasts of air
out of the mouth at 70 miles an hour. The body starts pumping adrenaline; the heart rate
increases; the brain releases endorphins and enkephalins—natural painkillers."[2]

Anyone would agree that our physical movements when laughing are unlike those for
any other emotional display, so it's no wonder that scholars and philosophers from Plato to
Arthur Koestler have written on the subject. Despite the efforts of hundreds of theorists to
understand the nature of comedy, however, disagreements continue. The essence of comedy
long has eluded analysts, most likely because comedy has no essence. Without repeating
here the dozens of theories that have been put forth, it may be said that the fallacy that sends
most analysts down in flames is their attempt to explain comedy as a single phenomenon:
*comedy is based on the ridicule of one whose behavior is unacceptable; comedy is the sudden
release of psychic energy;* and *comedy is found in those who show excessive physical or
mental rigidity.* These are but a few of the theories that attempt to define the essence of
comedy. But comedy isn't a single phenomenon to be summed up in a few catch phrases;
it's extremely complex. On the bright side, it can be said that nearly every single-minded
theorist did identify for us at least one legitimate aspect of the comic phenomenon, and in
so doing made a contribution to our understanding of this elusive entity we call comedy.

65

The earliest writings on comedy come from Plato (427?–347? B.C.), who wrote that those whose behavior is seen as ridiculous are rightfully the objects of laughter. He adds that when a person's behavior is foolish but doesn't lead to any serious harm to anyone, it's merely funny. He adds that a person whose swelled head is more threatening than silly is dangerous:

> Those who are both deluded and weak, unable to avenge themselves when laughed at, may rightly be described as "ridiculous"; but those who can retaliate might more properly be called "formidable" and "hateful." *For ignorance in the strong is hateful and ugly. . . But ignorance in the weak may be reckoned, in truth is, ridiculous.*[3] (Italics added)

We can apply this distinction to one of the most infamous figures of the twentieth century. When Adolf Hitler began his manic posturings in the early 1930s, he was seen as silly and laughable by most people in Europe and the United States. In 1930 the German humor magazine *Simplicissimus* ran a derogatory cartoon of Adolf Hitler, created by Thomas Theodor Heine, an outspoken critic of the Nazis from the earliest days (see Figure 8–1). In this drawing, two policemen are examining the head of a weak, scrawny Adolf Hitler. The caption reads: "An unproductive search of Hitler's house finds no cause for concern: It's remarkable how little it takes to put things right." Hitler is thus seen in 1930 as an empty-headed buffoon.[4]

During the early years of Hitler's rise, he was the butt of jokes and was shown as a buffoon in movies, including the film *The Great Dictator* and a Disney cartoon in which animal characters sing a derisive song with a refrain that ends, "Ven der Führer says, 've iss der master race,' Ve go 'heil!, heil!, right in Der Führer's Face'!" After each "heil!" the

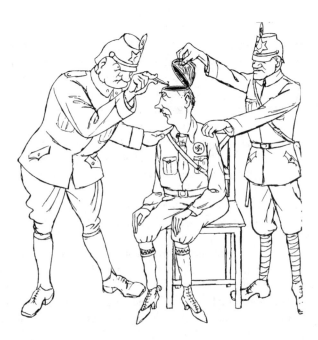

FIGURE 8–1

characters make the sound of a Bronx Cheer (the polite term from yesteryear for the sound of flatus).

Charlie Chaplin's film *The Great Dictator* represents common feelings about Hitler in the early years of his rise to power. Filming commenced in 1939, coinciding with the declaration of war by Britain and France against Germany. In the film, Chaplin plays both Adenoid Hynkel, a caricature of Hitler, and a timid Jewish barber. Chaplin savagely lampoons Hitler with all the skill acquired during his long career as a pantomimist. Perhaps the most memorable scene is that of Hynkel dancing with a large balloon that represents the globe; he embraces it, kicks it about, and collapses in tears as his bubble finally bursts. In the film, Nazi Brown Shirts are seen as stupid, crazed brutes, and Hitler is portrayed as imbecilic, ridiculous, and incompetent.

A few years later, after Hitler's hold on the German people had led to the invasion and destruction of nation after nation and the near extermination of Jews, Gypsies, Slavs, homosexuals, people with disabilities, and others Hitler considered to be subhuman, people no longer saw Hitler as a harmless buffoon; in the public arts he became an arch villain. A 1940 Pulitzer Prize–winning political cartoon shows a fierce Hitler, his right hand dripping blood, his left holding torn papers labeled "broken promises," and "treaty" (see Figure 8–2).

FIGURE 8–2

Edward Duffy,
The Baltimore Sun.

He stands over the prostrate bodies of those his armies have vanquished. The harmless clown of the 1930 cartoon had become the symbol of evil incarnate. Although some hostile wit continued to be directed at him, the hostility was less disguised and was, therefore, not very funny. The two cartoons, drawn ten years apart, illustrate Plato's distinction between deviants we perceive as weak and deviants we see as strong.

In his 1964 autobiography Chaplin wrote: "Had I known of the actual horrors of the concentration camps, I could not have made *The Great Dictator,* I could not have made fun of the homicidal insanity of the Nazis."[5] While Chaplin may not have read Plato's thoughts on comedy, his statement illustrates a gut-level understanding of the appropriateness of making fun of weak, foolish people versus those who are evil and strong.

Following Plato, Aristotle (384–322 B.C.) gave us additional insights into the comic vision. In his *Poetics,* he wrote:

> Comedy, is, as we have said, an imitation of characters of a lower type—not, however, in the full sense of the word bad, the Ludicrous being merely a subdivision of the ugly. It consists in some defect or ugliness which is not painful or destructive.[6]

Aristotle was writing about certain kinds of deviations from the norm that he believed to be ridiculous but not excessively threatening. In his *Nichomachean Ethics,* he used examples to clarify what he meant by the norm and deviation from it:

> . . . the man who flies from and fears everything and does not stand his ground against anything becomes a coward, and the man who fears nothing at all but goes to meet every danger becomes rash; and similarly, the man who indulges in every pleasure and abstains from none becomes self-indulgent, while the man who shuns every pleasure, as boors do, becomes in a way insensible; temperance and courage, then, are destroyed by excess and defect, and preserved by the mean.[7]

To Aristotle, as to Plato, those whose behavior or appearance was seen as deviant were legitimate objects of derision. The Greeks laughed to show disapproval of someone's bad behavior, or even of a physical deformity. We laugh less today over deformity or ugliness, but we still laugh at those whose behavior is annoying to us. To the Greeks (and, I believe, to us) people who deviate from acceptable conduct and are at an extreme of any quality, are ripe subjects for comedy. *Saturday Night Live* and *Mad TV* quickly seize on personality quirks or questionable actions to ridicule through exaggerated caricature. Think of recent jokes about people in the news: Isn't it true that most are understandable by Aristotle's definitions?

The comic vision, as understood by the ancients, is one that sees some forms of human behavior as unacceptable and asks that the comic spirit be invoked to deal with such behavior. Unkind as this may sound, it actually represented a major step forward in human evolution. Earlier societies punished social deviants by (1) putting them to death; (2) exiling them; or (3) shunning them. Niko Tinbergen came up with an amazingly insightful observation, based on his study of herring gulls. After netting a nesting gull for marking, he was surprised to see the gull, struggling in the net, being attacked and pecked by the other gulls. The reason? The trapped gull was *behaving strangely.* Tinbergen drew some fascinating conclusions:

In human society, "primitive" as well as "civilized," a similar instinctive reaction is very strongly developed. It is perhaps possible to distinguish three steps or gradations of rising intensity in the social-defense attitude of the crowd. The first is laughing at the individual who behaves in an abnormal way. This serves the function of forcing the individual back into normal, that is to say conventional, behavior. The next and higher intensity reaction is withdrawal; the individual has made himself "impossible," and his companions ignore him. This, viewed from the aspect of biological significance, is a still stronger stimulus to the individual person to behave normally. The highest intensity reaction is one of definite hostility, resulting in making the individual an outcast, and, in primitive societies, even of killing him. *In my opinion it is of great importance for human sociology to recognize the instinctive basis of such reactions, and to study them comparatively in other social species.*[8] (Italics added)

Tinbergen was right about the three stages although, by identifying them in order of rising intensity, he listed them in reverse chronological order from the way they most likely developed in human societies; he says that the first level is the laughter of ridicule, but it's likely that laughter at societal deviants came to human societies well after the other two stages he mentions.

VILLAINS AND COMICS

The most obvious and readily understood application of Plato's principle is found in nineteenth-century American melodramas. Throughout that century, staged melodramas featured four stock characters: heroes, heroines, villains, and comics. Heroes and heroines are discussed in Chapter 9, "Heroic Vision, Form, and Function." Villains and comics reflect two contrasting views of bad behavior, as illustrated earlier by changing attitudes toward Hitler between 1930 and 1940.

Villains of the nineteenth century, generally speaking, had two outstanding characteristics: they were evil, and they were powerful. Nineteenth-century understanding of human behavior was little changed from that of the Elizabethan age, in that villains were characterized as evil because they *chose* to be evil. Aaron, Shakespeare's chief villain in *Titus Andronicus,* knows he is evil, and revels in that fact:

> *Aaron: . . .*
> *Even now I curse the day . . .*
> *Wherein I did not some notorious ill:*
> *As kill a man, or else devise his death;*
> *Ravish a maid, or plot the way to do it;*
> *Accuse some innocent, and forswear myself;*
> *Set deadly enmity between two friends;*
> *. . . Tut, I have done a thousand dreadful things*
> *As willingly as one would kill a fly;*
> *And nothing grieves me heartily indeed,*
> *But that I cannot do ten thousand more.*
> *v, i, 125, 127–131, 141–144)*

A nineteenth-century villain, Coates, in William Bausman's *Early California,* demonstrates villainous conduct and motivation that parallel Aaron's:

> Coates: This note, ostensibly from her father, is ingeniously forged. . . . She will go where the note directs her . . . and she will be completely in my power. Since the stain of blood is on my hands, what further crime need I scruple to commit? I was respected once; but let that pass. Fate may now do her worst. The stake for which I play is worthy a great effort. If I fail, it only remains to curse mankind and die.[9]

In their conduct, both nineteenth-century and Elizabethan villains deliberately deviated from accepted standards of behavior. And because they were powerful, they represented a threat. It's amazing and discouraging to see that our understanding of human motivations didn't change for the nearly three hundred years that passed between *Titus Andronicus* and *Early California.*

Unlike their villanous counterparts, neither sixteenth- nor nineteenth-century comic figures were aware that their ludicrous behavior deviated from the norm. They, like villains, usually possessed two stereotypical characteristics, foolishness and weakness. But aside from deviant behavior, some figures on the nineteenth-century American stage were considered ludicrous mainly because they differed from the Caucasian, Protestant majority. Comic characters on the nineteenth-century American stage were of many types and backgrounds: ethnic minorities, including Negroes (African Americans), Chinese, Mexicans, Italians, Germans, Irish, and Indians (native Americans); and religious minorities, including Catholics, Jews, Mormons, and Buddhists.

Others who were fair game for the laughter of ridicule were rural Americans such as the Yankee peddler, the country bumpkin, and the clodhopper; the sissy or greenhorn, often an effeminate male from the big city or England; and stuffy professors who knew little about life apart from books and laboratories.

Why did audiences find these stereotypical agents funny? Here we return to Tinbergen's thoughts derived from the behavior of seagulls. When a dominant group in a society is confronted by those who differ from them by nationality, race, color, religion, physical appearance, behavior, or any other quality that it finds bothersome or disquieting, it has the options of exiling or killing them, shunning them, or laughing at them. Martin Grotjahn's *Beyond Laughter* substantiates these claims.

> Increasing demands for repression through the ages have changed aggression from assault into wit. Where we would have struck a person in earlier times, we restrict our hostility now, and often repress it entirely. Aggressive wit gives us a new way of admitting dangerous aggression to our consciousness—but it has to be done in a cleverly disguised form. . . . Hostile jokes lift repressions and open up otherwise inaccessible sources of pleasure.[10]

In nineteenth-century melodramas, stereotypes of those believed by the majority to deviate from the norm were portrayed on stage as comic figures. Every new wave of immigrants brought people to America whose differences threatened the security or values of those whose ancestors had taken an earlier boat. Hostility toward these interlopers was inevitable and, because they were seen as weak and also looked down upon by audiences, they became objects of ridicule. Generally, ridicule was enough of an outlet for audiences to release their annoyance or discomfort, but occasionally aggressive tendencies were strong enough for the majority to take direct action through lynchings, tar-and-featherings, or exile.

A significant exception to this generalization was the hostility directed toward Chinese immigrants to California during the California Gold Rush and in the decades that followed. After the discovery of gold in 1848, great numbers of fortune seekers arrived in San Francisco, among them thousands of Chinese from Canton. The European Americans who'd arrived earlier, and who subscribed to the nineteenth-century fantasy of Manifest Destiny, saw the Chinese as a serious threat to their land (recently taken by force from Mexico), their religion (which few practiced) and their wealth (which few possessed).

The Chinese were portrayed on stage as comic figures, but their characteristics were unusually distasteful, even by nineteenth-century American melodrama standards. A review of several plays with comic Chinese agents shows them as having a number of unsavory characteristics: They were guilty of lying, stealing, cheating at cards, being lazy, eating rats, smoking opium, drinking alcohol to excess, engaging in White slavery, and—most abhorrent—attempting to make love to White women![11]

As difficult as it may be to accept these notions, the fact is that an important facet of comedy involves pointing the finger of ridicule toward those whose behavior or appearance is considered unacceptable. Think of these comic deviants:

> Lucy Ricardo (*I Love Lucy*)
> Tim Allen (*Home Improvement*)
> Al Bundy (*Married . . . With Children*)
> George (*Seinfeld*)
> Archie Bunker (*All in the Family*)
> Ted Knight (*The Mary Tyler Moore Show*)
> Several therapy group patients (*The Bob Newhart Show*)

All of these comic characters—whom you can see in reruns or through rentals—were both laughed at and enjoyed by their audiences. Wait. . . . that sounds contradictory: if we find aberrant behavior annoying, why do we enjoy watching those who engage in it? Why do we find them funny? Why don't we try to avoid them?

The answers to these questions may be found by looking at three factors: we laugh at these characters if

> the *degree* and *nature* of their deviance is neither too outrageous nor harmful to others;
>
> we are a *distance* from them—that is to say, we don't have to live with them at home or at work;
>
> we find their personalities charming or even lovable.

Once we understand that we're not guilty of a sin, crime, or lack of sensitivity because we harbor low-level hostility toward others—including those we love most—we can acknowledge that hostile wit is the underlying basis of most interactions we find the funniest. It's entirely human for us to reject the notion that we harbor hostile feelings because we've been taught to be kind and forgiving and told we should love one another. But to deny that we sometimes have hostile intentions will keep us ignorant of one of the most striking aspects of being human: our ability to cope with the behavior of those who irritate us through hostile witticisms. Here's a brief example of how that works in close relationships from the popular television comedy *Home Improvement.*

Tim is in the kitchen seasoning a tray of meat when his wife, Jill, enters.

Jill: Hello.

Tim: How's school?

Jill: Oh it was great. I got my first A. [*holds up a paper*]

Tim: Congratulations. That goes on the refrigerator. [*takes page from Jill*]

Jill: No, no, Tim. This is the paper on abnormal sexuality.

Tim: Put it up in the bedroom.

Jill: We don't need it.

Here's a brief look at some of the theories of comedy that followed Plato and Aristotle. Most are attempts to explain laughter.

RELEASE AND RELIEF

From the mid–nineteenth century on, science-based approaches to understanding comedy gained in popularity. These theories explained laughter in an entirely mechanical-psychological way. Herbert Spencer (1820–1903) wrote that laughter occurs simply because an excess of nervous energy from a too-full reservoir has taken the quickest and easiest path toward release. Similarly, John Dewey (1859–1952) and others felt that laughter represented a release from some form of restraint or tension. Sigmund Freud (1856–1939), whose contributions to an understanding of comedy will later be explored in more detail, agreed that ". . . laughter arises when the sum of psychic energy, formerly used for the occupation of certain psychic channels, has become unutilizable so that it can experience free discharge."[12]

BIOLOGICAL INSTINCT

Both Charles Darwin (1809–1882) and James Sully (1842–1877) an English psychologist, saw laughter as being primarily a device whereby humans are able to communicate feelings of joy or happiness to one another. Darwin believed that some laughter arose from a recognition of the ludicrous, but he felt that such laughter was secondary: people were created to enjoy certain aspects of life, and laughter represents the manifestation of such enjoyment.

James Sully pointed out that babies quickly learn to smile and laugh to indicate a state of well-being. Later, as they acquire the ability to communicate with words, they continue to use laughter to indicate well-being. Sully calls this use of laughs and smiles the communication of the *play spirit.* A common application of this principle occurs in television studios daily, when a person—usually a cast member—goes before an audience minutes before the show goes on the air to tell jokes to *warm up* the audience. Most likely these actors have never heard of Sully or the play spirit, yet it's precisely that spirit that they are evoking.

INCONGRUITY, THE INCOMPATIBLE, EXPECTATION

The incongruity theory derives from the notion that comedy arises from ill-suited or conflicting ideas or situations. Schopenhauer (1836–1854) viewed the cause of laughter to be "simply the sudden perception of the incongruity between a concept and the real objects . . ."[13] Arthur Koestler, a modern critic, developed what he called the *bisociative theory* of comedy.[14] In brief, this concept, which is actually an extensive and complex reworking of the incongruity theory, tells us that we laugh because of a discrepancy between what we expect to happen, and what actually occurs. "Sometimes it is said that a laugh detonates whenever there is a sudden rupture between thinking and feeling. The rupture occurs the instant a situation is seen in another light."[15]

PSYCHOANALYTIC THEORY AND SIGMUND FREUD

In *Wit and Its Relation to the Unconscious,* Freud analyzes comedy under three categories: the *comic, humor,* and *wit.* In this rambling treatise he incorporates concepts developed by earlier scholars but adds details and explanations that expand our understanding. His analyses of humor and wit are of value to those who write and evaluate comedy, but his involved, sometimes incomprehensible discussion of the several categories of the comic is beyond the scope of this book and, I believe, the patience of its readers. In discussing comedy, I use some of Freud's categories without being committed to all of his psychoanalytical theories of causes, motives, deeper meanings, and so on. These categories are neither rigid nor mutually exclusive; they overlap and interconnect at many points.

The Comic

While accepting Freud's division of comedy into the comic, humor, and wit, it's important to note that several categories of the comic often work together, sometimes overlap, and are not always parallel in their meanings. The areas of the comic we examine in this section include most of those described by Freud, but incorporate ideas from other theorists as well.

superiority
naivete
motion
speech
expectation
incongruity
unmasking, deflation
caricature

the mechanistic
inadequacy

Superiority.   The comic of superiority is a category that supports the views of Plato and Aristotle, who believed that comic ridicule was and should be directed at those whose behavior is unacceptable by society's standards. Many scholars believe that, whatever other comic devices or techniques may be in play, our feeling of superiority over one who makes mistakes or behaves foolishly is a source of our laughter. Thomas Hobbes is quoted by Arthur Koestler in support of the superiority concept: "The passion of laughter is nothing else but sudden glory arising from a sudden conception of some eminency in ourselves by comparison with the infirmity of others . . ."[16]

Here's a joke that combines superiority with hostile wit, the unexpected, comic speech, caricature, and the naive:

The young wife of a Mafia enforcer has twins, a boy and a girl. In this closed society, one of the father's duties and privileges is to name the babies. However, the father is away on business, and returns a week after the baby's birth and announces that he's ready to name the babies:

> **Wife:**   Yer too late. Duh babies had to be named, and you wasn't here! Yer brother named um.
>
> **Husband:**   Dat jerk! Dat's terrible! He's ain't got no class. What'd he name 'em?
>
> **Wife:**   He named duh goil Denise (pronounced duh-NEECE)
>
> **Husband:**   Hey! Dat's not bad! What'd name duh boy?
>
> **Wife:**   Duh Nephew.

Another aspect of the superiority theory, the comic of speech, is seen when a joke is told that requires some specialized knowledge to understand the witticism. Such a story won't appear funny to one who doesn't know the meanings of two unrelated but similar-sounding words:

A fifth grade student was asked by his teacher to write an essay on a famous composer of his choosing. The child selected the eighteenth-century German composer Johann Sebastian Bach. He wrote: Johann Sebastian Bach was a famous composer. He had two wives and twenty children. Mr. Bach kept an old spinster in the attic to practice on.

Those who know that a spinster is an elderly, unmarried woman, and that a spinet is an eighteenth-century ancestor of the piano not only find this comic mix-up funny, but also feel self-gratification in knowing the meaning of two words not in common usage.

Naivete.   The comic of naivete relates to the speech, and sometimes the movements, of children and not-so-bright adults. In comedy of the naive, we laugh simply because the ignorance of a child is, in some sense, witty. A child of five or six has a limited vocabulary, which may not include such words as *attaché, indivisible, garment,* or *threshold.* So, on occasion, delightful mix-ups in speech occur. Examples: a child refers to her mother's attaché case as her *ricochet case*; a child pledges allegiance to the flag with these words, ". . . One nation, invisible, with liberty and justice for all"; and another, seeing that a piece of luggage remains in the trunk of the family car, says, "Mother—don't forget the varmint bag." My favorite example was said by my daughter at about the age of five. She'd seen a movie that included a marriage ceremony and its aftermath, and solemnly told us that "after the wedding, the man carried his bride over the fleshhold."

Comic of naivete works only if it's unplanned. The comic of the naive can be a naive joke or a naive obscenity. Freud gives this example of a naive joke: "A little girl, on being told that a certain man was a Hebrew, asks if his wife is a Shebrew."

Freud's funniest example of the comic of naivete tells the story of two children, a boy of ten and his sister of twelve. They produce a play for adult members of the family, setting its scene in the hut of a poor fisherman and his wife. Times are so difficult that the husband leaves on a voyage in search of wealth. After an intermission, the second act sees the fisherman return after several years absence with a sack of gold. As his wife greets him outside their shack, he boasts of his luck and the wealth he's brought home. His wife interrupts him:

> "Nor have I been idle in the meanwhile," and opens the hut, on whose floor the fisherman sees twelve large dolls representing children asleep. At this point in the drama the performers were interrupted by an outburst of laughter on the part of the audience, a thing which they [the children] could not understand.[17]

The naive joke occurs because the children had no idea how babies were created; it seemed logical to them that, while the man was away making money, the wife was busy making babies. Freud is obviously correct in stating that there's no hostile intent behind the joke.

Gracie Allen, of the comedy team Burns and Allen, was noted for her naivete, as seen in this paraphrase of one exchange:

George: What are you doing, Gracie?

Gracie: I'm knitting some socks for my nephew's birthday.

George: Good. So, why are you knitting three socks?

Gracie: Well, my sister wrote that he's grown another foot.

Motion. Freud asks, "why do we laugh at the actions of clowns?" He answers his own question: because their actions appear to be immoderate and inappropriate. Why does this make us laugh? "We really laugh over the excessive expenditure of energy." Also, we laugh when someone "wiggles his ears." Freud goes on to say that "all grimaces which exaggerate the normal expression of the emotions are comical, even if they are involuntary."[18]

In my opinion, Freud's view of the comic of motion is both tortured and limited. True, exaggerated movement is present in much funny pantomimic movement, as in the gestures of Ralph Kramden in *The Honeymooners,* of the Three Stooges in nearly all of their short comic sketches, and of Lucille Ball in scenes from almost every episode of *I Love Lucy.* But the key seems not to be exaggeration alone, but exaggeration combined with other factors:

with caricature, as in the famous episode of Lucy as a grape-stomper in an Italian movie; with violence, as in the eye poking and head smacking of the Three Stooges; and with hostility, as in the nonverbal gestures of Ralph toward his wife, Alice, in *The Honeymooners.* The comic of motion is seen in many guises—pie throwing, pratfalls, and wild auto chases—and in nearly all instances, the nature of the comic is best determined by noting what else, besides exaggerated movement, is being demonstrated.

The old *Dick Van Dyke Show,* still seen on rerun channels such as Nickelodeon, opens with Rob (Van Dyke) entering his living room, spotting his two writing colleagues, heading for them and, in one version, tripping over an ottoman and, in another version, skillfully skirting the piece of furniture at the last moment. When broadcast, both versions were rotated in an unpredictable order, and audiences watched as each episode opened, trying to guess whether on this occasion he'd fall or safely skirt the obstacle.

Speech.   The comic of speech refers to puns, plays on words, double entendres, clever uses of words, and so on. "Does the Pope have lips?" is a fusing of two common sayings, "Is the Pope Catholic?" and "Do chickens have lips?" This example is also comic of the naive if the words are spoken by a child.

Freud gives this example of the comic of speech: "He has a great future behind him," and adds that ". . . wit presents to the hearer a double face, and forces him to two different views. In nonsense-witticisms . . . one view, which considers only the wording, states that they are nonsense; the other view . . . follows the road that leads through the hearer's unconscious [and] finds very good sense in these witticisms."[19]

Oscar Wilde gives us many examples of the comic of speech: "I can resist everything except temptation," "I never travel without my diary. One should always have something sensational to read [on] the train," "There is only one thing in the world worse than being talked about, and that is not being talked about," and "To love oneself is the beginning of a lifelong romance."[20]

Expectation.   The comic of expectation involves a difference between that which was expected and that which happens. In a construction common to many jokes, there's a divergence between the speaker's vantage point and that of the listeners. To use a rather feeble joke from Freud as an example, the speaker asks, "Did you take a bath?" The response is, "No—is one missing?" We expect to hear either yes or no. But the term *take,* as used in this example, can mean "did you *have* a bath," or "did you *steal* a bath." The fact that we expected one answer, and received another quite different from that expectation, is said, by Arthur Koestler (among other advocates of this theory of the comic), to be the cause of the comic laughter.

A longer story with an unexpected punch line is that of two elderly former baseball players living in a retirement home. As they sit on the porch one night, they discuss the future:

Fred: Whatta you think, Mario? Do they play baseball in heaven?

Mario: I don't have a clue. I sure hope so!

Fred: Yeah, so do I! Tell ya what: whichever one of us goes first has to return and let the other one know.

They agree on that. A month later, Fred suddenly dies. Another week passes, and Mario is aroused from his sleep.

Mario: What's that noise? [*seeing Fred's ghost*] Fred, is that really you?

Fred: [Weakly] Yes, Mario. I have only a few seconds . . .

Mario: Quick, tell me—do they pay baseball in heaven?

Fred: I have good news and bad news. Yes, they play baseball in heaven . . .

Mario: Well, what's the bad news?

Fred: You're scheduled to pitch this weekend.

Incongruity. The comic of incongruity operates on the notion that comedy arises from ill-suited or conflicting ideas or situations. An example of incongruity is Woody Allen, New York accent and all, playing the part of a Russian conscript during the time of Napoleon in *Love and Death.* The discrepancy between Woody's thick New York accent and his characteristic whining personality are totally out of place in Napolean's army, and is almost the only source of laughter in this comedy. In the movie *Arthur* the perfect British butler, played by Sir John Gielgud, gets some laughs by using four-letter gutter terms as he vilifies his employer (Dudley Moore) under his breath. This is related to obscene wit.

Unmasking or Deflating. In brief, unmasking is the use of the comic to degrade the dignity of humans, most often the powerful or pretentious among us. Degradation occurs when attention is called to ". . . one of the common human frailties. . . . Unmasking then becomes equivalent to the reminder: This or that one who is admired like a demigod is only a human being like you and me after all."[21] Unmasking is also known as deflation of authority figures.

Most jokes that deflate authority figures are timebound, and are funny only when the audience is familiar with those being ridiculed. A newspaper cartoon that ran at a time when maverick political hopeful Ross Perot had built up a sizeable following ridiculed the appearance of several aspirants for Perot's endorsement. Six of these are seen dressed in swimsuits like Miss America contestants, as Perot snarls, "Y'all look worse than an armadillo's rump! Let's move on to the talent contest." This cartoon was quite funny when first published because both the event and those lampooned were known to the paper's readers. As time passed, and public recognition of Perot and his suitors waned, the cartoon lost much of its comic power.

Arthur Koestler condenses several ways scholars have described the theory of degradation:

> For Aristotle himself, laughter was closely related to ugliness and debasement; for Cicero "the province of the ridiculous . . . lies in a certain baseness and deformity"; for Descartes laughter is a manifestation of joy "mixed with surprise or hate or sometimes with both"; in Francis Bacon's list of laughable objects, the first place is taken by "deformity."[22]

Most of us relish examples of unmasking or deflating, which are readily available in political cartoons and on such satirical programs as *Saturday Night Live* and *Mad TV.*

FIGURE 8–3

Courtesy of Hugh Haynie, © *The Courier-Journal.*

Caricature.   The comic of caricature is a much-used technique of deflation. Caricatures are representations that exaggerate some aspect of a person's appearance or behavior (see Figure 8–3). Caricatures include cartoons of famous people (Nixon's nose, Carter's teeth). We also see caricature in the comic impersonations of Rich Little, Dana Carvey, and other impressionists.

Saturday Night Live and *Mad TV* make extensive use of caricature. During the drawn-out saga of President Clinton's impeachment trial, Dana Carvey and many other regular performers on SNL were adept at impersonating persons in the news, including President Clinton, Linda Tripp, Kenneth Starr, and several members of congress. By late 2001, these public figures had given way to others: Martha Stewart, Brittney Spears, Donald Trump, Michael Jackson, Vice President Dick Cheney and, of course, President George W. Bush. Caricature, by definition, carries with it the comic technique of unmasking as well as hostile wit. Successful caricature possesses these features:

It is timebound in that those caricatured must be known to the audience.

The person targeted must, in nearly all instances, be seen as a buffoon, a deviant, or a person with power who isn't fully trusted—caricature doesn't work if the butt of the impersonation is an object of pity, or is otherwise helpless.

The caricaturist must resemble the depicted person in physical appearance, movements, facial expressions, and speech.

The person doing the impersonation must tread a fine line between performing a mirror image of the victim, and overexaggeration to the point where believability is lost.

The Mechanistic.   The French philosopher Henri Bergson (1859–1941) was the chief promoter of the theory that much of our laughter is directed at those whose behavior or reactions are mechanical. Bergson refers many times to "the mechanical encrusted on the living." It was his belief that ". . . the main sources of the comic are the mechanical attributes of inertia, rigidity, and repetitiveness impinging upon life."[23] These three aspects each give rise to a different but related aspect of the comic.

Inertia.   Inertia is an aspect of the comic of motion. It occurs when physical movements seem out of sync with what's happening: Wily Coyote, who continues rapidly placing one foot before the other, even after stepping off a cliff and descending rapidly toward a crash at the bottom. Related to this is the failure of people to alter their physical movements to compensate for changed conditions that demand a different reaction. For example, we laugh at the bowler whose gestures after releasing the ball show that he feels he still is in control of the ball's path as it races toward the pins.

Rigidity.   Another aspect of the mechanical is seen in the psychological rigidity of individuals who don't alter their behavior when conditions change or when it would be to their advantage to change their ways. My favorite example of this is Captain Manly in William Wycherly's *The Plain Dealer* (1764). In this play, Manly is characterized as an excessively moral person who believes that one should always tell the truth. In acting on this simplistic notion, Manly alienates everyone because, even when he should tell a white lie—as when his fiancée asks him if she is beautiful—he tells her his true feelings, losing her for good. Even when he might avoid a touchy issue by making no comment, he plunges headlong toward disaster.

Repetitiveness.   In Bergson's view we laugh at the duplication of things or people that ought to be unique. He would undoubtedly agree that this description is funny exactly because everyone in it is a machinelike duplication of everyone else: A mass wedding ceremony of five hundred couples conducted by a charismatic minister illustrates the mechanical and is funny because it duplicates a rite which should be unique to each couple being wed, according to established practices in our society. On the other hand, a line of dancers, such as the Rockettes, kicking their legs in unison is mechanical but is not funny to us, most likely because dancing in unison is a characteristic of nearly all ensemble dances. In another example, the sight of a single Elvis impersonator may be slightly comical to us, but the appearance of ten or so fake Elvises gathered in one place is definitely laughable, especially so because Elvis was so unique.

Inadequacy.   A riddle, a joke, or a pun that is hopelessly insufficient in quality elicits a kind of laughter from the audience. Inadequate efforts at making a joke most often result in a chorus of amused groans.

Humor

Humor, according to Freud, is our way of controlling fears, anxieties, and sorrows. When we've managed to control these feelings sufficiently, we're able to make jokes about the very events that caused our embarrassment or suffering. We've all had embarrassing experiences which, at a later date, we've been able to recite to others (usually with some embellishment), in order to provide laughs at our expense. Freud explains this in these words:

> Only in childhood did we experience intensively painful affects over which today as grown-ups we would laugh, just as a humorist laughs over his present painful affects. The elevation of his ego, which is evidenced by the humoristic displacement—the translation of which would nevertheless read: I am too big to have these causes affect me painfully—he could find in the comparison of his present ego with his infantile ego.[24]

According to Freud, humor is related to *depression, narcissism,* and *masochism,* meaning that humor arises from *adversity,* is concerned with the *self,* and reflects a *cruel view* toward the individual with whom we are asked to identify.

My favorite example of humor, involves mistaken identity. One summer, I had my annual physical exam from a Dr. Rowden and, after checking me for blood pressure, and so on, he sent me to the lab for blood, urine, and other tests. He said he'd call me if there was a problem. About a week later the phone rang, and the conversation went like this:

> Hello.
>
> Hello, Mr. Hyde. This is Rowden.
>
> Oh. [*then, realizing it was my doctor*], Oh, yes. Is something wrong?
>
> Yes. You have dry rot.
>
> I have WHAT?
>
> You have dry rot. . . . In front.
>
> Wait a minute, Dr. Rowden—I . . .
>
> I'm not a doctor. I'm Rauben, the carpenter. Your wife called and said you have dry rot in your front steps.

Wit

Freud's analysis of wit was his most significant contribution to theories of comedy. To begin with, Freud divided wit into two categories: *harmless wit* and *tendency wit.* He believed that some witticisms were without any hidden or even unconscious motivation, "Sometimes wit is wit for its own sake and serves no other particular purpose."[25]

Martin Grotjahn, a modern Freudian, tells us that the existence of harmless wit was of theoretical importance to Freud because if there were such a thing, it would prove that the pleasure we receive from wit is the result of the technique, rather than from some hostile or obscene tendency. Grotjahn goes on to state that Freud can't produce a single valid example of harmless wit. Even Freud had to admit that his examples of harmless wit were not very funny.

Freud's major interest in comedy centered around what he called tendentious wit which stems from hostile or obscene motivations. "Whenever wit is not . . . harmless, it puts itself in the service of but two tendencies which might themselves be united under one viewpoint: it is either *hostile* wit serving as an aggression, satire, or defense, or it is *obscene* wit serving as a sexual exhibition."[26] (Note that Freud included jokes about bodily waste in the category of obscene wit.)

Martin Grotjahn describes the process through which we release our pent-up frustration or impatience with others by making jokes, that is, hostile witticisms:

> The first person, the one who makes the joke or perceives the idea, attacks the second person, the butt of the joke. The wish to attack is temporarily repressed, pushed down into the unconscious where it is disguised by the wit work. In order to test whether the work of disguising the aggressive tendency was successful, the first person tells his witticism to a third person . . . When the third person, to whom the joke is told, reacts with laughter, the first person, who had originally conceived the witticism, may join in the laughter with relief: the disguise has succeeded.[27]

At times and under certain conditions, hostile wit succeeds even though the tendency is *not* disguised. In the television show *Married . . . With Children,* for example, hostile wit directed at Al Bundy is fully understood to be just that by the audience. Audience enjoyment of the put-down is not lessened one bit because of the lack of a disguise. On the whole, though, undisguised hostile wit is more likely to result in anger and confrontation than in laughter.

Obscene wit has been popular throughout history. In ancient times, and in many cultures, a Lord of Misrule was annually chosen to guide bawdy, drunken, and blasphemous celebrations enjoyed by the entire populace. At the conclusion of the so-called period of license, the Lord was dethroned and punished—sometimes by being put to death! His punishment removed all guilt from the celebrants—the bad Lord had caused their misbehavior, and, with his death, all participants became pure and sinless once again.

COMIC FORM AND FUNCTION

Most theories of comedy come from the analysis of laughter or jokes, and if all comic experiences were confined to jokes, such analyses would be sufficient. However, because the type of drama we call a comedy often is a lengthy, structured story, it's important to briefly investigate comic form and the function it sometimes serves, a topic ignored by most writers on the subject.

If it's true that the genuine tragic form gains its power and uniqueness from the purgation of the emotions of pity and fear, from what does the comic form gain its power? And, what are the features of comic form?

Aristotle wrote that tragedy deals with persons who are better than ourselves, and comedy deals with persons who are worse than ourselves. This definition is true for the central comic figures of Greek dramas—as well as those in many plays since ancient times—but it doesn't fit very well with characters in comedies whose behavior isn't harmful or hurtful to others. Harpo Marx, in *A Night at the Opera* (among many other of his films), certainly was funny because of his deviant behavior, yet his antics were not of evil intent, nor were they injurious to others, so we don't see him as worse than ourselves.

By contrast, Max Bialystock, in the film *The Producers,* also was characterized by deviant behavior but, unlike Harpo, he did bring harm to others. It's appropriate that, at the end of *The Night at the Opera,* no punishment is bestowed on Harpo, while at the end of the film *The Producers,* Max is sent to prison. This is a key difference between comedies that focus on harmful deviant behavior and those based on harmless foolishness.

In the classic model, the comic figure is a person who deviates from normal behavior in specific, unacceptable ways. At the conclusion of a classical comedy, one of two related outcomes must occur: In the first, the deviant must recognize his or her shortcomings and promise to change—or at the very least, feel embarrassment or humiliation; in the second, the comic deviant is actually punished. Not only does retaliation uphold a society's concept of right and wrong, it also gives those who've enjoyed the antics of a deviant a means of avoiding self-criticism. "Yes, I laughed at so-and-so's pranks, but it was okay, because I was laughing *at* him, not *with* him—and, I knew all along that eventually he'd get his lumps!"

The function of both types of catharsis is to purge an audience of feelings of hostility, contempt, or derision toward those whose behavior is seen as unacceptable. Our belligerence must remain within bounds, though, for if our hostility is too strong, the comic disguise fails and the story becomes a melodrama rather than a comedy. We laugh at Archie Bunker because of the bad feelings he arouses in us when he mistreats Edith or Meathead, but we also laugh when Archie gets his comeuppance—an example of comic catharsis.

In earlier times, hostility toward rascals was greater than it is today, and the punishment more severe than any we'd want to see. In 1606, Ben Jonson, a drinking buddy of William Shakespeare, wrote his classic comedy *Volpone* about an unscrupulous man who preyed on greedy, trusting victims. Volpone, the central character, and his cohort, Mosca, are con artists who shark on those whose greed makes them living examples of W. C. Field's truism that "you can't cheat an honest man."

Volpone pretends always to be about to die, a victim of many life-threatening illnesses. The scam is to dupe unsuspecting victims into believing that Volpone is near death, and that he's named the sucker of the moment as sole heir. As one of his victims arrives, bringing a silver plate as a gift, Volpone speaks to Mosca: "Loving Mosca, It is well, my pillow now, and let him enter. Now, my fain'd Cough, my Pthisick, and my Goute, My Apoplexie, Palsie, and Catarrhe, . . . He comes, I heare him (uh, uh, uh, uh)."[28] At the end of the play, Volpone and Mosca are convicted of bilking their victims and are punished severely. Mosca is sentenced to be whipped and to spend the rest of his miserable life as a galley slave; Volpone, the mastermind, is (in the words of the judge) ". . . to lie in prison, cramp'd with irons, Till thou be'st sick and lame indeed."[29]

QUESTIONS

1. The two cartoons of Hitler used to help explain an important aspect of Plato's concept of comedy together provide an example of his theory. Can you think of any person who was similarly depicted (harmless buffoon to evil menace) during your lifetime? Your examples may come from jokes, cartoons, stories, or other media.

2. If you're a member of a group, does banter take place on a regular basis that you can identify as a means of releasing low-level hostile tendencies?

3. Where have you seen Sully's concept of the play spirit used to increase audience enjoyment? How was it used?

4. Give examples of the comic of motion, the comic of the naive, the comic of speech, and the comic deflation of an authority figure.

5. *Saturday Night Live* was discussed in this chapter, and several public figures who were objects of ridicule in late 2001 were mentioned. If these persons have been replaced on this program by others, who are the replacements? What (if anything) does their inclusion tell you about changes in public concerns or preoccupations?

NOTES

1. Henri Bergson, "Laughter," in *Comedy* (Garden City, NY: Doubleday Anchor Books, 1956), 61.
2. Linda Shrieves, "Giggles & Guffaws," *The Washington Post,* 25 May 1991.
3. Quoted in Paul Lauter, ed., *Theories of Comedy* (New York: Anchor Books, Doubleday, 1964), 7.
4. You may find a copy of this cartoon in the book, *Masters of Caricature* (New York: Alfred A. Knopf, 1981), 130.
5. Charlie Chaplin, *My Autobiography* (New York: Simon and Schuster, 1964).
6. Aristotle, *Poetics,* tran. S. H. Butcher (New York: Hill & Wang, 1961), 59.
7. Aristotle, *Nichomachean Ethics,* tran. Ingram Bywater (New York: The Pocket Library, 1958), 184.
8. Niko Tinbergen, *The Herring Gull's World,* cited in Robert Ardrey, *The Social Contract* (New York: Atheneum, 1970), 271.
9. William Bausman, *Early California* (San Francisco, 1872).
10. Martin Grotjahn, *Beyond Laughter* (New York: McGraw-Hill, 1957), 10–11.
11. In *Crawford's Claim,* written in 1887 by W. H. Benn, a scene begins with these instructions and words: (Enter LING, with a bouquet of flowers; kneels by ABIGAIL) LING: Chinaman mashed on Melican woman's shape. Bring bouquet allee samee likee Melican man. ABIGAIL: What is this? Ling at my feet with an offering of flowers? Are these flowers for me, Ling? LING: Chinaman mashed on your shape. Bring flowers to you. . . . Mally me, washee cost you nothing. ABIGAIL: Marry you, you wretch! I'll scratch your eyes out.
12. Sigmund Freud, *Wit and Its Relation to the Unconscious* (New York: Dover, 1993), 226.
13. Arthur Schopenhauer, *The World as Will and Idea,* cited in *Theories of Comedy,* ed. Paul Lauter (New York: Doubleday, 1964), 355.
14. Arthur Koestler, *The Act of Creation* (New York: Dell, 1964).
15. Wylie Sypher, "The Meanings of Comedy," in *Comedy* (Garden City, NY: Doubleday Anchor Books, 1956), 202.
16. Arthur Koestler, *The Act of Creation* (New York: Dell, 1964), 53.
17. Sigmund Freud, *Wit,* 293–94.
18. Sigmund Freud, *Wit,* 304–05.
19. Sigmund Freud, *Wit,* 346–47.
20. John Bartlett, *Familiar Quotatoins* (Boston: Little, Brown and Company, 13th ed., 1955), 767–70.
21. Sigmund Freud, *Wit,* 326.
22. Arthur Koestler, *The Act of Creation,* 53.
23. Henri Bergson, *Laughter* (Garden City, NY: Doubleday, 1956), 61ff.
24. Sigmund Freud, *Wit,* 380–81.
25. Sigmund Freud, *Wit,* 128.
26. Sigmund Freud, *Wit,* 138.
27. Martin Grotjahn, *Beyond Laughter* (New York: McGraw-Hill, 1957), 10–11.
28. These infirmities are now spelled differently: Pthisick (phthisic, asthma), Goute (gout, a painful inflammation of the joints), Apoplexie (apoplexy, a loss of muscular control), Palsie (palsy, a loss of control over body parts), and Catarrhe (catarrh, inflammation of the mucous membranes).
29. Freud, *Wit,* 380–81.

CHAPTER NINE

HEROIC VISION, FORM, AND FUNCTION

Chapter 9 describes the essential elements of stories told in the heroic mode. This mode comprises several variations including the epic, myth, legend, fairy tale, romance, and melodrama. The chapter includes a comparison of comedy, tragedy, and the heroic, and discusses variations of form employed by stories in the heroic mode with examples of heroic stories from antiquity. The connection between ancient stories of good versus evil and modern melodramas is demonstrated.

As the drama nears its climax, Gabrielle and Joxer rush in panic toward the cliff overlooking the river, their last hope of escape. The evil Gorgon's footsteps grow louder and louder, shaking the ground. A montage of closeups shows us the fearful, panting, perspiring, frightened faces of Gabrielle and Joxer. Then, at the very last moment, when all seems lost, Xena appears, leaping onto the path a few yards in front of the evil Gorgon. Fear contorts the Gorgon's face. He bellows a challenge. Xena shouts, "You came to conquer the Parthians, Gorgon, but I traveled hundreds of miles to thwart you, so prepare for battle!" The Gorgon roars in anger, then lunges toward Xena. With a back flip, then a forward flip, Xena knocks the Gorgon senseless, her heels to his chin. The Gorgon collapses, Parthia is saved, Gabrielle and Joxer are ecstatic. Fade to black, roll credits . . .

This scenario represents one extreme of the heroic mode, the *melodrama,* at its most spectacular. Another, more subtle and less violent version of the heroic mode appears in fairy tales and the romance. While there's some violence in *Beauty and the Beast,* for example, and the theme of good versus evil is present, the overriding message is one of true love. This fairy tale, with some differences, can be traced to ancient Greece, where it was told as the story of Cupid and Psyche.

ORIGINS OF THE HEROIC VISION

The heroic vision arose from our early ancestors because of their need to confront, in a controlled manner, the dangers that threatened them. Life was precarious, frightening, and mysterious. They were surrounded by danger, engulfed by fragmentary and apparently inexplicable sensory data, and victimized by the whimsy of a capricious and often unjust fate. To control their fears, they developed regulated nightmares and confronted the sources of their apprehension through stories, rituals, and ceremonies that addressed those fears. These stories conjured up heroes to do battle with villains and beneficent gods and demigods to confront evil supernatural forces. The function of the heroic story was to reaffirm a belief that good will always be threatened by evil, and that good eventually will win out.

Primitive people believed in spirits and developed beliefs and ceremonies related to witchcraft. In the absence of scientific explanations for a great range of unusual occurrences, evil demons were blamed. The shaman, or witch doctor, was a natural development because primitive groups needed someone to defend the clan against malignant and unseen forces.

Some spirits, such as the apparitions of departed ancestors, were friendly, so food was set out, prayers intoned, and doors thrown open to receive the ancestral ghosts. But other spirits were foreign, and were either the ghosts of enemies or weird otherworldly creatures who came in the night. Both the good and the evil spirits had to be dealt with, so societies developed rituals to welcome friendly spirits while shamans developed elaborate and mysterious rituals to cope with malignant ghosts and demons. Many rituals and ceremonies involved blood; many centered around human and animal sacrifice. Ceremonies involving the casting out of evil often meant stoning a human scapegoat to death.

These magical ceremonies were held at night, in caves. The celebrants wore grotesque masks, covered their bodies with feathers or animal skins, used tattoos or bright pigments on the exposed portions of their bodies, and, in short, used every device of the costumer's art to enhance the dramatic impact of the ritual. In Meso-America, priests costumed themselves in the bloody flayed skins of recently sacrificed victims. But masks and costumes were only the beginning. Flickering bonfires cast grotesque shadows on cave walls. Pantomime, dance, drum beats, and increasingly frenetic chanting gradually whipped the celebrants into a state of ecstasy. Participants ingested alcohol and hallucinogenic drugs to expand the mind. It's no coincidence that the word *spirits* means *ghost, soul*—and *alcoholic beverages*!

Aside from such ceremonies, our early ancestors developed stories to explain phenomena they otherwise could not comprehend. They created stories that explained the origin of the world; the origin of life; the causes of wind, thunder, lightning, and rain; the creation of the sun, the moon, and the stars; the reasons for growth, death, and decay; and the causes of such phenomena as echoes and reflections. They wove explanations into epics, myths, legends, fables, and other stories. The heroic vision, in its origins, dealt with the supernatural, good versus evil, adventure, heroism, imaginary creatures, horror and terror, and superstition.

Genres of the Heroic Mode

The heroic mode is the basis of several genres among the storytelling arts, but the most common are (1) epic, (2) myth, (3) legend, (4) fairy tale, (5) romance, and (6) melodrama. Although there are important differences among these genres, they have at least five features in common:

1. All serve as models of agents and actions, and thereby provide guidance as well as reinforcement of a number of human hopes or convictions; for instance, that evil exists and must be combatted; that virtue eventually will triumph over evil; or that true love eventually will win the day.

2. All require a double ending in which the sympathetic characters win and those opposing them lose. (Rare exceptions to this formula occur and are noted.)

3. Each of these genres makes use of the same themes, though not all in every story. Extreme melodramas (e.g., *The Return of the Mummy, Gladiator, 2001 Dalmatians*) often feature villains, fantasy, horror, terror, suspense, primitivism, heroism, good versus evil, and love versus duty.

Lighter melodramas (*Chariots of Fire, Babe*) employ antagonists pitted against sympathetic agents, but those opposing the protagonists are seldom one-dimensional villains; story elements create conflicts and reversals. Romances depend on romantic love, obstacles that obstruct the course of true love, misunderstood intentions, daydreams, etc.

4. In these genres, there's a threat against the protagonist(s), but the threat usually is losing one's life, one's loved one, or one's sanity, and not—as so often is the case with tragedy— losing life's ultimate meaning.

5. All of these genres are alike in the nature of their catharses (a subject explored below, in "Melodrama and Heroic Form").

Stories in the heroic form vary greatly in their degree of violence. Epic tales, including the *Iliad,* the *Odyssey,* the *Aeneid,* and *Beowulf,* are distinguished by violent heroism, villainy, terror, and horror, and are at one extreme of the heroic form. Some fairy tales that feature hapless victims falling prey to villains include violence (*Hansel and Gretel, Snow White, Sleeping Beauty, Little Red Riding Hood*), but violence isn't essential to all fairy tales, particularly those based on love.

Many stories in the heroic mode contain no violence at all. Some of the most enduring stories in this mode are best described as *romance*; for example, *Sleepless in Seattle* or *Sommersby*. Heroic romance is often mixed with comedy, as in *When Harry Met Sally* and *To Catch a Thief.*

Comedy, Tragedy, and the Heroic

Tragedy shows us how we believe we ought to be (better than ourselves). Comedy shows us how we believe we ought not to be (worse than ourselves). The heroic mode is more complex. It shows us what we believe, imagine, or dream we are; or what we imagine we could be; or what we fear we might be (or might become). To paraphrase this complex thought, the heroic is based on our feelings (what we believe); our daydreams (what we imagine and fantasize over); our dreams (what we wish we were); and our nightmares (what we fear).

Each of these concerns is appropriate to one or more genres of the heroic mode. An extreme melodrama such as *The Invasion of the Body Snatchers* gains its strength from a nightmarish fear that the human species will be taken over by aliens from another planet. *Field of Dreams,* a much lighter melodrama, bases much of its suspense on the products of daydreams and dreams.

Tragedy and comedy have their roots in ancient ritual, but neither seems to have become a recognizable art form in Western civilization until the time of the ancient Greeks, when the earliest extant plays were written. The epic, legend, and other forms in the heroic mode, on the other hand, go back thousands of years before the birth of the first playwright or actor. Tragedy and comedy are known primarily though the drama, while heroic tales descended from stories told by tribal storytellers.

EXAMPLES OF THE HEROIC FROM ANTIQUITY

Reviewing the earliest stories in the heroic mode that have survived offers an opportunity to test Aldous Huxley's assertion, found in the introduction, that human nature does not change. The examples from antiquity that follow begin with extreme melodramatic events and themes, then move to more reserved and internalized emotions found in stories from the same period and cultures. The origins of the heroic mode, reflected in three great civilizations tell us much about the universality of human needs and interests.

Mesopotamia

From *The Epic of Gilgamesh,* written on clay tablets in Mesopotamia somewhere between four thousand and five thousand years ago but existing in oral tradition for centuries before the invention of writing, we see many themes: the hero, lust, fantastic creatures, prostitution, seduction, hand-to-hand combat, friendship, and death and grief.[1]

The Hero.   The creation of Gilgamesh:

> When the gods created Gilgamesh they gave him a perfect body. Shamash the glorious sun endowed him with beauty, Adad the god of the storm endowed him with courage, the great gods made his beauty perfect, surpassing all others, terrifying like a great bull.

Lust.   Gilgamesh is unlike most modern heroes in that he uses his strength and good looks to satisfy his need for power and sex. Today, these practices by people of power characterize villains rather than heroes.

> . . . the men of Uruk muttered in their houses, "Gilgamesh sounds the tocsin [alarm] for his amusement, his arrogance has no bounds by day or night. No son is left with his father, for Gilgamesh takes them all, even the children; yet the king should be a shepherd to his people. His lust leaves no virgin to her lover, neither the warrior's daughter nor the wife of the noble."

Fantastic Creatures.   To tame Gilgamesh, the goddess Aruru takes a pinch of clay and creates Enkidu, a beast-man as strong as Gilgamesh himself. Her plan is to have him fight Gilgamesh on even terms, hoping that confronting a rival will cause Gilgamesh to leave the community in peace:

> His body was rough, he had long hair like a woman's; it waved like the hair of Nisaba, the goddess of corn. His body was covered by matted hair like Sumuqan's, the god of cattle. He

was innocent of mankind; he knew nothing of the cultivated land. . . . Enkidu ate grass in the hills with the gazelle and lurked with wild beasts at the water holes.

Prostitution.   To tame the wild creature, a frightened trapper asks his father for advice. The wise old man recommends that a prostitute be sent to Enkidu to seduce and thereby tame him:

> "[Find a] harlot, a wanton from the temple of love; return with her and let her woman's power overpower this man."

This is done, and the trapper and the harlot spend two fruitless days at the watering hole, waiting for Enkidu to appear along with the herds of grazing animals. Finally, on the third day they arrive. The trapper speaks:

> "There he is. Now, woman, make your breasts bare, have no shame, do not delay but welcome his love. Let him see you naked, let him possess your body. . . . teach him, the savage man, your woman's art, for when he murmurs love to you, the wild beasts that shared his life in the hills will reject him."

Seduction.   After seven days and nights of lovemaking, Enkidu tries to rejoin the herd, but is rejected. The harlot advises him to shun the animals and become a man. She takes him to Uruk to meet Gilgamesh.

Hand-to-Hand Combat.   When Enkidu arrives in Uruk, Enkidu and Gilgamesh engage in a mighty battle:

> . . . in the night Gilgamesh got up and came to the house. Then Enkidu stepped out, he stood in the street and blocked the way. Mighty Gilgamesh came on and Enkidu met him at the gate. Enkidu put out his foot and prevented Gilgamesh from entering the house, so they grappled, holding each other like bulls. They broke the doorposts and the walls shook, they snorted like bulls locked together. Gilgamesh bent his knee with his foot planted on the ground and with a turn Enkidu was thrown. Then immediately his fury died.

Friendship.   The hero and his fantastic adversary become friends:

> When Enkidu was thrown he said to Gilgamesh., 'there is not another like you in the world. . . . your strength surpasses the strength of men.' So Enkidu and Gilgamesh embraced and their friendship was sealed.

Death and Grief.   After many adventures, Enkidu is condemned to death for his part in the destruction caused by the pair. After several days of suffering, Enkidu dies:

> He touched his heart but it did not beat. So Gilgamesh laid a veil, as one veils the bride, over his friend. He began to rage like a lion, like a lioness robbed of her whelps. . . . he tore out his hair and strewed it around. He dragged off his splendid robes and flung them down as if they were abominations.

Gilgamesh laments:

> "I made you rest on a royal bed, you reclined on a couch at my left hand, the princes of the earth kissed your feet. I will cause all the people of Uruk to weep over you and raise the dirge of the dead. The joyful people will stoop with sorrow; and when you have gone to the earth I will let my hair grow long for your sake, I will wander through the wilderness in the skin of a lion."
>
> The next day also, in the first light, Gilgamesh lamented; seven days and seven nights he wept for Enkidu until the worm fastened on him. Only then he gave him up for the earth . . .

Egypt

Stories from ancient Egypt include adventurous happenings, not unlike the popular tales from Mesopotamia. The *Tale of Two Brothers* includes the themes of seduction, battling brothers, an unfaithful wife, emasculation, death and rebirth, revenge, and more. Two other stories, *The Shipwrecked Sailor* and *The Doomed Prince,* are filled with adventure and themes that arouse strong emotions.

At the same time, Egyptian popular tales also depicted low-key and acutely sensitive human interrelationships. A collection of stories, *King Kheops and the Magicians* (now spelled Cheops), written about four thousand years ago, includes a whimsical and amusing story dealing with the boredom of King Snefru. An advisor suggests that the king needs a diversion, and proposes a boating trip on the Nile, with young women at the oars. Snefru agrees to the plan, and issues this order:

> "Have brought to me twenty paddles of ebony inwrought with gold. . . . Have brought to me twenty women, of those with the fairest limbs, and with beauteous breasts and braided tresses, such as have not yet given birth, and moreover have brought to me twenty nets, and give these nets to these women instead of their clothes."[2]

This was done, and the king no longer was bored as he watched the lovely maidens at their labor. The lead rower suddenly lost her malachite fish pendant overboard, and ceased rowing, and all the other rowers did likewise. When informed of the problem, the king dismissed it as trivial, and offered a replacement.

But the woman wasn't placated, insisting that the replacement wasn't the real thing, and that she wanted the one she'd lost. When all reasoning failed, the king sent for his magician, who parted the Nile, set one-half of the water atop the other half, and retrieved the pendant. The lead rower was satisfied, the rowing continued, and ". . . his majesty spent the whole day in merriment . . ."[3]

A brief poem from the Egyptian New Kingdom (between c. 1580 and 1090 B.C.) expresses flirtation in a way that will be understood by anyone who has ever come on to an attractive would-be mate: The speaker is a young woman. The scene is a river. A short distance away is a young man whose appearance is found by the woman to be attractive.

> *Diving and swimming with you here*
> *Gives me the chance I've been waiting for:*

To show my looks
Before an appreciative eye.

My bathing suit of the best material,
The finest sheer,
Now that it's wet
Notice the transparency
How it clings.

Let us admit, I find you attractive.
I swim away, but soon I'm back.
Splashing, chattering,
Any excuse at all to join your party.

Look! a redfish flashed through my fingers!
You'll see it better
If you come over here,
Near me.[4]

Greece

Greek literature is noted not only for its powerful tragedies and hilarious and racy comedies, but for sensitive and intimate poems and narratives as well. Sappho, who lived about 600 B.C., was the most honored female poet of antiquity. She wrote with subdued passion about her most intimate feelings and, although she married and gave birth to a daughter, her deepest love was reserved for young women. This brief poem demonstrates her gift of words, and the depths of her passion.

I have not had one word from her

Frankly I wish I were dead
When she left, she wept

a great deal; she said to me, "This parting must be
endured, Sappho. I go unwillingly."

I said, "Go, and be happy
but remember (you know
well) whom you leave shackled by love

"If you forget me, think
of our gifts to Aphrodite
and all the loveliness that we shared

"all the violet tiaras,
braided rosebuds, dill and
crocus twined around your young neck

"myrrh poured on your head
and on soft mats girls with
all that they most wished for beside them

"while no voices chanted
choruses without ours,
no woodlot bloomed in spring without song . . ."[5]

The Odyssey.   Two scenes from Homer's *Odyssey*[6] show ageless themes that link the greatest poetry of antiquity to us, to our own times, and to our capacity for sharing in the emotions of our brothers and sisters who lived more than twenty-five centuries ago.

Odysseus spends ten years fighting at Troy and, after the war is won, another ten years on his perilous journey through the Mediterranean to his home in Ithaca. After his twenty-year absence, he returns as a ragged, bearded, stranger and is met by his son, who doesn't recognize him. The son decides to offer the stranger his hospitality and orders Eumaios, a swineherd, to lead Odysseus to the family home. On their way, the timeless theme of man and dog is poignantly expressed as Odysseus sees an old dog, which he believes to be his faithful hunting companion of years past, Argos:

> As they were talking together, a hound that was lying there lifted his head and pricked up his ears. This was Argos, whom Odysseus himself had bred and trained. . . . There lay Argos the hound covered with vermin. When he knew it was his old master near him, he wagged his tail and dropped both his ears; but he could not move to approach him. Odysseus saw, and secretly wiped a tear from his eye . . .

Eumaios tells Odysseus that the dog belonged to a man who died in Troy, and goes on to describe the dog, Argos, when he was in his prime. After the two leave to enter the palace, Argos dies, happy at seeing his master one last time.

Even more moving is the scene in which Penelope, the faithful wife of Odysseus, meets her long-gone husband. When he arrives in her presence, having been told by their son Telemachos that the stranger is her husband, she refuses to accept him, She tells her son that if the stranger is indeed her husband, she will know because of the secrets they alone share.

Odysseus is taken away by servants who bathe and clothe him in elegant robes. When he rejoins Penelope, she remains unconvinced. Odysseus then reveals details of their wedding bed, facts known only to the two of them and a few intimate servants. Penelope, at last, melts:

> She was conquered, she could hold out no longer when Odysseus told the secret she knew so well. She burst into tears and ran straight to him, throwing her arms about his neck. She kissed his head, and cried:
> "Don't be cross with me, my husband, you were always a most understanding man! The gods brought affliction upon us because they grudged us the joy of being young and growing old together! Don't be angry, don't be hurt because I did not take you in my arms as soon as I saw you! My heart has been frozen all this time with a fear that some one would come and deceive me with a false tale; there are so many impostors! But now you have told me the secret of our bed, that settles it. No one else has seen it, only you and I, and my maid Actoris, the one my father gave me when I came to you, who used to keep the door of our room. You have convinced your hard-hearted wife!"

Odysseus was even more deeply moved, and his tears ran as he held her in his arms, the wife of his heart, so faithful and so wise. She felt like a shipwrecked mariner, when the stout ship has been driven before the storm and smashed by the heavy waves, but a few have escaped by swimming. How glad they are to see land at last, to get out of the water and stand upon solid ground. . . . So glad was Penelopeia to see her husband at last; she held her white arms close round his neck, and could not let him go. Dawn would have risen upon their tears of joy, but Athena had a thought for them. She held the night in its course and made it long.

These few excerpts adequately represent the heroic mode in classical antiquity.[7] Certainly, Aldous Huxley's point has been made: We are, indeed, the same species of being as those for whom these stories and poems were created so many centuries ago. Huxley's conviction that humans are unchanged in their response to human relationships is an important guide to the creation of stories that work today and will continue to work forever.

THE HEROIC MODE AFTER THE GOLDEN AGE

Following the Golden Age in Athens, plays continued to be performed, but both output and quality rapidly declined. When Athens fell to Sparta in 404 B.C., the life of the world's first democracy was extinguished, and with it the creative spark that had seen the birth and fruition, not only of heroic tales, but of tragedy and comedy as well.

Little need be said about the heroic mode during the years of Roman dominance that saw its empire expand to Britain, Asia, North Africa, and all lands between. The need or desire to be engrossed by heroic themes—at least the most bloody and revolting of them—was served by the horrors of gladiatorial combat, as well as the public slaughter of prisoners of war and early Christians. The plays of Seneca—which most likely were intended for reading rather than for staging—mirror the horror found in the arena. Comedies continued to be written and performed, and those of Plautus and Terrence remain noteworthy accomplishments. Perhaps their comedies offered relief from an otherwise too-stimulating diet of horror. Elements of melodrama may be seen in these comedies—as they are today in *Ally McBeal, City Slickers,* and *Mrs. Doubtfire*—but essentially they were cast in the comic mode. After the fall of Rome, night descended on the arts and sciences of the Western world, and one of the casualties was the dramatic art.

A thousand years elapsed before the rebirth of staged drama in England. The plays of Shakespeare, the most brilliant playwright in the Elizabethan Age, offer significant insights into the diverse elements that made up the heroic mode in his era.

Shakespeare's plays traditionally are categorized as tragedies, comedies, and histories (sometimes classified as chronicles). Yet a broader and more instructive understanding of the heroic mode tells us that these categories have little to do with the realities of his plays. It's true that *Hamlet* is a tragedy, *The Comedy of Errors* is a comedy, and all of the histories dealing with the rulers of England do, indeed, base their stories on English history.

At the same time, Shakespeare's so-called tragedy *Titus Andronicus* is essentially a blood-and-thunder melodrama of the most violent type, featuring human sacrifice, abduction, rape, mutilation, insanity, murder, cannibalism, and torture.[8] Of the twenty-two characters in the play, fourteen suffer violence—most of them violent death—in the course of the action.

Most of Shakespeare's history plays are likewise melodramas, though of a less violent sort. Henry V is portrayed as the prototypical hero, fighting traitors at home while setting out to conquer French provinces he believes belong to England. In *Richard III,* Richard, Duke of Gloucester, is a stereotypical arch villain who kills his way to the throne and is crowned Richard III.

The label *comedy* accurately describes such farces as *The Comedy of Errors, The Taming of the Shrew,* and *The Merry Wives of Windsor.* But several of Shakespeare's plays designated as comedies lean toward the romance, one of the heroic models many guises. *As You Like It, The Merchant of Venice,* and *Twelfth Night* have comic moments, but all are distinguished by their romantic views of love and the delicious struggle between a man and a woman seeking to establish a working partnership. Shakespeare's gift to subsequent ages was that of expanding the potentials of the heroic mode to include gentler stories that attract and hold our attention without reliance on external spectacle.

THE CHANGED VIEW OF HUMAN NATURE

From the Elizabethan Age to the mid-nineteenth century, beliefs about human nature underwent relatively little change. Humans were born to particular stations in life: some were born to be heroes, others to be rulers and, in descending order of importance, professionals, skilled workers, unskilled workers, and, at the lowest level, slaves. A corollary to this was the belief that all people were born either good or evil, and were destined to live out their lives as they reflected their inborn qualities.

A sixteenth-century treatise proclaimed throughout England states this concept in very clear terms:[9]

AN EXHORTATION CONCERNING GOOD ORDER AND OBEDIENCE
TO RULERS AND MAGISTRATES
Almighty GOD hath created and appointed all things in heaven, earth, and waters, in a most excellent and perfect order. In Heaven, he hath appointed distinct and several orders and states of Archangels and Angels. In earth he hath assigned and appointed Kings, Princes, with other governors under them, in all good and necessary order. . . . and all manner of every degree of people in their vocation, calling and office, hath appointed to them their duty and order: some are in high degree, some in low, some Kings and Princes, some inferiors and subjects, Priests, and lay men, masters and servants, fathers, and children, husbands and wives, rich and poor, and every one have need of other, so that in all things is to be lauded and praised the goodly order of GOD, without the which no house, no City, no Commonwealth can continue and endure, or last. For where there is no right order, there reigneth all abuse, carnal liberty, enormity, sin, and Babylonical confusion. [Spelling changed from Elizabethan to modern for easy comprehension.]

The radical turnabout in beliefs about the nature of human beings began with the Age of Enlightenment (sometimes called The Age of Reason), roughly the eighteenth century. In brief, John Locke in England, Voltaire and Rousseau in France, and many other scholars and philosophers swept away centuries of misconceptions about the innate nature of the human species. Gone forever was the concept that people were born to occupy fixed roles in life, and that all humans possessed unchangeable characteristics. These fallacies were replaced by the conviction that all humans are created equal, and that the mind of each originates as a "blank tablet" on which the events of each person's life determine the ways in which they behave.

It took nearly a century to see the impact of these new concepts, but out of this new understanding of human qualities grew a new style of dramatic characterization. By the late nineteenth century Maxim Gorki and Anton Chekhov in Russia, Henrik Ibsen in Norway, Gerhart Hauptmann in Germany, George Bernard Shaw in England, and August Strindberg in Sweden wrote plays that revolutionized the depiction of stage characters. Melodramas continued to be written and enjoyed even though their depictions of one-dimensional heroes and villains no longer held validity, but ground had been broken for a new kind of melodrama—dramas with deeper and ultimately more gripping stories in which the forces pitted against each other were neither all-bad nor all-good.

From the nineteenth century on, melodrama has been the most popular form of drama in the United States on stage, film, and television.

MELODRAMA AND HEROIC FORM

The most common form in the heroic mode follows this pattern: The story begins with the identification of those who are essentially good and those who oppose them. The opposition threatens the life or security of the good person or of an upright community. Throughout the story, the opposition has the upper hand, and anxiety and fear are aroused in the audience. At the last moment (and, in the least realistic melodrama, sometimes in an improbable way) the good person defeats the evil one, the hero and his love are saved, the community is spared. As spectators to this, we're purged of our feelings of anxiety and fear. This is the heroic catharsis for traditional and essentially extreme melodramas.

While this description is true of most works in the heroic mode, it's not true of all. *Jack and the Beanstalk* follows this formula, but *Cinderella* does not. This makes *Cinderella* more of a romance than a fairy tale because fairy tales that emphasize romantic love often lack the good versus evil concept of the heroic vision. The hero of *The Frog Prince* and the Beast in *Beauty and the Beast* are both under the spell of an evil being (the Beast by an evil fairy, the Frog Prince by an evil witch), but neither antagonist appears in these stories, so these tales are to be seen more as romances than melodramas. In many episodic works, such as *Sir Gawain and the Green Knight,* the Arthurian cycle, *Robin Hood,* and *Gilgamesh,* the hero dies at the end of the final story, but this occurs only after all of the major battles have been fought and won.

A glance at the entertainment section of a contemporary newspaper shows how popular the heroic (melodrama) is today.[10] A few popular melodramatic films of recent years include *Boogie Nights, Pulp Fiction, Scream, An American Werewolf in Paris, The Postman, Midnight in the Garden of Good and Evil, Alien Resurrection, Titanic, Fallen, Whispers in the Dark, Tomorrow Never Dies, Cliffhanger, Twister, Independence Day, The Shawshank*

Redemption, and *The Perfect Storm.* Films that combine melodrama and comedy include *Honey, I Shrunk the Kids* and *Home Alone.* Television melodramas include *NYPD Blue, St. Elsewhere, ER, CSI* (*Crime Scene Investigation*), *Survivor, Nash Bridges, The X-Files, Law and Order, The West Wing, Walker, Texas Ranger,* and *Touched by an Angel,* as well as professional wrestling matches.

An article in the *New York Times,* reporting on the phenomenal success of the film *Harry Potter and the Sorcerer's Stone,* listed the top fifteen box-office first-weekend earnings:

1. *Harry Potter and the Sorcerer's Stone*
2. *Jurassic Park*
3. *Planet of the Apes* (2001 version)
4. *The Mummy Returns*
5. *Rush Hour 2*
6. *Star Wars, Episode 1*
7. *Monsters, Inc.*
8. *Pearl Harbor*
9. *Hannibal*
10. *Mission Impossible 2* (2000 version)
11. *Toy Story 2*
12. *How the Grinch Stole Christmas*
13. *Austin Powers: The Spy Who Shagged Me*
14. *X-Men*
15. *Mission Impossible* (1996 version)

Every one of these is a melodrama. And the details of each reinforces the claim that the heroic mode is the most versatile of all forms. Of the fifteen, numbers 1, 11, and 12 were produced for children; numbers 11 and 13 are comedy-melodramas; and the remaining eleven are blood-and-guts melodramas. Taken together these fifteen films include themes of cannibalism, war, alien invasion, spies and espionage, monsters, magic, sorcery, horror, terror, sex, heroism, revenge, mutilation, treachery, good versus evil, evil punished, virtue rewarded, inanimate objects coming to life, life in outer space, and so much more. The heroic form lives and prospers in twenty-first-century America!

QUESTIONS

1. Select any three of the fifteen high-grossing films listed above and analyze them in terms of universal themes, listing every theme you can identify.

2. Choose a melodrama from any medium whose details are fresh in your mind. What does the story tell us about the following clues identified by Kenneth Burke (see Chapter 3: scene, act, agent, agency, and purpose)?

3. Select a melodrama that includes comic moments. In the list of fifteen films, listed above, these are likely candidates: *Toy Story, Austin Powers,* and *How the Grinch Stole Christmas.* What techniques of the comic and wit are used?

4. Select five fables—Aesop is a good and readily available source—and analyze them in terms of the practical or moral lessons they were intended to teach.

5. Choose any melodrama—whether a violent story such as *Gladiator,* or a more subtle one such as *Forrest Gump,* and analyze it in terms of any cathartic effects it may have had on you.

NOTES

1. *The Epic of Gilgamesh,* trans. N. K. Sandars. (Middlesex, England: Penguin Classics, 3d ed., 1972), 61ff, 95–96. Permission to use these excerpts from *The Epic of Gilgamesh* was kindly granted by The Penguin Group (UK).
2. Adolf Erman, ed. *The Ancient Egyptians* (New York: Harper and Row, 1966), 39.
3. Ibid., 40.
4. Anonymous, trans. by Noel Stock from *Love Poems of Ancient Egypt,* 7. Copyright 1962 by Noel Stock. Reprinted by permission of New Directions Publishing Corp.
5. Mary Barnard, *Sappho: A New Translation* (Berkeley, CA: University of California Press, 1958). Permission granted by the Regents of the University of California.
6. Homer. *The Odyssey,*, trans. W. H. D. Rouse (New York: Mentor Classics, 1937), 196ff. Rouse uses the name "Odysseus," rather than "Ulysses," and both names are to be found in various translations.
7. Note to readers: I began this chapter intending to touch briefly on heroic tales of the ancient world. As I moved deeper into this literature—which I'd first encountered years ago—it once again took possession of me, and I found myself unable to merely skim the surface in a paragraph or two. On reviewing what I'd extracted from the past, I decided to leave it as I wrote it. The fact that these tales once again captivated me is eloquent confirmation of the power inherent in well-conceived stories, and a reminder that you'll succeed as a professional storyteller if you remember always to project yourself into the minds and feelings of your audience, creating dramas that meet their needs, desires, and fears, while touching on timeless themes.
8. A few scholars refuse to accept this play as being written by Shakespeare. Regardless of its authorship, the play was both popular and Elizabethan, and is different only in its degree of bloodiness compared with other so-called Elizabethan tragedies—*Tamerlane* (Marlowe), *The Duchess of Malfi* (Webster), and Shakespeare's history play, *Richard III.*
9. *Elizabethan Homilies,* "An Exhortation Concerning Good Order and Obedience to Rulers and Magistrates." http://anglicanlibrary.org/homilies/bk1intro.htm.
10. Inevitably, all examples given here may very well be forgotten by the time you read these words. Such is the reality of the transient arts of our time, including most popular novels, comic strips, films, television dramas, and popular songs.

CHAPTER TEN

TRAGIC DRAMA THROUGH THE AGES

Chapter 10 distinguishes what we see as tragic *events* from the tragic *form* that developed millennia ago in ritual, and later in tragic drama. The Egyptian myth of Osiris and Isis and the celebration that grew from it establish the connection between myth and ritual. Later, in ancient Greece, tragic ritual evolved to dramatic art. Some modern views of tragedy are cited, and major arguments for the continuing relevance of tragic drama are presented. Arthur Miller's definitive essay, "Tragedy and the Common Man," which sets forth criteria for tragic drama in our own time, is quoted in some detail.

An understanding of tragedy is important to all storytellers, despite the scarcity of tragedies in today's television and films. Writers for the public media should have a grounding in all modes of storytelling, including tragedy, long considered the supreme achievement of the dramatic arts.

A discussion of tragedy will help you see what tragic drama once was about; will help you understand its place in the history of the public arts; will clarify the connection between tragic stories and public ceremonies and rituals; and will help you understand the nature and power of catharsis. Without an understanding of tragedy, a view of the storytelling arts would be incomplete. The broader your store of knowledge, the more choices you have as you search for ways to express your creative visions.

The literature of tragic theory is vast, and it would take this entire book to do it justice. For those who haven't studied tragic drama and theory, this chapter, brief though it is, should serve as an introduction to some of the most profound accomplishments of the human imagination.

THE ORIGIN OF TRAGEDY

In outlining tragedy's origin, it's important first to contrast tragic drama with events most of us think of as tragedies. Horrible occurrences are conspicuous in today's public arts. Murders, rapes, assassinations, wars, terrorist attacks, and torture are depicted in films and television, are seen in history-based documentaries, and are a staple of television news. There's no question that such calamities stir our emotions and cause us pain, so it's not unreasonable for us to think of such events as tragic. The term is appropriate for the *events*, but it doesn't describe tragedy as a *form* and a *vision* in the dramatic arts.

It's believed that the earliest appearance of anything approaching tragedy as a concept arose in ancient Egypt. It began with the legend recounting the murder and dismemberment of the Egyptian god-king Osiris. This tale gave birth to a ritual that eventually created the form, vision, and purpose of tragic drama. The structure of the Osiris and Isis legend, and later the ritual that grew out of it, is outlined here. What's important and unique about the murder and the mourning that ensued is that *grief eventually gave way to rejoicing* as Osiris rose from the dead. In ancient times, orators recited legends and myths before rapt members of a clan, and priests and others performed rituals and dramas in the tragic mode, not only for the sake of suffering (which has its own therapeutic value), but for the transmutation of suffering to joy though the tragic catharsis. In this context, it's important to distinguish between tragic *events* and the tragic *form* in order to understand tragic drama.[1]

Out of the Isis and Osiris legend grew the ritual. Osiris, the god-king of Egypt, together with his sister-wife Isis, the goddess of birth, was the first to cultivate wheat, barley, and grapes. Before his time, people were savage cannibals, but Osiris was a civilizing influence; people saw him as the principle of good, and celebrated him as a hero. His evil brother, Set, the principle of evil (darkness), killed Osiris and cut his body into fourteen pieces, scattering them throughout Egypt. Isis searched for his remains and, with the help of the god Thoth, reassembled his body, restored his life, and Osiris became the ruler of the underworld, given the task of judging the dead. Because he returned from the dead, people worshipped him as the god of resurrection and life eternal.

Out of this legend of Osiris came a public ritual that resembled a massive dramatic production. The ritual took the form of a passion ceremony, lasting eighteen days and performed annually throughout Egypt. There are obvious connections between this ritual and the annual cycling of the Nile. Once each year the Nile, Egypt's river of life, mysteriously rose, overflowing its banks and depositing fertile mud to replenish the rich soil of the delta. Living in an area which saw little rainfall, Egyptians saw no meteorological cause for the yearly inundation. They assumed that the floods occurred because of munificent gods, so they praised them for this magical rebirth that fostered the sowing, growing, and harvesting of crops (the death and rebirth of vegetation).

The festival opened with the people in mourning for the dead Osiris. It began with the plowing and sowing of three types of seed in a special field. Small images of Osiris, composed of rich earth were made and embedded with wheat kernels, then were cast from a gold mold. On the tenth day, they were taken on a voyage attended by thirty-four images of deities, and illuminated by three hundred and sixty-five lights. On the twelfth day an image of Osiris in a coffin made of mulberry wood was laid in a grave as a similar image, placed there the previous year was removed and, on the eighteenth day, placed in a holy sepulcher. At a certain point in the ceremonies, the wheat kernels that had been embedded in the earthen figures of Osiris sprouted, a sign of rebirth. Celebration replaced mourning, and the festival came to an end with rejoicing. The transition from this and similar ceremonies to tragic drama took many centuries, but the essence of tragedy as a process of moving from mourning to joy and as an affirmation of good defeating evil was present in the myth and ritual of Osiris.

There's no evidence that tragic ritual developed into formalized tragic drama in Egypt; that development occurred later, in ancient Greece, as religious rituals were converted into dramatic performances. These performances dealt with the struggles and the inevitable deaths or downfalls of the mighty but, as was true of the Osiris festival, the purpose of these dramas was not to bring about unhappiness. They were structured to have an audience first confront the catastrophe and then be elevated above suffering.

All tragic stories stem from the belief that there is meaning to human life, however obscure and unfathomable. Although a tragedy need not be religiously oriented, it must acknowledge that both good and evil exist in the world, and that good is to be sought, and evil is to be shunned. Critic Richard Sewall tells us that:

> . . . tragedy discerns a principle of goodness that exists with evil. This principle need be nothing so pat as the Moral Order, or the "armies of unalterable law," and it is nothing so sure as the orthodox Christian God. It is nearer the folk sense that justice exists somewhere in the universe. In this sense, the opposite of tragedy is not comedy or satire but cynicism and nihilism.[2]

Tragedy asserts that humans, as thinking, knowing beings, are obliged to make serious choices. As beings who understand the difference between right and wrong, we are morally obligated to make the most ethical of all possible choices; as imperfect beings, living in an imperfect world, we find difficulty in determining the truth and following its dictates—especially when the possibility of our own downfall might be caused by our actions.

Tragedy, then, represents an upward look at the human species. It presents people who are better—or at least greater—than the average. It assumes that we occupy a special and important place in a meaningful universe. We aren't merely another species of animal and, no matter how degraded the leading characters of a tragedy may be (Macbeth and his wife, for example), their unique humanity is apparent if only by their deviation from acceptable conduct. Tragedy is associated with important issues, with codes of conduct, and with morality. Tragedy shows us, through the suffering and destruction of the protagonist, that there is meaning to life beyond mere physical existence.

TRAGIC FORM AND FUNCTION

The form of a story or play is the action pattern of that story. It presents its incidents in a step-by-step manner and, in a well-written or well-told story, each incident motivates the next one. When we experience a tragic protagonist as a functioning member of society, we move inevitably to the tragic story, and tragic form, vision, and purpose meet in the culminating act of the tragic process.

In his *Poetics,* Aristotle very economically defined tragedy, including the vision, the form and the function:

> Tragedy, then, is an imitation of an action that is serious, complete, and of a certain magnitude; in language embellished with each kind of artistic ornament, the several kinds being found in

separate parts of the play; in the form of action, not of narrative; through pity and fear effecting the proper purgation of these emotions.[3]

Modern scholar Murray Krieger explains the cathartic principle:

> The cathartic principle itself, in maintaining that pity and fear are not merely to be aroused but to be purged, is evidence of the need in tragedy to have dissonance exploded, leaving only the serenity of harmony behind. . . . The purging of dangerously aroused emotions, following as it does upon the satisfaction, the soothing grace, bestowed upon wayward materials by aesthetic completeness, uses form to overcome the threat of these materials and, consequently, these emotions.[4]

Krieger supports the belief that tragic drama was the outgrowth of tragic rites and festivals held in ancient days, and that tragic dramas were developed, not for the sake of suffering but to arouse suffering, and then to relieve it through a catharsis. Today, we tend to call any story that ends in the death or downfall of someone we care about a tragedy. That's okay. There's no point in not enjoying stories such as *Braveheart, Brian's Song, A Streetcar Named Desire,* or *Love Story* just because they don't fit the traditional mold. They're outstanding in their own right, and need no excuses; we can be overwhelmed by their power, even though they don't conform to long-established definitions of tragic drama.

TRAGIC DRAMA TODAY

Arthur Miller, perhaps the most honored playwright of his time, is convinced that tragedy does not require a noble or otherwise exalted person as the tragic figure. His 1949 drama *Death of a Salesman* was both praised and panned by critics, some of whom felt that his central character, Willy Loman, was too common to be a fit subject for tragedy. Miller answered his critics in a now-famous essay, "Tragedy and the Common Man."[5] Miller makes several points in spelling out his thesis, but perhaps his most telling argument deals with the false notion that exalted status—god, hero, or king—is demanded for a character to be a truly tragic hero.

> In this age few tragedies are written. It has often been held that the lack is due to a paucity of heroes among us, or else that modern man has had the blood drawn out of his organs of belief by the skepticism of science . . . . For one reason or another, we are often held to be below tragedy—or tragedy above us. The inevitable conclusion is, of course, that the tragic mode is archaic, fit only for the very highly placed, the kings or the kingly, and where this admission is not made in so many words it is most often implied.[6]

Miller then notes that because of modern psychiatry we know what the Greeks—and indeed all societies up to the end of the nineteenth century—did not know: that every human being, from king to laborer, shares the same characteristics and potentials and has the capacity to react the same way in similar emotional situations. From prehistoric times, all recorded societies believed that individual humans were born to unchangeable stations in life. Some were born to rule, others to serve. Some to be masters, some slaves. Only those high born were worthy of depiction in tragic drama. This fallacy helped make for great tragedy as long as it was believed—and we can still thrill to plays thus conceived—but it has little relevance to tragedy written for our times.

Miller continues with the assertion that the tragic feeling is present when we see a character who is willing to die ". . . if need be, to secure one thing—his sense of personal dignity. From Orestes to Hamlet, Medea to Macbeth, the underlying struggle is that of the individual attempting to gain his 'rightful' position in his society."[7]

In all times there have been those who act against that which degrades them

> . . . and in the process of action everything we have accepted out of fear or insensitivity or ignorance is shaken before us and examined, and from this total onslaught by an individual against the seemingly stable cosmos surrounding us—from this total examination of the "unchangeable" environment—comes the terror and the fear that is classically associated with tragedy.[8]

Miller observes that a person who's compelled to fight even to death for principles and for his freedom to follow his conscience reveals a wrong or an evil in the environment, and this revelation shows us the enemy of our freedom.

Miller concludes with these remarks:

> It is time, I think, that we who are without kings, took up this bright thread of our history and followed it to the only place it can possibly lead in our time—the heart and spirit of the average man.[9]

If we accept Miller's basic argument, it helps us understand why we have such a powerful experience with dramas such as *Death of a Salesman, The Crucible, West Side Story, The Death of Klinghoffer, Dead Man Walking,* or *The Green Mile.* In some of these dramas, only the tragic vision, as described by Krieger, carries the tragic impact. In others, including *A Streetcar Named Desire,* the impact is there even though the tragic protagonist is not fully aware of the nature of her struggle to reclaim her dignity.

A television drama from the Golden Age of television (roughly from the 1950s to the early 1960s) followed the form and the vision of tragedy.[10]

The Collar, set in nineteenth-century America, centers around the growth to full humanhood of a young Episcopalian priest serving in New England. The priest is bright, popular, articulate, and ambitious. When he's passed over for appointment to a choice position as leader of a large congregation, he protests to the bishop, claiming that the older priest who was appointed was dull and out of touch with the modern world. The bishop acknowledges the charges, but tells the young man that he is too worldly, and lacks a deep spirituality. The visit ends as the bishop tells the priest that he's being assigned a missionary post in the American West where he might grow to become a fully realized human being.

The priest is captured by an Indian tribe and is told by the Chief that years earlier, when a captive of White settlers, he was placed on public display wearing an iron collar. As retribution for that act, the priest is sentenced to like treatment. After months of humiliation, the chief tells the priest that he is free to go—that the Indian encampment is surrounded by

U.S. military troops, and there is no way out for the Indians. The priest leaves with sincere misgivings.

When he reaches the headquarters of the army, the priest learns that the encampment is to be taken by force the following day, and that all Indians will be "exterminated."

It's at this point that we recognize the priest's evolution to spirituality, through suffering and, later, empathy. After vainly arguing against the assault, he decides that his place is with the Indians, and he returns to be killed with them.

Other plays could be cited, but *The Collar* makes the point that tragedy deals with humans who are placed in situations in which they must make moral choices, even when such choices lead to their destruction. In the presence of truly significant acts, we are reminded of the infinite capacity of the human spirit to place some values above comfort, wealth, fame, and even above life itself.

QUESTIONS

1. Read the entire essay by Arthur Miller in Appendix C. After considering Miller's arguments, view or read a modern play on stage, screen, or television that is serious and has a catastrophic ending for the protagonist(s). Determine the characteristics of the central agents in terms of station in life, relationships with others, degree of self-indulgence or concern for others, manner of making important decisions—expediency, self-interest, greed, selflessness, concern for others, ethical or moral considerations, etc.—and nature of the actions that lead to the protagonist's downfall.

NOTES

1. This outline of the Osiris myth and celebration is paraphrased from Frazer's *The Golden Bough,* as edited by Theodor Gaster. It is found in Part IV, Dying and Reviving Gods.
2. Richard Benson Sewall, *The Vision of Tragedy* (New Haven, CT: Yale University Press, 1980), 121–22.
3. Aristotle, *Poetics,* trans. S. H. Butcher. (New York: Hill and Wang, 1961), 61.
4. Murray Krieger, *The Tragic Vision: Variations on a Theme in Literary Interpretation* (New York: Holt, Rinehart and Winston, 1960), 3–4.
5. This article originally appeared in the *New York Times,* February 27, 1949, Sec. 1, p. 1. It was reprinted in the March 1951 issue of *Theatre Arts,* Vol. XXXV, No. 3. Throughout the article, Miller writes of the "common man." If he were writing this piece today, he very likely would use gender-sensitive language. The entire Miller article can be found in Appendix C.
6. Arthur Miller, "Tragedy and the Common Man," in *The Theater Essays of Arthur Miller* (New York: Da Capo Press, 1996), 3.
7. Ibid., 4.
8. Ibid., 4.
9. Ibid., 7.
10. A search on the Internet failed to locate a source where this drama can be viewed or purchased.

CHAPTER ELEVEN

FROM THEORIES TO PRACTICE

This chapter is the connecting link between Parts I and II. It places theoretical considerations of Part I into contexts that apply theory to actual challenges of conceptualizing and writing scripts. The chapter begins by tracing a public service announcement (PSA) campaign from the initial challenge to the completion of scripts for broadcast. The second part introduces and elaborates on the practice of using your sleeping mind to assist you in creative problem-solving. The chapter then moves to the writing of scripts, from conception, to first drafts, and then to the completion of final drafts. The chapter offers a discussion of sight and sound in scriptwriting, and ends with a discussion of various facets of stereotyping.

Tracing an actual writing challenge from inception to completion allows us to connect theories to specific writing challenges. Eventually, you'll face the challenge of complex writing tasks such as feature reports, comic sketches, or commercial campaigns, but it's best to begin with a simpler first step, such as the relatively uncomplicated process of creating a public service announcement (PSA) campaign. A more comprehensive examination of public service productions, including slide presentations and announcements is the subject of Chapter 17, "Media in Community Service."

Public service campaigns are ideal for practicing scriptwriting because the announcements that flow from them are brief and straightforward in structure, needn't involve music or complicated special effects, and can intensify your writing experience by allowing you to write for an actual client or cause. This, in turn, means you can promote social programs in which you truly believe, and there's no better motivating force than writing with an urgency to communicate. The case history that follows is a PSA campaign process that takes you from start to finish to see how the principles discussed in the preceding chapters apply.

A PUBLIC SERVICE ANNOUNCEMENT CAMPAIGN: A CASE HISTORY

The head of a local AAU (Amateur Athletic Union) Swim Committee has asked you to create public service announcements to promote its age-group-competitive swim program. If you accept this request, the AAU committee will become your client. As is true of most lay people working as volunteers for nonprofit organizations, this committee knows next to nothing about media. One of your collateral duties will be to educate your client.

Background Check.   Without yet committing yourself, you set out to find answers to two basic questions. First, does this organization qualify for PSA status? Second, is this a cause you want to support?

The committee assures you that the swim program and its sponsor, the AAU, meet the criteria for PSA eligibility, but to be safe you decide to check with the AAU itself. To access the AAU, you enter Amateur Athletic Union on a search engine such as Yahoo! or Alta Vista. A click of the mouse and you have the answer: its nonprofit status is set forth on its home page.

After determining that your agency is, indeed, eligible for PSA consideration by stations, the next step is to gather enough information about the association to decide whether or not you want to support it with your efforts. Before committing yourself, you begin researching the AAU age-group swim program.

Among other things, you learn that age-group swimming is an exciting, noninjury sport for both boys and girls. You find much specific information about its value to children and their parents, and you decide that it's a program you can enthusiastically promote. At this stage, you've formed a vision—a general attitude about the project, the details of which are not yet clear, but which you'll approach with interest and dedication. Your vision carries with it a notion of the mood, style, and "flavor" of the project.

The Fact Sheet.   Now that you know what information is available to you, and having made preliminary decisions, it's time to prepare a fact sheet. Creating a fact sheet comes before writing your scripts because it's an outline of the campaign's major selling points and you'll draw on these as you write your scripts. Your fact sheet includes many more points than you'll use when writing your spots, but you include every item because, at this point, you're not ready to settle on the content of each spot.

You will share your fact sheet with Swim Committee members and you'll also send it to radio and television stations to inform programming personnel of the scope and importance of the swim program. If your sheet is successful, it may encourage stations to schedule your spots during their best available time periods. Before using it yourself as a guide to creating your campaign or sending it to stations, you meet with the Swim Committee to make sure of your facts, and to keep them informed of where your project is heading. It's always important to avoid running ahead of those who've commissioned your work—even if the job is pro bono.

FACT SHEET ON AAU SWIMMING PSA CAMPAIGN

1. The campaign runs from November 15 through December 23.
2. Sponsor is the swim committee of the Amateur Athletic Union. The AAU is a nonprofit organization dedicated to the preservation and expansion of amateur athletics.
3. There are more than twenty AAU swim teams in your three-county area, with more than one thousand swimmers.
4. The AAU sponsors swim meets nearly every weekend. Swim meets are classified according to ability. "B," "A," and "AA" meets are held so that everyone has a fair

chance to compete with others of the same age, sex, and current ability. At these meets, swimmers compete for the sport of it, for time improvements, and for medals and ribbons.

5. The AAU also sponsors dual meets, in which teams compete for league championships.

6. Outstanding swimmers also compete in invitational meets, national championship meets, and Junior Olympics.

7. It's good to start young. Most AAU swimmers begin when they're under ten years old, and many begin at age five or six.

8. The AAU also has a master's program. Competition is for those ages twenty-five and over, with competitive categories to over eighty with five year increments.

9. AAU swimmers are healthy people. Swimming builds their bodies and sharpens their reflexes.

10. Swimming is a noninjury sport.

11. Swimming gives absolutely equal treatment to boys and girls.

12. AAU swimming is family fun. At meets, the kids swim while parents judge, time, record, or just watch and cheer.

13. Younger swimmers practice about an hour a day, five days a week. Older swimmers practice longer, depending on their motivation.

14. AAU swimming has its practical side, too. AAU swimmers can take care of themselves in nearly any emergency that may arise on the water. They're also trained to save the lives of others.

15. Now is the best time to join an AAU swim team. Practice goes on all winter, in heated pools. By the time spring and summer arrive, swimmers will be built up for exciting team competition.

16. FOR FURTHER INFORMATION ABOUT AAU SWIMMING, PHONE 555-3777.

When you and the committee agree that the sheet is accurate and covers the main points about age-group swimming, you prepare copies on AAU stationary that later will be sent to radio and television stations to inform station personnel of the scope and importance of the swim program.

Beginning. After these preliminary assessments, you begin, not at the beginning, but at the end. That is, before deciding on which medium to use (radio or television) or the number and length of spots, and before touching a keyboard, you look for answers to these questions:

If the PSAs are totally successful in achieving our agency's objectives, what will have changed?

Who will we have reached, and for what purpose?

What motivational devices will be appropriate for this cause?

How will those who respond to the PSAs benefit?

How will the swim program be better off than before?

Who will have been helped, and in what ways?

These questions seem obvious, but careful monitoring reveals that many PSAs leave us with little or no useful information and without motivation to write or to give. The starting point in developing a PSA campaign, then, is to determine as specifically as possible its purpose.

Purpose and Vision. You meet with the AAU Swim Committee to determine objectives for the campaign. The committee has a limited vision which sees but a single purpose—that of increasing membership on local swim teams. You believe the campaign can achieve additional goals because well-conceived messages for the program can include both a primary statement—in this case one directed at recruitment—as well as sub-messages to meet such secondary goals as: establishing name recognition for the AAU and its programs; making the public aware of the contributions of amateur athletics to our nation's international sports competitions; and building enthusiasm—and esteem—among swimmers already participating. Your broader vision, shared by the committee, expands the original purpose to present the swim program in an exciting yet factual manner to listeners and viewers.

Target Audience. Having determined your purpose and vision, the next step is to define your target audience. Do you want to reach the young, the elderly, those from twenty to middle-age, or all ages? Is ethnicity a factor? Is gender a factor? Do you want to reach people of a particular economic group?

In deciding on your target audience, a problem surfaces. You want to reach children between the ages of six and ten, because they're the ones who'll become the swimmers; at the same time, because heavy parental involvement is required, you also must gain the interest of parents. So you actually have two audiences to reach, and this suggests three types of spots: one addressed to children, a second meant for parents, and a third appealing to families. Having identified your target audiences, you'll next consider motivational appeals. You anticipate a solution to the problem of reaching three audiences through an analysis of motivation.

Motivation. You begin with an assessment of needs and desires, as discussed in Chapter 3. Here are some obvious needs or desires shared by children you want to reach:

> the need to have shared experiences with others;
> the desire to identify with a group you consider special;
> the need or desire to achieve physical excellence;
> the need for recognition by others;
> the need for self-improvement;
> the need or desire to excel;
> the need or desire to have fun;
> the desire to imagine oneself a hero or heroine; and
> the desire to please ones parents.

And, for the parents:

> the desire to share experiences with your children;
> the need to see your children excel;

the need to feel successful as a parent; and

the need or desire to be an important part of a team effort through timing, judging, or other volunteer activities.

Most parents will have some needs or desires satisfied through their children's' participation, and while others will feel rewarded by their own involvement in the swim program. You realize that you must advertise a program that involves the whole family, one that encourages familial love and support.

After a discussion with the Swim Committee and a careful analysis, you decide to place primary emphasis in some spots on the family. Children will give almost anything a try, and swimming is among the activities most children love best. But it would be inappropriate to excite hundreds of young children about AAU swimming if they ultimately would be disappointed by uninterested or uncommitted parents. Other spots will be addressed to children. All spots will give basic information, such as a telephone number to call or where to fax, e-mail, or write for details.

There's a further opportunity. The AAU Swim Committee is concerned because there are very few so-called minority children in the program. They believe this is so because minority families are infrequently represented in private swim clubs, where information about the AAU swim program is generally available. There also is a belief that many African American, Latino, and Asian American families are not sure they'd be welcome in an activity that, historically, has been dominated by Whites. These assumptions won't change the motivational appeals you'll use, but they strongly suggest the medium of radio, because there are, in your area, Black-, Spanish-, and Asian-oriented radio stations, and audience demographics show that these stations are popular with the families you want to reach. There's no need to create special scripts in Spanish or Chinese (for example) because most children raised in non-English-speaking homes are bilingual.

Your best chance of gaining and holding viewers and of creating excitement about the program is to show a video taken at a swim meet. You also know that television spots are more difficult to produce and more costly than are radio spots. You decide to create both a radio and a television campaign, with the radio spots aimed at narrow target audiences and the television spots aimed at the general audience.

Videotape is your choice for television spots. Even though your budget is limited, you can produce good quality videos at very low cost. Color 35mm slides would be another possible visual medium, but you believe that motion and sound will be far more effective in attracting and holding the interest of viewers.

Conceptualizing.   It's time to begin conceptualizing your scripts. You want to reach both children and parents, so you decide to produce two television spots, one narrated by a child, the other by a parent. You will create and produce several scripts for radio broadcasts. You don't consider using voice tracks of the television spots for radio. If those tracks are as effective on radio as on television, then you're not making compelling use of the visual medium.

As you conceive your scripts, concentrate on one at a time. Trying to include every appeal in any one spot would guarantee muddled results. The longer the spot, the more information and appeals you can inject. In the shorter messages, you'll mention only key points, including a way listeners can receive more information about the swim program. The following scripts are examples of what you might create.

Script No. 1

Twenty-second radio. Purposes are to catch the attention of girl listeners; to let them know that they can become part of a team; to reinforce messages made on your other spots; to state and repeat the phone number for information.

SWIM COMMITTEE
AMATEUR ATHLETIC UNION
20-SECOND RADIO
VOICE OF 7–8-YEAR-OLD GIRL

If you're between the ages of six and ten, you're lucky. Because you're ready to start competitive swimming. Join an AAU swim team now, and start preparing for swim meets. You can find out all about AAU swimming by phoning 555-3777. 555-3777. See you in the pool!

Script No. 2

Twenty-second radio. Purposes are to attract attention of boys; provide reinforcement and basic information; make the appeal individual and personal; promote the need or desire to compete; stress the fun aspect; tie in to the concept of self-improvement.

SWIM COMMITTEE
AMATEUR ATHLETIC UNION
20-SECOND RADIO
VOICE OF YOUNG BOY

Hi! I'm an AAU swimmer. I started a year ago when I could barely swim across the pool. Now I swim in meets two or three times a month. It's fun, and it's exciting. Would you like AAU swimming? Call us and learn how to reach the swim team nearest you. Phone 555-3777. 555-3777.

Script No. 3

Thirty-second radio. Purposes are to reach parents with news of a valuable program for families; to give concrete reasons for considering AAU swimming; to stress competition and winning; to list benefits, such as the development of strength, health, and sharpened reflexes; to indicate that this program is open to all ages.

SWIM COMMITTEE
AMATEUR ATHLETIC UNION
30-SECOND RADIO
VOICE OF FEMALE OR MALE ADULT

We're all proud of the showing made by American swimmers in the last Olympics. Many of these swimmers started with an AAU swim team when they were only five or six years old. The competitive swim program gave them goals in life, built their bodies, sharpened their reflexes, and gave them good health. Most swimmers don't go to the Olympics, of course, but all benefit from the program. The AAU offers competitive swimming for all ages, from under 6 to over 80. If you want to see if AAU swimming is for you or your children, call us at 555-3777. 555-3777.

Script No. 4

Thirty-second radio. Purposes are to cover many of the persuasive points listed on the fact sheet. Major purpose is to let adults know that their active participation is a requirement, but that the program is rewarding for both parents and their children.

SWIM COMMITTEE
AMATEUR ATHLETIC UNION
30-SECOND RADIO
VOICE OF MALE OR FEMALE ADULT

May I have 30 seconds of your time? I want to tell you about a program that might be just right for your family. I'm talking about AAU competitive swimming. A year ago, our children joined the Orlando Dolphins swim team. Janie's eight and Mike's eleven. They've developed strength, poise, and skill. At swim meets kids swim and we parents judge, record or just watch and cheer. The ribbons and medals are great, but best of all, we're there as a family. For information, call 555-3777. That's 555-3777.

Script No. 5

Thirty-second radio. Purpose is to stress the equality of all swimmers, regardless of age or gender.

SWIM COMMITTEE
AMATEUR ATHLETIC UNION
30-SECOND RADIO
VOICE OF ADULT FEMALE

Hello! Our children, Sara and Stanley, are swimmers for the Orlando Dolphins. I'd like to share my excitement about this wonderful family program. The Dolphins belong to the Amateur Athletic Union's national swim program. This sport is great for everyone, both children and parents. Most important for me is our children get equal treatment. The youngest girl on a team earns the same number of points in a meet as does the oldest boy. How's that for building confidence and esteem? There's a swim team near you. Phone the AAU at 555-3777. 555-3777.

The television spots are, of course, more complicated. You begin by connecting the selling points you want to make to both visual images and spoken dialogue.

Script No. 6

Twenty-second television. Addressed to parents and children. Purpose is to show the thrill of achievement, and that a young person can be a hero through ability and hard work.

SWIM COMMITTEE
AMATEUR ATHLETIC UNION
20: VIDEO

VIDEO	AUDIO
SCENE IS POOL AT SWIM MEET.	(SFX: CHEERING. CRACK OF STARTER'S GUN)
	ANNCR:
OPEN ON WIDE SHOT, THEN ZOOM IN TO GIRL SWIMMER. FOLLOW HER THROUGH ENTIRE LENGTH OF POOL.	This message will last 20 seconds. Before it's over, this eight-year-old girl will swim 25 yards of butterfly.
	She belongs to an AAU swim team. She practices an hour a day, and travels to swim meets two or three times a month. If you'd like to know more about AAU swimming, Phone 555-3777. 555-3777. (SFX: CHEERING UP AND OUT)

Script No. 7

Twenty second-television. Purpose is to show swim activities, with shots showing the entire team in team sweats and jackets, swimmers being cheered on, swimmer receiving medal. Most shots are to feature activities of young swimmers, ages ten and under.

SWIM COMMITTEE
AMATEUR ATHLETIC UNION
20: VIDEO
VOICE OF CHILD

VIDEO	AUDIO
SHOTS OF SWIMMERS ACTIVITIES, TO MATCH ACTION ON SCREEN.	(SFX: CHEERING, CRACK OF STARTER'S GUN) I go to swim practice several days a week. Two or three times a month I compete in swim meets.
	At some meets, I swim to improve my times. At other meets, I swim for my team.
	When we swim an event, our whole team cheers us on.
	If we set a record, we get a medal. Would you like to swim for a team?
SUPER: 555-3777.	Call 555-3777 for information about AAU age-group swimming. Sponsored by the Amateur Athletic Union. Remember— call 555-3777.
	See you in the pool!

This completes the PSA campaign employed as an example of a systematic approach to creating scripts that connect theory with practice. Every writer must modify details of work methods, conceptualization, and writing to conform to individual preference, background, and work routine. Experience through trial and error will help you learn what works best for you.

STARTING A PROJECT

Conceiving and writing scripts should begin with a clearly defined assignment. Whether the project is a commercial, a comic sketch, a documentary narration, or any other project common to the broadcast media, the clearer the guidelines, the easier it is to get started. Here's information that should be clear from the outset:

> details and facts about the topic, product, or project
> intended audience
> choice of medium
> deadline for completion
> limitations of budget
> desired outcome

If you're a copywriter for an advertising agency, a staff writer for a production company, or a reporter or writer for a broadcast news department, you'll receive your charge from an account executive, an editor, or a producer, and expectations will be quite specific. In other circumstances, as a freelance writer, you may be hired to write scripts for a wide range of media productions, such as scripts for:

> technical training lessons
> travelogues or promotional pieces for vacation destinations
> museum guided tours
> nutrition and fitness programs
> promotional pieces for trade shows
> single-subject descriptions of a great range of medical conditions for patient education
> instructional videos for at-home and classroom use
> training visuals for company employees

Written contracts will likely include precise instructions for your guidance. If significant questions remain unanswered, be sure to ask them before embarking on the project. It will be far too late to clarify fuzzy concepts when you deliver your first draft.

You may at times choose your own project—an essay, a commentary, a script for an existing television drama or comedy, an idea for a new show—in short, any piece you're interested in writing on speculation. In this chancey arena you must make your own determinations of the intended audience, the audience's level of sophistication, and all the other essential considerations that guide the development of your script. You should sort all of this out before you pitch your idea to a potential client or send the synopsis of a story idea to an agent or producer.

Once details of your assignment are clearly understood, you'll go through preliminary steps much like those outlined at the beginning of this chapter with the AAU swim project as a model. With experience, you'll make adjustments to suit your personal style and work habits.

After you have the objectives and other aspects of the work clearly in mind, and have made a run-down of its salient points, you're ready to start conceiving stories that you'll encode as scripts, which eventually will be turned into performances.

There are many ways of stimulating your creativity. One is to use a well-known activity called "brainstorming." As you think about the project, pen in hand, jot down all ideas that come to mind. At this stage, don't question the gifts that spring forward; write them down, and resist analysis or any other rational process until you're ready to examine what your mind has offered. If you're focused on the challenge and free from external distractions, you may fill up several sheets with the fruits of this exercise. A different but related activity asks you to listen to ideas that come to you courtesy of your sleeping mind.

USING WHAT YOUR SLEEPING MIND GIVES YOU

One of your most useful creative tools is your unconscious mind. This may sound mystical or far-out, but it's anything but that. Perhaps you've already discovered how your unconscious mind can help you solve creative challenges. If you haven't, try to cultivate this amazing tool. Studies have observed that our unconscious minds work on, even during sleep, without our being aware of it. Suddenly after awakening, and without consciously attempting to put your mind to work, a solution to a problem or an idea for a script, pops into your head.

Gayle Delaney, in *All About Dreams,* expresses her belief that the answers we seek to life's problems and creative challenges lie in our dreams.

> Usually people dream about their feelings about themselves, their work, and their relationships. Apparently more rare are the dreams that help us solve concrete problems. Yet I wonder whether, if more people were taught to incubate and remember their dreams, and if they were encouraged to use their dreams for problem solving, this would still be the case.[1]

Delaney cites the experience of a noted physiologist, W. B. Cannon, in describing his use of dreams in problem solving:

> As a matter of routine I have long trusted unconscious processes to serve me—for example, when I have had to prepare a public address. I would gather points for the address and write them down in a rough outline. Within the next few nights, I would have sudden spells of awakening, with an onrush of illustrative instances, pertinent phrases, and fresh ideas related to those already listed. Paper and pencil at hand permitted the capture of these fleeting thoughts before they faded into oblivion. The process has been so common and so reliable for me that I have supposed that it was at the service of everyone. But evidence indicates that it is not.[2]

Delaney gives another example, of murder mystery writer Sue Grafton (*B Is for Burglar, C Is for Corpse*). She regularly incubates dreams for her alphabet novels as well as for her TV screenplays. She explains:

> I reach a point in many of my books, when I'm very heavily engaged in the process of writing, where I have a problem that I can't solve. And as I go to sleep I will give myself the suggestion that a solution will come. Whether this is from a dream state I'm not certain. I know that I will waken and the solution will be there. I attribute it to right brain activity. I don't know the relationship between right brain and dreams but I know when the analytical self, the left brain, finally releases its grip on us and gets out of the way, the creative side of us, which often surfaces in sleep, comes to the fore and in its own playful and whimsical manner will solve many creative problems.[3]

These testaments to the value of dreams as creative aids echo my own experiences. As an undergraduate drama major, I had the task of quickly learning my lines in a one-act, two-character play. In bed one night, I read the script as I was falling asleep. I was astonished to awaken the next morning with the entire play committed to memory! I've used my sleeping mind as an indispensable and priceless companion ever since.

To incubate your dreams, Delaney gives these suggestions, which I have paraphrased and slightly amended to relate better to solving creative writing issues.

1. Choose the right night. Be free of alcohol and drugs, including sleeping pills.
2. Before going to sleep, write a few lines about the emotional highlights of your day. This will help you relax and help you recall your dreams much better.
3. Use your conscious mind to review the writing challenge.
4. Write down the one-line question that best expresses your challenge.
5. In bed, repeat this "incubation phrase" over and over as you fall asleep.
6. Sleep!
7. Record in detail your dream memories as soon as you awaken. Don't try to judge or evaluate them. Try to re-experience the dream.
8. Interview yourself about your dream.

Because the interview step completes the incubation process, these final suggestions from Gayle Delaney are of extreme importance:

> Don't try to force your dream to answer your question. Since your dream could possibly be about another topic, explore your dream with an open mind. . . . When you figure out what your dream is about, only then ask yourself if it sheds light on your incubation phrase. Remember that dreams don't tell you what to do. Your dreams are your own mind working. Let your dreams give you insight—that is, let them open your eyes.[4]

Becoming efficient in directing the unconscious mind is possible through the cultivation process of which Delaney speaks, but most of us, even if we don't want to explore her suggestions in depth, can still benefit greatly if we simply learn to listen for the voice from our sleeping mind. We can't demand that our unconscious mind give us its thoughts—the sleep work or dream work is much too elusive and fragile for that. And although we tend to think of ourselves as being either fully asleep or fully awake, there's a brief period when we inhabit both territories; during this time we can attempt, consciously, to listen to what our unconscious mind is suggesting, and find solutions to creative problems that are its gifts.

If you find that you can't, at this time, tie into your dream work in any useful way, don't abandon the search; it may take time and practice before it works for you. Please know, though, that what follows can still be of immense help in preparing and writing your first drafts. The use of the sleeping mind is only one way to foster creative solutions to writing challenges.

The unconscious mind offers solutions to creative problems at times other than when we first awaken. If we remain open to receiving its messages, they may pop into our consciousness at random moments—when waiting for a bus, when exercising, or when simply looking out the window.

You may have heard a person say, "I'd like to sleep on it." This usually is said when the speaker is asked to make a difficult or a hasty decision. The decision to "sleep on it" may be much more than a delaying action; it can be a wise decision, based on experience that has shown that something important happens during sleep, something that helps us with problem solving and decision making. The cultivation and application of the time-honored concept of "sleeping on it" may help you become a better writer!

Here are some suggestions for developing the use of your unconscious mind.

- When you receive a writing assignment, carefully think through the specifics of the assignment, and determine the objective (purpose, vision) of the piece to be written.
- Assuming that you don't have to meet an imminent deadline, put the project aside, and turn to other matters. Let your mind return to the project from time to time to see if ideas relevant to the script are emerging. Watch carefully for suggestions from your unconscious mind. Make written notes of any and all ideas that come up.
- Just before falling asleep each night, mentally review the project. Next morning, give your unconscious mind a chance to speak to your conscious mind, preferably before becoming wide awake. By this time, your unconscious mind may have many suggestions to offer. It's no surprise that most successful writers begin their work early each morning; they do this because they've awakened with ideas that ask or demand to be incorporated into their script-in-progress.

BEFORE WRITING YOUR FIRST DRAFT

Some aspects of the writing project will, of course, be givens, which you must fully understand and keep in mind throughout the development of your script:

- whether the script is to be broadcast or not
- whether it's to be written for the aural or the visual medium
- the purpose of the script (to sell a product, to explain a concept or a process, to evoke laughter, etc.,)
- the deadline for delivery

These are realities that you must take into account as you approach every writing project.

Before you begin, write a statement that clearly outlines the basic facts about the writing challenge. New questions, together with a paraphrase of the questions asked in regard to the public service campaign that opens this chapter, are appropriate here:

What's the purpose of my message? Who am I trying to reach? (Be as specific as possible.)

What characteristics are relevant? (age, gender, ethnicity, occupation, economic status, etc.)

If my script is successful what will have changed?

What motivational devices are appropriate for this script?

How will those who receive the message benefit?

Who will have been helped, and in what ways?

When you've answered these questions, move on to more specifics:

What mood and style are appropriate for this piece?

What structure (form) is best suited to it?

What resources will be available to those who produce it?

If you're unclear about these matters, especially the objective of the piece to be written, chances are you're in for a struggle.

After determining objectives, target audience, and so forth, and before attempting to write anything resembling a script, sit down and scribble notes about anything and everything that you conceivably could use in the script—in brief, brainstorm. Make no attempt to rule anything out at this point—even a bad idea can lead to a creative breakthrough, if only by suggesting its opposite. (You may choose to do your "scribbling" on a computer and, if that works for you, great!)

To repeat, always keep in mind that your script will be spoken by interpreters, and that your dialogue will be heard, but never seen, by your audience. Keep the sounds of your script in mind as you develop ideas for it. If appropriate, think of music and sound effects as well as words. (Music is appropriate to many commercials and dramas, but generally is inappropriate for radio essays or most instructional tapes.)

Make written notes—or an audio recording—of whatever comes to you. Do not, at this stage, analyze or question the ideas you're receiving.

Organize your notes. This most likely isn't necessary for a short script, such as a commercial, but is very helpful for documentary narration and other lengthy scripts. Then, if it's appropriate to the writing task, arrange your ideas by categories. Do this according to some principle, such as logical sequence, ascending order of importance, or whatever you choose. Then organize your categories into a logical sequence. This organization gives your story its form, or structure. The importance of form in the story arts is discussed in more detail in Chapter 5, "Form in the Arts."

Next, eliminate ideas that no longer fit, or that you realize are inappropriate. This is difficult for most writers; ideas that seemed brilliant when they first emerged are painful to abandon when we sense that they no longer work.

WRITING YOUR FIRST DRAFT

Don't assume that a script written at this time will be your final version. If you make such an assumption, you'll likely end up trying too hard, and this can cause writer's block. Adopt a more casual attitude. Attach no pride of authorship to your early efforts on any script. You may wind up discarding everything from your first draft, but no one need ever know.

Your computer allows you to manipulate your words easily and often. You have spelling and grammar checkers available, so use them for the help they can give you. At the same time, don't allow any program to edit your copy! Most style or grammar checkers flag conversational conventions including brief simple sentences, split infinitives, prepositions at the ends of sentences, slang, and other so-called problems that writers often use precisely because they are conversational. I wonder what these programs would have told Shakespeare, or even Ernest Hemingway or Steven King, about weaknesses in their writings?

Use your computer to sketch out a page, document, or script, with little attention paid to any dumb things you set down and will later discard. At this stage of brainstorming, disregard structure, order, precise language, correct spelling, pagination and paragraph-a-nation (I just invented a term), proper grammar, or precise syntax. Instead, jot down your ideas while they're at their hottest. Write in a stream-of-consciousness style. Become the boss of the machine, rather than its servant. There'll be time later to refine your script, but if you try simultaneously to engage in free-flowing creativity and copy editing, you'll do neither very well.

As you write your phrases and sentences, speak them aloud. Listen for such problems as sentences or phrases that are too long; not enough contractions; awkward sentence structure; too many sibilant or plosive sounds; copy that is too difficult for easy reading or for ready aural comprehension; or statements that could cause confusion. Here are examples of each of these writing problems.

Sentences That Are Too Long.   Read this sentence aloud:

> Hermann's Delicatessen features the best Kosher foods in the Twin Lakes Area: pastrami, salami, chicken liver, gefilte fish, knishes, Hungarian goulash, kreplach, matzoball soup, borscht—both cabbage and beet—and for dessert, strudel, Hamantaschen and ice cream, or blintzes with sour cream.

You may have noticed that it leaves no convenient places for the announcer to take in air, to breathe. If an announcer is forced to sneak short breaths because there are no built-in pauses, chances are listeners will hear distracting gasps as the announcer struggles to avoid running out of breath.

The sentence also presents listeners with a serious overload of information. When too many details are mentioned, listeners often are unable to remember more than one or two. It's far better to limit a list to three or four features that audiences will remember than to list thirteen (as in the delicatessen spot), all of which will get lost. Good writing for aural delivery contains short sentences, clarity and simplicity, and directness.

Not Enough Contractions.   Use contractions, unless the style of the piece calls for more formal address. Nothing sounds more "read-y" than a person saying every syllable of every word without using contractions. Good narration or dialogue almost always is characterized by the use of contractions to give it a conversational quality. The following overlong and complex sentence underscores this point:

> Mayor De Bellis is being ingenuous in not telling us all that is involved in her plan to restrict trucks over a certain length and weight from unloading their

goods while double-parked on downtown streets that often are congested and that do not have sufficient parking places or adequate restricted loading zones.

This sentence suffers from terminal length, convoluted sentence structure, unnecessary detail, tortured syntax, and murky meaning. Here's the same sentence written in simpler language, and with contractions:

Mayor De Bellis wants to ban large trucks from downtown streets at peak hours, but she doesn't offer a practical alternative. She's correct in her concern about double-parked trucks, but is the only solution a complete ban on deliveries? Why not enlarge loading zones? Is that too simple?

Awkward Sentence Structure.

In southern Nepal, where it is too high and cold to grow crops, and where the weather is an ever present menace, life is a struggle not only for humans, but is only slightly more tolerable for llamas, mountain goats, and other indigenous wildlife.

This sentence has the distinction of being both awkward *and* too long! To become comprehensible to a listener, this sentence would have to be rewritten using more and shorter sentences:

Southern Nepal is too high and too cold to grow crops. The weather is fierce, constantly menacing humans and animals. Llamas, mountain goats, and other wildlife survive, but they're only slightly better off than the Nepalese.

Excessive Sibilance.   Read this bad sentence aloud.

This session is the second of a series that shall set forth significant circumstances that may cause "sick sinus syndrome."

Do you hear the hissing caused by the sibilant sounds—those created in sounding the letters s, sh, z, and the medial sound in vision? These sounds amplify and become very hissy when spoken into a microphone. You can't avoid sibilant sounds, because they're part of our spoken language, but you can de-emphasize them somewhat by careful writing. Reading and recording your scripts should help you spot problems of excessive sibilance. When you do, paraphrase as necessary to avoid as many "s" sounds as possible, without losing or distorting the meaning.

Excessive Plosive Sounds.   Here's another "poorly put" sentence:

Apparently the pilot permitted the private plane to pass too closely on its port side.

The plosives—p, b, t, d, k, and g—are made by a sudden release of air, creating a distinct popping sound on a microphone. As with sibilant sounds, plosives are unavoidable, but you can keep them under control by finding other words to express the same thoughts, words that don't begin with plosive sounds: "Apparently the pilot allowed the small plane to fly too closely to the airliner's left side."

Copy That Is Difficult to Read or Hear.   The next point is of critical importance, and warrants emphasis: *As you finish each draft, read the copy into an audio recorder. Play it back and listen carefully to detect any of the problems just described. You MUST know how your script will sound to those receiving your message. Silent reading gives some information, but it doesn't tell you how your words will sound when your script is produced. Here are just two examples of careless copy:*

> In the animated feature-length cartoon *Pocahontas,* an Indian warrior tells the Chief that he wants to marry his daughter. The Chief replies, "That would make my spirit soar!" The problem here should be obvious: "soar" and "sore" are homonyms, so to the listener, the father's response can be taken in either of two diametrically opposed ways!
>   A newswriter, reporting a story from central Africa, wrote that "thousands of people have died from ebola virus." This reads okay, but because this deadly virus was little known to Americans at that time, their ears heard it as "thousands of people have died from a bowl of iris."

The lesson to be learned: watch those homonyms!

If you've been given a time limit for your script—as is true of nearly all commercials and much other copy—time your reading and make adjustments as necessary.

Statements That Cause Confusion.
Misleading Statements.   Carelessly written statements can lead an audience to false conclusions:

> Here's good news for farmers—the legislature has approved a reduction in property taxes on family farms.

Anyone not familiar with the legislative process would assume that the reduction had become law. In practice, legislative committees may pass tax bills, but approval must still be gained by the entire legislature or assembly, and in many states, a senate. After passing both houses, the bill still faces a possible veto by the governor!

Statements That Are Too Abstract   Writers for the electronic media should pay special attention to what semanticist S. I. Hayakawa called the abstraction ladder. This concept refers to the fact that several terms are usually available for the same object or condition.

Here's an example of this concept. Look at the words *vehicle, automobile, Mazda, sports car, Miata.* The Miata is a sports car, which is one kind of automobile made by Mazda and which in turn is a vehicle. All five terms are correct and, at one time or another, useful.

The term *vehicle* is a high-level abstraction; *automobile* is below it on the abstraction ladder; *Mazda* is quite specific and is at a lower rung; *sports car* becomes still more precise, and *Miata* takes us as low on the ladder as this example will accept. As a writer, you should be sensitive to the "rung" on the "ladder" occupied by the words, allusions, phrases, or examples you use or cite.

There is, however, a BIG EXCEPTION to this rule. This doesn't mean that everything you write must or should be at the lowest level of abstraction. It means, rather, that you should match the level of abstraction to the nature of what you're writing, and to the knowledge level of those for whom your script is being written—in other words, your intended audience. A training tape for electronic technicians about a new product will appropriately use terms that would be unsuitable for, or even incomprehensible to, those not of their group.

In general, you'll be most effective as a writer for a general audience if you avoid vague and ambiguous terms and look for more precise ones. Following is an example of a statement that is too vague or unspecific for easy audience understanding. It contains a high level of abstraction.

> The general expressed his belief that the B-1000 will make the U.S. capable of destroying ICBMs and SAMs, thereby protecting both the lives of citizens and the nation's infrastructure.

Translating this to a lower level of abstraction, you might say

> General Burns claims that the new stealth bomber, the B-1000, will be able to shoot down intercontinental ballistic and surface-to-air missiles. The general added that this weapon will save lives and protect roads, bridges, buildings, and other essential structures.

"General Burns" is less abstract than "the general"; "stealth bomber" is more precise than "the B-1000"; "intercontinental ballistic and surface-to-air missiles" is clearer than "ICBMs and SAMs"; and "roads, bridges, and buildings" is more specific than "the infrastructure." When you find problems such as these, make appropriate changes in your next draft.

EDITING YOUR DRAFTS

You'll likely write several drafts before achieving the version that best measures up to your initial vision. It takes experience and discipline to continue working on a script to move it from "acceptable" to "outstanding." Here are several suggestions that may help you as you engage in the painful experience of self-editing.

■ *Copy edit.* After completing each draft, force yourself to be a ruthless editor. Often in early drafts you'll have retained an idea or a phrase that's been with you since you began work on this project; you now sense that it doesn't work, or doesn't fit, yet you've become fond of it. Force yourself to change or eliminate it!

■ *Be Objective.* As you read each version of your evolving script, try to be objective. Put yourself in the place of a listener or viewer, and ask yourself such questions as: "Is this piece clear to me?" "Am I interested in what's being said or shown?" "Do I feel what the writer intended me to feel?"

■ *Edit, rewrite, edit, rewrite.* Do this as often as necessary, until you honestly believe that you can't further improve your script. However, remember that time and distance can provide objectivity. Most writers become so involved with their scripts that they lose objectivity. If your deadline permits, put your "best effort" aside, and approach it with a fresh mind after a wait of from one to several days. You most likely will see your script in a new light, and any weaknesses that were earlier hidden from you should be apparent.

■ *Save, save, save.* When working on a script, be sure you ask your computer to remind you every x-number of minutes to save your work. Most writing programs have this feature, and you can ask to be reminded to "save" every ten minutes or every half hour or some time in between. There are few experiences more frustrating than that of working for hours on a script, only to have your computer crash, taking with it all of the gems you've struggled to bring to life during those hours.

At the end of every work session, save your script on your hard disk, and also on an external storage device: a writable CD, a Zip disk, or even a floppy. It may not be overkill to place stored copies of your scripts in a safe-deposit box.

■ *Mark your place.* As you work on a lengthy script, type "STOPPED HERE" when you're finished for the day. This will help you get back to that point when you resume work by hitting "find" and entering "STOPPED HERE." Your screen will at that point take you to the place where you left off.

If you create several drafts while searching for the final one, give a name and number to each draft, and make a simple log of key details in each. This simple action can spare you much time spent in rummaging through your drafts to find the one that included that "especially well-cast paragraph." The longer your script, the more important it is to number and log each draft.

When you write your scripts, it's important to write it in a style that makes for easy communication with those who'll judge or interpret your messages. Effective script formatting is the topic of the next chapter.

WRITING SIGHTS AND SOUNDS, NOT WORDS

Sights

Robert Pritikin, who modestly calls himself an "ad man," created one of the most successful advertising agencies in broadcast history. He criticizes commercials that are based on the old saw, "don't sell the steak, sell the sizzle," and adds,

> This perverse wisdom has persuaded legions of copywriters to create TV commercials that do not effectively identify the product or its label. Instead, a bread commercial will dwell on

insipid unctuous children romping on a playground to illustrate energy (the "sizzle") and then tag the spot with a quick shot of the bread package (the "steak"). Viewers, dizzy from hours of jumpy, nervous television visuals, can hardly be expected to remember that particular brand of bread, the label of which was permitted only a few seconds on the screen.[5]

Pritikin's understanding of television's potential, along with his years of experience, convinced him that most television commercials fail to take advantage of the medium's intimate nature. When faced with the challenge of creating a commercial campaign for Fuller Paint, he began by asking key questions about the product:

What to show? What to say? For years paint companies had been selling interior and exterior paint by talking about its maintenance characteristics—durability, washability, the like. But, I mused, that's not why people buy paint, especially for inside walls. They buy paint for the same reason they buy cosmetics—to beautify.[6]

Pritikin placed a can of Fuller paint on his desk, pried it open with a screwdriver, and looked at the paint, trying to find the essence of its appeal:

The paint was the whitest I'd ever seen. I tilted the can just a tad. Like undulating marshmallows. Not just beautiful, but sensual. Had anyone ever really *seen* paint before? Not on the TV screen they hadn't. . . . No one had ever really seen paint before, not as I was seeing it then.[7]

He eventually devised a commercial that focused on several open paint cans, visible on the television screen from start to finish. To retain attention and create motion on the television screen he had hands dip into the paint at appropriate times while the voice-over script read the lines:

Dr. Freud might have had something to say about this paint.

There's something about the way it pours and flows and undulates.

And goes on so smooth and easy—you almost don't need a brush.

Your walls are very personal things. They surround you and protect you.

And covered with color they can warm you up. [*orange paint*]

Or cool you off. [*green paint*]

Or excite you! [*magenta paint*]

Fuller believes paint is very personal, and with over a thousand colors there's a Fuller color just for you.

Fuller Paint, since 1849, painting the colorful West—the best.[8]

His commercial was able to retain audience attention because the hands, in interacting with the paint, *told* a story, and the story and the sales message were one.

Pritikin validates his example by pointing out that qualified critics don't judge a commercial on whether or not they liked it, whether it was entertaining or not, whether it was offensive or inoffensive. "The only criteria should be: *is it remembered? does it persuade?*"[9] (Italics added.)

What can you learn from these observations by Bob Pritikin? First, when writing for television, remember that a significant part of your story will be carried by its visual impact. Don't write a story first, and then look for ways to make it "visual." Try to conceive it in terms of pictures and, later, write words to support and clarify what is seen. Second, exploit television as the intimate medium it is. Huge movie theatre screens demand that actors be shown in medium or longer shots, otherwise mouths and other facial features would be a dozen or more feet wide. Wide shots work well on film because even from a distance we can see a wink of the eye or a faint smile. Television, despite ever-increasing screen sizes, favors close-up shots of the actors. Your audience will view your work at home, and the visual scale appropriate to theatre audiences is not as effective for home viewing. Perhaps you've seen a film in the theatre, and again later on television. You've likely enjoyed the film less because the medium shots that were huge but compelling in a movie theatre were too small to be nearly as effective on your much-smaller television screen. Television is best used for portraying intimate relationships, while film favors stories with more physical action. Many films lose much of their effectiveness on the home video screen—*Jurassic Park, Raiders of the Lost Ark, Gladiator*—while others lose little impact because they were conceived on a less physical scale—*Enchanted April, 84 Charing Cross Road,* and *Cross Creek,* for example. Search for stories whose intimate nature makes them appropriate for the living room and the home video screen.

Sounds

Radio and television, despite obvious differences, have some things in common, and the most important of these is sound. Radio, the first medium to enter our homes by wireless transmission, was limited to sound alone, so writers had to choose words, music, and sound effects with great care. Television, considered by most to be a visual medium, is nearly as dependent on sound as is radio. See for yourself how important sound is on television by watching a range of programs with the volume turned all the way down; you'll find that most programs so viewed deliver little useful information. The lesson here is that, while you communicate your ideas to interpreters with written words, it's the transformation (the reconstitution, really) of those written symbols into sounds and sights that makes your vision come alive.

Because sound is so critical, it's important that you listen to your scripts much as an audience will. An indispensable tool for media writers is a good-quality audio recorder. Read your scripts aloud and record them—even fragments of them when you want to check the flow of specific passages—then listen critically to the way they sound. When split-second precision is required, as with commercials, time them. As you listen to your scripts, look for the many things this chapter discusses. Regular use of a recorder to hear your script will inevitably make you a better writer for the electronic media.

Radio scripts are written to be heard, and television scripts to be seen and heard, so writing for these media is a unique challenge. Most writers new to scriptwriting need constant reminders that their scripts will never be seen or read by their audiences. Writers for the print media have it easy—what they set down on paper is exactly what their audiences see. Scripts, on the other hand, will pass through the eyes, ears, voices, and minds of others. So scripts require a different kind of writing than print media. You should consider your scripts to be blueprints for productions because, after you write them, they'll be interpreted by producers, directors, performers, and, at times, by graphic artists and composers.

For television, the challenge is to use words that instruct and inspire your interpreters to re-create your vision on screen and speaker. For radio, you must put together words that create pictures in the minds of listeners. Keep these considerations in mind as you work to create clear, straightforward, easily understood, and effective scripts.

Clear writing for the electronic media is a necessity, not because your audience is simple-minded, but because our ears process words and sentences differently than do our eyes. If you learn nothing else from this book, I hope you'll become skilled at writing for the ear!

AVOIDING DISCRIMINATION

As you invent your stories, keep in mind the sensitivities of those who historically have been undervalued by the public media. Although you may not need this reminder, it's better to err on the side of caution.

Stereotypes

Stereotypes are much like caricatures, but they relate to *groups* rather than to *individuals*. Political cartoons of prominent public figures exaggerate features to make them recognizable, while at the same time depicting them as ludicrous, dangerous, foolish, or even (in a very few instances) noble.

Writers find stereotypes an efficient and time-saving means of establishing the nature of agents in their stories. They use traits believed by great numbers of people to be true, and incorporate them into agents that embody them. You've undoubtedly heard jokes or comments based on stereotypical assumptions: Scots are thrifty, the French are amorous, Germans are meticulous, Greeks love to dance, and Italians are great singers. So long as those stereotyped aren't members of a group that suffers from the prejudice of others, they're relatively harmless.

Years ago, groups now free from negative stereotyping were ridiculed as stupid or evil (or both); for example, the Irish during the 1800s, and Germans during World War I. Today Italians generally are treated as individuals rather than types, except when they're shown as mobsters in Mafia-related stories.

At the same time, other groups within our society continue to ask for fair, multifaceted characterization in popular stories. These include African Americans, Native Americans, Asian Americans, and Latin Americans. Americans of Jewish heritage, as well as those of

Armenian, Middle Eastern, and Caribbean backgrounds, are also frequently victims of discrimination and stereotyping.

Members of certain groups not defined as *ethnic* minorities also suffer from stereotyping, and include gay men and women, convicted felons (both in and out of custody), and those who practice certain trades: dentists, lawyers, car sales personnel, and politicians.

There has, of course, been some change to more sensitive portrayals of nearly all categories of people, and there's every likelihood that positive changes will continue. Until that Golden Age arrives, though, writers for the public media should be careful when using stereotypes.

It's easy to see why some stereotypes should be avoided by writers, but what about so-called "harmless" stereotypes? Maureen Dowd, writing in the *New York Times,* tells us what's wrong with stereotypes, regardless of who is being so depicted:

> We are living in a golden age of coarse generalizations. All the politesse and tiptoeing in the office has created a robust hunger for vulgar stereotypes in popular culture.
>
> It turns out that stereotypes are not only offensive, they are also comforting. They wrap life in the archetypal toastiness of fairy tale and myth. They make complicated understandings unnecessary. They permit people to identify the appearances with the realities, and so exempt them from any further mental or emotional effort. They keep familiar things familiar. *They are not completely false, but they are completely shallow.*[10](Italics added)

When you select the characteristics of agents in your stories, giving them individualized, multifaceted personalities will enhance your characters' credibility while greatly improving the dimensionality and significance of your work.[11]

Outdated Terms of Gender. Just a few decades ago male terminology dominated our language; *the man in the street, salesman, spokesman,* and so forth. For most users of American English these terms have become obsolete and are seldom heard today. But there remains a concern that has not yet been addressed. Years ago, as women increasingly moved into careers formerly open only to men, it was assumed that a special term was needed to describe their roles: hostess, actress, comedienne, drum majorette, and so forth. But, the roots of each of these terms—host, actor, comedian, and drum major—are not gender specific. If we're to truly go beyond the condescension that produced these terms, we should stop using them in our stories. A female protagonist is a hero, a female who creates statues is a sculptor, and a female who tells jokes is a comedian.

Age Referents. It's incorrect to assume that people over the age of sixty are elderly. Some people are elderly at the age of fifty, while others are still relatively youthful at seventy-five. Most people in the upper age brackets, who've retained their youthful zest for life and who continue to make contributions to our society, rightfully resent depictions that they see as discriminatory and inaccurate. When you create characters for your stories who are above the age of sixty-five, don't show condescension by writing dialogue that makes them seem like old fogies—unless, of course, you're depicting such a person for a reason, as in the commercial for Jetson Travel in Chapter 13.

This chapter demonstrates the importance of creating and drawing upon a reservoir of theories as you approach the actual writing of scripts. Conceptualization—which relies on a knowledge of human needs, interests, and motivations, as well as a keen sense of storytelling as an art—should guide you toward establishing a vision, purpose, and structure for every story you're going to create. The extended example that took a public service campaign from start to finish is but a single example of how to make such connections. Taking the creative process beyond the limits of this chapter is now in your hands. Over time you'll find it ever-easier to slip into a creative conceptualizing mode on acceptance of an assignment. Working toward that end should be your goal.

QUESTIONS

1. Choose a television drama—serious or comic—that you find outstanding. Record and then watch a few episodes. Start, stop, and review as appropriate to give you time to make notes about your perceptions. Analyze these dramas in terms of the quality of their *visualization* and their use of *sounds,* including speech, music, and sound effects. Determine the effectiveness of the programs according to their use of sounds and sights.

2. This chapter identifies several levels of abstraction, using an automobile as its example. Apply the lessons learned to the levels of abstraction found in radio and television: newscasts, commercials, and dramas.

3. Experiment with the suggestions of Gayle Delaney on using your sleeping mind to help you solve problems, especially creative writing challenges. Record the results.

4. Find stories written for print media such as newspapers or magazines. Select three stories you feel are written in a style inappropriate to the broadcast media—use of overlong sentences; sentences too complex to be effective when heard rather than read; unconversational writing style; and words or concepts that are too abstract. Rewrite them for more effective aural comprehension.

5. Borrow or rent a video version of a film you enjoyed in a movie theatre. Watch it critically in your home environment, and look for answers to these questions:
   - Did I enjoy the video as much as I did the theatre experience?
   - Were there times when I wished for closer views of people, objects, scenery, and so forth?
   - If there were written words—title, credits, a letter, something written on an object—did I find the words hard to read?

NOTES

1. Gayle Delaney, *All About Dreams.* (San Francisco: HarperSanFrancisco, a division of HarperCollins, 1998). 229. Reprinted by permission of the publishers.
2. Ibid., 200.
3. Ibid., 200.
4. Ibid., 208–9.
5. Robert C. Pritikin, *Christ Was an Ad Man.* (London: Bay Court, 1997), 191.
6. Ibid., 193.
7. Ibid., 194.
8. Ibid., 196, 197.
9. Ibid., 192.
10. Maureen Dowd, "Cuomos vs. Sopranos," *New York Times,* 22 April 2001.
11. Of course, if you write skits for programs such as *Saturday Night Live* or *Mad TV,* you'll be required to use some stereotypes. But when writing stories with more permanence and depth, it's best to create *individuals* rather than *types.*

SCRIPT FORMATS AND NOTES ABOUT SCRIPTS

Chapter 12 describes and illustrates several script formats in common use throughout the radio, television, and film industries.

Not all television and radio programs rely on scripts, but for those that do, scripts are the blueprints that guide producers, designers, directors, and performers as they turn your written words into sights and sounds. Some programs or program elements begin with a script; some have a script written only after most program material has been collected; and some never have a script. Here are some of the variations:

Programs in which writers conceive scripts and turn them into words on paper. These include nearly all dramas, comic sketches, television essays, commentaries, news copy read by anchors, and most commercials.

Shows made up of recorded and edited material connected by narration. These include most documentaries, America's Most . . . or America's Funniest . . . programs, feature reports, some essays, and many satiric comedy sketches.

Shows made up of recorded and edited material, without connecting narration. A small number of documentaries tell their stories entirely through visual images and words spoken by their subjects. For these, a script consists of notes on paper identifying the segments, and listing them in the order in which they'll be assembled. After completing the production, the script may be prepared for closed-captioning. One outstanding example of such a production is the documentary *Moving Mountains,* the story of the Yiu Mien people of Laos who emigrated to America after the Vietnam War, settling in Oregon and California. It documents problems of homesickness and culture shock, told by the Mien themselves.[1] Radio features made up exclusively of sounds, including actualities, music, and sound effects, are called *sound portraits.*

Scripts written by college students for a class in writing for the electronic media are identified by an asterisk (*) appearing after the author's name.

Unscripted programs include game and talk shows, DJ music programs, sports play-by-play, interviews, and news reports from the field. When making packages—recorded and edited stories—reporters usually record their narration not from scripts, but from sketchy notes.

Audiences never see scripts for radio and television. Because of this, the starting point of any script for the electronic media is a *conceptualization* of the sounds and/or visual images you wish to have conveyed.

We think of scripts as being made up of words and, of course, from a literal point of view, that's true. But here are six different ways that a television commercial can dispense information:

- One script calls for only visual images, sound effects, music, and printed words on the screen.
- A second asks only for music and visual images.
- A third uses visual images and song to convey its message (such as a soft drink commercial without spoken dialogue).
- A fourth is a dramatization, where actors discuss a topic; for example, a concern about health or insurance policies.
- A fifth is a montage of shots (either still or in motion), together with voice-over narration.
- In a sixth, an on-screen announcer speaks the sales message directly to us, without visual embellishment.

Of these, only the last three—dramatization, voice-over narration, and direct address—are dominated by spoken language. Even radio scripts that rely heavily on spoken dialogue or narration often make use of sung lyrics, instrumental music, and sound effects. The lesson for you, as an electronic media writer, is to conceive the sounds and pictures that will convey your message *before* begin to turn your vision into written symbols.

SCRIPT FORMATS

The term *format* has several meanings in broadcasting, but in this book, the format refers to the physical layout of a script, the way in which dialogue, sound effects, music, visual images, and other program elements are set forth on the page. If you're new to scriptwriting, without an agent or a track record, you'll want to present your script in its most comprehensible form. And you'll communicate your intentions most accurately if you follow established script formats.

Good formatting is important because it presents your story in its most reader-friendly form. Unless your script is easily read by agents or producers, chances are it won't be read at all! You can create all script styles with whatever writing program you have; specialized software is not needed. Formatting can be difficult, however, especially the two-column television format, so you may want to consider a writing program designed for film, radio, and television writers. Such programs allow their users to change scripts from one format to another at the push of a button. If you don't have access to a scriptwriting program, you must devise serviceable formats for your scripts. Agents, producers, and others who evaluate your scripts must read the words you've set down, and convert them into aural and visual images in their mind's eye. Anything that prevents an easy conversion is damaging to your effort. Busy people lack the time and patience to struggle over scripts that use unfamiliar formats, so it's crucial that you make your vision as easily and effectively retrievable as possible.[2]

Script formats aren't completely standardized, but you should follow the radio and television formats found here and throughout this book. They're not meticulously followed—no format is. Scripts in Part II show acceptable differences in formats prepared by various people, agencies, and networks. All of the script examples shown are accepted and effortlessly read and evaluated by agents, producers, directors, and performers.

Radio Script Formats

Script Terminology. One of the first elements of script formatting you should learn is the terminology. As you begin to turn your ideas into scripts, you'll find yourself stumbling if you don't know and use the vocabulary that tells interpreters what you desire in the way of special effects, music, interpretation of lines by an announcer or character, and so forth.

TERMS USED IN RADIO SCRIPTS

ANNCR   Designation of announcer.

board fade   To fade out all sound going through the audio console.

bridge   A means of moving from one program element to another, usually by way of a short musical passage.

continuity   A term used for all script material.

crossfade   An overlapping of sound and sound, music and sound, or voices. As one sound is faded out, the second is faded in (see also *segue*).

echo chamber   A means of adding an echo to the sounds being broadcast or recorded. This effect is used in many ways: to give a dreamlike quality to a voice, to create the illusion that a voice is from the grave or from from the past, or to simulate speech delivered in a crypt or a haunted house. The term *echo chamber* continues to be used, even though echoes are created electronically.

sound effect   All sound other than voices or music. The abbreviation is SFX. This is usually placed on the left side of the script, just before the desired effect which is written in capital letters. When the effect is an interruption of dialogue, omit the term SFX, and place the direction at the point of the interruption: I'll come right over. (PHONE RINGS) Hello?

filter mic   A microphone that can significantly alter the sound of a person's voice. It's used to simulate a voice being heard over a telephone or an intercom speaker.

segue   The ending of one sound (such as music) followed after a barely perceptible pause, by another sound.

SFX   Abbreviation for sound effects.

sneak in   An instruction to slowly fade up the volume of sound, music, or voices.

UNDER FOR   Volume of SFX or MUSIC is faded down as voice comes in.

UP: Volume of SFX or MUSIC is faded up.

To add music, write MUSIC: in left column, as you do with SFX. On right side, indicate the type of music: (BUGLE CALL) or (UP-TEMPO INSTRUMENTAL).

To give an interpretative direction in the script, write it in capitals, put it between parentheses, and enter it at the spot where you want it, as in (GRUMBLING) in the air conditioner commercial that follows. Other indicators are (BEGIN FADE) and (SEGUE). SEGUE (pronounced SEG-way) is defined above.

Script formats for radio vary, not in style, but according to complexity. The simplest script format is written for a single voice delivering a message, unaccompanied by sound effects, music, or other embellishment. Commercials, essays, analyses, and public service announcements of this genre are simple, as these examples show.

Single-Voice Radio Scripts. Radio scripts using a single voice—as an announcer delivering an unembellished message—employ a bare-bones format. The two scripts that follow are equally acceptable:

Safety Belt Education[3]
Live Announcer Copy
:20

When you're just driving around the block or up the street, you don't need to wear a seat belt, because you know you're not going to be in a car crash, right? Wrong! Because anybody who's ever been in a car crash can tell you, they never saw it coming. So always buckle up. Always. A message brought to you by the U.S. Department of Transportation and the Ad Council.

AGENCY: VOLTAIRE VILLANUEVA*
CLIENT: SAN FRANCISCO STATE UNIVERSITY ADVISING CENTER
LENGTH: :30

ANNCR: (SOMEWHAT TENSE AND SERIOUS) Are you stressed because you think you can't graduate anytime soon? Are you undeclared, without a clue as to what major matches your interests and abilities?

              (CALM, SPOKEN MORE SLOWLY) Well, you're ready for a visit to the Advising Center.

              The Center's a university service that offers academic guidance and information for students just like you. There are workshops for students who are undecided about a major, and unclear about general education requirements. Our professional staff wants to help you graduate on time. But, we can't help you if we don't see you. So call us at 338-2101 or visit us in Administration 212 for more information.

Radio Production Scripts. Radio scripts that call for sound effects, music, special effects, and/or dialogue are written in a *production script format.* SFX means "sound effects," and both SFX and suggestions for interpretation are capitalized and usually are placed within parentheses. Here's a radio PSA that asks for a minimum of production: two voices and sound effects. Note the ways sound effects are designated.[4]

The Advertising Council, Inc.

"Watts on Your Mind"[5]

AS RECORDED RADIO TEXT—"Another Illuminating Idea" :60

SFX: (WE HEAR THE CLASSIC SOUNDS OF THE BUBBLING BEAKERS, ELEC-TRONIC WALLA, ETC., COMING FROM MAD'S LABORATORY. WE ALSO HEAR THE SOUND OF A TELEVISION SET PLAYING IN THE BACKGROUND.)

SIGGY: Master, why is it so important not to waste energy?

MAD: Because, Sigmund, wasting energy increases air pollution.

SIGGY: Oooo, that's not so good.

MAD: No, Sigmund, it's not. But there are things we can do to stop wasting energy.

SIGGY: Really? Like what?

MAD: Like turning off the TV when we're not watching it.

SIGGY: Good idea.

SFX: (WE HEAR THE SOUND OF THE TV BEING SWITCHED OFF. WE HEAR THE SOUND OF A REFRIGERATOR DOOR BEING OPENED.)

SIGGY: Let's see . . . what do I want . . .

MAD: Like deciding what you want from the refrigerator *before* you open the door.

SFX: (WE HEAR THE SOUND OF THE REFRIGERATOR DOOR BEING QUICKLY CLOSED.)

SIGGY: I knew that.

MAD: Like turning off electric lights when you . . .

SFX: (WE HEAR THE SOUND OF SOMEONE TURNING OFF THE LIGHTS.)

MAD: Sigmund?

SIGGY:	Yes, Master?
MAD:	You just turned off the lights.
SIGGY:	Yes, Master!
SFX:	(WE HEAR THE SOUND OF MAD FUMBLING FOR THE LIGHT SWITCH AND WALKING.)
MAD:	Sigmund, I appreciate you not wanting to waste energy but don't you think it would be better to wait until we leave the room before you turn off the . . .
SFX:	(WE HEAR THE SOUND OF MAD TRIPPING, EQUIPMENT FLYING AND EVERYTHING LANDING ON THE FLOOR WITH THUDS AND CRASHES.)
MAD:	. . . lights?
SIGGY:	Yes, Master.
ANNCR.:	Another illuminating idea brought to you by the U.S. Environmental Protection Agency, Earth Share, and the Ad Council.

Here's another SAMPLE RADIO COMMERCIAL SCRIPT FORMAT

AGENCY:	Name of your choice
CLIENT:	Brigham Air Conditioners
LENGTH:	:30 (to indicate 30 seconds)
WRITTEN BY:	George Spelvin

ANNCR:	(ON SLIGHT FILTER) Ah, the sounds of summer. . . .
SFX:	(BIRDS CHIRPING, SPLASH OF DIVING INTO SWIMMING POOL)
ANNCR:	(FILTER) Today's forecast calls for temperatures in the low to mid-eighties, low nineties in our inland valleys. (UNDER FOR:)
MAN:	(GRUMBLING) It's too darn hot!
MUSIC:	(RADIO SCANNING ACROSS STATIONS. STOP ON UPTEMPO MUSIC. MUSIC UNDER.)
MAN:	(GRUMBLING) The more I hear that weather person, the hotter I get! (MUTTERINGS. UNDER FOR:)
MUSIC:	(MUSIC UP AND OUT.)
ANNCR:	If this scene is all too familiar, listen to another sound of summer . . .

SFX: (AIR CONDITIONER STARTING UP. LOW VOLUME. UNDER FOR:)

ANNCR: That slight murmur you hear is the sound of relief! It's the all-new Bingham air conditioner. Inspired by space-age technology, the Bingham Climate Commander lowers your energy costs, as it raises your spirits. This summer, get out of the hot . . . come into the cool. The Bingham Climate Commander!

LIVE TAG: The Bingham Climate Commander's on sale this weekend at the Appliance Club, in the Northside Mall.

This script format is also useful for comedy sketches, radio feature reports, and radio documentaries.

Television Script Formats

Television scripts are written in various formats. Those produced as television (rather than film for television) follow a two-column format, with all of the visuals in the left column, and all of the sound, including dialogue, narration, SFX, and music, in the right column.

As with the discussion of radio script formats, it's important to know television terms for special instructions before starting to write a script. It should be noted, however, that camera and on-camera personnel movements are not indicated in all scripts. News copy, for instance, is formatted with two columns, but the left column is blank, providing space for notations by the camera director.

CU close-up

ECU or XCU extreme close-up

LS or XLS extreme long shot

IN: indicates the words that open a sound bite

MCU medium close-up

MS medium shot

OS over-the-shoulder shot (usually over a reporter or interviewer's shoulder and showing the person being interviewed face-on)

OUT: indicates the words that end a sound bite

PAN camera moves right to left or left to right, without movement of the pedestal

RS reverse shot (reporter or interviewer listening to person being interviewed)

SLO-MO slow motion

SLUG the slug line, a brief title given to a news story for identification purposes

SOT sound on tape

TILT camera moves up or down, without pedestalling up or down

TRT total running time

TS   tight shot

TWO-SHOT   a shot with two people in the frame

VO   voice-over

WS or LS   wide shot or long shot

Four television script formats are illustrated here. The first is a complete, detailed, two-column format. The second is a scaled-down, one-column format, used for scripts with a single performer and no changes in scene. The third is a script with storyboard, and the fourth shows the format for scripts shot as film. In subsequent chapters, you'll see television scripts with slight variations that are acceptable by most producers and agents. While including them in this book may be a bit confusing, it would be misleading to omit or reformat them.

The first example includes all audio and video information, and is quite specific in its details.

CLIENT: The San Francisco Zoo
AUTHOR: Samantha Wiedmann*

"Parents and Kids" :30 TV Spot

VIDEO	AUDIO
MS OF A MOTHER WITH A BOY, GIRL, AND BABY IN STROLLER	(MUSIC: GENTLE BUT UPBEAT. IN AND UNDER) ANNCR: (VO) Enjoy a special day with your family at the San Francisco Zoo.
CU OF AYE-AYE	Check out some of our new exhibits, including the mysterious Aye-Aye.
CU OF BABY RHINO	See the biggest baby at the zoo—a 75-pound rhinoceros.
CU OF BABY AND MOTHER GORILLA	Or come meet Nneka, our baby gorilla. Of course there're all the other favorites. . . .
:08 MONTAGE OF MOST POPULAR ANIMALS	
LS OF FAMILY ON LITTLE PUFFER TRAIN	FAMILY: (LAUGHING) (CHILD'S VOICE) Thanks, Mom! This is fun!
GRAPHIC: SF ZOO LOGO WITH PHONE NUMBER	ANNCR: Rediscover your world. The San Francisco Zoo. Open daily. (UPBEAT MUSIC TO CLOSE)

The second example is a television script that has no significant visual complexities. In this example, there are no scene changes, and talent is on-camera throughout.

AGENCY:	Anna Heidt and Associates
CLIENT:	Rosale's Tamale Parlors
LENGTH:	30 seconds

SUPER: Miguel Rosales, Super

MIGUEL: (STANDING BEHIND DISPLAY TABLE LOADED WITH ROSALE'S FOOD PRODUCTS)

I'm proud of the tasty and wholesome food prepared here in the Rosale's Kitchen. (PICKS UP A CRISPY TACO) Like this Taco Grande.

A crisp corn taco shell, made without lard, and baked, not deep-fried. Filled with chorizo-seasoned beef, shredded lettuce, grated cheese, and topped with an olive for looks and taste! (TAKES A BITE) Um, muy sabroso! (PICKS UP TAMALE ON PLATE) But our especialidades are the famous Rosale's Tamales! Words can't express their taste, but you'll get the message by watching my joy as it disappears before your very eyes. (EATS TAMALE WITH OBVIOUS PLEASURE)

ANNCR: (VO) Rosale's Tamale Parlors. Muy Sabroso!

Some scripts, most often those prepared by advertising agencies, include a storyboard to show artists or producers who'll turn the script into a finished production how they want the spot to be visualized. The drawings needn't be slick or photographic in appearance, but they must show the basic shots that matter.

AGENCY:	Gordon Lee Advertising
CLIENT:	Best Times Foods
PRODUCT:	Roquefort Salad Dressing

ANNCR (VO): Best Times Foods presents a taste sensation for your salads!

Goat's milk cheese from the caves of Roquefort!

Virgin olive oil from Sunny Spain,

Herbs and spices from the slopes of Vesuvius!

It's the international taste sensation that has salads singing in three languages!

(SINGING, VO) (IN FRENCH) The best cheese from the best caves;

(IN SPANISH) We press the olives only once for the sweetest taste;

(IN ITALIAN) And, we bring out the nippy flavor with herbs and spices from Italy!

ANNCR VO: Try the new Roquefort dressing!

From Best Times, for the Best Salads of your life!

Script Formats for Television Dramas and Comedies. Scripts written for television dramas, whether shot on film or tape, almost always use a quasi-film format. Although film script formats aren't totally standardized, in general they follow these principles:

> Names of characters (MARY) are ALL CAPS.
> All important information (SCENE B) is ALL CAPS.
> Visuals (DROPS HER GLOVE) are ALL CAPS.
> Dialogue (Hello, Ramon. How's It going?) is in upper and lower case.
> *Omit directions,* such as cut to or fade to black.

Make your script as easy to read as possible—use double- or triple-space, wide margins, lots of white areas.

Brief excerpt of television script written in film format

SCENE A

INTERIOR OF UNDERGROUND PARKING GARAGE. WALKING TOWARD THEIR CAR ARE MARIA, RAMON, AND FRED. MARIA IS CARRYING A LARGE SHOPPING BAG. RAMON HOLDS LARGE HEAVY BOX.

RAMON

Wow! This box weighs a ton.

RAMON STOPS, AND ROUGHLY PLACES BOX ON THE HOOD OF A JAGUAR XKE.

MARIA

Careful, Ramon—that's some yuppy's sixty-thousand-dollar toy!

RAMON

Hey, what's the problem. . . .

MARIA

(INTERRUPTING) Ramon! Some guy's in the back seat!

FRED

Not to worry—he's asleep.

MARIA

(MOVING CLOSER TO CAR) Better take another look—he isn't breathing!

Additional examples of script formats of all kinds may be found in Appendix B, as well as in several other chapters.

NOTES ABOUT SCRIPTS

Printing the Scripts

Always print your scripts double-spaced. Why? Because your work should be as reader friendly as possible. Busy agents have no patience with scripts that require extra effort to read. And agents, editors, AND TEACHERS! will want to make notes or write suggestions between the lines of your script; single-spaced scripts leave no room for these comments. At the production stage, your script will be marked for interpretation by directors and performers, which again demands double-spacing. If it's space-and-a-half or single-space, it's very frustrating. Computer writing programs undergo change from time to time, so the comments that follow may or may not apply at the time you read this.[6]

When setting up your computer, choose 12-point type. Titles and headings should be in larger type, usually 14 to 18. With Microsoft Word 5.1, to use one example, choose "format" from the menu bar (very top of display screen), and select "character."[7] Word-processing programs permit the selection of spacing of letters to give your script the best possible appearance. When using scripts, select an unembellished font, rather than one with serifs. Serifs are the added lines that embellish letters to make them more attractive. Here's a sentence printed in Helvetica, a font without serifs: "Scriptwriters should always work for clarity." Here's the same sentence written with Palatino, a font with serifs: "Scriptwriters should always work for clarity." While the Palatino font is more eye-appealing and works well for letters and memos, it's less appropriate for scripts that often are in the form of dialogue that is to be spoken by a performer.

Make sure your printer has ink in it because sometimes scripts that are otherwise excellent—well formatted, accurate spelling, etc.—can be all but impossible to read because the print is too faint.

Use both UPPER- and lowercase letters for all words that are to be spoken, as in "John, I asked you for Mary's address, and you merely said she lived in Dover, Maryland. That's not helpful!" There's a practice, especially in newsrooms, of WRITING EVERYTHING IN CAPITAL LETTERS. Please don't do that. This is a holdover from the days of mechanical teletype machines that were set to print in capital letters only. There's a reason for uppercase and lowercase, and generally in a script, DIRECTIONS such as sound effects (SFX) are written in UPPERCASE. Frequently you'll also find directions placed in parentheses.

Make sure you identify your scripts! When printing a script for submission to an agent or producer, it's good practice to list your name and other pertinent information on a cover sheet, and to list your name at the bottom of every page. Don't staple your pages together, and don't use paper clips or plastic folders.

Always number your pages. When you deliver a twelve-page script, and an editor or agent finds something on page six that she wants to comment on, she can't write "on page six you did such and such." That editor will have to go through, page by page, counting and numbering them, or will have to write "somewhere toward the middle of your script, where I've made a great big X, you'll find. . . ." It's very unlikely that any busy reader will bother to add what you've failed to include on your script. Number your pages. It's easy. Your computer will do it automatically—if you know how to tell it to.

Estimating the Running Time of Scripts

Many scripts are written to exact time limits. A thirty-second commercial must be produceable in exactly thirty seconds, and an hourlong drama must, with time omitted for commercials, be exactly forty-two minutes—to use the requirements of one network. Other scripts, including essays, editorials, and sound portraits must conform to time requirements set forth by program or station producers. Feature reports on newscasts vary in length, but those who produce them are given a ballpark figure to guide them.

Given a time frame to fill, how do you estimate the time represented by each page of script? Seasoned professionals can look at a piece of paper and say, "that's sixty-five seconds." Most likely, you're not yet able to do that. The best advice I can give is this: whenever you write a script, read it into a tape recorder, play it back, and time it. Experience will give you a sense of how much physical space on a piece of paper represents how many seconds or minutes of time. Sit with a stopwatch when you play back your words and time them. Soon, you'll develop the ability to look at the paper, and say that it's too long or too short.

Radio and television scripts differ in pages per minute. Because television scripts are divided into two narrow columns, one for video and the other for audio, they generally run to about two pages a minute, while radio scripts average one page a minute. Obviously, some passages are delivered slowly, others more rapidly, and sometimes a musical passage will occupy more time than the space it occupies would indicate. So, take all aspects of pacing into consideration when estimating the length of a script on which you're working.

The sample scripts in this chapter, as well as the many scripts in Appendix A and the chapters that follow, demonstrate a variety of formats. You can use them as models whenever you're in doubt.

QUESTIONS

1. The several scripts in this chapter illustrate various ways of formatting. Choose two radio and two television scripts, and analyze them in terms of:

   - structure (form)
   - vision
   - mood
   - effectiveness

2. Find a radio commercial in Chapter 13 and turn it into a television spot, complete with storyboard. Rewrite—or even reconceive—the spot to make the best use of television.

NOTES

1. *Moving Mountains* was produced and directed by Elaine Velazquez, and is distributed by Filmakers Library, 124 East 40th Street, New York, NY 10016. Phone: (212) 808-4983, website: http://www.filmakers.com.

2. In years to come, when you've achieved success and recognition, you may become more casual about formatting. Established writers know exactly how far their scripts can vary from established formats, but as a beginner or only slightly experienced writer, you're on safer ground if you follow the formats given as examples in this chapter and in Chapters 13–17.

3. Courtesy of The Advertising Council.

4. When you examine both radio and television scripts in Appendix A, you'll find some variation in small details such as capitalization of music, sound effects, and interpretation instructions.

5. Courtesy of The Advertising Counsil.

6. At one time, Microsoft Word required thirteen steps to insert page numbers on a script! Later versions, of course, became far more user friendly.

7. I once had the latest version of Microsoft Word installed on my computer, but I eventually dragged it to the trash because it kept stopping me in mid-sentence to say that I'd misspelled a word or to make suggestions that weren't relevant to my needs or interests.

CHAPTER THIRTEEN

COMMERCIALS

Chapter 13 is a key chapter in *Idea to Script*. While it focuses on conceiving and writing commercials, many of its lessons apply equally to script writing for all types of broadcast messages. The emphasis on opening your message with words or pictures that attract attention, causing audiences to stay focused to see what's coming, is applicable to many other types of programs, including comic sketches, essays, commentaries, and feature reports.

This chapter considers radio and television commercials as creative challenges that can, at times, have an awesome effect. One noteworthy commercial was shown for Apple Computers only once. Apple paid $500,000 to broadcast the sixty-second spot on the 1984 Superbowl. It resulted in $4.5 million in sales within six hours. Many other outstanding commercials in this chapter illuminate ways of conceiving and creating commercials that sell.

Noted playwright George Bernard Shaw, in a letter to Mrs. Patrick Campbell, apologized for the letter's unusual length. He wrote that he lacked sufficient time to write a shorter message. This remark may seem flippant and little more than a joke, but it contains a noteworthy truth that applies to scriptwriting: it's far more difficult to write compelling stories with fifteen- to sixty-second time limits than it is to write much longer pieces—news stories, essays, or reviews, for example.

This reality dictates why this chapter of *Idea to Script,* the first devoted to conceiving and writing scripts, centers around commercials. Once you've developed your ability to focus sharply on a clearly determined objective and produce a tightly written, persuasive message of less than one minute's duration, you'll be well prepared to take on more complex and lengthy writing challenges. Here's an extremely effective example of getting one's point across with a minimum number of words:

Scripts written by college students for a class in writing for the electronic media are identified by an asterisk (*) appearing after the author's name.

```
AGENCY:   CHUCK BLORE & DON RICHMAN, INC.[1]
CLIENT:   KGO-TV
OCCASION: 6:00 O'CLOCK MOVIE

MUSIC:    (HARP GLISSANDO)

ANNCR:    Tonight's six o'clock movie is Alfred Hitchcock's production of
          The Birds. It's too exciting for words.
          The Birds
```

    The first objective of any commercial is to capture the attention of listeners or viewers. Here's how Eric Poole accomplished that in this commercial for a bakery.

```
AGENCY:   ERIC POOLE, SPLASH RADIO[2]
CLIENT:   La Belle's French Bakery
PRODUCT:  LOW FAT DESSERTS
SFX:      (BIRDS CHIRPING)
```

MAN: So let me get this straight. You grow fat?

GUY: Uh-huh, I'm a fat farmer.

MAN: Where do you grow this fat?

GUY: Right here. On my fat farm.

MAN: Mm-hmm.

GUY: See, I plant the little fat globules in the furrows, and they grow into these giant majestic stalks of fat!

MAN: Stalks of fat . . .

GUY: Well, you know all those fatty snack foods you ate as a kid . . .

MAN: Uh-huh . . .

GUY: Well, I grow the fat they put in 'em.

    These words capture our attention at once. You can read the complete commercial later in this chapter, but the opening is here as an example of the chief requirement of a commercial: to grab the attention of those you want to reach and make them want to hear more! Commercials present writers with special challenges. To succeed as a writer of commercials, you must

- awaken interest in a message that interrupts whatever program the audience is enjoying (remember—you're butting in, so your message could be as unwelcome as a telemarketer's phone call during dinner. Your opening should not give people a reason to "tune out");
- retain audience attention for the duration of the message;
- sell a product or a cause in thirty seconds or less (sixty seconds for some radio commercials); and
- motivate individuals to take an action—buying a product, phoning for more information, or placing an order over the phone or on the Internet—to mention but a few possibilities.

Some very fine scripts are written as commercials. Perhaps you've seen awards ceremonies for television commercials, or you've tuned to a program featuring great commercials of the past. Each of us undoubtedly can name at least a few commercials that are favorites. Famous spots include the "Mean Joe Greene" commercial for Coca-Cola; the "Joe Isuzu" spots, notorious for Joe's outrageous lies; "Where's the beef?" for Burger King; Ray Charles and three lovely backup singers, serenading us on behalf of the "Pepsi Generation"; Budweiser commercials showing the Clydesdale horses; and the Taco Bell commercials featuring a talking Chihuahua.[3]

While many broadcast ads are dull, irritating, or raucous, others stand out as entertaining, amusing, and sometimes moving. Pay careful attention to commercials; note the characteristics of those that amuse, charm, or otherwise please you, as well as those that irritate or offend you. Force yourself, if necessary, to pay close attention to commercials that neither offend nor please; see if you can identify the characteristics of spots that make no impression and leave you with little memory of them, because these are the ones that misfire.

Analyzing commercials is the first step toward learning to create effective spots. While audiences may try to ignore or avoid commercials, even to the point of zapping them, you, as a writer for the electronic media, mustn't allow yourself that luxury: pay close attention because you can learn much by studying not only the best, but the most offensive and insipid of commercials as well. It's been known for years that the two types of commercials that audiences remember are at the extremes: those they love, and those they hate; analyzing both can tell us a lot.

DETERMINING THE PARTS AND THE STRUCTURE

Earlier chapters considered structure and explored various arrangement formats, such as chronological, logical, and thematic. This chapter applies these principles of structure to specific types of scripts.

Almost any example of well-written copy shows clearly differentiated parts. On the most basic level, copy may be broken down to a beginning, middle, and end. The beginning is the introduction and customarily gains our attention. The middle, or body, contains most of the information, at times including advantages of this product over others. The end generally sums up the most important points. It frequently urges action or repeats the name, address, and telephone number of the sponsor. On television, this is done by showing a phone number or e-mail address.

THE INTRODUCTION—GAINING ATTENTION

How do you get listeners to pay attention to what's essentially an intrusive message? Some ad agencies believe that any means of attracting attention is justified. Bob Garfield, ad critic for *Advertising Age* magazine, disagrees and gives one reason why many openings are counterproductive:

> So much advertising fails because it imagines the world is hanging on its every word. Other advertising fails because it is so intent on getting noticed it simply grabs viewers by the lapels and shakes, which is attention getting, but leaves an unfavorable first impression.[4]

Attention can be gained in a number of ways. One of the easiest and least defensible is to use trickery. If you begin your spot with "Attention! This is a traffic alert!" and your message turns into a commercial about a sale or similar event, you'll just invite anger from your listeners. An attention-getter *must* be motivated and justified by what follows. An audience-catching opening establishes a promise you're obliged to keep. Here are regrettably common ways of capturing attention:

False Alert

ANNCR: (AUTHORITATIVE VOICE) Your attention, please . . . (OR) This is an emergency message. . . .)

Raucous Noise:

MUSIC: (LOUD BLAST FROM TRUMPETS)

Screaming Actors:

(ACTORS SCREAM WITH HIGH VOLUME AND PIERCING PITCH.)[5]

MAN: Whadda we do now?

WOMAN: Yeah, Mr. Wiseguy! What next?

MAN: We shoulda done something sooner!

WOMAN: Yeah!

(SPOT CONTINUES, WITH UNHAPPY COUPLE YELLING AT HIGH PITCH AND VOLUME AT THE TOP OF THEIR VOICES. SCREAM VOLUME IS REDUCED AS VOICE-OVER ANNOUNCER TRIES UNSUCCESSFULLY TO CONNECT THIS CACOPHONY TO THE SPONSOR'S PRODUCT, A FINANCIAL CONSULTATION FIRM.)

These attention-getters may make us listen—at least until we hit the mute button or switch to another station—but all are counterproductive. The first is a bogus announcement that works only because listeners—especially those in cars—are tricked into believing they're about to hear an important safety message. The second and third efforts work because loud and piercing noises startle listeners into paying attention, but again, arouse resentment because people are annoyed by uninvited loud and unpleasant noises blaring from their speakers.

For radio, the most effective commercials frequently begin with a comment or question that invites attention without resorting to extreme volume or outlandish promises. The waterbed commercial that follows opens with the comment, "Your most treasured possession is your body," which gently gains our attention. The remainder of the spot is pleasant to the ear, has a logical structure, and delivers a worthwhile message. As you read this spot, note the use of imagery enhanced by music.

AGENCY: Pritikin & Gibbons[6]
CLIENT: BODY COMFORT WATERBEDS
LENGTH: 60 SECONDS

(READ ALL ANNOUNCER COPY IN THIRTY-NINE SECONDS)

MUSIC: GENTLE-CONTEMPORARY

ANNCR: Your most treasured possession . . . is your body.

MUSIC-VOCAL: COMFORT YOUR BODY IN A BODY COMFORT
                    WATERBED
                    WHAT A BEAUTIFUL WAY
                    TO LAY YOUR BODY DOWN

ANNCR: Every single day—your body has the opportunity to engage
                    in a marvelous, sensual, almost spiritual experience. It's
                    called . . . sleep.

                    Body Comfort Waterbed is the distinguished name in
                    waterbeds. They helped pioneer the most important
                    advances in waterbed comfort.

                    And, take comfort in this: at Body Comfort there's a
                    thirty-day trial guarantee. Open every day 'til ten . . . and,
                    you get the lowest possible prices commensurate with the
                    highest quality.

                    Perhaps you should spend that important one-third of your
                    life in a Body Comfort Waterbed.

GENTLE VOCAL: WHAT A BEAUTIFUL WAY TO LAY YOUR BODY DOWN.

ANNCR TAG:	Take 101 to Whipple or Holly exit on Industrial Road just north of Circle Star Theatre.

This commercial is noteworthy because every word, every phrase, contributes to an overall, cohesive message. No wasted verbiage; no exaggerations; no false enthusiasm. And, the spot is pleasant to the ear.

Many commercials begin with a dramatized joke. They work well if the joke is amusing and *if the build-up connects logically with the sales message.* Here's an example of a humorous spot that works:[7]

AGENCY:	KKTD RADIO
CLIENT:	SOLOMON'S APPLE GARDEN
LENGTH:	:60
AUTHOR:	Sharon Yamane*

SFX:	(SOUND OF BIRDS CHIRPING)
EVE:	(SEXY) Hey Adam! Wanna bite of my forbidden fruit?
ADAM:	Got no time for that, Eve. I'm headed to Solomon's Apple Garden for the back to school sale. They've got iMacs starting at $899, Titanium Powerbooks from $1999, and so many more tempting offers I can't even count!
EVE:	And, when is this alluring sale?
ADAM:	August 30th through September 15th.
EVE:	Sounds too good to be true.
ADAM:	Oh come on Eve, it's for real! What've you got to lose? You've already been kicked outta the Garden of Eden!
EVE:	True, but what do I tell the boss?
ADAM:	Tell him we're off to get school supplies for Cain and Abel. We can get them new games at 50% off, too! It might get them to stop fighting over the pet snake.
EVE:	Good idea! By the way, I need to get some clothes on the way there. My fig leaves are coming loose.
ANNCR:	Solomon's Apple Garden. On the corner of Chapman and Pixley in Larkspur. Visit us now, for a heavenly sale.

By contrast, here's a commercial that spends fifty seconds on the joke, leaving a scant ten seconds for the commercial message. Even if the joke were worthy of a listener's time, the result is a wasted effort because the joke doesn't connect with the product. This spot is a close paraphrase of an actual broadcast commercial!

AGENCY:	MERRIAM, SUZUKI, & JEFFERSON
CLIENT:	MIDWEST FON-EZE DSL
TIME:	:60

SFX:	(TELEPHONE RINGS)
CLERK:	(CHEERFUL) Jetson Travel—how may we help you?
MAN:	(MAN IS STEREOTYPED OLD CRANK. HIS ANNOYANCE BUILDS THROUGHOUT SPOT) Got my plane tickets, and there's somethin' wrong!
CLERK:	I'm very sorry, sir. We go all out to get things right, and if there's a . . .
MAN:	(CUTTING HIM OFF.) I don't have all day to listen to that stuff. Just fix the problem.
CLERK:	(SLIGHTLY SHAKEN) Oh. Sorry, sir. I didn't mean to upset you— I just wanted to say that Jetson . . .
MAN:	(CUTTING HIM OFF) You're doin' it again!
CLERK:	(SOMEWHAT COWED) Please, let's start over. What's your complaint?
MAN:	Time's are wrong on my ticket.
CLERK:	How are they wrong?
MAN:	You got me flyin' out of Detroit (DEE-troit) at 8:20 A.M. and gettin' to Chicago at 8:33 A.M. That's only thirteen minutes!
CLERK:	Well, actually it's not a mistake. You see, Detroit's on Eastern time, and Chicago's on Central time.
MAN:	What? What the dickens does that mean?
CLERK:	There's a time change.
MAN:	A WHAT?
CLERK:	Let me explain. . . .
MAN:	Don't explain. Change the darn tickets!

CLERK: (GIVING UP) Sir, the tickets are correct. (GETS A BRIGHT IDEA. SPEAKS WITH MOCK CONFIDENTIAL TONE.) You see, you're flying on a new plane that's very, very fast.

MAN: Well, why the devil didn't you say so in the first place?

SFX: (RECEIVER BEING SLAMMED DOWN)

ANNCR: Slow computer? Is yours giving you fits 'cause it's not fast enough for your work? Call MIDWEST FON-EZE (pronounced FONE-ease), and join the magic world of DSL! It's as speedy as a jet plane!

In this example the connection between the alleged speed of a "new jet" and a speedy computer is flawed because it's illogical to compare physical speed (a jet) with the speed of electronic transmission. Additionally, nearly the entire spot is taken up with a joke that, while fairly funny, leaves a scant ten seconds for the sales pitch; finally, it's damaging to any advertiser's message to depict unpleasant fictitious customers to promote a product or service. Have you ever seen a commercial whose main character was stupid, gross, or offensive? Did you get the impression that it reflected the advertiser's concept of its customers?

Faulty Logic

Examples of faulty logic abound in radio and television commercials.[8] One, a television spot for a muscle car, sets its scene in the high desert. The car appears and drives past a black figure dressed as a knight. He's mounted on a black horse and, as the car passes by, the knight sets off on an effort to overtake the car. As the knight pounds along the two-lane road in pursuit, we see that he's brandishing a scythe, and we realize that he's the symbol of Death! As he nears the car—which, a super at the bottom of the screen informs us, is driven by a professional driver on a closed track—the driver shifts gears, takes off, leaving Death in the dust. Furious at losing a customer for the morgue, he flings his scythe to the ground in disgust.

So, what are the lessons here? If we buy this particular automobile, we'll be able to escape death, *if* we become a professional driver, and confine our jaunts to a closed track? It's obvious that the creator of this spot flunked Critical Thinking 101.

In another lapse of logic, we see the Big Bad Wolf attempting to blow down a house that shields the three little pigs. But the wolf fails because the house is protected by a security alarm system. Apparently, the creator of this spot believes that an alarm system will make a house resistant to high winds!

An even more curious spot shows us an SUV in profile. Behind it is an immense pile of luggage of many sizes and shapes. A man proceeds (for twenty-five seconds!) to struggle with the bags as he places them in the trunk. We hear him grunting (ten times) and making comments under his breath about the extreme weight of one large bag. At the twenty-five-second mark, he flings one last bag, a small one, into the trunk and slams down the lid. He turns away and moves toward the house, bent over and holding his back in obvious pain. In the final four seconds a VO announcer identifies the SUV's maker and tells us that it holds a lot of luggage. Because the vehicle is seen only in an unflattering side view, we're left without a visual image that could create a positive feeling about it. What we're left with is a memory of how difficult it is to load heavy suitcases into the car's trunk—not exactly what the sponsor had in mind.

Failure to Connect

Some spots are not illogical, but instead lack a structure that connects part one with part two. One ill-conceived commercial campaign for a bank opens its spots with questionable statements intended to capture our attention. The announcer asks: "Suppose you could have free gasoline for a month! Great, huh? Better still, what if you could have free gasoline for a year? What if you could have free gasoline forever." The pitch continues with a few more pointless questions, and then tells listeners they can have free checking at such-and-such bank. The disconnect between the opening attention grabber and the product being peddled should be apparent to all.

Another weird commercial shows a person in a canoe paddling toward the precipice of a very high waterfall. The canoe goes over the edge, and we follow its frightening descent all the way down to its destruction at the bottom. We then see a man and a woman who've observed this standing in front of an SUV. They shrug, get in their car and drive away. End of commercial.

Why is faulty logic so prevalent in radio and television commercials? The reality is that it's easy for creative minds to come up with several possibilities for making a particular point in sixty seconds or less; it takes restraint and judgment to recognize when a creative thought is just plain stupid.

RETAINING INTEREST DURING THE BODY OF A SPOT

Most good copy retains an audience's attention by giving concrete reasons for continued interest and attention. Two ways to do this are by explaining why this product or service is superior to its competition or, if the product aims at a highly specific audience or lacks significant competition, by simply explaining what's being offered. Late evening television commercials, especially on cable and independent stations, offer products that are of interest to those who might need them, and ignored by those who don't; for example, ads for ink-jet refills, big-band classic CDs and tapes, instant leak-sealer, first-aid kits, scratch remover, and solar garden lights. The main challenge of such copy is to get to the point ASAP, give a convincing sales pitch, and end up by revealing that the actual cost is less than the viewer had been led to expect. At times, this is accomplished by offering two items for the price of one. You'll find these commercials every evening on your television set.

Here's an example of a commercial written with sustained interest as its goal. It works within limits and, while not very imaginative, it offers reasons why people may want the product as well as explicit information as to where to get it. Many merchants shy away from fancy or artsy advertising, preferring instead a straightforward sales message.

AGENCY: Jefferson Advertising, Inc.
CLIENT: Mertel's Coffee Mills
LENGTH: 60 seconds

ANNCR: Are you a coffee lover? Most Americans are. Would you like to enter the world of gourmet coffees? Mertel's can help.

SFX: SOUND OF COFFEE BEING POURED INTO CUP

ANNCR: Gourmet coffee begins with whole beans, carefully selected, freshly roasted.

SFX: SOUND OF COFFEE BEANS BEING GROUND

ANNCR: Gourmet coffee is ground at home, just before brewing. Choose your coffee according to your taste and the time of day. Rich but mild Mocha Java for breakfast. Hearty French Roast for that midday pickup. Nutty Arabian with dinner. And Colombian decaf before bed. Sound inviting? You bet. Sound expensive? Not so. Mertel's feature forty coffee beans from around the world, and some are only pennies more per pound than canned coffees. And there's always a weekly special. This week, its Celebes Kalossi, at just $6.99 a pound! Remember—if you want gourmet coffee, begin with whole beans, and grind them just before brewing. Come to Mertel's Coffee Mills, and move into the world of gourmet coffee! We're located at the Eastside Mall, and on Fifth Street in downtown Russell. Mertel's Coffee Mills.

By contrast, here's a radio commercial that's creative and has flair. It has no difficulty retaining our interest regardless of our attitude toward the product. It's opening line immediately grabs our attention but, unlike the bad examples cited earlier, the payoff is worth our time.

CREATION AND
PRODUCTION: Chuck Blore & Don Richman, Inc.[9]
CLIENT: Campbell Soup
LENGTH: 30 seconds

DON: You're eating chunky chicken soup with a fork?

JOHN: Well, you've got to spear the chicken to get it into your mouth. Look at that. Look at the size of that. You gotta use a spoon for the noodles.

DON: You got some noodles on your fork.

JOHN: Yeah, but they slide through.

DON: Well, you use the spoon, you use the fork.

JOHN: That's right.

DON: Is chunky chicken a soup or a meal?

JOHN: I leave that up to the experts, but I personally . . .

DON: (OVER LAUGH) Why'd you say that?

JOHN: I know, but I mean, you know, I'm not a connoisseur in the food department but I would say it's a meal.

DON: But it's a soup.

JOHN: It's a meal within a soup can. Let's put it that way.

DON: Campbell's Chunky Chicken . . . it's the soup that eats like a meal.

THE STRUCTURAL CONCEPT OF "THE RULE OF THREE"

Most outstanding commercials are both subtle and complex. Chapter 5 provided some analysis of the structure of stories; another consideration is added here—the so-called rule of three. This long-recognized principle says that the sharpness and punch of one's comments are diluted by going beyond three words or phrases in a given sequence. Note how the rule of three is followed in this commercial script.

AGENCY: Ketchum Advertising, San Francisco
CLIENT: The Potato Board[10]
PRODUCT: Potatoes
TITLE: "Versatile"
LENGTH: 60 seconds

ANNCR: Here's another message from The Potato Board. Don't we Americans love food? Fast food . . . slow food . . . all kinds? But, above all, don't we love that good food—the potato? Today, the potato stands alone as the number one vegetable of versatility. And our friends at The Potato Board remind us that Americans crave potatoes in any and every form, for every meal. Why, Americans love potatoes as appetizers, in soups and salads, as entrees and side dishes, and, yes. . . . even as desserts.

   The Potato Board says any way you serve the all-American potato, you'll be getting an economical vegetable that has lots of nutrition, but not—I repeat not—lots of calories. So, whether you serve potatoes scalloped, hashed, or mashed . . . sliced or diced . . .

> French fried, boiled, or baked, in all their delicious versatility, The Potato Board says potatoes are America's favorite vegetable. Well, aren't they in your house?

Note that in this commercial the first grouping of three comes early: "Fast food . . . slow food . . . all kinds?" Also note that the first three sentences (beginning with "Here's another-" and ending with "—the potato?") form a complete expository unit and should be read in such a way as to give a sense of a beginning, a middle, and an ending—though not so obvious an ending as to make what follows seem tacked on.

The next set of three is less obvious. Here are the three parts of this segment of The Potato Board commercial:

1. "Why, Americans love potatoes as appetizers—"
2. "—in soups and salads,—"
3. "—as entrees and side dishes,—"

Then comes what seems to be a fourth element, ". . . even as desserts," but the ellipses indicate that this is to be set apart from the preceding sequence of three by a pause. These words become a group of three in themselves if an announcer pauses slightly between each word—"even . . . as . . . desserts." In analyzing this copy, you should not see *appetizers, soups, salads, entrees, side dishes,* and *desserts* as six points with equal stress.

The final set of three consists of the phrases "scalloped, hashed, or mashed," "sliced or diced," and "French fried, boiled, or baked." Two of the three phrases in this sequence are made up of three units each.

While the rule of three works well most of the time, like all other rules, it doesn't guarantee success, and its misuse can create a terrible commercial, as in this spot for an economy automobile. (This spot was written to make a point. It isn't a real commercial, or even a paraphrase of one, but it was fun writing it!)

ANNCR: Y'know, I'm an easy-going kinda guy. Just give me pizza, a burrito, chow mein—I'll get by just fine. No sushi, steak tartare, chardonnay—just plain American grub. Like I say, I'm easy to please.

The same goes for the car I drive. I don't need a satellite telling me how to get from here to there; I'm annoyed by a computerized voice telling me to fasten my seatbelt; and I don't believe the name of a car model has anything to do with masculinity—"the Cheeta," the "Grizzly," the "Coyote." I'd drive a car with a name like "the Poodle" if it had what I wanted: good looks, a smooth ride, and jackrabbit starts. Zero to sixty in five seconds. That's my kinda car!

Most of all, though, I want a car that's priced right, gets good mileage, and has a 100,000-mile warrantee. So, when I saw that

> Melikian's Motor Mart was having a sale on all Jupiter cars in stock, I headed right down to Auto Row, and staked my claim on their economy model. No frills, no deluxe paint job, and no fancy upholstery.
>
> Now, I just laugh when I pass those monster, bulked-up, gas-guzzling SUVs, park next to a $75,000 import, or see a luxury car being towed by a very un-luxurious tow truck!
>
> Like I say . . . . I'm just an easy-going kinda guy.

This pseudo-commercial uses the rule of three eight times in just sixty seconds! Read it aloud, and you'll see that the device actually becomes predictable and annoying. The ultimate rule, then, is to be skeptical about rules! Let a rule help you when it works, but be free to abandon it if it leads you to write bad copy!

When you set out to create a commercial, it's best to follow a systematic plan. The plan must be one that suits your personality, your creative aptitude, your work habits, and your persuasive abilities—*and* it must meet the needs (and whims!) of your client!

Only you can develop and follow a system that works well for you. As experience dictates, you should fine-tune your system, and learn from both successes and failures. With practice, you should tackle a commercial assignment with confidence and a minimum of wasted effort.

Commercials are created with very specific objectives. In conceiving a commercial, ask yourself three initial questions (yes, we're back to those fundamental questions again.):

1. *Who am I trying to reach?* This involves audience demographics—such factors as age, gender, ethnicity (if relevant), income level, educational level, and area of employment. It also involves defining the special interests of those you want to reach.

2. *What message do I want to convey?* Am I to describe a product? A service? Advertise a sales event? Establish the name of a product or business? Cultivate interest in an upcoming event? Underscore the prestige of a company? Stress the reliability of a product? These are but a few possibilities, but a clear answer to the question is mandatory if you hope to create an effective spot.

3. *What outcomes do I hope to bring about?* If I'm successful in reaching my target audience and in getting my message across, what will have changed? Will people buy the product or a service next time they make a purchase? Will they place an order over the toll-free number that's included in the message? Will they call for more information? Will they have a more positive attitude toward the sponsor?

It's obvious that the goal of commercials is to sell something. Radio and television are effective media for reaching the public with sales pitches for nearly any product and service imaginable. The most effective way to sell something is to persuade listeners/viewers that they need what you're offering. This in turn suggests that you offer arguments that will sway people to choose your product over its competitors.

NARRATIVE COMMERCIALS

The simplest commercials are straight narration without music or sound effects. Their purpose is to present a sales message without gimmickry and with no attempt to entertain. Here's an example of such a radio commercial. It sets out to make you hunger for the product and, if completely successful, will cause you to buy it next time you're near the client's bake shop.

AGENCY: Millar Advertising, Inc.
CLIENT: Andre's International Bakery
LENGTH: 60 seconds

ANNCR: Hot, fresh, breakfast rolls, glistening with melting butter! Croissants and cafe au lait. Raisin bran muffins to go with your poached eggs. Andre's has these delicacies, and they're waiting for you now. For afternoon tea, Andre suggests English crumpets, served with lemon curd. Or scones and pomegranate jam. For after-dinner desserts, how about baklava, the Persian delicacy made with dozens of layers of paper-thin pastry, honey, and chopped walnuts? Or, if your taste runs to chocolate, a German torte? These and dozens of other international delights are created daily by Andre and his staff. Made only of pure and natural ingredients—Grade-A cream and butter, natural unrefined sugar, pure chocolate and cocoa, and imported spices. For mouthwatering pastries, it's Andre's International Bakery. We bring you the best from the gourmet capitals of the world. Visit Andre's today! In the Eugene Shopping Center. Andre's!

Here are two straight narrative commercials written by Gerry Sher, Accounts Executive for KABL radio. With nothing but words and a single voice he manages to deliver his sales messages without extreme measures to force our attention. To Gerry, selling the product in this manner isn't merely the simplest and most economical way to get a message across—it's frequently the most effective. Single-voice spots, unless they're delivered by those who are instantly recognizable to an audience, are usually delivered by a "generic" announcer—that is, an announcer with a pleasant voice, good articulation, the ability to interpret copy for maximum effectiveness, and so forth.

CLIENT: Houston Hearing Aid Center[11]
LENGTH: 60 seconds
BY: Gerry Sher

ANNCR: Good evening, this is Angelina Bellini. Listen to me whisper this sentence. (WHISPERING) Do you have difficulty hearing someone speaking in a low voice? (NORMAL VOLUME) If you couldn't hear my whispered message, then you might need hearing assistance. Al Sawyers and associates at the Houston Hearing Aid Center are licensed hearing aid dispensers and offer a complete audiometric service. The Houston Hearing Aid Center has been helping the hearing-impaired since 1947 with sales, service, and repairs on all brands of hearing aids. Offering a senior citizens' discount, 30-day free trial, and credit terms, Al Sawyers of the Houston Hearing Aid Center can help you create a brighter outlook on life with the correct hearing aid. Call Al Sawyers at the Houston Hearing Aid Center, 555-3333, for an appointment, or for their free in-home service. This is Angelina for the Houston Hearing Aid Center.

CLIENT: Norwegian Designs
LENGTH: 60 seconds
BY: Gerry Sher

ANNCR: If I told you I have a hang-up for you, would that be misleading? I'm Nanette of Norwegian Designs. We're the new and exclusive working wall system store in the Financial District. At Norwegian Designs, our hang-ups are leasable. It's probably the first time anyone has offered your walls a new look with suspended furniture. I could describe the file systems, or the hidden bar, or many of the other features of space-saving wall units for your office, but I'd much prefer if you'd walk in on me, and look at them in all their displayed beauty. I'm at the corner of State and Michigan. Norwegian Designs. Oh, I wasn't fooling about the leasing part—we really do lease this office furniture. We carry major systems of suspended furniture, with great varieties of wood, tones, and colors. Your office may need just an inexpensive facelift that's totally utilitarian. Stop by and see us at Norwegian Designs. What a hang-up!

DIALOGUE FOR TWO OR MORE VOICES

A step beyond single-voice commercials in complexity and cost are those featuring two or more voices. Introducing a second speaker almost always turns a sales message into a brief dramatic scene. In going in this direction, characterization becomes a factor.

Here's an effective commercial written for two actors. The spot's opening gives no clue as to where the story is going, but it immediately grabs our attention. Note how Chuck Blore establishes the shopper's personality before getting to the final humorous exchange.

CLIENT: O'Neill's Department Store[12]
AGENCY: Chuck Blore & Don Richman, Inc.

DEPARTMENT STORE CLERK, YOUNG WOMAN

CLERK: May I help you, sir?

MAN: Oh, uh, yeah. I was looking for a uh, birthday present for my wife.

CLERK: Did you have anything particular in mind?

MAN: Well, I was thinking about maybe getting her some, uh, under, uh, some . . .

CLERK: O'Neill's has a lovely selection of lingerie. What size do you think she would take?

MAN: Whadda you take—about a large?

CLERK: Ah, no I take a small . . .

MAN: You're both really about the same size.

CLERK: Uh huh . . .

MAN: Your neck is a little longer . . .

CLERK: (EMBARRASSED LAUGH) O'Neill's prides itself on its lingerie.

MAN: Oh. that's good. She has, uh, winter pajamas, y'know . . .

CLERK: She has winter, uh, pajamas . . .

MAN: Yeah, they're flannel, and I thought maybe she'd like something with a little more air in there . . .

CLERK: Uh, yes . . . I see what you mean. Well, how about something a little sexy? Uh, maybe a lovely peignoir set . . .

MAN: One of those black . . .

CLERK: Uh huh.

MAN: Well, I don't think so . . . We're married, see, and her mother's staying with us.

MUSIC: (FEMALE CHORUS) It's happening now at O'Neill's. (REPEAT, AND FADE TO CLOSE.)

This commercial is written to make only a few points: to mention the name of the sponsor three times—twice in the dialogue, the third in the jingle; to let listener's know that O'Neill's clerks are friendly, helpful, and have a sense of humor; to mention women's lingerie; and to put a human face on the sponsor's store. The customer is funny as he bumbles toward finding a gift for his wife, but he's also sympathetic. O'Neill's doesn't insult potential customers by portraying the man as a buffoon. It's important, with but thirty to sixty seconds available, to focus on a few important points to avoid clutter and information overload.

Here's another two-voice commercial that takes a comic approach to evoke friendly and positive feelings about its sponsor. This commercial for AT&T long distance services was created before deregulation. Today, because deregulation brought with it strong competition, AT&T has adopted aggressive and often irritating approaches to sell its services, and humorous institutional advertising has been lost as a consequence.

CREATION AND	
PRODUCTION:	Chuck Blore & Don Richman, Inc.[13]
CLIENT:	AT&T
LENGTH:	60 seconds

CATHIANNE:	(ON PHONE) Hello.
DANNY:	Uh, hi. You probably still remember me, Edward introduced us at the seminar.
CATHIANNE:	Oh, the guy with the nice beard.
DANNY:	I don't know whether it's nice . . .
CATHIANNE:	It's a gorgeous beard.
DANNY:	Well, thank you. uh, listen, I'm gonna, uh, be in the city next Tuesday and I was, y'know, wondering if we could sorta, y'know, get together for lunch?
CATHIANNE:	How 'bout dinner?
DANNY:	Dinner? Dinner! Dinner's a better idea. You could pick your favorite restaurant and . . .
CATHIANNE:	How 'bout my place? I'm my favorite cook.
DANNY:	Uh, your place. Right. Sure. That's great to me.
CATHIANNE:	Me too. It'll be fun.
DANNY:	Yeah . . . listen, I'll bring the wine.
CATHIANNE:	Perfect. I'll drink it.
BOTH:	(LAUGH)
DANNY:	Well, OK, then, I guess it's a date. I'll see you Tuesday

CATHIANNE:	Tuesday. Great.
DANNY:	Actually, I just, uh, I called to see how you were and y'know, Tuesday sounds fine!
SOUND:	(PHONE HANGS UP)
DANNY:	(YELLING) Tuesday . . . AHHHH . . . she's gonna see me Tuesday. (FADE)
SUNG:	(REACH OUT, REACH OUT AND TOUCH SOMEONE)

This commercial for AT&T is entertaining and would seem on the surface to lack a logical appeal. Yet, because the product (long-distance phone calls) is important to listeners separated from family or friends, the spot plants the idea of reaching them by long distance.

Another spot by Blore and Richman tells women a great deal about men, especially when they're together doing "men's things." In the commercial, we hear the voice of the main character but not that of those on the other end of the line. Additional voices are from Ernie's co-workers who have a good time heckling him.

AGENCY:	Chuck Blore & Don Richman, Inc.[14]
CLIENT:	AT&T
TITLE:	"Rock-A-Bye-Baby"
LENGTH:	:60
ERNIE:	(ON PHONE) Yeah, hi, honey, it's me . . . well it was a piece of cake actually. We all got here. We've got about 17,000 feet of snow out here.,
CHUCK:	(OFF MIC) More 'n that!
SUNG:	(REACH OUT, REACH OUT AND TOUCH SOMEONE)
SFX:	(GUYS TALKING, LAUGHING, BUILDING A FIRE, TAUNTING, BEHIND)
ERNIE:	We got ourselves a ton of firewood and a great fire goin' . . .
CHUCK:	Card game goin' . . .
ERNIE:	I'll be right there, guys . . . uh? (LOWERED, INTIMATE VOICE) Course I love you . . .
CHUCK:	(FALSETTO) I love you too, honey!!! C'mon and play cards!!!
JOHN:	(LAUGH)
ERNIE:	Just the guys . . . mmm . . . put him on, put him on. . . .

CHUCK: C'mon Ern!

ERNIE: (LOW VOLUME, HOPING NOT TO BE HEARD) Good night, doggy woggy woggy woggy . . .

CHUCK &
JOHN: (LAUGH)

CHUCK: Woof-woof! ! !

ERNIE: Bye-bye, bye-bye, doggy. These guys are razzin' me here . . .

CHUCK: Woof-woof, Ern!

JOHN: Woof-woof!

ERNIE: (WHISPERS) Now, c'mon, I'm gonna . . . honey, be reasonable . . .

JOHN: (HOWLS)

ERNIE: . . . will ya? The guys . . . put him on.

Hello, baby, this is Daddy—Daddy, woogy-woo-doo.
Mmmm, oh, I wouldn't let a night go by without our little song . . .
ROCK-A-BYE-BABY . . .

CHUCK &
JOHN: (JOIN IN) on the tree top, when the wind blows the cradle will rock . . .

SUNG: (REACH OUT, REACH OUT AND TOUCH SOMEONE)

PRODUCTION COMMERCIALS—MUSIC, SOUND EFFECTS, VOICES

Many commercials make effective use of music. Bob Pritikin nearly always opens his spots with music. At times the music is instrumental, and it both opens and accompanies the dialogue throughout the commercial. Pritikin's radio commercial for Fuller Paint became an instant hit, as listeners called radio stations across the country to ask where copies might be found. Here is the spot and Bob Pritikin's comments about it and radio as a creative medium.

AGENCY: Pritikin & Gibbons Communications[15]
CLIENT: Fuller Paint Company
MEDIUM: Radio
LENGTH: 60 seconds

ANNCR: The Fuller Paint Company invites you to stare with your ears at . . . yellow. (FLUTE ARPEGGIO) Yellow is more then just a color. (FLUTE TWEETS) Yellow is a state of mind. (FLUTE—FLURRY

OF QUICK NOTES) A way of life. (FLUTE) Ask any taxi driver about yellow, he'll tell you. (FLUTE) Or a banana Salesman. (FLUTE) Or a coward. (FLUTE—DESCENDING NOTES) They'll tell you about yellow.

SFX: (PHONE RINGS)

ANNCR: Oh, excuse me. Yello! (GONG) Yes, I'll take your order. (GONG) Dandelions, a dozen (FLUTE); a pound of melted butter (FLUTE); lemon drops and a drop of lemon (TINKLING OF TRIANGLE), and one canary (PICCOLO TWEETS) who sings a yellow song. (LONGER PICCOLO ARPEGGIO) Anything else? (GONGS AND FLUTE)

SFX: (CALLER HANGS UP)

ANNCR: Yello? Yello? Yello? (GONG BETWEEN EACH "YELLO") Oh, disconnected. She'll call back. (MUSIC: RICKY-TICK IN BG WITH GUITAR TWANGS TO PUNCTUATE—UNDER TO END) If you want yellow that's yellow-yellow, remember to remember the Fuller Paint Company. A century of leadership in the chemistry of color. For the Fuller color center nearest you, check your phone directory.

           The yellow pages, of course.

SFX: (MUSIC UP AND OUT)

This radio commercial by Bob Pritikin was written for Fuller Paint in the 1960s. It was so novel and effective that it was included as the only commercial in a presentation album, *The First Fifty Years of Radio*. When played on radio stations announcers, including DJs, invariably commented on its creativity and its unique use of radio as a medium. Pritikin made these comments on his motivation for this breakthrough commercial.[16]

> That radio commercial was one in a series designed to paint dazzling colors on the screen of the listener's imagination. It blended music effects and word pictures into a statement that I believe is far more graphic than could ever have been achieved in the more literal pages of a magazine or, for that matter, on a television screen.

He continues by stressing that the medium of radio demands a conception that respects its uniqueness:

> When you write radio for the eye, you must know the magic of words. You must know that verbs are more visible than adjectives, and that a silent pause can be the most dramatic language of all. . . . Perhaps a psychologist could best explain the phenomenon of radio and its incomparable potential to carve deep recollective impressions. I believe it has to do with the fact that listeners are required to create their own mental pictures. . . . What's the key to writing great radio? Engage the listener as your co-author.[17]

Here are two more commercials by Bob Pritikin, each of which makes effective use of music.

AGENCY: Pritikin & Gibbons Communications[18]
CLIENT: Selix [PRONOUNCED SEE-lix]
LENGTH: 60 seconds

MUSIC: (ORCHESTRA WITH DEFINITE BEAT. PLAYS UNDER ENTIRE
            SPOT)

SINGER: (MALE) Y'know, penguins are cute, penguins are fun,
            but you wouldn't want your daughter to marry one.
            Penguins are wild in the arctic zone,
            but don't dampen the prom with a penguin clone.
            (MUSIC UP FOR THREE SECONDS)
            When you rent for a formal event,
            Don't turn yourself into a penguin,
            Turn yourself in to Selix.

MUSIC: (UP TWO SECONDS, THEN UNDER)

ANNCR: Getting married? Don't look like a penguin at the altar—
            The penguin look is for the birds.
            Selix is THE expert in formal wear for weddings, featuring the great
            designers—Cardin, Yves St. Laurent.
            For your wedding, be sure of perfect taste with a little dash.

SINGER: Don't turn yourself into a penguin,
            Turn yourself into Selix.

ANNCR: Get married in a Selix tux—low as 59.95.

MUSIC: (UP TO CLOSE)

AGENCY: Pritikin & Gibbons Communications
CLIENT: Swenson's Ice Cream
LENGTH: 60 seconds

SINGING: (FEMALE VOICES) Turn on your tongue, Turn on your tongue,
            Turn your tongue on to Swenson's Ice Cream Factory.

MUSIC: (INSTRUMENTAL—AFTER ACCOMPANYING VOICES, MUSIC
            CONTINUES UNDER THROUGHOUT)

ANNCR: (INSTRUMENTAL MUSIC IN BG THROUGHOUT) Oh, what a
            marvelous instrument is the tongue. Bring your entire tongue to

Swenson's Ice Cream Factory, and let your tongue actually watch the fresh wild blackberries fold into thick, rich, ice cream. It's true! It's made before your very tongue—the creamy caramel cashew, banana brickle, the chocolate eclair ice cream. Now, let your tongue luxuriate in the crescendo of fresh almonds on top of a hot apple sundae—or the pure vanilla ice cream cone that weighs a full quarter pound . . .

SINGING: Turn your tongue on to Swenson's Ice Cream Factory.

MUSIC: (UP TO END)

The Folger Coffee commercial that follows features a song by a popular male singing group, The Limeliters. Glenn Yarbrough, the lead singer, sang lyrics written by Bob Pritikin in a mellow, hauntingly pleasing voice.

AGENCY: Pritikin & Gibbons Communications
CLIENT: Folgers Coffee
LENGTH: 60 seconds

MUSIC: (LIMELITERS SING BEHIND GLENN YARBROUGH)

SINGING: When I say coffee, this I mean,
Coffee from the mountain bean,
Nurtured by the mountain soil,
Coffee beans for Folgers.

ANNCR: Y'know, this coffee business is a pretty crazy business. Every company says it has the best coffee. Yuban says theirs is best. Hills Brothers? They say theirs is the best. Maxwell House . . . well, they say they're the best. MJB's the best as far as they're concerned. And, Folgers? Well, we say we're the best. Now, it stands to reason that all these coffees can't be the best. If there is a "best," only one can be the best. If you left it up to a popular vote, I know which one would win. The top-selling coffee in the west—could it be that that's the best?

SINGING: When I say coffee I mean Folgers.

WRITING FOR PRODUCTS THAT LACK LOGICAL APPEAL

Commercials for many products avoid any pretense of logical appeal because there really is little that sets them apart from their competitors. In the United States, most commercials for soft drinks and American mainline beers (as contrasted with imports and microbrewed beer and ale) are contrived to achieve two modest objectives: to make friends for the product while conveying the impression that in choosing it, one becomes a member of an in-group.

Television commercials for Budweiser, Coors, Miller, O'Doul's, Molson, or Old Milwaukee, for example, are created to achieve these ends. One brewer tells us that "it's the water"; Budweiser says its beer is "beechwood aged," and that it's "the King of Beers"; Miller Lite advises us that "Life is Good!," while its spots for cold-filtered draft implore us to "Stay Cool." It's hard to imagine a customer rushing out to buy a six-pack of anything because of such slogans! Many beer commercials shamelessly exploit women with the heavy-handed message that beautiful young women will trade anything they possess for a six-pack of beer—so long as it's offered by a virile hunk of a man!

Soft drinks have a related problem. In a commercial for Diet Coke, a singer asks us to buy it "just for the taste of it."[19] For the same company's Classic Coke, we're told it's "the real thing." A competitor responds with Ray Charles and a backup chorus telling us that "Pepsi's the right thing, Baby—uh-huh, uh-huh." In another spot, Pepsi hardly surprises us with the news that "nothing else is a Pepsi." A soft drink (7-Up) that competes with both colas, once was promoted as the "Uncola." It's doubtful that these phrases make a difference to consumers.

Unlike most popular beers, soft drinks vary greatly in flavor (e.g., cola, root beer, orange, lemon-lime, etc.), yet all are made from essentially the same ingredients: water, sweetener, coloring, and flavorings. There truly is no logical reason to prefer Sprite over Dr. Pepper, so we aren't given rational reasons to buy one or the other; we're not told that one is more nutritious, nor are we asked to believe that a particular cola will cure us of anything other than our thirst. Because of this, ingenuity is required to produce commercials that grab and hold our attention, mildly entertain us, and leave us with agreeable feelings toward the product.

This spot by Blore and Richman makes its case for Rainier Ale with the help of singer Pearl Bailey.

AGENCY: Chuck Blore & Don Richman, Inc.[20]
CLIENT: Rainier Ale
TALENT: Pearl Bailey

PEARL: (SINGING, FADE IN) . . . The Rainier Ale . . .

ANNCR: (SINGING CONTINUES UNDER) That's Pearl Bailey. She says her canary taught her that song

PEARL: Well, that's true, honey. And, it's funny because he used to just mope around in his cage all day. That canary really had the blues. And he was afraid of the cat.

ANNCR: He was yellow?

PEARL: Who you talking about, the canary?

ANNCR: Yeah.

PEARL: Of course, darling. One day, listen, I poured some Rainier Ale in that child's watercup . . .

ANNCR: Rainier Ale?

PEARL: And that canary tore the bars off his cage, he chased the cat out of the house, and came back in singing.

MUSIC: (PEARL, SINGING) You're down with a case of the blues, and you've got a face that refuses to smile. Here's how you get up off the ground, you keep some Rainier Ale around, and every li'l old pound of you will wail—oh, honey, go get that Rainier Ale. (SPOKEN, AS MUSIC ENDS WITH A FLOURISH) This is the greatest ale, well, what can I tell ya?

ANNCR: (CANARY TWEETS THROUGH TAG) Sick's Rainier Brewing Company, Seattle, Washington.

Standing apart from other types of commercials in this category is a small number classified as "institutional." Institutional advertising, where the objective is to create or maintain a favorable public attitude toward a particular company, is less obviously devoted to "selling" than are most commercials. Chevron features spots that, in several instances, show a wildlife area that has been rehabilitated and dedicated by Chevron as a bird or animal sanctuary. The conclusion of the spot asks: "Do people really care about wildlife?" It then supplies the answer to its own question: "People Do!" Nothing is said about the quality of the fuel Chevron manufactures, and no attempt is made to sell anything. It's produced simply to generate a positive feeling toward the company.

Here are some suggestions and tips for conceiving and writing commercials for radio.

1. Try to avoid copy that's contrary to your principles.
2. All other things being equal, avoid trite or hackneyed copy. You may, on a rare occasion, want to write a cliché-ridden commercial, but you'd need to justify it on the basis of selling your product. Especially poor is the commercial that has this structure:
   "Do you (feel, need, hate, etc.)" . . .
   "Well, we've got just the thing for you . . ."
   "_____ (name of product) has _____ (invented name of nonexistent magic ingredient), and it's guaranteed to relieve (control, eliminate, improve— choose your own promise)
   "So, run on down to . . ."
3. Always attempt to create copy that has merit, is well written for oral delivery, and demonstrates a creative approach.
4. Humorous commercials are fine, but remember that a clever commercial that doesn't sell is rather easy to write, but misses the point of commercials.

In later years, you may have to write copy that violates all of these principles. Right now, though, it's to your advantage to practice writing effective and tasteful commercials while you're learning your craft and before impossible demands and deadlines force you into compromising your creative judgment.

Here are radio spots that I believe make good use of the aural medium. Eric Poole, whose opening lines for La Belles French Bakery began this chapter, is the winner of many awards for creative and effective commercials, and one of his most amusing spots follow. His structures his radio ads to attract attention and retain listener interest, while hitting home with sales messages.[21]

AGENCY: SPLASH RADIO, ERIC POOLE
CLIENT: PUPSICKLES
PRODUCT: INTRO
"Research Lab"   AS PRODUCED

SFX: FOOTSTEPS

MAN: And this is our motivational research center. . . .

GUY: Wow . . .

MAN: Where we do all our doggie-treat research.

GUY: Doggie treat?

MAN: Yeah, dogs are capable of much more than you think.

GUY: Really?

MAN: Oh, yes. They've just never had the right motivation.

GUY: Oh.

MAN: What does your dog do?

GUY: Well, he rolls over, plays dead . . .

MAN: Exactly. Now in here . . .

SFX: DOOR OPEN, PIANO, TAP DANCING

CHOREO-
GRAPHER: Okay, girls, big finish!

GUY: Dogs tap-dancing?

MAN: Yeah, they want the new frozen treat for dogs, Pupsickles.

GUY: Pupsickles?

MAN: It's like snow cones for your dog. Now in here . . .

SFX: DOOR OPEN, JAZZ COMBO PLAYING

GUY:	A jazz quartet!
MAN:	You should hear Muffin's tenor sax solo.
GUY:	Wow.
MAN:	We've found dogs will do anything for Pupsickles. And over here . . .
SFX:	DOOR OPEN, TYPEWRITERS
GUY:	Secretarial school?
MAN:	Typing, dictation, and shortpaw.
ANNCR:	Unleash your dog's potential with Pupsickles, the world's first frozen treat for dogs. There's never been anything like it. It's full of flavor, but has no calories, fat, or sugar. And unlike real popsickles, it won't upset your dog's stomach.
SFX:	DOOR OPEN, MUSIC UP
MAN:	And this is our malt shop.
GUY:	Lotta dogs eating Pupsickles . . .
MAN:	Uh-huh. Smart as they are, they still think it's the real thing.
ANNCR:	Pupsickles, the world's first frozen treat for dogs. New in your grocer's ice cream freezer. Go fetch some today.

This commercial for Allison's Pet Center captures our attention, and eventually justifies our interest by giving us a good laugh.

CLIENT:	Allison's Pet Center
OCCASION:	Christmas Sale
WRITTEN BY:	Brian Underwood*
LENGTH:	:60

SFX:	QUIET APPLAUSE, AS IN A CONCERT HALL
ANNCR:	(DIGNIFIED, OVER SFX): Good evening. I'm here at the Civic Opera House where the renowned dancer Vladmir Brokoyov (VLAD-uh- meer bro-KOY-off) is here to dance his interpretation of the Christmas Season.
SFX:	BALLET MUSIC UP FULL. UNDER AFTER FOUR SECONDS.
ANNCR:	Brokoyov enters stage, and begins with a beautifully executed pirouette, revealing a sign on the back of his leotard that reads,

"Allison's Pet Center shares the holiday spirit with a Christmas Sale." He's actually spinning rather fast now as a chorus of guppies and goldfish enter, each wearing a letter spelling out "Ninety-nine cents each." Brokoyov is now spinning extremely fast, doing his famous interpretation of a squirrel monkey, which according to the program now sell for only two-hundred-fifty each.

SFX: SPLASH

ANNCR: Such grace—Brokoyov just dove straight into the ten-gallon aquarium, which Allison's is offering for only thirty-nine ninety-five, including the filter.

SFX: LOUD CRASH

ANNCR: I don't think Brokoyov was counting on that filter. . . .

SFX: SIREN

ANNCR: . . . And the paramedics have arrived; they are wheeling Brokoyov away, and his flowing eloquence is still apparent, despite the probable hernia. He should be out before Christmas so he'll still have a chance to get to Allison's Pet Center, at Hewitt and Oak, in Richmond. Good night from Civic Opera House.

At times, the occasion requires a sincere—but not heavy-handed—style. This commercial for Hallmark Cards invokes the themes of young love, separation, and giving. It was created by Chuck Blore and Don Richman, two of the most creative and honored commercial writers in the history of American radio:

CREATION AND
PRODUCTION: Chuck Blore & Don Richman, Inc.[22]
CLIENT: Hallmark Cards
LENGTH: 60 seconds

JOSH: My dad says we'll only be gone 4 to 5 weeks, tops.

NANCY: You're going to call me, aren't you?

JOSH: You know I'm gonna call you.

NANCY: I have a surprise for ya.

JOSH: Oh.

NANCY: Pick a hand . . .

JOSH: Right hand . . .

NANCY:	Okay, see this?
JOSH:	What is it?
NANCY:	It's a charm. All you do is rub his stomach and you'll have luck for the rest of the day.
JOSH:	Thanks, I have something for you also.
NANCY:	You got me something?
JOSH:	Here, it's a card.
NANCY:	Ohhhh!
JOSH:	It's a Hallmark card.
NANCY:	(LAUGHS)
JOSH:	You're gonna read it, aren't ya?
NANCY:	Of course. (PAUSE) Ohhh! I love you too. (LAUGHS)
JOSH:	You don't have to get all choked up about it.
NANCY:	Gimme a hug, man.
UNISON:	(LAUGHING)
ANNCR:	Sharing caring feelings, one-to-one, heart-to-heart. How could you give anything less than a Hallmark Card? Hallmark Cards. When you care enough.

Gerry Sher, longtime radio account executive and scriptwriter, gives us a commercial that calls for characterization:

LENGTH:	60 seconds[23]
MUSIC:	INSTRUMENTAL FROM "FIDDLER ON THE ROOF"
AUTHOR:	GERRY SHER

ANNCR:	Ah-ha, it's a New York flavor in music . . . and at David's you'll get the New York flavor in deli. How can the true taste be transferred to Des Moines? It's simple. You just serve true Eastern beef, cured and pickled to David's unmatched palate, and sliced to your order. Of course, there's hot New York corned beef . . . hot pastrami . . . Hebrew National Salami . . . lox . . . bagels . . . and much much more—all with David's taste buds controlling the taste that hasn't been in Des Moines until now. At David's, when you taste the

Kosher pickles and the sour tomatoes, you'll remember those days. How about a knish—potato, kasha, or beef? If you've never had a David's knish, then you're in for a gourmet's delight. Actually, David's wife makes them, but where would David be without her anyway? Mrs. David also makes the matzo ball soup, the borscht, and the change. David's isn't easy to find, but it's worth the look. To find David's, first find the Flatiron Building, and there, practically in its shadow on Oak Street, is David's. Actually, it's next to Logan's Irish Pub. David's—777 Oak Street . . . A New York tradition in Des Moines.

These radio commercials are effective, creative, and frequently entertaining. Perhaps you also like them, or perhaps you don't—but at least you can see how each tries to make use of radio's unique qualities.[24]

As promised earlier, here's the complete La Belle's French Bakery "Fat Farm" commercial.

AGENCY: SPLASH RADIO[25]
CLIENT: La Belle's French Bakery
PRODUCT: LOW FAT DESSERTS

SFX: (BIRDS CHIRPING)

MAN: So let me get this straight. You grow fat?

GUY: Uh-huh, I'm a fat farmer.

MAN: Where do you grow this fat?

GUY: Right here. On my fat farm.

MAN: Mm-hmm.

GUY: See, I plant the little fat globules in the furrows, and they grow into these giant majestic stalks of fat!

MAN: Stalks of fat . . .

GUY: Well, you know all those fatty desserts you ate as a kid . . .

MAN: Uh-huh . . .

GUY: Well, I grow the fat they put in 'em.

MAN: So you'll be closing down soon . . .?

GUY: (GASP) Closing down?

MAN: Now that LaBelle's has introduced the world's first low-fat desserts . . .

GUY:	Low-fat desserts?
MAN:	Uh-huh. Four different mouth-watering goodies, like Napoleons, petit fours . . .
GUY:	Oh, boy . . .
MAN:	And they're baked by LaBelle, so they taste great.
GUY:	And they're light?
MAN:	Yep. No cholesterol, and 98% fat free.
GUY:	Fat free?
MAN:	Fat free.
GUY:	But this is a fat farm. I grow fat!
MAN:	I know you do.
GUY:	If La Belle's making fat-free snacks, what'll I grow?
MAN:	Well, they still need those delicious fillings.
GUY:	Well, there you go. I'll plant pudding.
ANNCR:	New LaBelle low fat desserts. No Cholesterol and 97% fat free. Now you can have your cake and eat it, too.

TELEVISION COMMERCIALS

Television commercials differ from radio commercials in obvious ways. They're usually briefer, running from fifteen to thirty seconds; they use music and sound effects more often; and they seldom are performed live. Because television is a visual medium, most advertisers want to show their products or services. This means that the majority of television commercials feature voice-over narration. The face of a television commercial announcer rarely appears on the screen, unless that person is a famous actor, singer, or dancer. Commercials that feature an on-screen announcer, usually confine the appearance to a few moments of introduction at the beginning.

Television scripts are often storyboarded. The standard arrangement for a storyboard is to sketch key visual aspects in boxes on the left side of the page, and match the sketches with the audio portion on the right side. Storyboards are much like cartoon strips in newspapers. The cartoonist matches ongoing dialogue with drawings showing key visual moments. You can learn much about storyboarding from the comics. You'll find a storyboarded script in Chapter 12, "Script Formats and Notes about Scripts."

The following television scripts were created by students in a course titled Writing for the Electronic Media. The author's analysis follows each script.

AGENCY: VIRTUAL IMPACT
CLIENT: BRIGGS COFFEE COMPANY
PRODUCT: JUMPIN' JAVA
AUTHOR: BRIAN UNDERWOOD*

VIDEO	AUDIO
	NOTE: ALL SOUND IS SLIGHTLY MUTED TO DRAW MORE ATTENTION TO THE VISUAL.
LARGE PILE OF COFFEE BEANS	SFX: BRIEF PHONE RINGING, FOLLOWED BY A CLICK, AS IF THE PHONE WAS PICKED UP
MCU MAN (AGE: LATE TWENTIES)	MAN: Hello, Claire? (PAUSE) You didn't stick around for breakfast the other day. (PAUSE) Don't you like coffee?
FREEZE FRAME: VO ANNCR:	ANNCR: Some companies would have you believe that coffee and sex are closely linked.
UNFREEZE FRAME, MAN CONTINUES	Hello? Hello? (PAUSE, MAN SIGHS) SFX: DIALING PHONE NUMBER
FREEZE FRAME	ANNCR (VO): At Jumpin' Java, we want to dispel these myths of causality between coffee and sex.
UNFREEZE FRAME	MAN: Hello, Debbie? (PAUSE) Remember me? (PAUSE) No, from last month. (PAUSE) No, this isn't Ted. I took you to that little theater with all the sexy . . .
FREEZE FRAME	ANNCR (VO): If you're interested in the former, we suggest you try dark, rich, Jumpin' Java. If you're interested in the latter, you're on your own.
HUGE PILE OF COFFEE BEANS. CAN OF JUMPIN' JAVA RISES FROM WITHIN THE PILE OF BEANS	SFX: DIALING PHONE, RING, PICKED UP ANNCR (VO): Break new grounds with Jumpin' Java.

HOLD ON CAN   MAN (VO): Hello, Doris? (PAUSE,
                                     PERVERTED LAUGH) Guess who this
                                     is. Hello?

ANALYSIS OF JUMPIN' JAVA TELEVISION COMMERCIAL
BRIAN UNDERWOOD
After seeing as many coffee commercials as I have, I've noticed that most if not all of them appeal to sexual urges, most by showing potentially romantic situations with a "wink-wink" as to what happens next. To make this one different, I turned it around, by clearly saying that this coffee is not at all suggested to be helpful in that arena. This is said slightly to take aim at the competitors who blatantly do. There is also some hostile wit directed at the gentleman on the phone who can't seem to get a second date. Hopefully the implication is clear enough that there is a reason why he can't get a second date, and thus he provides a cathartic outlet for anyone who has tried dating like that and recognizes his antics. Not even a really good coffee can save this guy.

AGENCY: THE ASSOCIATES
CLIENT: PURE SANANI
LENGTH: 30 seconds
AUTHOR: Voltaire Villanueva*

VIDEO AUDIO

MCU OF MAN IN AN   SFX OF AIRPLANE AMBIANCE
AIRPLANE WAITING FOR COFFEE

MS OF FLIGHT ATTENDANT
GOING THROUGH AISLES
SERVING COFFEE

TWO-SHOT OF MAN AND
FLIGHT ATTENDANT

XCU OF FASTEN SEAT BELT SIGN   SFX: BELL RINGING SEAT BELT
TURNING ON

LS OF MAN WALKING AWAY FROM   SFX: WIND BLOWING
CRASHED PLANE IN THE HOT
DESERT

WS OF MAN PASSING BY AN OASIS   SFX: WATER CRASHING ONTO
WITH A WATERFALL   ROCKS

WS OF MAN PASSING BY AN OASIS
OF WOMEN OFFERING BEER   MUSIC: REGGAE MUSIC

WS MAN RUNNING TO AN OASIS OF PURE SANANI COFFEE

MUSIC: HALLELUJAH CHORUS

SUPER OF PURE SANANI GRAPHIC

ANNCR: (VO) Pure Sanani. Arabian Mocha, slowly roasted to perfection.

FADE OUT

ANALYSIS OF TELEVISION COMMERCIAL FOR PURE SANANI COFFEE
VOLTAIRE VILLANUEVA

This television commercial appeals to those who basically are coffee drinkers. It opens with a man on a plane waiting for his coffee to be served. Once the flight attendant reaches him though, the seat belt sign goes on and in the next shot, the plane has crashed in the desert with him being the lone survivor. So he walks past several mirages, but none seems to capture his attention, except the one with Pure Sanani coffee. So he runs over, picks up the cup and rejoices. The purpose of having the man pass the first two mirages, especially the one with women and the beer, is to give the idea that nothing could be better than a warm cup of Pure Sanani. The Halleluiah chorus at the end gives the idea of rejoicing over the finding of the coffee. The chorus also explains one need, the need to believe in the miraculous.

QUESTIONS

Select 5 radio and 5 television scripts from Appendix A and analyze them in terms of:

1. Intended audience

2. Device(s) used to gain attention

3. Means of selling the product or service: does it use logic, humor, enticement, other?

4. Development of the story: does it flow easily? is it "seamless?"

5. Conclusion: does it justify the means used to gain attention?

6. Finally, is it persuasive?

NOTES

1. Courtesy of the Chuck Blore Company.
2. Courtesy of Eric Poole, Spash Radio, Los Angeles.
3. These particular commercials may be found only in archival sources. Collections of commercials are produced and sold to libraries and college audiovisual (AV) centers on a regular basis. These include annual CLIO Award winners, as well as collections of "The Best Commercials You Never Saw," "America's Funniest . . . ," and so forth. Use the Internet to find what may be available at AV departments near you by using San Francisco State University as a model: enter its name on a search engine; select AV/ITV; click on "media catalog," then enter "TV commercials" in a box on the upper left of the screen. Click on "submit."
4. Bob Garfield, writing for *Advertising Age,* July 23, 2001, http://www.adreview.com
5. This absurd opening is a paraphrase of an actual spot for a finance company!

6. Courtesy of Robert C. Pritikin.

7. This excellent spot was written by Sharon Yamane while a student in Writing for the Electronic Media, spring, 1999.

8. Don't look for the commercials paraphrased in this section. By the time you read this they will have been consigned to wherever bad commercials go when they die.

9. Courtesy of Chuck Blore Company.

10. Courtesy of The Potato Board.

11. This and the Norwegian Designs commercial courtesy of Gerry Sher Creative Sales.

12. Courtesy of Chuck Blore Company.

13. Courtesy of Chuck Blore Company.

14. Courtesy of Chuck Blore Company.

15. Courtesy of Robert C. Pritikin.

16. Robert C. Pritikin, *Christ Was an Ad Man* (San Francisco: Bay Court, 3rd ed., 1997), 106.

17. Ibid., 109.

18. This and the next two commercials for Swenson's and Folgers courtesy of Robert C. Pritikin.

19. Slogans for beers and soft drinks are changed periodically by manufacturers on the premise that if slogans becomes too familiar, people will notice them less.

20. Courtesy of Chuck Blore Company.

21. Eric Poole is the recipient of nearly fifty major awards, including CLIOs and Sunny, American Advertising Federation, New York Festival, and London International Festival awards.

22. Courtesy of Chuck Blore Company.

23. Courtesy of Gerry Sher Creative Sales.

24. Scripts for study and analysis may be found in Appendix A.

25. Courtesy of Eric Poole, Splash Radio.

CHAPTER FOURTEEN

NARRATIVE SCRIPTS

This chapter describes, discusses, and provides extensive examples of scripts written for delivery by a single voice, most often that of its creator. Most of the narrative scripts in this chapter were written for radio. Chapter 15, "Production Scripts," features television productions.

Narrative scripts come with a variety of descriptive labels: essays, commentaries, editorials and, in some instances, reviews. Regardless of designation, all are statements that a single speaker presents, on-camera for television and on microphone for radio. This chapter examines one- to five-minute scripts expressing opinions, sharing perceptions, or presenting facts. They're considered together because they don't involve production, such as recorded interviews or sound bites, although some television narratives may have visual components added for visual variety.

ESSAYS AND COMMENTARIES

Most narrative scripts are written and delivered by persons who've established themselves as qualified to express positions on topics of importance. Noteworthy commentators of our time include Roger Rosenblatt, Ann Taylor Fleming, Clarence Page, and Richard Rodriguez. Essays created and delivered by these authors represent their positions on a great range of subjects and, while often inspired by news events, the essays go deeper than headlines, giving us insights and an understanding of causes. Of those whose essays appear with frequency on national television, none is a more gifted storyteller than Richard Rodriguez.

This narrative written for PBS demonstrates the author's ability to discern story potential in societal trends not apparent to others; to select and arrange elements into narratives that attract and hold our attention; and to conclude with observations that leave us with a heightened consciousness of how our public arts shape our perceptions of reality.

Scripts written by college students for a class in writing for the electronic media are identified by an asterisk (*) appearing after the author's name.

PACIFIC NEWS SERVICE
PNS-DEATH
COMMENTARY-725 WORDS © COPYRIGHT PNS

VAMPIRES: AMERICA'S NEW OBSESSION WITH DEATH
BY RICHARD RODRIGUEZ, PACIFIC NEWS SERVICE[1]

Was it so long ago when discretion ruled the TV newsroom? At a car crash or a murder scene, the TV camera used to shy away from intimate postures of death. Not any more.

Something is changing in America. We are growing more interested in death, even besotted by death.

We Americans used to be famous for ignoring death. People didn't die in America, they "passed away." Violence and death were not unknown to us—the Civil War, the Wild West. But perhaps because there was so much death, we turned away and made youth our national theme.

Today, it is precisely the death of the young that astonishes us and makes death so inescapable. The old are living longer. The young are in jeopardy.

In East Oakland, in the broken heart of the city, stands a mortuary, a thriving business these days. The undertaker says he buries the young more often than he buries the old. And he says: "Kids in the neighborhood often come by, hang out; the littlest kids come in to look at the corpses."

Throughout this century young Americans went off to foreign wars, Many returned, dazed, shell shocked; we didn't understand what they were trying to tell us about the horror of war. In today's America, young children live with Death as a schoolmate. Death lingers in the high school hallway. Death walks behind you on the way home. Death peers out of a passing car. One boy recently told me: "I'm either going to grow up to be a rap artist or I'll be murdered."

It is not only the young in the inner city who are haunted by death. Teen suicide is on the rise in the American suburbs. And to American children both in the suburbs and the inner city who say they are numb, Death promises ultimate sensation. Death becomes a trip beyond drugs.

The fatalism of the young has changed adult perceptions of death. When I was a kid, Halloween was no big deal. You put on a mask; you went out; you filled your bag full of candy. You got sick on all the candy. As a kid, I would never have imagined that Halloween would ever become an adult celebration.

Yet on Halloween this year there were bank tellers and typists throughout downtown San Francisco, in broad daylight, in costume.

Homosexuals were the first to make Halloween an adult festival in the 1970s. Gays knew all about costume long before that. What was interesting on Halloween night in the Castro district was that Death was everywhere in the crowd of masks: Nicole

Simpson, vampire lovers. At a time of AIDS, Death was the invited guest at the street fair.

Ancient cultures learn to make their peace with death. Early in November, in Mexico, for centuries, on the Dia de los Muertos (the Catholic Feast of All Souls) Mexicans visit the graves of their relatives. Mexicans bring food for the dead; they clean up the grave site; they linger and talk to the ghosts; they sing; get drunk; they even poke fun of death by sucking on candy skulls.

There is a thin line between morbidity and the acceptance of death. Here in the United States, we have never had an easy relationship with death. Now that death is everywhere—in the morning paper, on our TV screen—now that the young are dying of guns, of AIDS, of drugs, we cannot use the idea of youth to evade death. Death forces its way into our lives. We have turned morbid. We linger over every detail of Ronald Goldman and Nicole Simpson's murders. We expect to see the bodies taken away from the bus in Tel Aviv after the terrorist bomb has exploded. We are like children.

Anne Rice, the novelist, has caught the spirit of these times with her romances about death. These days Tom Cruise appears on the movie screen as Anne Rice's leading man, a vampire.

Here is the ultimate irony: the boy next door has become an erotic lover as Death. It is a decadent fantasy, appropriate to a time when children murder children and young people pass a virus to one another in a fevered embrace.

We pay seven bucks to see death disguised as Tom Cruise, the boy next door, stealing his way into our bedroom.

END   © COPYRIGHT PNS

Here's a statement full of anger that pulls no punches and makes no pretense of being objective. It was written by syndicated columnist Dave Barry, whose disgust with certain types of advertising brought about this well-conceived article. It is a newspaper commentary—rather than a broadcast script—but it's style is conversational, and would make an excellent piece on an NPR program such as *All Things Considered.* Note how Barry uses comic speech, caricature, imitation, and most notably, hostile wit.[2]

THE MIAMI HERALD
Copyright " 1996, The Miami Herald
SOURCE/CREDIT LINE: DAVE BARRY Herald Columnist

ANNOYING ADS MAKE YOU WANT TO SHOUT

So I turned on my car radio, and the first thing I heard was the Shouting Car-Dealership Jerk. You know the one I mean. He sounds like this:

"BELOW DEALER COST!! MAX SNOTWICK FORD DODGE ISUZU CHEVROLET NISSAN STUDEBAKER TOYOTA IS SELLING CARS AT BELOW DEALER COST!! WE'RE LOSING MONEY ON THESE CARS!! WE HAVE TO MAKE ROOM FOR MORE CARS!! SO WE CAN LOSE MORE MONEY!! WE HAVE PROCESSED CHEESE FOR BRAINS!! THAT'S WHY WE'RE SELLING CARS FOR BELOW DEALER . . ."

I immediately did what I always do when the Shouting Car-Dealership Jerk comes on: I changed the station. I will listen to anything—including Morse code, static and the song "A Horse With No Name"—before I will listen to those commercials, and I think most people feel the same way. So the question is: why are they on the air? Why are car dealerships paying good money for Commercials that people hate?

My theory is that these commercials are NOT paid for by car dealerships; they're paid for by competing radio stations, who hope you'll switch to them. I developed a similar theory years ago to explain the infamous "ring around the collar" TV commercials for Wisk. Remember those? They always featured a Concerned Housewife who tried and tried to get her husband's collars clean, but when her husband, who apparently did not wash his neck, would put on a shirt, people would point out that his collar was dirty. You'd think he'd have punched them in the mouth, but instead he just looked chagrined, and these extremely irritating voices—voices that would kill a laboratory rat in seconds—would shriek "RING AROUND THE COLLAR! RING AROUND THE COLLAR!" And the Concerned Housewife would be so embarrassed that the only thing preventing her from lying down right on her kitchen floor and slashing her wrists was the fear that the paramedics might notice that she had waxy yellow buildup.

There was a time when the ring around the collar campaign was arguably the single most detested aspect of American culture. Many people swore that, because of those commercials, they would not purchase Wisk if it were the last detergent on Earth. Yet the commercials stayed on the air for years. Why? Because somebody was buying Wisk. The question is: Who?

My theory is that it was the Soviet Union. These ads ran during the height of the cold war, when the Soviets would stop at nothing to destroy America. I believe they sent agents over here with the mission of purchasing huge quantities of Wisk; this convinced the Wisk manufacturers that the "ring around the collar" campaign was working, so they kept it on the air, thereby causing millions of Americans to conclude that they lived in a nation of complete idiots, and thus become depressed and alienated. I believe that virtually all the negative developments of the '60s and '70s—riots, protests, crime, drug use, The Gong Show—were related, directly or indirectly, to Wisk commercials. I also believe that to this day, somewhere in the former Soviet Union, there are giant hidden underground caverns containing millions of bottles of Wisk.

I'll tell you another kind of ad I hate! The ones where they give you information that could never be of any conceivable use to you. For example, there was a series of ads for some giant chemical company, I forget which one, where they'd show you, say, a family watching television, and the announcer would say something like: "We don't make televisions. And we don't make the little plastic things that hold the wires inside the televisions. We make the machines that stamp the numbers on the little plastic things that hold the wires inside the televisions." When I saw those ads, I wanted to scream: WHY ARE YOU PAYING MILLIONS OF DOLLARS TO TELL ME THIS?? WHAT DO YOU WANT ME TO DO??

I also do not care for:

- Any ad featuring a demonstration of a product absorbing an intimate bodily fluid.

- Any ad where a singer sings with deep emotion about something nobody could possibly feel deeply emotional about, such as cotton, Hoover vacuum cleaners, and Jiffy Lube. Builders Square has a commercial wherein the singer bleats this hyper-patriotic song that makes it sound as though the people shopping there are actually building America, whereas in fact they are looking for replacement toilet parts.

- Any of endless series of ads by long-distance companies accusing other long-distance companies of lying. LISTEN LONG-DISTANCE COMPANIES: WE DON'T BELIEVE ANY OF YOU ANY MORE. WE'RE THINKING OF GOING BACK TO SMOKE SIGNALS,

Excuse me for shouting like the Car-Dealership Jerk: I get emotional about this. I'm sure you do, too, which is why I'm inviting you to write to me at One Herald Plaza, Miami, Fla., 33132, and tell me—BRIEFLY—what advertisements, past or present, that you really hate, and why. I'll write a column about this, which will benefit humanity in general by enabling me to write yet another column without doing any research. Don't thank me: I do it all for you. At WAY below dealer cost.

For a change of pace and mood, here's a delightful piece on the meaning of time. Its tone is one of annoyance rather than outrage. The style is tongue-in-cheek, and the structure takes the piece full circle. It begins with a tease, occupying an entire paragraph, that intrigues us but gives no clue as to where the story is heading. The second paragraph gradually reveals the source of the author's annoyance: the invention of devices, beginning with the calendar, that have enslaved us. The story ends with the author driving home his point as he excuses himself to rush to an appointment. Once the author conceived the basic point, the writing became relatively effortless.

RADIO ESSAY: A Matter of Time
AUTHOR: Brian Underwood*

There's one conspiracy that even "The X Files" has failed to explore. True, it has to do with aliens planning to conquer the Earth, as most conspiracies these days do. But in the highly competitive market of global conquest, this particular set of aliens uses a technique that involves slowly stripping humans of all their common sense.

Because the process is so slow, it's unclear how long ago they started, but they're doing a fantastic job at present.

The earliest evidence of alien intervention was the calendar. Before the aliens sprung their plot, most cultures had no concept of the passage of time—they had no need for it. But after the first calendars mysteriously cropped up, those societies that had calendars started to worship them, basing much of their lives on their understanding of where they were on the calendar.

A few thousand years passed, and humanity had accepted calendars so wholeheartedly that the aliens moved to the next phase. That was when they brought us clocks. All of a sudden, it wasn't enough to know what month it was, or even what day. Suddenly the day was divided into hours, the hours into minutes, and the minutes into seconds, creating the intense precision by which humans started to live.

Time passed, and people measured it. Around the 1800s, the sadistic aliens intensified their plot even more. Heavily disguised as Englishmen, they called a global convention of humans in Greenwich. There, they unveiled their next two weapons against the waning human common sense: time zones and daylight savings time.

Despite the overwhelming foolishness of measuring time at all, never mind with such great precision, the alien's latest layer of pointlessness made us change our clocks periodically. We were led to believe that the sun should rise and set at about the same time every day, which it doesn't. We were led to believe that the sun should rise and set at about the same time in different parts of the world, which it doesn't. And we were led to believe that whenever it didn't, we should change our clocks to more accurately reflect the sun's rising and setting habits, which they don't.

The alien's reasoning was that as we worshipped our timepieces more and more, we'd eventually spend every waking moment setting and resetting the clocks in our homes. As extra insurance, they sent down all kinds of consumer appliances: televisions, VCRs, computers, pagers, even bread makers—all with clocks in them. The most Huxleyan product of all is the wristwatch. Most people willingly wear wristwatches, and they're almost a necessity to survive in our heavily schedule-oriented society. And all the clocks that we let into our lives take control of us as we set them over and over. Yet they never actually tell us anything that could be construed as useful, in the grand scheme of things.

Why would the aliens do this to us? Well, partly for a good laugh at our expense. And partly so that we'll all be so wrapped up in our schedules and our punctuality that we'll be in too big a hurry to do anything between appointments. We'll be too busy to give ourselves an afternoon to go to an art museum. Or to frolic in a meadow. Or to stargaze. Or even to look up and notice the alien ships overhead when they finally mount their long-planned attack.

Is there hope for humanity? Or are we too gullible to survive? It's hard to say. Maybe some kind doctor will someday step forward and point out that stress-related diseases are real, and that our modern lifestyle is killing us. Maybe then people will learn.

But I can't waste any more time thinking about it. I need to be downtown in twenty minutes.

Chanel Perez touches on an age-old myth, one learned by hundreds of generations of girls who were encouraged to believe that one day a handsome man would appear, win her love, and take care of her forever.

ESSAY
"The Love Myth—Prince Charming, where are you?"
Chanel Perez*

When I was a little girl, I knew that of all the accomplishments in my life, the most important would be finding my true love. Was this a dream? Did I want to find love like I wanted to be a dancer? Did I keep saying to myself "when I grow up I want to be someone's girlfriend?" Yes. All the women around me were single. Despite that, I was told by them, by mommy, and by television that a man would make me complete. My grandest desire should be that for male companionship,

Now that I've grown up, things are a little different. Well, I see them differently. Love of the fantasy kind is a myth. Sure, women want to believe in some magical force that drives two people together. I would love it if money grew on trees. The fact is money does not show up in my backyard, and neither does Prince Charming. So many centuries have passed with little girls being told to find a man. Is this society blind? Love and relationships take work. A choice is involved when starting a relationship. When in love, couples need to compromise, argue, disagree, and make the effort to build a healthy, caring partnership.

The Cinderella story is beautiful. But, it's just that, a story. Women need to wake up and stop looking for the white horse outside their front door. Men do not come to sweep you off your feet and instantly make all your troubles disappear. What happens to a woman's dreams, her passion, her calling? Don't we have an obligation to fulfill our mission as individuals?

Anyone who comes into your life to share it is a bonus. Last time I checked my math skills, one plus one still equals two.

Don't get me wrong. I'm a true advocate of soul mates and passionate love affairs. This can only be accomplished, though, by two people deciding to work on their love. When you fall in love and out of infatuation, you realize it goes much deeper than Sleeping Beauty could imagine. Not having a perfect romance is what makes it worthwhile. You grow with your mate through the ups and downs. When you appreciate your independence and differences, when you stop defining yourself as a woman only in the presence of a man, and when you truly love yourself, this is when "true love" becomes possible.

It's time to take a realistic view of love and relationships. It isn't carriages and flowers every day. It's not being awakened from a deep sleep by one kiss. It's not having a man rescue you. Love is about rescuing each other. Love is about growth, healing, learning and sharing your most prized possession, your life. Romance and passion, fairy tales and dreams are nice. Caring and friendship, understanding and sincerity are invaluable.

Commentaries are basically essays, and many are indistinguishable from editorials. The essay that follows was initiated by an arrest in Lebanon, Pennsylvania. The motivation for turning this into a commentary was not merely the story's basic facts, but the irony of the event as well—adults failing to see how their behavior might well result in unacceptable activities by their children. The author goes beyond the drug theme to question other parental behaviors that serve as negative models for children.

COMMENTARY: KIDS WILL BE KIDS
LENGTH: 3 Minutes Radio
AUTHOR: John Sidhom*

The woman in Lebanon, Pennsylvania, did the right thing. She saw kids selling drugs and she called the police. The police investigated and found the culprits to be between the ages of seven and nine.

Only it turns out they weren't selling drugs, they were selling grass. As in lawn grass. You see they were just "playing" drug dealers and their props were baggies of dried up St. Augustine, not Acapulco Gold. Somehow the image of mere children acting out drug transactions cuts to the heart of my sensibilities. Much the same way I cringe when I see a youngster pretending to gun down his little friends with an ominous looking Uzi submachine gun aka water pistol. I'm not suggesting that every kid who plays with a toy semi-automatic will become a mass murderer, or the kids who sell baggies of lawn cuttings will become dope dealers. Some of them will, but that's no reason to pull the water pistols and baggies out from under them. Children are just that, children. They don't have enough information or life experiences to understand the real-life consequences of selling drugs or aiming guns.

It occurred to me that if my mother had seen me peddling baggies of marijuana, even pretend marijuana, from behind my lemonade stand she probably would have gone directly into cardiac arrest. After her revival, I'm sure she would have dismantled the lemonade stand and given me a long lecture on the evils of drugs. Then she would have retired to her bedroom and taken a Valium. Upon my fathers' return home from work, I would have to sit before him, listening to another lecture along the same lines, while he mixed himself a drink.

It doesn't take a Rhodes scholar to see the incongruities here. Perhaps my parents didn't have enough information or life experience to understand the real-life consequences of pills or alcohol. No, I'm afraid they used their "drugs" to escape—to take the hard edge off reality.

The problem of mind-altering substances has and probably always will exist. What's so frightening is the scope with which these substances are affecting society. The age of users is decreasing as the toxicity of the drugs increases. If this trend does not turn around, we'll soon have three generations of mindless wonders roaming the streets.

As individuals we need to take stock of ourselves and the world around us. What have we done to ourselves that has made us so eager to escape?

Why are we so unhappy with our lot in life? Why are we so threatened by a car wanting to change lanes in front of us on the freeway? More important, what can we do to appreciate more what we have, and stop this incessant feeling that we can't let the other guy win? In short, we need to stop escaping and start enjoying what we have.

Now back to the mini–drug dealers in Lebanon, Pennsylvania. Are they trying to escape from reality? Hardly. They're simply mirroring life as they see it. This is what children do. It's our responsibility as adults to improve the society they mirror, starting with a good look at ourselves. As caretakers of the children, we must do a better job. We can't just meet their physical needs, we must nurture their emotional and intellectual needs as well. Our failure to do this has produced seven- and nine-year-olds who don't "play" drug dealers—they believe they *are* drug dealers. Isn't it ironic that this incident took place in a town called Lebanon?

STATION EDITORIALS

Editorials are identical to other types of commentaries in most details. Both identify an issue, move ahead with an explanation of why the issue's important, offer information about the issue, and state a position and give reasons for the stance taken. Editorials often suggest action that may be taken by those swayed by the presentation.

Few broadcast stations take advantage of their right to editorialize. Deregulation gave broadcasters a green light to eliminate services that brought them little or no revenue. So, if station editorials are no longer a force on radio and television, why bother to discuss or analyze them? Editorials will remain worth considering for as long as station licensees retain their constitutional right to editorialize. Perhaps, in the wake of terrorist attacks that shook the complacency of most Americans in the fall of 2001, broadcasters will look for ways to make a more positive impact on those they serve. Editorials are an obvious way of doing this. They are waiting to be rediscovered.

At those stations where editorializing reflects a commitment to serve the public interest, management teams meet to examine issues, usually issues that affect people of their community. Members of the team assemble lists of potential topics and rate the importance of each. They debate the position the station might take but, because the editorial position taken represents an official view of station management, a general or station manager makes the final decisions.

Here are a few types of issues that could become station editorials: the treatment of panhandlers by local officials; the problem of voter apathy in elections; an appeal for donations to holiday food distributors; a salute to firefighters who saved lives and property in a firestorm; or praise for volunteers who helped restore parks and playgrounds following a storm.

Those stations that continue to editorialize need personnel capable of researching and writing editorials. If you work for such a station, you may be assigned a topic, with the station's official position on it. You, then, must create an editorial script, usually which the station manager will read on the air. For radio, your script will be a straight narrative recorded in a studio for later broadcast. Television editorials usually are read and recorded in their entirety in-studio, before cameras, but file footage—SOT bites—may be added for variety or to show still photos, charts, and graphs that help in understanding an issue.

Keys to success in this assignment are doing effective research; having a clear concept of the people you're trying to reach; deciding how you want to affect those persons; and determining what will have changed if you're successful in persuading them to your station's point of view. Here are some suggestions:

STRUCTURING A STATION EDITORIAL

1. State the problem or issue clearly, and in a way that relates it to your audience. People aren't usually interested in problems that they can't identify with or feel are unimportant. Without relying on grocery-store check-out-line scandal sheets or any other type of sensationalism, get your listeners' or viewers' attention.

2. Provide facts or examples to support your claim that there is a problem. The management team that discussed this editorial topic undoubtedly had some information about its pros and cons, but now you will need specific facts supported by evidence.

3. If appropriate, give the conflicting opinions of responsible persons or groups. (In some instances, you may want to give the views of those you feel are irresponsible—as with hate groups or the "lunatic fringe.")

4. State the editorial opinion of your station. Support your position with logic, facts, statistics, or opinion. Be as specific and factual as possible. Answer the claims of those who oppose your position.

5. Conclude with a recap, a summary, or a restating of both the issue and your position on it. In some instances, you may want to urge your listeners to take a particular action: "write your legislator"; "call _____ , and let your opposition (or support) be known"; "send your donations to _____ ."

6. Make sure your editorial flows from point to point. Avoid jumping from one point to another without transitional words or phrases.
7. Keep complex numbers simple: change "8,895,000 people" to "nearly nine million people."
8. Use plain language. Your editorial will be read by a person, such as your station manager, who wants the audience to see her or him as a real, down-to-earth human being, not an elocutionist using stilted and unconversational language. Here are two versions of the same statement, one stilted and the other in conversational English:

    First version: As manager of this station, I sincerely hope that you will take time out from your busy schedule to study the ballot propositions before you make final closure on each of them.

    Second version: I'm Marge Cortes, manager of KKZZ. If you're like most of us, you probably have far too much to do. But, I truly hope you'll make time for a close look at the propositions on this November's ballot.

9. Use contractions. Here's the same sentence with and without contractions. Read both versions aloud, and hear the difference:

    First version: "We are lucky to live in the Greater Chicago Area for many reasons, but public transportation is not one of them. If you are tired of dirty and unsafe city buses—yet feel you cannot do anything about the problem—we urge you to . . ."

    Second version: "We're lucky to live in the Greater Chicago Area for many reasons, but public transportation isn't one of them. If you're tired of dirty and unsafe city buses—yet feel you can't do anything about the problem—we urge you to . . ."

    Sometimes, however, contractions are less effective; for example, when you want to emphasize a word: "You *are not* required to pay in advance . . ."

The following list outlines the steps you may want to take as you practice editorial writing:

1. Examine the major issues facing your region today.
2. Select an issue of importance to you.
3. Research this topic if appropriate.
4. Contact anyone who may be able to contribute to your statement.
5. Outline your presentation.
6. Write your script. Rewrite as often as necessary to make it clear, direct, appealing, and persuasive.

Here are two editorials by award-winning editorial writer Nicholas DeLuca.[3] They were selected for inclusion here because each addresses an unresolved question or issue. The processes that identified the issues and the positions taken on them by the radio station vary. DeLuca and the general manager (who read the editorials on the air) constituted the "editorial board." In some instances editorial ideas came from the G.M., at other times from DeLuca. Most topics were mutually agreed on before research and scripting were undertaken. The final script was always subject to the G.M.'s approval.

The first KCBS editorial included here, titled "The Washing of Hands" attacks those who, in opposing abortion, resort to murder.

A KCBS Editorial
Written by Nick DeLuca for
The Management of KCBS, San Francisco

ANNCR: Here is KCBS General Manager Frank Oxarart With an Editorial Opinion.

THE WASHING OF HANDS

"The Christian principle is to do unto others as you would have them do unto you." So said Paul Hill, an antiabortion activist, in an Interview earlier this year.

So how did that same Paul Hill come to stand accused of killing a doctor and his escort outside a women's health clinic last week? And how did a religion that advocates love for one another come to inspire a man who advocates violence to stop abortion?

KCBS believes a heavy share of that responsibility falls on the antiabortion movement and its leaders, many of whom are also leaders in the Christian faith. They could express their heartfelt opposition to abortion in strong, but reasoned terms, in a language that allowed for some possibility of discussion with the other side—and all too often, they don't.

There are some antiabortion leaders who actually say, It's okay to kill someone in the name of preventing abortion . . . but even the day-to-day rhetoric of the more numerous, more moderate voices opens a door to violence.

You can't whip people into a frenzy about abortion . . . calling it murder, a holocaust, a singular act of evil . . . in a religious context of absolute right and wrong . . . then walk away from the consequences. And it can hardly come as a surprise . . . that for some antiabortion activists, those consequences Include violence, even murder.

It's just not enough to condemn the act of killing after the fact, as many antiabortion leaders did. And Christians have a powerful symbol for the refusal to take responsibility. We suggest the leaders of the antiabortion movement turn to the Bible, to that moment when Pontius Pilate washes his hands, literally and symbolically—before turning over Jesus Christ to certain death at the hands of the crowd. It didn't absolve Pilate of responsibility then. KCBS believes it doesn't work now.

In Deluca's next editorial, retailers of upscale clothing are exposed as supporters and beneficiaries of sweatshops in which women workers—most of them immigrants—work long hours for meager pay. As is true of most editorials, "Dream Worlds" ends with a suggestion of actions that may be taken by those who agree with the editorial's stand.

A KCBS Editorial
Written by Nick DeLuca for
The Management of KCBS, San Francisco

ANNCR: Here is KCBS General Manager Frank Oxarart With an Editorial Opinion.

DREAM WORLDS

Jessica McClintock sells a world of dream and romance . . . long lacy dresses of another time, But Jessica McClintock's dreams are made in a very different world. A world of long hours, hard work, and low pay.

In fact, behind much of the dream world that fashion offers us . . . stands a real world of sweatshop labor . . . mostly woman, mostly immigrant . . . working behind closed doors and blacked-out windows . . . earning the smallest fraction of what their work brings in the finest stores.

In between that real world, and the dream world . . . stand the contractors who run the sweatshops. Designers and clothing manufacturers contract out the cutting and sewing, and choose not to ask questions about how that work gets done.

So if working conditions are substandard, as they often are . . . if the sweatshop goes out of business, as it often does . . . the sweatshop workers are often left without jobs, without back pay, without recourse. Designers and the clothing companies are insulated by the law from any responsibility.

So part of the answer is corporate accountability. The companies that reap so much benefit from that sweatshop labor should share in the responsibility for those laborers. And chances are whatever you buy . . . Jessica McClintock, Ralph Lauren, Esprit . . . wherever you shop . . . Macy's. the Gap, Banana Republic . . . your world of dreams is built on the reality of the sweatshops.

KCBS thinks you should ask before you shop. Call your favorite designer or store . . . ask them how their clothes are made . . . and if you don't buy their explanation, don't buy their clothes.

REVIEWS

Film critic Jan Wahl wrote this review for multiple purposes: it was written as an article to be printed in several regional newspapers and a monthly magazine. She divided the review into three segments, which she would read on the radio. It's suitable for both print and broadcast because it's written in a conversational style.

FILM REVIEW
by Jan Wahl[4]
A Bought Rating for "Potter"

Someday soon there will not be movie critics, only "entertainment reporters." It will be all about promotion of Hollywood products, with journalism being replaced by ballyhoo. It is happening now, from the inclusion of Larry King and Liz Smith as "critics" in movie ads to Katy Couric breathlessly presenting an hour special on Harry Potter. Can we now expect intrepid journalist Couric to take on the issue of a possibly inappropriate rating for the Potter film, or would that mean giving back all her Potter perks?

Forgive the cynicism in my tone, but it's obvious that any negative comments toward the new Potter movie is tantamount to crying "the Emperor has no clothes." The pressure is enormous to be part of the marketing and merchandising climate that proclaims magic and wonder for *Harry Potter and the Sorcerer's Stone.* Going along with the marketing hype flow gives the reporter access to stars, both now and in future Warner Brothers films, as well as the goodwill of newsrooms hoping that braying loudest and happiest will lead to ratings or readership.

The good news is that the Harry Potter series has made readers out of a generation of kids oversaturated with electronic media. To talk with young people about their love of all things Potter is to re-acknowledge the power and beauty of the written word. As a voracious reader myself, I purposely stayed away from Potter, hoping to review the film as a movie that stands on its own as adventure and across-the-board entertainment. While this two-and-a-half hat fantasy will thrill those who love the books, the movie itself is visually stylish but lacking in a script that keeps us emotionally invested in the outcome.[5] The book's fans, of course, will be hooked on what happens next, but as a non-Potter-reading adult, it was just another pleasant, if overly long, children's fantasy film.

What could have made this film work as a generational crossover, like the Indiana Jones series or the original three Star Wars? One element missing from the Potter epic is a backstory for promising side characters, played by Maggie Smith, Richard Harris and Alan Rickman. It's always delightful to see these wonderful performers, but here they are present to move the plot along, without an identity or explanation of their own. Robbie Coltrane is the comic relief, but if one hasn't read the book, he's merely a funny giant, serving to let us in on plot devices and chase details.

The three main children, led by likeable and sensitive Daniel Radcliffe as Harry, are engaging but would've been far more interesting if we had insight into how his friends ended up at the school along with him. The hype reminds us that over seven-hundred-fifty special effects shots were used, from three-headed dogs to ferocious trolls, but without a compelling reason to care, they are just more cinematic eye candy.

The negatives I heard from people coming out of the movie: parents upset at the scarier images in a PG movie, and a teenage girl worried that her favorite character from the book was shown to be helpless and in need of male rescuing. But ninety percent of the people there truly loved the books and this film.

Good for them, and a big hats off for those who can go beyond the hype and social pressure to look for possible flaws or suggestions. The entire world shouldn't be one, big, Hollywood-kiss-up episode of "Entertainment Tonight."

IMPRESSIONS

Some radio and television essays are personal statements, created with no purpose other than to reveal and share experiences and feelings. Like more conventional commentaries, they represent the feelings or opinions of their authors, but they differ in that they don't deal with hard news, and they needn't be timely. Most essays in this style explore a situation, a tradition, a movement, or similar topic of interest, and present an analysis and a personal point of view. Because of their intimate nature, I call such essays "impressions."

Impressions are revelations of experiences or feelings you had at one time, often the experiences of childhood. They're similar to personal comments found in diaries, with the obvious exception that they're written to be shared. While impressions differ from conventional essays only in their degree of introspection, it's useful to consider them separately because a recognition of the boundaries of each will help guide you as you work to create one or the other. Before writing an essay of any kind, you should determine where you want it to be on the scale of fact versus feeling.[6]

When searching for an idea to turn into an impression, don't reject things you believe to be commonplace. It's not important that a topic be extraordinary or exceptional; it's the special feelings or insights you bring to it that matter. Having been in a shipwreck or having spent time in jail may seem exciting and promising material for a story, but neither topic would automatically produce a good essay. Conversely, sharing your feelings about some very personal experience—the end of a romance, a dispute and reconciliation with a best friend, a recounting of your special memories of a grandparent—could become fascinating listening for others.

You may feel you've led an undramatic or commonplace life, and that others who've grown up in similar circumstances would find your story boring. But remember, some of the most poignant stories ever told are memorable, not because of the story outline, but because their authors were able to see commonplace events in unique ways, and to tie into universal themes and needs.

Here's the assignment sheet given to students:

BECA 370—WRITING FOR THE ELECTRONIC MEDIA

Impressions from My Past

This assignment is intended to help you appreciate some of the rich (and seldom used) potential of the aural medium of radio. The only broadcast service where you would likely hear such a piece would be noncommercial radio—National Public Radio (NPR), Public Radio International (PRI), Monitor Radio, a college station, or an independent such as KPFA.

Write a narrative script giving your "listeners" an impression of some event or situation in your life that has special memories for you. In three to four minutes, give us a "word picture" of this memory. Don't be completely factual and literal, but instead try for an evocative, a poetic effect. Try to convey the feelings you once had—establish an ambiance, a mood; convey your feelings of anticipation, of fear, of melancholy, of joy, or sorrow—whatever's appropriate. It's as fitting to write a humorous or sardonic script as it is a sad or melancholy piece. The only requirements are that your reminiscences be true, that they be evocative, and that they make use of radio's special capacity for introspection. USE SOUND EFFECTS AND/OR MUSIC, IF APPROPRIATE.

(*Very important note—please let me know on the back of your last page if it's all right for me to share your paper with the class. This is important. I want you to feel free to dig as deeply as you like into your memories, without fear of embarrassment.*)

YOU DON'T HAVE TO WRITE AN ANALYSIS OF THIS SCRIPT. I hope you have fun with this piece—I think you'll find it a stimulating challenge. I look forward to reading your impressions, and sharing them with our classmates.

The impression that follows was written by a student who lives in the United States but who grew up in a culture other than the United States. This author could have felt that his story would be of little interest to others because it isn't in any usual sense dramatic. Or, he might have thought that because people in his homeland wouldn't find it unusual, no one else would. But because the story is so well told, it makes the point that anyone's story, if told in a unique way, will interest others. And, while details may be unfamiliar to us, the story touches on human feelings that are universal and eternal. YiLi Liang was born in a village in southern China, Guang Dong, and emigrated to this country seven years ago.

IMPRESSION
"A Camping Trip"
YiLi Liang*

MUSIC BACKGROUND: ACOUSTIC GUITAR

For the last seven years, ever since I came to this country, I have been living in San Francisco. It is a city beautiful and charming, but all my senses of connection with mother nature are numbed by its fast pace of life. Life in a city is routine, sometimes good, yet not complete. Sometimes I feel like my father's goldfishes in the tank, though everything needed is in that small box, they are never free.

I grew up in a farming village, where intimacy with mother nature was a part of daily life. My childhood was nurtured by nature. My family planted and harvested according to the season. Our village celebrated solstices and equinoxes. I remember waking up to rooster calls. I remember the colors of the seasons: bright and colorful in the spring; turning green in summer; yellow in the fall; then, concluding with an earthy brown in winter. I also remember the sounds of seasons—spring's frog calls, summer's thunders, fall's bird songs, and winter's restful silence.

Maybe it was because for me to adapt to the city life, I had forced myself to disconnect from my childhood. Last summer, a couple of friends and I went to Lake Tahoe for a camping trip. It was in my first camping trip,and on it I rediscovered mother nature and my childhood.

I remember we were driving on the highway 89. After a couple turns, the mountains gave way to a vast opening. In front of us was a body of deep blue water, intimately surrounded by mountains that were dark on the horizon, and green in the far distance. Patches of snow were still visible on the taller mountains. Powdery clouds were high in the sky and their beauty was captured by the lake as its calm water provided their perfect reflections. Heaven and earth seemed to merge together on the horizon. Nearby was Emerald Bay. In the middle of Emerald Bay is a lonely island, guarding the lake like a fortress.

I spent my first night in awe and in recollection of my childhood. Above the canopy of pine tree, stars lit up the sky. I saw my old friends, the constellations, for the first time since leaving my country home. The summer night in that high elevation was chilly, but crispy and refreshing.

Magnifying the mood were occasional solos by the forest, as the mild wind gently waved the branches.

MUSIC: ACOUSTIC GUITAR (FADE UP & UNDER FOR)

The sights and sounds gave me courage to revisit my childhood. And, I was happy and complete.

MUSIC: ACOUSTIC GUITAR (FADE OUT)

The next impression is one that most of us who've had a friendly rivalry with a close relative can appreciate. The story is about baseball, but the relationships and the emotions could apply to nearly any competitive setting.

IMPRESSION
"Little League Days"
Ryan Nobrega*

I was just going through some old boxes and I came across a baseball from my little league days. I instantly knew what it was. It had some scores on it, a date, and two signatures. It was the game ball from the most memorable little league game of my life.

My best friend growing up was my cousin, Damon. We used to spend hours playing baseball and bragging about which of us was the better baseball player. He was the power hitter on his team. It seemed like he could crack one out of the park on command. I, on the other hand, was usually the lead off or second batter. I was more of a defensive player. A good, solid third baseman. We lived in different cities so our teams never got a chance to play against each other during a normal season. There was one time though, when our parents got together and organized a game between the Beavers of Belmont, which was my team, and my cousin's team, the Burlingame Colts.

I remember it so well—it was June of 1982—one of those hot, dry summer days. School was out for the summer and it felt so good to be carefree. The parents were all there, friends, a big barbecue . . . even my dog, Dylan, came to watch the game. We'd spend a few hours in the dirt and grass battling it out and, in the end, the Beavers would win. But that's not what I think of when I look back on that game. . . .

It was the bottom of the 3rd inning. Coach Curran had decided to make some changes in the lineup so the kids who were on the bench could get some playing time. Somehow I ended up in center field. It wasn't really where I wanted to be, but since I was having so much fun, I didn't really mind. So there I stood, way out in center field and who comes to the plate? My cousin the slugger.

He stepped up and went through his I-want-to-look-like-a-pro-ball-player warm-up routine. I just smiled. The pitcher paused, looked to first base as pitchers always do, and went into his windup. As the ball left his hand, the whole world went into slow motion. The ball sailed right over the center of the plate—waist high. Damon's eyes almost popped out of his head as he took that first step towards the ball. He swung with everything he had. I didn't even hear the crack of the bat. All I saw was the ball rocketing high over the pitchers head right towards me. I started stumbling back, trying to keep one eye on the ball and one eye on where I was going. I remember taking that final step—stretching my arm up into the air, leaning back, and watching as the worn leather ball with faded red stitching fell into the deepest part of my glove. My foot caught the ice chest they used as the home run marker which sent me sailing through the air and landing flat on my back. I laid there and the first thought that came into my mind was "I just earned myself bragging rights for the rest of our lives."

The ironic thing about this story is not that I robbed him of a home run, but where we ended up in life. I only played baseball for a few more seasons. I finished high school, went on to college and got a "real job." Damon, on the other hand, not only continued to play baseball, but was drafted into the major leagues right out of high school. Sitting here looking at this ball brings back so many memories. It makes me think about who we were and how much things can change.

I think I'll give him a call today, just to remind him I'm still the best baseball player of all time.

A low-key reminiscence about growing up with a special mother includes lessons for all of us. Themes include nostalgia, parent-child love, death, and parenting values.

TITLE: My Mom
AUTHOR: Michéle Haydé Gelow*

Yesterday, my husband, Bill, and I were at Crown Books. As he looked for a book on home brewing, I wandered around the store. On the coffee table display, I ran across a book: *A Norman Rockwell Christmas.* The large, white book with Santa sitting on a stool, the red suit jumping out at me, immediately reminded me of Mom. Mom had this book. Unfortunately, I'm not sure why, and this is just one of the mysteries of Mom.

Mom was unique; then again, though, don't we all think that of our Mom? She was born in Indonesia during the Japanese occupation of World War II, moved to Holland at 15 and went to college in France. She had a very close relationship to her mother, something I am now jealous of.

Mom was a very no-nonsense person. Standing only 5′ ¾″, she could silence us kids with just a few words. Her "No, and that's final!" never received an argument. Getting Mom mad wasn't something we wanted to do, though I can't remember her being mad very often.

We weren't rich, but she was happy. Unlike my father, Mom was not at all materialistic. Things didn't interest her; family, health and education did.

We kids were her priority. She was always there when we came home from school, something that meant a lot to me. Most of my friends were latchkey kids, and I was grateful to her for not making us latchkey kids, too. Though Irvine is one of the safest cities in the nation, Mom always walked us to the bus stop in the morning; she wasn't taking any chances with her babies.

Mom was also interested in broadening our horizons. After studying about England in school, my sister and I decided that we wanted to have afternoon tea. So, every afternoon at 4:00, Mom would call us in from playing, and there on the coffee table would be a pot of tea, cups, milk and sugar, and scones or finger sandwiches. Of course, as fickle as kids are, we soon lost interest. But Mom wasn't offended. She was happy to have given us our afternoon tea and was ready for the next request.

Unfortunately, a lot of what I've learned of Mom lately has come from her friend Amina who lives in Berkeley. Mom died on the 29th of November, 1984, of breast cancer; she was 42 years old. She and Amina met in 1971 in a gardening class in Santa Monica. Both were thrilled to have found another Eurasian. Amina is very much like Mom in her ideals, tastes, and hobbies. By spending time with Amina, I learn about Mom and feel like I'm spending time with her. Amina is also the only person I know willing to speak of Mom; who she was, what she liked to do and the fun they had together. Like me, Amina has refused to give Mom up, and we firmly believe that she's still with us, even if it's only in spirit. As long as we love and remember Mom, she'll always be alive.

The way Mom raised us has become very important to me now that Bill and I are getting closer to having kids of our own. Bill was a latchkey kid and turned out just fine, but I don't want to do that to my kids. Mom was always home when we returned from school, and that's something that I want my kids to have, too.

Bill is very much like Mom, and I don't think that's an accident. I really wish the two could have met, because I think that they would have gotten along great. I miss her, and always will, and miss getting to know her as an adult. But, with my love, memories, and myself she will always be with me and alive in my heart.

IMPRESSION: John Sidhom
LENGTH: "PANIC SYNDROME" 4 Minutes Radio
BY: John Sidhom*

At 4 this morning I had the good fortune of going from the depths of utter despair to complete exhilaration, all because of a 10-year-old cat named Katie.

Two days ago Katie didn't show up for breakfast, which was very unlike this cat. She didn't get her nickname, The Incredible Bulk, for nothing. Still, there are other things more important to her than food. Not many, but there are some.

That evening on returning home, I noticed her face was missing from among the other three in the front window. I became a little concerned and hurriedly opened the door. No Katie. I called out and still no Katie. I assumed this was some kind of a new game we were playing and she forgot to leave me the rule book. I casually changed my clothes, only occasionally calling out to her. Nothing. Food ! That would do it. She's never been able to resist the sound of a can opener. Six opened cans later there was still no sign of her. It was then that I knew this was serious.

I searched high, I searched low. I searched in, I searched out. I didn't like this new game.

Several hours later, after calling on all the neighbors and circling the block many times, I was exhausted and feeling depressed. To say nothing of my newly tarnished image in the neighborhood.

When one of the neighbors heard me calling out, she offered to join in the search for Katie. She wanted to know what she looked like, so I told her Katie was black and white with a little black moustache. She looked quite puzzled and I realized she thought Katie was a child. Her help only lasted two houses.

I finally gave up the search and went back home. Weary and frazzled, I dropped into bed and tried not to think about it. I knew she'd come home.

I awakened before the alarm and rushed out to the kitchen. I just knew she'd be waiting. She wasn't. My heart sank. The other kitties looked at me as if sharing in my disappointment, their spirits dimmed but not their appetites. I combed the neighborhood once more before leaving for work. I queried everyone I saw and left my work number with a neighbor to give to the mail carrier, so he could be on the lookout. The search was intensifying.

From work I called Animal Control and every pet hospital I knew of. At least she was wearing her collar and tags. Between making "Lost Cat" posters and phone calls I didn't manage to get much work done. It occurred to me I was taking this rather badly. I couldn't help it. I left work early. As I drove home, stories I had heard of cats missing for days then suddenly turning up raced through my mind. Katie had never left home before. How could she do this to me?

Once home I gathered together a group of friends and we covered Redondo Beach with "Lost Cat" posters. I offered rewards. I begged, I pleaded. I put individual notices on doors for blocks around—in case the occupants had somehow missed seeing the signs on every telephone pole. Returning home I stared at the flashing red light on my answering machine. Could this be it? Did someone see the signs and find her raiding their refrigerator? No, it was my dentist's office calling to remind me it was time for a checkup. Now I'm not too fond of dentists in the first place, but this clinched it. Eventually my friends went home and I was left with a silent phone. I tried to sleep—no luck. So I planned my attack for the next day. I would borrow a doctor friend's stethoscope and listen at every garage door. I would crawl under every house. I would rent a plane to carry a banner—hoping she hadn't left town.

Just as I was deciding which news media to call—it happened. At 4 A.M. I heard a "meep." It didn't sound like Katie, but it didn't sound like anyone else either. I meeped back. She meeped. I meeped. I was getting closer. It was the drawer. The drawer was meeping. I opened it and looking back at me was my child with the black moustache. I hugged her. I kissed her. I cried. After a whole can of food and a trip to the sand box, I began to realize the nightmare was over, for both of us. Not that I had overreacted, of course.

Katie didn't look too much the worse for wear after her two days in solitary confinement. I looked a wreck. After the "good news" phone calls were made and the posters were down, Katie and I had a long talk. We both decided not to play this game anymore. The good people of Redondo Beach are still calling with reports of sighting her. I happily report to them she was found. One woman called to say not to give up hope. Another woman did try to convince me I had the wrong cat and she had actually found the Real Katie.

No, there she had been the whole time, right under my nose. Just like many of the solutions to our problems, if we only knew where to look.

The next impression takes us back to high school, exploring some of the emotional roller-coaster rides most of us experienced. Themes include romance, adolescent insecurity, nostalgia, wish fulfillment, beauty, and the thrill of feeling "special"—if only for an evening.

TITLE: Precious Moments
LENGTH: 3 minutes and 30 seconds
AUTHOR: Voltaire Villanueva*

VOLTAIRE:

It was a warm spring evening during my junior year in high school. after weeks of planning I couldn't believe it was here. We've all seen movies glamorizing the fun one can have on this special night, as well as the different incidents that can possibly go wrong. It's the first opportunity high school students have, not only to dress up in tuxedos and fancy dresses, but also the first opportunity to share the evening with a special friend. It's the evening all high school students know as . . . The Junior Prom.

MUSIC: (MOZART; CROSSFADE)

My evening started with a beautiful dinner at a restaurant here in the city called the Magic Flute. It was a classy restaurant with unique Italian decor and music by Mozart playing all through the night. It was a bizarre evening. It had only been a month since Jean first called my house and asked if I wanted to go to prom with her. For months I'd been trying to get a date with her, and here I was having dinner and taking her to the Prom.

It was a momentous occasion. It was just out of the blue when she called and asked me to go. I couldn't believe it myself, out of all the guys that she knew, she asked me.

There was a good reason why a lot of guys liked her. I mean, how can someone ignore it? She was attractive. Guys would come up left and right asking for her number. Jean had long brown hair, a beautiful complexion, and a voice sweet as honey. But what was most attractive about Jean were her eyes. She had the prettiest eyes that seemed to shine like pools of water. It's no wonder I was mesmerized throughout dinner.

After we ate, we hitched a ride with her friends and headed toward Union Square. The Junior Prom was at the Grand Hyatt and was entitled "Precious Moments," after a popular 1970s melody. As soon as we arrived, we found a table and sat pretty close to the front. Unfortunately, there weren't enough chairs for us and her friends, so I asked Jean if she wanted me to find another seat. She said it was okay, and instead she took a seat on my lap. Now things started to become a little intense.

I asked myself, what now? What are people gonna think? First she asks me to the prom, and now she's sitting on my lap. Does she like me or is she just playing with my mind? I was under the impression that when she asked me to the prom, we were just going as friends and nothing more. Sure, I hoped something good would come out of all this, but this was all happening too soon.

So to get this off my mind, I asked her to dance. I hoped the music wouldn't change to a slow one, but it did, and here we were standing face-to-face in the middle of the dance floor. In shock, I was stiff. So she placed her arms on my chest, and I slowly wrapped mine around her waist and we started to slow dance. Still stiff, she told me to relax. So her body came closer to mine and then she rested her head on my shoulder.

I then asked myself if this would be one of those movie endings I saw so many times when I was a kid. It was too good to be true. As we danced, I saw all my friends looking at us and smiling. My friendship with her seemed to turn more affectionate, and as we continued dancing, it almost seemed magical and we kissed.

Later that night, we spent the rest of the evening holding hands and acting pretty much like a couple. Ultimately we did end up having one of those high school relationships, but it never lasted since we both had to head off to college.

When I look back at my first prom, it seems like a fairy tale. The feelings I shared with Jean weren't only spontaneous, but also shared. The events surrounding the Junior Prom are among the most "Precious Moments" of my life.

Monique Linyard shares with us memories of her childhood dream of becoming an actress. Many of us whose early wishes for a particular career didn't come true may identify with eight-year old Monique; if we're as philosophical as she, perhaps we, too have no regrets that our path led elsewhere.

ACTING MEMORIES
By Monique Linyard*

I was just eight years old when I told my mother that I wanted to be an actress. She was so happy that she immediately put me into the acting programs at the Black Repertory Theater in Berkeley. I grew up watching famous television sitcoms such as *Good Times, Different Strokes*, and *Silver Spoons*. These were the shows that inspired me to make that decision as a young kid. I was also very lucky because I saw a performance of *The Wizard of Oz,* and that really inspired me to try to succeed as an actress.

I remember this day as clear as Evian. It was a sunny day and my mother was taking me for an audition to be in a play. I was told that I had to sing a song of my choice because that was to be the audition. I was *really* nervous because there were a lot of people watching and I didn't know much about singing.

The four judges called my name and I'd already decided to sing "The Greatest Love of All" by Whitney Houston. Everything in the theater was so dark and mysterious looking. All I could see was the spotlights on the four judges and my mother smiling at me and giving me encouragement from her eyes.

I began to sing, and what lasted for five minutes seemed like a lifetime. I was terribly scared but I wanted to show my mother and the judges that I could suceed at this audition.

I finished the song with flying colors and I felt good about myself. I'd always been the child who was scared of proving herself to people. I was more of a private individual, and I now know that in order to succeed in the business of acting you have to have a lot of self-confidence and motivational support.

In the end I didn't get the part but I was happy that I was even considered for it. I'll never forget the encouragement my mother gave me as a child. She's the reason I have high confidence in myself. I know firsthand how important it is for children to have the support of the mother who gave them life. Support given to children will shape their personality and help them find their own identify.

Even though I didn't pursue a career in acting I had the opportunity to be a star for five minutes and that made my day.

The impression that follows is very personal and carries a message that may touch you deeply. If you have grandparents, this impression could motivate you to spend more time with them, including time to learn about their lives when they were your age. It's generally acknowledged that the United States is a youth-oriented culture, and this is most likely true. There's nothing wrong with that, of course. But Ben McClintock reminds us that we can benefit from spending some priceless hours learning about times past as we develop a closer relationship with our grandparents.

IMPRESSION
"Missed Opportunities"
Ben McClintock*

We've all got things that we regret in lives.

Especially missed opportunities.

When we look back at those kinds of things, the act of reminiscence can be very bitter.

When they say hindsight is twenty-twenty, boy they aren't kidding.

This is the regret in my life that I wish to share with you.

Throughout the course of your life, your family, more often than not, is a constant.

They're always there and you can't pick them.

Like my dad says, "You can pick your friends, but you can't pick your family."

This constancy can be a double-edged sword though.

While it can provide a sense of permanence, it can also lead to the mistaken assumption that they will always be there.

When you're thirteen, you think that your family members will be there forever.

The reason I bring this up is because when I was thirteen, my grandfather, my mother's father, was diagnosed with lung cancer.

Three months later, he died from complications caused by it.

I still remember the last time I saw him.

He was a tall man, with a great, booming voice.

That day I don't remember him talking much louder than in a soft whisper.

I didn't know it at the time, but the reason my parents took me and my sister down to see him was because they knew he wouldn't be alive much longer.

When I look back on my memories of him, my regret as a young man, is that I never really got to know my grandfather.

I don't really blame myself.

After all, I was only thirteen, and we all know that the priorities of adolescents differ greatly from older people.

Sure, I saw him at family get-togethers and camping trips, but I have to ashamedly admit that I don't really know the person behind the title of grandfather.

I know that he was kind, and he had a laugh you could hear a mile away.

But as far as talking with him, finding out what he was like, I never did that.

Now that chance is forever denied to me.

It's amazing how we can interact with people for years and years and never truly know much about them.

When I decided to go to San Francisco State, my big dilemma was figuring out where I was going to live.

When my dad's parents said they would be glad to have me live with them while I went to school I jumped at it.

It was a great opportunity, if anything else because they laughed at me when I asked them how much they wanted me to pay them a month.

Now I see it as an even greater gift, one I'm glad I've not squandered.

I missed the chance to get to know my Mom's dad, but here was the perfect opportunity to get to know my other grandfather.

Living with your grandparents has its own unique set of drawbacks, but I wouldn't trade it for any dorm room or apartment in the world.

I get to see them on nearly a daily basis and know what they're really like outside the weekend visits and holiday cheer.

I feel lucky not only because I had this chance, but because I saw it for what it was and took advantage of it.

I'm old enough to realize that my grandparents won't always be there and one day, all I'll have of them are memories.

One thing I've learned in life is that it's not often you get second chances to do certain things,

I feel very lucky to have gotten the chance to live with them.

It has given me the chance to build up memories of them that will last me the rest of my life after they're gone.

Treasure your family.

Take the time to see them.

Take the time to talk with them.

Life has a way of moving all too fast, and when you're young, it can be hard to put on the brakes and take a look at those around you.

But it's important to do just that.

I missed my chance to get to really know one of my grandparents.

I'm glad I had enough sense to not make the same mistake with my other ones.

Narrative scripts, whether they're called commentaries, essays, opinions, or impressions are written to entertain, to move, or to enlighten. There isn't a big market on radio and television for such material, but the challenge is exciting, and the process of creating them can be a valuable learning experience. Developing the ability to spot the storytelling potential in seemingly commonplace events or activities, and to turn that potential into narratives is easily transferrable from a script to the creation of stories for print media. Many newspapers and magazines publish (and pay for!) stories that meet their standards and are in keeping with their stylistic tenor.

QUESTIONS

1. Select a narrative script from Appendix A and analyze it in terms of needs/desires it touches on, and the universal themes it addresses.

2. Select any of the narrative scripts in this chapter, and determine the parts—beginning, middle, and end. What is used to attract our attention at the outset that causes us to want to hear more? List the sequence of incidents or ideas that make up the middle. Are these logically or chronologically arranged? How does the end justify the story's opening? Does it make a point based on what went before? Does it leave us satisfied?

3. Write an "impression." Write it for you alone, as though it never will be seen by anyone else. After you're done, you may or may not decide to share it with others, but it's important as you conceive, structure, and set your impression into written words that you not write them as though someone is looking over your shoulder.

NOTES

1. Reprinted by permission of the author and Georges Borchardt, Inc.
2. Reprinted here with the gracious permission of the author.
3. Nicholas DeLuca is seven-time winner of the yearly Distinguished Service Award given by the Society of Professional Journalism; has twice won the National Headliner Award from the National Headliner Club; and has received awards from the Associated Press and the Radio and Television News Directors Association.
4. Courtesy of Jan Wahl, Entertainment Reorter for KRON-TV and KCBS Radio, San Francisco.
5. Jan Wahl is noted for her collection of hats, so instead of assigning "stars" to films, she awards hats.
6. A word of caution: it's important to avoid hairsplitting in determining whether a particular essay is a conventional one or an "impression." There's no solid line between them. Categories can be useful when they clarify or organize our thinking, but become counterproductive if we try to use them as though they're rules. Keep in mind that the difference is subtle, with essays being on the objective side of the scale, and impressions being on the subjective side.

CHAPTER FIFTEEN

PRODUCTION SCRIPTS: REPORTS AND SOUND PORTRAITS

This chapter discusses scripts that require production, and in many instances, more than one speaker. Scripts presented in this chapter generally involve recording on location, and employ music, sound effects, special visual effects, postproduction editing and/or electronic manipulation. Most, but not all, of the scripts in this chapter were written for television.

Developing your ability to spot topics that may make compelling narrative scripts can be of real benefit to you as a writer. Bob Davy, whose scripts are found in this and other chapters of *Idea to Script,* made these tacit observations:

Feature Ideas: Where do they come from?
Everywhere, that's where!
Lots of things come from newspapers:
    Endangered Species Act hearings
    horses used in logging
    ferry trip through the San Juan Islands
    a visit to the *Queen Mary* (retired classic ocean liner)
    Anti-Aryan nations rally
    Free Willy—Keiko flown to new home
    woman applies to all-male Elks for membership
    a visit to a game preserve
    cemetery art[1]

Scripts written by college students for a class in writing for the electronic media are identified by an asterisk (*) appearing after the author's name.

Davy maintains that interesting stories are before us at all times, and spotting them and turning them into good radio or television production requires only the ability to detect the potential in raw material.

FEATURE REPORTS

Feature report is an elastic term. It stretches enough to encompass everything from brief stories on current events to lengthy examinations of topics that have only glancing relationships to news. Feature reports are seen and heard on newscasts, but similar stories are also told on magazine-type shows, including *Good Morning America* and *Today,* current events programs, and such news-related shows as as *60 Minutes, Frontline, 20/20, Nightline,* and *CBS Sunday,* with local variations on regional stations and community-access cable outlets.

Reports come under a variety of labels: backgrounders, essays, commentaries, reviews, op/eds, editorials, and features. All tell their stories in greater depth than items on conventional newscasts, and topics, if they relate to news events at all, are most often of the soft news variety.

This chapter makes no attempt to categorize and label the boundless variety of stories that make up feature reports. The scripts and the commentaries that follow them merely reflect the range of endeavors and sequence that this genre offers. The scripts have but one thing in common: all are of excellent quality. To simplify matters, and for the sake of clarity, all scripts in the section that follows are called "reports."

Whether for radio or television, reports are made up of edited *bites* (television), or *actualities* (radio), arranged and held together with narration. Bites and actualities are statements made by persons other than broadcast personnel—spokespersons, eye witnesses, experts on particular subjects, and even people on the street randomly selected to express feelings or offer opinions.

Reports, aside from those dealing with hard news, often appear on newscasts. Typically, a reporter conceives or is assigned a human interest story; the closing of a once-popular night club; the college graduation of a fifty-year-old returnee and her son; the anniversary of the opening of an important landmark such as a bridge; or the story of a championship Little League team.

In nearly all instances, a reporter gathers information at the scenes of a story, records interviews and statements in the field that will be logged as sound bites or actualities, and makes notes for later reference. At the station, the recordings are reviewed, selected, edited, and assembled in sequence. The reporter writes and records an introduction and voice-over narration, and submits the story as a complete package needing only a lead-in by an anchor. *Route 66, Slang*, and *Ohlone Humane Society* are examples of that process appearing in this chapter.

News departments represent features as being factual, and for the most part, they are. However, because reporters can't avoid having feelings about stories they cover, they often reveal their personal opinions in the selection and arrangement of bites and in the connecting narration. As a writer-producer of feature reports for newscasts, it's important to try to put personal feelings aside and present balanced reports that permit audience members to form their own opinions. If, on the other hand, the story isn't presented as news, it's acceptable to take a position, as in an editorial, commentary, or essay.

Features appear on both radio and television, and are common on PBS programs. Radio features are regularly heard on National Public Radio, and Public Radio International. Assignment editors at most local television stations send reporters into the field to create feature reports for their newscasts.

Some feature reports center on important social, political, environmental, or similar issues of special significance; others explore topics of less urgency, but are worth investigating and producing as features because they're illustrative, informative, humorous, or otherwise attractive to audiences.

Backgrounders are reports that present insights or implications of stories in the news. Reporters may refer to important developments from the past that help assess ongoing issues. Some concepts can be documented in sound or pictures: for example, a feature on a proposed law to make English our official language could include some historical information, complete with file recordings on bilingual societies such as Canada, Belgium, and Ethiopia.

Topics of feature reports concern people, problems, events, or anything else of general interest that lacks the hard news character demanded by coverage on a regular newscast. News events frequently inspire feature reports, but such reports differ from news stories in that they provide more detail, offer greater perspective, and sometimes express a point of view.

The feature report *Free Willy* was written, produced, and narrated by Bob Davy, a freelance writer-producer of essays, sound portraits, and features for National Public Radio (NPR), Public Radio International (PRI), Voice of America (VOA), the BBC, and, occasionally, NBC Radio News. His script *Free Willy* follows a format preferred by National Public Radio, on which *Free Willy* was broadcast. The script includes all spoken words and sound effects. Narration uses both capitals and lowercase letters. Actualities and the introductory words of the program host are ALL CAPS.

"FREE WILLY" FEATURE[2]
BOB DAVY

HOST INTRO:
ON JANUARY 7, THE KILLER WHALE NAMED KEIKO (KAY-KOH) WILL BE FLOWN FROM MEXICO CITY TO HIS NEW HOME IN NEWPORT, OREGON. KEIKO WAS THE STAR OF THE 1993 SURPRISE HIT MOVIE *FREE WILLY,* SEEN BY MILLIONS OF CHILDREN. KEIKO'S NEW HOME IS A MODEL SEA MAMMAL FACILITY, FOUR TIMES LARGER THAN HIS PRESENT POOL IN MEXICO. IT WAS A RUSHED CONSTRUCTION JOB BECAUSE OF KEIKO'S DECLINING HEALTH. BOB DAVY HAS THIS REPORT FROM THE OREGON COAST AQUARIUM.

SFX #1: MOVIE TRACK I EXCERPT FROM FILM *FREE WILLY* (WE HEAR WHALE SOUNDS AND BOY'S VOICE "YOU CAN DO IT, WILLY")

DAVY:

The motion picture *FREE WILLY* is the story of a boy and his friend, a killer whale he releases from captivity into the ocean. It was filmed at an amusement park pool in Mexico City where its animal star named Keiko lived. A LIFE magazine article appearing after the filming of FREE WILLY reported that Keiko was in poor health, caused partly by his living in a small, overly warm chlorinated pool . . . and possibly by the pollution and high altitude of Mexico City. Prompted by that article, children across the nation raised money to help move their friend Keiko to a new eight-million-dollar home here at the Oregon Coast Aquarium at Newport. Thousands of letters with contributions including pennies, nickels and dimes came to the film's producers at Warner Brothers Studios in Hollywood.

Oregon Coast Aquarium President Phyllis Bell says she was first contacted by people from Earth Island Institute, an environmental action organization of San Francisco, the group that had been asked by Warner Brothers to find a new and better home for Keiko.

SFX # 2: FEEDING SEA MAMMALS AT AQUARIUM

ACTUALITY #1 (PHYLLIS BELL)
THEY CAME TO VISIT HERE, LOVED THE AQUARIUM, LOVED WHAT WE WERE ABOUT, LIKED OUR MISSION STATEMENT, TOURED THE ENTIRE FACILITY, BEHIND THE SCENES ALSO, AND SAW HOW WE TREATED ANIMALS AND HOW OUR LIFE SUPPORT SYSTEM OPERATED, AND THAT DAY THEY MADE A DECISION THAT THIS WAS THE PLACE WHERE THEY WOULD LIKE TO SEE KEIKO GO (OUT).

SFX #3: CONSTRUCTION SOUNDS

DAVY:
Because of Keiko's declining health, a deadline for completion of the new facility required it be built in only 18 months. It took some hustling to get Keiko's new home finished by that time. But even in the rush to complete the project by January 7, Bell says the Aquarium staff did not want this to be just another showplace where sea mammals amuse people by jumping out of the water.

ACTUALITY #2 (BELL)
WE DON'T DO SHOWS HERE. WE HAVE NORMAL FEEDINGS OF THE ANIMALS AND THE PUBLIC CAN OBSERVE THAT—BUT WE DON'T ANNOUNCE THE TIMES—WE WANT TO MAKE IT AS NATURAL AS POSSIBLE. THAT WAS VERY IMPORTANT WITH KEIKO. NO GRANDSTAND SEATING. WE MADE A COMMITMENT EARLY ON THAT KEIKO WOULD ONLY BE VIEWED FROM UNDERWATER VIEWING WINDOWS AS NATURAL AS POSSIBLE.

DAVY:
Allen Monroe, Director of Animal Husbandry at the Aquarium, says Keiko's basic living environment will change for the better when he moves to Oregon.

ACTUALITY #3 (MONROE)
MEXICO CITY IN GENERAL IS AT AN ELEVATION OF 8,000 FEET. THERE AREN'T TOO MANY MARINE MAMMALS THAT ARE ADAPTED TO LIVING AT THAT KIND OF ELEVATION. SO WE THINK THAT BRINGING HIM DOWN HERE TO SEA LEVEL WILL BE A BIG IMPROVEMENT FOR HIM. WE'VE TRIED TO CREATE A MORE NATURAL ENVIRONMENT HERE BY INCLUDING ABOUT 5,000 SQ FT OF REEF AND ARTIFICIAL ROCK WORK IN THE BOTTOM OF THE POOL. IT PROVIDES NOOKS AND CRANNIES HE CAN SWIM AROUND AND GO AROUND, SWIM BETWEEN, HIDE BEHIND.

SFX Cut #4: HARBOR SOUNDS

DAVY:
Keiko is nearly full grown. He's 21 feet long, but the normal male killer whale of 14 years is about 30 feet. Keiko has skin lesions on his body, a compromised immune system with poor over-all muscle tone from inactivity in overly warm chlorinated city water in his pool. Oregon Coast Aquarium Curator of Marine Animals Mike Glenn will be in charge of Keiko's day-to-day management.

SFX #5: SOUNDS OF FEEDING SEA MAMMALS AT AQUARIUM

ACTUALITY #4 (GLENN)
WE HOPE IN A YEAR WE HAVE A VERY ROBUST KILLER WHALE. HE WEIGHS BETWEEN 9 AND 10 THOUSANDS LBS. HE'S CURRENTLY ABOUT 2,000 LBS UNDERWEIGHT, AND WE FEEL THAT'S SOMETHING WE CAN CORRECT RATHER QUICKLY, ONCE HE ARRIVES, BECAUSE OF THE QUANTITY OF FOOD WE'RE PREPARED TO FEED HIM AND THE TEMPERATURE OF THE WATER. WE'RE GOING TO FEED HIM SEVERAL DIFFERENT SPECIES OF FISH, A VARIETY OF FOOD, AND FATTEN HIM UP.

DAVY:
Releasing Keiko back into the Icelandic waters where he was captured 12 years ago has been suggested as a future goal for Keiko. But Glenn says Keiko would have to learn a number of skills for this to happen.

ACTUALITY #5 (GLENN)
ONE WOULD BE A HUNTING INSTINCT. WE'D HAVE TO STOP FEEDING HIM THE DEAD FISH WE'D GIVE HIM. AND WE'D HAVE TO START INTRODUCING LIVE FOOD AT IRREGULAR INTERVALS AND WATCH HIS BEHAVIOR. HE'D HAVE TO RECOGNIZE THE FACT THAT HE'S HUNGRY . . . RECOGNIZE THE FACT THAT THERE ARE FISH IN THE POOL, HUNT THEM DOWN AND EAT THEM. BEING A MALE IT'S VERY POSSIBLE HE'D HAVE DIFFICULTY IN TRYING TO GET BACK INTO A GROUP OF WHALES OR POD OF WHALES OUT IN THE WILD. THE PODS OF KILLER WHALES ARE FEMALE DOMINATED. AND NORMALLY THERE'S JUST ONE LARGE MALE, THE GROUP IS CONTROLLED

BY FEMALES. IF HE EVER HAD TO FIGHT OR DEFEND A TERRITORY, WE DON'T KNOW IF THAT WOULD BE POSSIBLE.

SFX #6: CONSTRUCTION SOUNDS

DAVY:

If Keiko recovers fully, another sea mammal might be introduced into his pool—a buddy for him to socialize with—even a mate. Right now the excitement for friends of Keiko is in flying him here from Mexico City with arrival on January 7, a dream come true for thousands of school children who collected all those pennies, nickels and dimes to help pay for Keiko's new home.

SFX # 7: MOVIE TRACK II EXCERPT NARR (cut #7):

DAVY:

For National Public Radio, I'm Bob Davy at the Oregon Coast Aquarium in Newport, Oregon.

The drama inherent in *Free Willy* unfolds at the very opening of the script, as the narrator focuses on the concerns of children about the fate of Keiko. Their contributions of pennies, nickels, and dimes; the success of their campaign; and the preparations being made in Oregon for the rehabilitation of Keiko complete the story. Take away that introduction, and the story becomes one of facts, statistics, and plans about the construction of Keiko's new home and the regimen planned for his recovery. Take out the children's crusade and the story loses its most important human quotient. When planning a story, it's important to look for themes inherent in the total picture that are most likely to attract, hold, and move an audience.

The chain of events that leads to the creation of a television feature begins with an idea in the mind of a writer or, when created for a newscast, by a reporter or an assignment editor. Each of these follows a different production path. One path sees the writer creating a script, after which visual and additional production elements are added to fit and underscore the narrative. Richard Rodriguez's *Death of a Church* reflects this process well. All visual images were obtained and assembled after the script was written. Richard Rodriguez describes how he works with a coproducer:

> About how the essays are assembled. Generally, I talk to my producer when we're shooting an essay about how I imagine the material visually. And, then we try to find the right images. sometimes we're not able to find images for some of the ideas, and they have to be computer generated. That part is done in collaboration. The writing part, the idea for the piece always comes from me, so that's my major contribution. As a writer. But, as a collaborator, I co-produce the visual essay. I make suggestions, and then my producer goes ahead and creates it.[3]

Rodriguez's television reminiscence *Death of a Church* is both feature report and and impression. It outlines facts about the closing of one Catholic church among several in San Francisco, and that's the essay aspect of the piece. At the same time, the author involves himself, his memories, and his emotions in the story, to give the piece the intimacy of an impression.

DEATH OF A CHURCH
BY RICHARD RODRIGUEZ
PACIFIC NEWS SERVICE[4]

VIDEO	AUDIO
PANORAMIC VIEW OF SAN FRANCISCO NEIGHBORHOOD SHIPYARD CRANES IN DISTANCE	(VO) For over a century, All Hallows Catholic Church has stood on its hill in San Francisco.
SLOW ZOOM OUT TO ALL HALLOWS CHURCH	Such a plain old building it is. Like thousands of nineteenth-century churches all across America. Architectural historians call the style "Carpenter Gothic."
CUT TO: CU OF ST. BRIGID'S CHURCH	Last year the Catholic Archbishop of San Francisco announced the closure of eleven churches all around the city. Reasons for the closings varied.
MONTAGE OF FACADES OF FOUR CLOSED CHURCHES	According to church officials, it was too expensive to make some churches earthquake safe. Or, it was a case of the grandchildren of the original immigrant founders moving off to the suburbs. One official claimed that All Hallows Church was no longer a viable Parish.
MCU RICHARD RODRIGUEZ BEFORE ALL HALLOWS	A few weeks ago I received a letter from a woman who attended All Hallows Church. She wrote, "I would be extremely gratified if you would come to our last Sunday Mass.

SUPER: RICHARD
RODRIGUEZ
PACIFIC NEWS SERVICE

The reason I am forced to write to you," she said, "is because we face a gaping need. We need to believe that we still matter."

MUSIC: CONGREGATIONAL SINGING

SHOT OF PROCESSION
DOWN AISLE IN ALL
HALLOWS CHURCH

That last Sunday mass at All Hallows is preserved now on homemade videotape. You can see what it was like: the crowded pews. That warm summer morning.

SHOTS TO MATCH
NARRATION

The knowing faces of the old, the screaming babies. The entire Parish had gathered one last time for a mass that went on, with tears and much music, for over two hours.

MS OF LARGE CRUCIFIX
SLOW ZOOM TO FACE OF
CHRIST

All Hallows was constructed in 1886 with dollars earned by working-class people. Generations tended this church. Painted and repainted it. Warmed it in winter, lit candles and sang hymns, and took communion and found a meaning for their lives. Finally, however, legal title to the building belongs to the Archbishop; it was his decision alone that locked the doors.

EXT SHOT OF ALL
HALLOWS

MONTAGE OF SHOTS OF
NEIGHBORHOOD

All Hallows, perched on its hill, saw generations pass beneath it. The founding neighborhood was predominantly Irish. There are still White families on these blocks. The nearby shipyard brought African Americans to this section of San Francisco during the war. Today, there is a growing Hispanic population, mostly Central American. And increasing numbers of the neighbors are Samoans and Tongans. "Pacific Islanders" they're called by bureaucrats.

SHOT OF VARIOUS RACE CHILDREN RUNNING	People in universities go on and on about multi-culturalism. People in neighborhoods like this one live multi-culturalism.
	MUSIC: IN AND UP
CHURCH FROM ABOVE SHOTS OF WORSHIPPERS IN PEWS, THEN RISING TO COMMUNION	On that last Sunday in the small church White and Black worshipped together. The singing was in Spanish and in Samoan. Huge Samoan men in ceremonial skirts sang like cherubs.
	Ideas about God do not create religion. Religion does not exist in the solitude of the theologian's mind or in the philosopher's high tower.
	Religion comes into being when people gather together, whether in a Mosque, or a temple, or a church. When people gather together to share their beliefs, and to worship. Religion creates community; religion requires community. Religion is a public thing, a neighborhood event, over time.
	In a neighborhood that many San Franciscans today regard as dangerous and violent, All Hallows Church was a place where people met.
MCU RICHARD RODRIGUEZ ADDRESSING CAMERA	Years ago, when I was an altar boy, I served at hundreds of masses, I saw more weddings and funerals in a year than baseball games. I grew up with the ritual rhythms of sorrow and joy.
	At a Catholic funeral there comes a moment, just after the communion, when the undertakers approach the altar. The mass is coming to a close.
	Suddenly, the mourners anticipate the journey to the cemetery. All the preparation, all that stands between life and death, the wake, the meals with

	visiting relatives, the funeral mass, all that keeps mourners from bidding their last good-bye is over.
BAGPIPER IN KILT, PLAYING AND WALKING AROUND INTERIOR OF CHURCH	MUSIC: AMAZING GRACE ON BAGPIPE At All Hallows that last Sunday, just after communion, the altar servers started extinguishing the candles. The altar was stripped of its starched white cloth.
MUSIC: AMAZING GRACE BAGPIPE, UP & UNDER	From the back of the church came an Irish bagpiper. He circled the congregation of Samoans and Nicaraguans, grandmothers and babies, all the while playing "Amazing Grace."
	MUSIC: UP AND UNDER
WORSHIPPERS LIGHTING ONE ANOTHER'S CANDLES. CHURCH LIGHTS OUT	The Church exists to see us through the seasons of our lives. Babies are baptized. Children take their first Holy Communion. Teenagers are confirmed. Young people get married. The old are buried.
	Fall, Spring, Christmas, Easter. We expect the church to last forever. To see us through our comings and goings. We do not expect to witness a funeral for a church.
	When the mass was finally over at All Hallows, even before we left the building, the lights were extinguished.
	MUSIC: UP TO CLOSE
FADE TO BLACK	I'm Richard Rodriguez.

The most creative and forceful passage in *Death of a Church* is near the end, in the paragraph that begins, "The Church exists to see us through the seasons of our lives." Here is the culmination of the entire piece, a summing up that conveys the true tragedy, in human terms, of the closing of a house of worship for financial reasons. The entire report, including its opening lines and the empathy established with those who built the church and those now worshiping there, are a skillful prelude to Rodriguez's summing up: his comments transmute our concern over the destruction of a physical object, an old church building, into an awareness of the unwitting cruelty of an act that deprived faithful but powerless church members access to their God while destroying their faith that the Church would always be there for them.

Wayne Freedman's *Route 66* demonstrates the other path. Once Freedman decides to explore a story, he moves to the scene of the action accompanied by a camera operator. On site, the story begins to suggest itself through Freedman's observations, interviews, and his feelings generated by the general ambiance of the place. They record the story elements and Freedman writes the bulk of the script after editing and assembling the bites. The script of *Route 66* follows Freedman's comments about creating expressive reports.

As mentioned earlier, Wayne Freedman of ABC News takes a path quite different from that taken by Richard Rodriguez. After coming up with the idea for a story, he engages in on-site research, usually accompanied by a camera operator. This exploration occurs before he writes one line of a script.

On site, he speaks with several likely candidates as he searches for the focus of the story. As he engages in what seems on the surface to be merely amiable conversations, he listens for clues as to what resides below the surface of each person he speaks with. When his story is to depict an event, he uses these interviews to select three or four individuals for sound bites, and one other who seems most likely to carry the spirit or mood of the occasion for an in-depth interview. That person will carry most of the story's exposition and whatever emotional depths there are to plumb. In *Route 66,* the story has but one principal on whom Freedman focuses. Freedman enjoys exploring the nature of people with interesting stories to tell. He tells us the factors that motivate the path he follows:

> I think television needs someone to remind viewers that, even with all the lunacy in this world, normal people still exist. I look for the untold story, and the person—a main character—and that person's simple truth. Hard news is impersonal; a feature report should be the opposite. Simple stories. Simple truths.[5]

As Freedman gathers facts and feelings about the story, his partner, a camera operator with whom he's worked for years, scouts for and records physical sites that may embellish, explain, or otherwise add to the story forming in Freedman's mind. At times, Freedman asks that a certain shot be taken from a particular distance and perspective. The visualization of his story is already forming in his mind.

> Day to day, this is a business of little stories. Learn to do those well, and the big ones will fall into place because you've learned how to tap into concerns and values, not only of the people whose stories you tell, but also of those who are moved by them. Television should be an emotional medium. The path to the head runs through the gut. You'll serve a piece better by staying out of the story's way.
>
> You mustn't invent the story, but instead try to discover it from the inside. You'll inevitably be *in* the story, but it's your responsibility to *tell* the story without *becoming* the story. Respect the viewers and let the person in the story be the star of that story. Even the

simplest story contains layers and subtleties. A good feature story is often about something other than the main subject. If I do my job exceptionally well, viewers may not remember me, but they'll remember the story—not for minutes or days, but for years.[6]

Route 66 is a splendid example of Wayne Freedman's credo translated into practice.

ROUTE 66
ABC NEWS
REPORTER: Wayne Freedman (WF)[7]

VIDEO	AUDIO
OPEN ON SHOT OF DESERTED, CRACKED, OLD, TWO-LANE HIGHWAY, DISAPPEARING INTO DISTANCE.	MUSIC: TWANGING CHORDS ON GUITAR
DISS TO LOG SHOT OF GARAGE AND JUNK YARD	
DISS TO GAS STATION, OLD SIGN SWAYING IN THE WIND.	
DISS TO OLD GARAGE, SEEN THRU TALL WEEDS.	
DISS TO OLD FADED SIGN SUNDAY SCHOOL 1000 MORNING WORSHIP 1100 AFTERNOON WORSHIP 700 EVERYBODY WELCOME	WF: According to the sign, there will be worship at the Chambers Pentecostal Church this Sunday. Though, from the look of things only termites will attend. Not far away, another sign says they still sell gas for 38.9 cents a gallon.
TERMITES ON LOG	
GAS PUMP SIGN	
FADED SIGNS BY ROADSIDE OF OLD 66	But on Route 66, signs may be deceiving. They have a way of pointing to the past, not to the future.
CU OF NILE ROCKWELL PULLING DOWNED SIGN FORWARD SIGN READS "NATIONAL ALL-TRAILS ROAD"	SFX: (CLANGING SOUND)

NILE: Can you read that??

OLD GRASS-COVERED, RUTTED
DIRT ROAD

WF: Sure can. National All-Trails Road,
it says.

WF: Around Chambers, the National
All-Trails Road is a dirt path bumping
out of the desert.

CUT TO DESERTED ROUTE 66

It is the trail that begat Route 66,

CUT TO BUSY ROUTE 40

that begat Interstate 40,

that begat the sad ending of Nile
Rockwell's once-thriving wrecking
business and road house.

2-SHOT OF WAYNE FREEDMAN
AND NILE ROCKWELL BEFORE
CRUMBLING STRUCTURE

WF: How many cars used to go through
here every day?

NR: Oh, about 600.

WF: Did they stop?

NR: . . . as many as I could fool.

MONTAGE OF THREE SHOTS OF
JUNKED CARS. WF IN LAST SHOT,
WALKS TOWARD CAMERA

WF: When Nile Rockwell took this place
over on 1954, he was buying a piece of
the American Dream. The business
would come to him, and for eleven years
business that was very good. But then,
Interstate 40 replaced Route 66. The
government did not build the overpass
it promised him, and nobody stopped
any more.

CARS DRIVING VERY FAST ON
RTE 40

SFX: (CARS DRIVING BY)

WF AND NILE IN 2-SHOT

WF: What did it do to your business?

NR: Well, it cut me out, dammit.

WF: And, for the last 26 years, he's
watched that business roll by his front
door. Thousands of cars a day,
separated by a fence. Cars that for Nile

Rockwell, might as well be in another galaxy.

WF: For them to get to you, how far do they have to drive?

NR: Well, five miles down, and five miles back.

SFX: (CARS DRIVING BY)

WF: It's gotta make you angry—or are you past that now?

NILE TURNS AWAY

NR: Well hell, I'm past that now. . . . hell.

PANORAMIC VIEW OF JUNKED CARS

MUSIC: STRAINS ON GUITAR, MELANCHOLY.

CU OF CAR HOOD. 1650 WRITTEN ON IT

WF: These days Nile Rockwell sees more rainstorms than customers. What'd they offer you?

NR: Probably offer me 500.

WF: You wouldn't take 500?

CU HOOD ORNAMENT: HUDSON

NR: Why, hell no . . . I'd get 500 for the hood.

SEQUENCE OF SHOTS OF OLD DECAYING CARS

WF: So, the rain falls and his cars slowly dissolve into the desert. Like the man who owns them, they are leftovers from prosperous times on a once busy road. Rusty dream machines, with stately lines, classic lines, and stories from the highway.

CU OF WF WITH HAND ON PASSENGER SIDE DOOR HANDLE

NR: Now, open the door and look in there. There was a man and wife and five children in that car. And, I haven't taken anything out of this . . .

WF POKING AROUND INSIDE CAR	WF: He remembers it as if it were yesterday. The car broke down. Nile took the family to town. The father asked him to keep an eye on their things.
	NR: Shut it.
WF SLAMS DOOR. MCU OF NILE	WF: That's all their stuff in there?
	NR: That's all their stuff.
	WF: How many years it been sitting here??
	NR: Oh, about, oh, around ten . . .
	WF: You don't expect them to come back now?
NILE TURNS AND WALKS AWAY	NR: No.
	WF: Just like the old days, and the old roads, and the business that once filled his garage.
INTERIOR GARAGE	NR: This is a good welder here . . . very good welder. And . . .
	SFX: (GRINDER)
	grinders.
	WF: Seems a shame to have all this stuff out here, and not be able to use it.
STOPS, PAUSES, LOOKS AT WF	NR: (DEFENSIVELY) I use it.
	MUSIC: TWANG ON GUITAR.
SHOTS OF OLD, RUSTED HULKS WF: LAST SHOT SHOWS WF IN BG. WF WALKS TOWARD CAMERA	And, Nile Rockwell will stay, he says, because after all the years, and all the trouble, this is still home. 400 acres, cut off from the highway. On a stretch of road no one travels anymore.
SLOW DISSOLVE, MONTAGE OF 8 SHOTS OF CARS	
DISS TO OPENING SHOT OF DESERTED ROUTE 66.	MUSIC: TWANGS ON GUITAR, SLOW AND MOURNFUL, TO CLOSE.

Simple story, simple truths.

Bob Garfield is cohost of NPR's *On The Media*, a frequent contributor to NPR's *All Things Considered*, and columnist and editor at large for *Advertising Age* magazine.[8] He delivered his essay, *Jerome the Pig* on *All Things Considered*. The essay is representative of his penchant for offbeat stories, a penchant that has taken him throughout the United States in search of bizarre Americana. Robert Seigel, host of *All Things Considered*, says this about Garfield: "Bob Garfield is the funniest correspondent on *All Things Considered*. While that is a lot like being the skinniest sumo wrestler in Hawaii, I am convinced that even if the rest of us were trying to be funny, Garfield would still be funnier."[9]

Jerome the Pig is funny, but it's more than that. The story reflects several aspects of Garfield's approach to his work: a keen eye for spotting the story potential in the traits of unusual, not-so-ordinary people; meticulous and thorough research; effective step-by-step structuring of story incidents; and the ability to formulate a report in crisp writing that allows us to savor his delight while not in any way arousing ridicule. We follow the story of Victoria Herberta and her pig, Jerome, with growing attachment to both. Garfield's narration is in italics.

Jerome the Pig[10]
By Bob Garfield

WOMAN:
[from the cab of a pickup truck traveling down the highway] I have always loved the name Jerome. I mean, since I was eight years old, I just love the name Jerome, and I always thought at that time, if I'm ever married and I have a son, you know, his name is going to be Jerome. . . .

This is the story of a pig, and the woman who loves him. The pig's name is Jeffrey Jerome. The woman is Victoria Herberta, and for the umpteenth time this year, she's making the three-hour pickup truck ride between Houston and San Marcos, Texas, to visit her beloved hog.

VICTORIA HERBERTA:
[still In truck] I'm the only mommy he knows, and he's like a son to me. I mean, he's like a child. So what I've been doing, I come to San Marcos. I stay thirty days at a time, go back to Houston for four or five days, which he will not eat during the time I'm gone . . .

This has been going on for a year, ever since last October 31 when Jerome, all 700 pounds of him, was exiled from the city of Houston. The charge: being a pig.

MAN:
Section 6-dash-11 of the City Code: the keeping of swine and goats, which are prohibited, with the exception of milk goats. That's the particular ordinance, and it just says where you can have these kinds of animals and where you can't.

That's Dr. Robert Armstrong, chief of animal regulation in Houston, a man who in Victoria Herberta's view falls somewhere between Simon Legree and Oscar Mayer. It was he who, upon learning that Ms. Herberta was keeping a pig within city limits, enforced the century-old law. But what began as a routine pig eviction has become a Texas cause celebre. Dr. Armstrong didn't realize that Ms. Herberta is not your typical 50-year-old pig-owning housepainter. And he didn't know Jerome is not your ordinary pig.

HERBERTA:
No, he's no ordinary pig. You know, he's got very good heritage, being the son of Priscilla. He's done a lot of good work. I mean, I've taken this animal and I've done good with this animal.

She's done well with all of her pigs. Jerome's mama, Priscilla the swimming pig, became internationally famous after saving the life of a drowning retarded boy at nearby Lake Summerville. This was in 1984, a hot July day when an ordinary outing with twelve people and a swimming pig would change Victoria Herberta's life. Press interviews, talk show appearances, even a Priscilla the Pig Day in Houston.

HERBERTA:
It was really something. I wasn't expecting it, because all I wanted was a pig to have as a pet and to raise as a pet and live in obscurity, you know, and just enjoy my pig.

That's all she ever wanted, but the universe wouldn't cooperate. Six months after Priscilla's water heroics, Herberta's pride and joy overdosed on backyard morning glories, and was retired to the farm in a porcine stupor. This left Herberta temporarily pigless, until, two pigs later, Jerome came into the picture. He lived with her from July 1987 to last fall, a period through which Herberta devoted her mother love to Jerome, and her leftover human compassion to the area's homeless. Most of her meager housepainting income went to feed needy men and women. Her purple frame house—the one with the antique signs and the giant hog on the porch—was a conspicuous oasis for the down-and-out. Whether the procession of hungry visitors angered neighbors, Herberta doesn't know. But somebody complained to the city, and all of a sudden she was being cited for an illicit pig.

HERBERTA:
They had to admit that he was totally clean. His quarters were clean. He had absolutely no odor. And I took them around the yard and there was no excrement or no urine in the yard.

Didn't matter. Jerome was still a pig. Swine non grata. Herberta engaged a lawyer, but that was no help. Dr. Armstrong's department was burdened by the tragic and overwhelming daily duty of putting down stray animals and protecting the health of an irresponsible public. In that unpleasant context, the problems of a woman and her pet pig seemed trivial. Armstrong's only concession was to let Jerome remain at home for one last hurrah: a charity fling, a Halloween party for the homeless. Then it was to the farm.

Now that may seem like a fitting venue for a pig, but that presupposes that the pig is a pig at heart, Jerome—terrific, radiant Jerome—is some pig, Herberta says, by virtue of being not very piglike at all.

HERBERTA:
He's humanized. All he knows is human companionship. He is totally afraid of other pigs. He will never, ever adjust to being a farm animal. I mean, he sees another pig—even his own mother—and he screams, and he runs and hides. He's terrified.

Not that the farm is inhospitable. Owner Ada Davis, who trains all the diving pigs for the nearby Aquarena Springs amusement park, has made her home Victoria and Jerome's home. When Herberta stays on the farm, Jerome does fine. But when she leaves, he goes . . . well, he goes hog wild, crying, squealing, laying in ant beds, starving himself, And it tears his owner up inside. After a year of living with her pig three weeks out of four in a 14 x 14 pump house—a tiny farm outbuilding with neither toilet nor kitchen facilities nor even hot water—Herberta can no longer bring herself to leave, and no longer afford to stay. There's no work for a fifty-year-old housepainter in rural San Marcos. Unless the city of Houston relents, she says, she'll have to put Jerome to sleep—if she can bear the agony of doing it.

HERBERTA:
[choking back sobs] I don't really know. I don't want to live without him, and I don't think he deserves that. I just don't think he deserves that.

Nor is she alone in that sentiment. Jerome's fate has become the focus of a campaign by concerned Houstonians, an eclectic assortment of citizens led by an unlikely advocate. She is Caroline Farb, the city's highest-profile socialite—she of the Christmas Food Basket Program and the Cancer Challenge Telethon, of the notorious $20 million divorce settlement and the 2,000-square-foot bedroom closet. Can it be that Caroline Farb, owner of the sprawling River Oaks mansion called Carolina, is now Houston's foremost champion of wronged hogs?

CAROLINE FARB:
Well, I'm not interested in all pigs. I'm interested in this specific pig, because he has done a lot of good, and he is truly a ham-bassador.

The effort has included a Save Jerome billboard, a letter-writing campaign (music begins to fade up from background) and even a specially recorded song called "The Ballad of Jerome."

SONG:
"This is the ballad of Jeffrey Jerome. He feeds the people without any home. Collects the food, all in cans, and takes it to his homeless fans. ohhhhh, ohhh Jeffrey Jerome (fades under) . . ."

Unfortunately for Farb and her volunteers, the campaign has been a bust. Attempts to pass special legislation have failed in city council and the Texas statehouse, on the principle that legislative exemptions for specific barnyard animals constitute bad government. As for Dr. Armstrong, the law is explicit, and because it all began with a citizen complaint, unavoidable.

ARMSTRONG:
Either say it is a pig, or it isn't. It is in the city, or it isn't. That's how you enforce ordinances.

But that sways Victoria Herberta not one whit.

HERBERTA:
You tell me rules are rules, and I will tell you rules are made to be revised and amended. Look at the amendments to the U.S. Constitution. And also we've heard that there is an exception to every rule, and I am sure that the mayor and the City Council—every member of City Council—at one time or another in their life has had a rule bent for them.

[To the sounds of the truck on a dirt and gravel driveway] *At last the ride is over, another separation ended, another happy reunion.*

HERBERTA:
[slamming truck door, walking around the vehicle as geese and ducks are heard in background] Have to watch the rocks and the mud. . . . I seeeeee you! Yes I dooooo! How's my little pumpkin, huh? How's Mr. Swoonie?

There's nothing quite like the feelings between a pet owner and a pet, even if the pet is a snorting third of a ton of highly saturated fat. [Jerome is heard panting and snorting]

HERBERTA:
Look at my pretty boy! Look at Mama's boyyyy! [animated snorting] Hey! Heyyyy!

Sitting in the old pump house, Herberta pulls out snapshots of Jerome the way some people show off their grandchildren.

HERBERTA:
Okay, this is Jerome when he was ten days old, just a little ol' bitty handful [laughs]. Okay, now here he is when he was about three months old and I was teaching him to pray. He knows how to pray. And here's his Halloween party. Here he was dressed like the Vampig, in his cape and orange feather tutu. And this is where we had over 1,000 people show up. This is his birthday cake, shaped in a pig face. The inside is dog food and the outside is cream cheese. [laughs] And here's a picture . . .

[With her continuing to show off snapshots in background] *What will become of Herberta and Jerome is still uncertain, but something has to give. She's sold virtually everything she owns to sustain herself this past year. Her only asset is her house, against which the city has placed tax liens. With no solution in sight, now she's just a lady with a pig, enjoying whatever time the two have left together.*

HERBERTA:
[to the pig] You're gonna get a treat! Yeah, you're gonna get a treat! [she rustles the cellophane wrapper of a muffin] Come on! You want a snack? Huh? [pig noisily gobbles muffin from her hand] That good? That's a bran muffin. Yeah, Mom give you a treat. Say, "Oh, I like that!"[11]

The feature that follow tells the story of a most unusual humane society—one whose sole mission is to save the lives of discarded pets and place them in caring homes. In this report, the nearly universal human affection for animals, especially dogs, is used to involve and move viewers to applaud the efforts of the all-volunteer Ohlone Humane Society. The piece is carefully constructed to capture the attention of viewers, to hold their attention, to lead them through some emotional moments, and to leave them with knowledge of this unique organization. It may, in fact motivate some to give support by contributing money or by becoming a volunteer.

OHLONE HUMANE SOCIETY
REPORTER: DORA RIVAS*

VIDEO	AUDIO
MS TO CU SHOT OF TASHA, A 125 LB. MALAMUTE MIX DOG. TASHA'S EARS ARE DOWN AND SHE'S STICKING HER TONGUE OUT.	NATURAL SOUND OF TASHA BREATHING RIVAS: Meet Tasha, a four-year-old Malamute cross with a gigantic heart.
LS OF TASHA AS SHE BEGINS PLAYING WITH A BALL. TASHA IN FRONT YARD AS SHE RUNS BACK AND FORTH, ROLLING THE BALL AROUND.	It's hard to believe that every year; hundreds of unwanted animals like Tasha find themselves without a home.
MS OF REPORTER STEPPING INTO THE PICTURE. PLAYS WITH TASHA AND THE BALL. SERIES OF SHOTS OF A VARIETY OF EVERYDAY HOUSES. SHOTS INCLUDE VARIETY OF PEOPLE FEEDING AND CARING FOR ANIMALS.	Hundreds of loving animals crowd shelters across the country, in search of a home, love and nourishment. Many times, they find death instead.
LS OF RIVAS AND TASHA IN FRONT OF HOUSE.	One Tri-City group is making great efforts to change the fate of these unwanted animals. This group, The Ohlone [o-LONE-ee] Humane Society

is not an ordinary animal shelter. In fact, the society doesn't even *have* a shelter.

REPORTER POINTS TO THE HOME WHEN SHE/HE SAYS, "HERE." SERIES OF MS AND CU SHOTS OF DIFFERENT FAMILIES TAKING COMPANION ANIMALS HOME. ONE SHOT OF A LITTLE GIRL HOLDING A GRAY FURRY CAT INSIDE PARENT'S CAR.

All animals are housed in homes like the one you see behind me. Here, in the homes of Volunteers.

The primary objective of the Ohlone Humane Society is to find homes for companion animals.

ANOTHER SHOT OF VOLUNTEER WEARING AN OHS SHIRT, SPEAKING WITH PROSPECTIVE OWNERS.

Despite this urgency, don't expect the process to be simple.

SUPER "NANCY LYON" WITH A PORTRAIT OF FAMILY AND PETS BEHIND HER. NANCY IS SITTING ON A BURGUNDY RECLINER.

Nancy Lyon, the OHS Publications Director says applicants go through a stringent interview process.

(N. LYON) IT'S GOT TO BE GOOD FOR THE PERSON AND GOOD FOR THE DOG.

MIX IN LS, MS, CU SHOTS OF DIFFERENT ANIMALS WITH VOLUNTEERS AND PROSPECTIVE OWNERS.

OUR BOTTOM LINE IS, WE FIND GOOD PERMANENT HOMES FOR ANIMALS. MOST OF THEM HAVE BEEN THROUGH SO MUCH ALREADY. EVERY TIME YOU BOUNCE THEM FROM ONE SITUATION TO ANOTHER THEY BECOME LESS SECURE.

CU SHOTS OF OHS INTERNET WEBSITE PAGES.

RIVAS:
The Ohlone Humane Society also focuses on expanding the knowledge and appreciation of animals through education and interaction.

SUPER
"CHERYL LYON,
PRESIDENT."

(C. LYON) WE TRY TO EMPHASIZE THAT ANIMALS NEED TRAINING. THEY HAVE TO TAKE THE TIME TO TEACH THE DOG

KILL SUPER

HOW TO BEHAVE. A LOT OF PEOPLE JUST AREN'T WILLING TO DO THAT.

	THEYRE BUSY WITH THEIR LIVES, THEY DON'T WANT TO BOTHER WITH ALL THE TRAINING. I MEAN IT'S A COMMITMENT. IT'S LIKE HAVING A BABY.
CU OF CHILD HOLDING PUPPY AND CRADLING IT LIKE IT'S A BABY.	
MS OF A CAT BEING SPAYED.	RIVAS: The Ohlone Humane Society also works to encourage the spaying and neutering of pets.
CU SHOT OF THE SAME CAT BEING SPAYED.	
SUPER ""NANCY LYON."	(N. LYON) 30 TO 60% OF ALL ANIMALS BROUGHT TO SHELTERS IN THE UNITED STATES ARE EUTHANIZED.
KILL SUPER	
CU SHOT OF A SAD-LOOKING CAT.	PEOPLE NEED TO ASK THEMSELVES WHY THESE ANIMALS ARE EUTHANIZED.
SHOT OF OLDER DOG.	IT'S BECAUSE THERE AREN'T ENOUGH HOMES.
MS OF RIVAS AND NANCY LYON.	RIVAS: Why do you suppose owners neglect to spay or neuter their pets?
MS OF OLDER DOG SURROUNDED BY PUPS. CU SHOT OF OLDER DOG. PANORAMIC SHOT OF A VARIETY OF ANIMALS IN CAGES.	(N. LYON) SOME PEOPLE WANT TO SHOW THEIR CHILDREN THE MIRACLE OF LIFE, WELL THERE'S LOTS OF GOOD MOVIES THAT SHOW IT BETTER. IF YOU WANT TO SHOW THEM LIFE, SHOW THEM DEATH TOO.
	TAKE THEM TO THE SHELTER.
CU SHOT OF A NEEDLE.	THEY PUT HUNDREDS OF ANIMALS TO SLEEP EVERY YEAR.
LS OF ANIMALS IN CAGES.	
LS OF OLD DOG LIMPING.	RIVAS: While overpopulation contributes to the euthanizing of animals, so does a lack of responsibility and the role of abandonment.

SUPER "CHERYL WILLIAMS."	(WILLIAMS) ONE OF THE REASONS IT'S DIFFICULT TO FIND HOMES, IS THAT PEOPLE WANT YOUNG PETS. MOST OF OUR ANIMALS ARE OLD. IT'S A RESPONSIBILITY TO YOUR
KILL SUPER. LS OF CHERYL WITH HER OLD DOG FILLING HIS DISHES WITH FOOD.	ANIMALS, THAT WHEN THEY GET OLDER, THEY'VE LOVED YOU FOR YEARS, IT'S YOUR RESPONSIBILITY TO TAKE CARE OF THEM IN THEIR OLD AGE.
RIVAS ON CAMERA WALKING DOWN AISLE AT THE TRI-CITY ANIMAL SHELTER WHERE ANIMALS ARE PUT TO SLEEP ANIMALS IN CAGES SURROUND REPORTER. MS AS REPORTER CONTINUES.	RIVAS: The Ohlone Human Society provides vouchers for low-income Tri-City residents who are interested in spaying or neutering their pet. And no pets leave the Society without having been spayed or neutered.
TALKING INTO CAMERA.	Now that's commitment and putting your money where your mouth is. So, let's you and I join the Ohlone Humane Society and make the same commitment. If you're interested in adopting a pet or in donating time or
SUPER WITH PHONE NUMBER.	money, you may reach the Ohlone Humane Society at (510) 490-4587. For Ohlone Network News, I'm DORA RIVAS.

Bob Mackenzie is a multifaceted reporter for KTVU, Oakland. His reports range from straight news to offbeat, whimsical observations of American life.[12] Bob isn't attracted to those who are eccentric or bizarre; such candidates are best left to the private care of their families. To be worthy of a feature report the story must include redeeming aspects—it must be informative, unusual, and often humorous. Most important of all, it should focus on human activities or beliefs that are out of the ordinary, but not painful or embarrassing to those he features. His special report on American slang is typical of his work: it's informative, compelling, and funny.

In this report, his interviews with teenagers, car salesmen, and gamblers were recorded on location and later skilfully edited and sequenced. His last step in producing this report was writing and narrating the connecting transitions. In this script, his voice-over (VO) narration is ALL CAPS, and words spoken by Bob and his guests during the interviews are in upper- and lowercase.

SLANG—BOB MACKENZIE[13]
SEGMENT TWO

VIDEO	AUDIO
MCU OF ANCHOR AS SHE GIVES LEAD-IN IN TO REPORT	LEAD-IN BY NEWS ANCHOR: ON SEGMENT TWO TONIGHT) . . . IF "TOE UP FROM THE FLO" UP MAKES SENSE TO YOU, YOU MIGHT JUST HAVE A SWEET SENSE OF SLANG. WHO USES IT AND WHY—AND A FEW CHOICE MEANINGS—ARE THE SUBJECTS OF BOB MACKENZIE'S SPECIAL SEGMENT TWO REPORT.
ON CAMERA, FRONT OF TV STATION	BOB: There's slang in every language, but probably America has more slang than anyone else.
MALL. SUPER: WALNUT CREEK CU BILL	BILL/STUDENT: It's sweet, awesome . . .
MS STUDENTS	BOB: Do those mean "good"?
KILL SUPER	BILL: Yeah.
	BOB: When something's good, what do you say about it?
CU CHERYL	CHERYL/STUDENT: Pimp.
	BOB: Pimp? That means good?
CU CHERYL (ALL GIRLS HAVE BRACES ON TEETH)	CHERYL: Yeah. Like cool.
	BOB: Really?
CU MELISSA	MELISSA/STUDENT: He hella fine. That means . . .
	BOB: He's really fine?
	CHERYL: Yeah.
SHOTS OF PEOPLE WALKING IN MALL	BOB: (VO) USING SLANG CAN BE A WAY OF SIGNALING THAT YOU'RE

	AN INSIDER, THAT YOU'RE CONNECTED.
CU TRACY	TRACY/STUDENT: They say, she's all, he's all, they're all, when they're trying to say he said or she said. When they talk about a big group of people, they say, they're all! O' my Gawd, y'know, it's totally Valley Girl, and that's one of the big ones.
	BOB: What else do they say?
CU MELISSA	MELISSA: 24-7.
	BOB: Twenty-four seven?
	MELISSA: Yeah, 24-7.
CU DANA	DANA/STUDENT: Yeah, it means, um, 24 hours, 7 days a week. They say, like, they talk on the phone, twenty-four seven.
MCU DANA, MELISSA, TRACY	MELISSA: Bones means money.
	BOB: Bones? Would you say to somebody, got any bones, meaning you have money today?
	TRACY: Yeah, money on ya.
CU KIMMIE HOLDING CELL PHONE	KIMMIE/STUDENT: OK, you know federal, you know . . . Yeah, you federal?
	BOB: Federal?
WAVES CELL PHONE	DANA: Federal is mobile phone, y'know what I'm sayin'? Stuff like that, OK?
	BOB: Federal meaning . . .
CU DANA	DANA: Federal means, y'know, like you ballin' outta control, ya know. Ballin' outta control is like, you got major money, right?

MLS YOUNG PEOPLE WALKING IN MALL	BOB: SLANG IS RICH IN ADJECTIVES, PARTICULARLY FOR THINGS WE DON'T LIKE.
CU BRIAN	BRIAN/STUDENT: It's bogus. Bummin'. It's weak.
	BOB: Bogus?, bummin', weak? And . . . bunk?
CU KIMMIE	KIMMIE: Yeah. And cheesy. Cheeseball. Cheese factor of 20 on a scale of 10.
2 SHOT LIANNE AND KIMMIE	LIANNE/STUDENT: I say that's really tight.
	BOB: Tight—meaning you don't like it, or meaning . . .
	LIANNE: Yeah. That's just so wrong that they have those rules, that it's really tight.
LS YOUNG BOYS PLAYING BASKETBALL IN GYM	BOB: SLANG CHANGES NOT ONLY FROM REGION TO REGION, BUT FROM ONE NEIGHBORHOOD TO ANOTHER. IF TIGHT IS A NEGATIVE WORD IN THE SUBURBS, IT'S A POSITIVE WORD IN THE INNER CITY.
CROWD OF KIDS, ELBOWING WAY TOWARD CAMERA	BOB: When you see something you think is really good, what do you say about it?
	BASKETBALL PLAYERS: You say it's saucy.
	BOB: Saucy?
	PLAYER: Tight.
	BOB: Tight?
	PLAYER: Yeah, sweet.
	BOB: What about something you don't like? Whatta ya say?
	KIDS: Boosie, boosie, boosie . . .

	BOB: Boosie, huh?
	KID: Nasty, ugly. Toe up . . .
	KID: Toe up from the flo' up.
	BOB Toe up from the floor?
	KID: Toe up from the flo' up.
	BOB: Toe up from the flo' up.
FILE FOOTAGE: CYCLISTS IN HELMETS	BOB: EVERY SUBCULTURE OR INSIDER GROUP HAS SLANG OF ITS OWN. FOR INSTANCE, MOTORCYCLISTS CALL HELMETS BRAIN BUCKETS . . .
FILE FOOTAGE: PERSON WORKING COMPUTER	COMPUTER WIZARDS REFER TO WET WARE, MEANING PEOPLE . . .
FILE FOOTAGE: BASEBALL PLAYERS	BASEBALL PLAYERS SAY A SLOW RUNNER IS DRAGGING A PIANO. AND, WHEN A PITCHER IS WORN OUT FOR THE DAY THEY SAY, STICK A FORK IN HIM—HE'S DONE.
USED CAR LOT	A RICH SOURCE OF INSIDER SLANG IS THE USED CAR BUSINESS.
RAY MILLER WALKS TO CAR, RAISES HOOD, LOOKS ENGINE	RAY MILLER OF ISLAND AUTO SALES IN ALAMEDA SAYS A CAR THAT COMES IN JUNKY IS A ROACH OR A POOCH OR A HOOPTY. A CLEAN NEWER CAR IS A JEWEL, A CLEAN OLDER CAR IS A PUP. A CUSTOMER WHO'S EASY TO SELL IS A LAY-DOWN.
CU RAY	BOB: Now, upside down, what's that?
	RAY: Upside down means, uh, say someone owes four thousand dollars on a vehicle, and it's worth about twenty-eight hundred—that's way upside down.

BOB: They owe more than the thing is worth.

BOB: Now, when somebody comes in, in that situation, and think they're gonna trade out their car for something cool . . .

RAY: OK, it's called, basically they're on ether. Y'know, they want something they basically can't afford.

MS INT POKER PARLOR

BOB: THE GAME OF POKER IS ALSO AN ABUNDANT SOURCE OF SLANG. AT THE OAKS CARD CLUB IN EMERYVILLE, WE LEARNED THAT SOMEBODY THAT LOOKS A THE DISCARDS AT THE END OF A HAND IS RABBIT HUNTING; THE PEOPLE WHO STAND ON THE SIDELINES WATCHING THE GAME ARE RAILBIRDS.

CU JOHNNY

JOHNNY: On the river—that's what generally beat me.

BOB: On the river?

JOHNNY: Yeah, that's the last card in Hold'em.

CU ROGER

BOB: Is there a name for a guy who comes in and is kinda, y'know, ripe for the picking in this game?

ROGER: Shoe salesman. You wanna keep them in the pot.

EXTERIOR MCU OF BOB, ADDRESSING CAMERA UNTIL CLOSE

BOB: (IN OAKLAND) As best we can get it, it's still cool to say cool, but it's no longer cool to say hot. Groovy, rad, and bitchin' are dead, that is, they're toe up from the flo' up. Best advice is save your bones and don't be bogus.

In Oakland, Bob MacKenzie, and that's the deuce . . . uh, I mean Segment Two.

At times, essayists craft reports that carry a bite. The essay *American Mix,* by noted essayist Richard Rodriguez, reveals his frustrations as an American of Hispanic descent who has always felt omitted from discussions of race in America.

AMERICAN MIX
NEWSHOUR WITH JIM LEHRER
RICHARD RODRIGUEZ[14]

VIDEO	AUDIO
FILE TAPE OF JURY FOREMAN	SOT: We the jury in the above (DELIVERING) entitled action find the defendant, Orenthal James (SOUND UNDER) Simpson . . . RODRIGUEZ: Since the verdict in the O. J. Simpson murder trial, many have voiced pessimism about race relations in America. Tired cliché s resurface, like "we are a nation polarized by race." "There are two Americas, one white, one black." VO: (VOICE OF LEAD JUROR UP AND OUT)
CUT TO SHOT OF CROWDED SIDEWALK	Beyond such anxieties, beyond proclamations of racial separatists, beyond official handwringing, on the real American street, there is evidence of complexity and mixture.
CUT TO MCU OF MIXTURE OF RACES WALKING ON SIDEWALK	Look. There are Americans who are neither black nor white. In the American crowd are Chinese faces, Indians, Samoans, Guatemalans.
CUT TO BUSY STREET SCENE. PULL BACK TO MCU OF RICHARD RODRIGUEZ	Increasingly, Americans are claiming to be of more than one race.

SUPER: RICHARD
RODRIGUEZ

LOSE SUPER

In Washington, the Bureau of Labor
Statistics is now considering a
new multiracial category for
future surveys.

The census bureau estimates that
there are two million children of
interracial marriages. In fact, there
are many millions more. For example,
among the 24 million Americans
we call Hispanic, most are of
mixed race.

COLIN POWELL AT BOOK
SIGNING IN STORE

A few weeks ago, thousands of
Americans lined up to buy the
autobiography of Colin Powell. General
Powell tells us early in his book that his
ancestors carried a variety of blood
lines—African, English, Scotch, Irish,
and Indian. He also says that his father
carried a Jewish strain.

CU POWELL GREETING
ADMIRERS

Why then do most Americans think of
Collin Powell simply as black?

PHOTO OF OIL PAINTING BY
CABRERA; MOTHER, FATHER.
DAUGHTER

In French America, and even more
commonly in Latin America, there was
an early Colonial awareness of racial
mixtures.

CUT TO CABRERA PTG: WHITE
MAN, AFRICAN WOMAN; THEIR
CHILD

Consider these depictions of racial
varieties by the 18th-century Mexican
painter Miguel Cabrera.

CUT TO PTG. OF PILGRIMS
LANDING IN AMERICA

One searches in vain for similar
depictions from Anglo-America. The
United States has lived less easily than
Latin America with the fact of
miscegenation.

CUT TO DRAWING OF SLAVE
AUCTION

For generations, there was rape,
romance, even marriage among blacks
and whites, in America. And, not only
among blacks and whites. The story of

MIXED MARRIAGE PTG

the Indian and black marriage in America is one little told in our history books.

LATIN AMERICAN FAMILY, MAN, WOMAN, BOY AND GIRL

Latin America has terms like mestizo, quadron, mulatto, to describe racial varieties. We in the United States have only a black and white checkerboard.

PHOTO OF O. J., NICOLE, AND THEIR THREE CHILDREN

But, where do the children of Nicole Brown and O. J. Simpson belong on that checkerboard?

The census bureau reports that 66% of the children of black and white marriages describe themselves as black. In other words, the child must choose one parent over the other.

PHOTO OF BLACK MAN AT COLORED ONLY DRINKING FOUNTAIN
PHOTO: BLACK MAN LEAVING COLORED ONLY WAITING ROOM

In the anti-black South of segregated lunch counters and colored-only water fountains, any recognizable measure of African blood defined you as black. You were forced to the back of the bus.

FILM OF HUGE CROWD OF BLACKS IN FRONT OF LINCOLN MONUMENT

Oddly enough, that old racist logic has become internalized in today's America. Black Americans tell me there is no freedom of choice. That they are black, regardless of any racial mixture, as long as a policeman or the banker, or the realtor sees them as black.

(SPANISH LANGUAGE SPEAKER, UP AND UNDER; THEN OUT)

FILM: CROWD OF HISPANICS IN PUBLIC PARK

Editorial writers, civil rights activists, politician and pundits, insist on describing a black and white Los Angeles, despite the fact that the majority population is actually Hispanic.

PHOTO OF HISPANIC FAMILY, MAN, WOMAN, CHILDREN

L.A., the largest Hispanic city in the United States, is therefore the most racially mixed.

FILM: HISPANICS DANCING

Hispanics carry a mixture of both Indian and Spaniard, with African and Asian.

OF CROWDED SIDEWALK	One can, after all, be Hispanic, and still carry the blood of any race in the world.
MCU RICHARD RODRIGUEZ OF BEFORE CROWDED SIDEWALK	I grew up chagrined by talk of a white and a black America. All my life I heard it.
	As someone who thinks of himself as neither white nor black, I use to hear such talk as a kind of family quarrel— it went over my head.
SLOW ZOOM IN TO CU	Today, I sense a weird nostalgia to such talk. . . . and a vanity.
	It is as though many whites and blacks cannot imagine an America peopled by anyone except each other.
	On the other hand, the other day I met a young junior high school student. She, the daughter of a marriage of Africa and Mexico, she proclaims herself a Blaxican.
MUSIC AND VIDEO: MICHAEL	She is the prophet announcing the united colors of Benetton.
JACKSON VIDEO FOR BENETTON. MONTAGE OF YOUNG PEOPLE ON CU DISS FROM ONE TO THE OTHER TO END.	The many faces in the Michael Jackson video. . . . a new America I become We.
	What race are you? Are you white? Are you Hispanic? Are you black? Are you a Pacific Islander? Are you Asian?
	I tell students all the time now to mark yes to everything on official forms.
	Yes, I am black, soi negro.
	Yes, I am white.
	Yes, I am Chinese, or Chino.
	Yes.
	MUSIC: TO CLOSE

If you're preparing for a career that might include feature reporting, you may find the script that follows instructive. The author, Sharon Yamane, without a camera operator or production capabilities of any kind, used her curiosity about an unsettling film to tell a story. Aside from some basic research, her report was filled out by conducting interviews with moviegoers before and after a screening. Comments made by author Dean Koontz were taken from a newspaper interview. The visualization of the report simply indicates what viewers might see if the report were to be produced.

Fear Equals Fun
By: Sharon Yamane*

VIDEO	AUDIO
OPEN ON MS OF REPORTER IN FRONT OF A MOVIE THEATER.	REPORTER: Good evening, I'm Cora Wopat for News Central. I'm standing in front of "The Bridge" for an advanced screening of "The Blair Witch Project."
	FADE UP EERIE MUSIC.
CUT TO FILM FOOTAGE OF THE WOODS.	REPORTER (VO): The Blair Witch myth started in the Township of Blair, located in North Central, Maryland.
PAN ACROSS THE TREES TO THE REENACTMENT OF THE EXILE OF KEDWARD.	In 1785, several children claimed Elly Kedward lured them into her house to draw their blood. She was accused of witchcraft, was exiled, and presumed dead.
	In 1786, all of Kedward's accusers disappeared. Half of the town's children vanished as well, never to be seen again.
PAN THE EMPTY AND DARK WOODS.	Since then, many other mysterious disappearances and murders have occurred around the Blair site.
CUT TO PICTURES OF HEATHER AND HER FRIENDS.	This legend provoked Heather Donahue, a Montgomery College student, to make a documentary film about "The Blair Witch." She set off to the woods near the Blair site with two friends. They never returned, but their

	film footage was discovered a year later. "The Blair Witch Project" is their story.
	FADE MUSIC OUT.
CUT TO MS OF REPORTER.	REPORTER: The legend was used to instill fear in little children so they wouldn't wander off into the woods.
	Today, people are lined up on this clear but cold night to experience the bone-chilling tale for themselves. According to "The Journal of Psychology," "Fear is an emotion characterized by unpleasant, often intense feelings and by a desire to flee or hide." It causes the heart to pound, palms to sweat, and muscles to tense. Horror stories and movies tend to cause fear. This brings me to the question, "Why do people like 'scary' books and films?"
	FADE IN "HALLOWEEN" THEME MUSIC.
CUT TO BITE OF PERSON TOSSING AND TURNING IN BED. CUT TO BITE OF PERSON WATCHING TV, HIDING FACE BEHIND FINGERS AND PEEKING THROUGH THEM.	Americans spend millions of dollars a year on horror movies and books, We consume them at the risk of having nightmares, but we seem helpless to stop ourselves.
CUT TO MS OF REPORTER.	To help us understand this "horror craze," I'm here to interview some of tonight's moviegoers.
ZOOM INTO CU OF REPORTER, TURNING TO A YOUNG MAN IN LINE.	REPORTER: Excuse me, sir. What made you want to see this movie?
	MAN: I heard it was gonna be "hella" scary.
	REPORTER: Why do you like scary movies?

MAN: I dunno, I guess it's sorta fun. Gets the adrenaline goin.'

PAN TO YOUNG WOMAN IN LINE.

REPORTER: Why do you want to watch this movie?

WOMAN: It kinda reminds me of a book by Stephen King, "The Girl Who Loved Tom Gordon." That story takes place in the woods, too. It got me curious.

PAN TO WOMAN'S FRIEND.

FRIEND: I don't like bein' "creeped out." I only came 'cause I'm her ride.

PAN TO MS OF REPORTER.

REPORTER: Not everyone appreciates a good scare, but fear seems to sell. It is evident because Wes Craven, director of "A Nightmare On Elm Street" and "Scream," is a big box-office draw. Stephen King and Dean Koontz have also found success as best-selling authors of horror novels.

BITE OF DEAN KOONTZ INTERVIEW.

REPORTER (VO): I was fortunate enough to interview Dean Koontz, author of the chilling suspense thrillers, "Intensity" and Mr. Murder."

2-SHOT WITH DEAN KOONTZ.

REPORTER: Why do you like to read and write horror stories?

CU OF KOONTZ.

KOONTZ: Storytellers became my heroes because they provided me with temporary escapes. Through their characters, they made me feel less isolated and more connected to human experience. And they brought joy and wonder into my life at a time when I would otherwise have known little of either. All I have ever wanted to do is give that same gift to others.

CUT TO CU OF REPORTER OUTSIDE OF THEATER, WHILE PEOPLE ARE EXITING.

REPORTER: Once again, I'm standing in front of the Bridge Theater. The *Blair Witch Project* has ended. Let's find out how it was.

ZOOM OUT TO MS OF REPORTER
WALKING UP TO SMALL GROUP
OF COLLEGE STUDENTS (C.S.).

ZOOM INTO CU OF REPORTER.

REPORTER: So what did you think about the movie?

CUT TO MS YOUNG MAN (YM).

YM: Oh, man! It was the scariest movie I ever saw!

CUT TO MS YOUNG WOMAN (YF).

YF: It was too real! I don't think I'm sleepin' tonight!

ZOOM OUT TO GROUP, ALL OF
WHOM WANT TO MAKE A
COMMENT.

YM: Me either!

YF: I thought the ending was lame.

(MONTAGE OF LOUD VOICES)

Are you kidding me? That was the best part!

I'm just glad it wasn't happening to me!

I'm never goin' camping again!

I didn't really like the movie, but it was fun 'cuz the place was packed.

(LAUGHING) You had your eyes closed the whole time, you chicken!

REPORTER: ON CAMERA) Why do people like horror novels and movies? Some people seem to find them intriguing because the stories tend to be outrageous ... a way to temporarily escape into another world. Others seem to enjoy the sense of danger and excitement.

Psychiatrist Martin Grotjahn believes that seeking out horror stories helps us conquer our fears of the real horror that abounds in the world. By going out of our way to seek horror in stories, we are telling ourselves and the world that we can take it—that horror can't touch us because we've diminished its power by embracing it in a movie.

Horror films and stories also create shared experiences among people. It can give them an excuse to huddle close together in their seats, or gather around a cozy campfire to listen.

As for me, I think horror stories are great . . . just as long as I'm not one of the characters.

Until next time, this is Cora Wopat for News Central, suggesting that you leave the lights on tonight.

Sharon Yamane's analysis of her feature report reveals her thoughts as she worked on its conception and development:

My target audience is college students and young adults because they are more likely (than any other age group) to be interested in horror stories and films. I went to the advanced screening of *The Blair Witch Project* and the audience really was made up of college students and young adults. I interviewed a few people, and some of them couldn't quite explain why they liked horror. This inspired the topic of my feature report, "Why do people like horror novels and films?"

Ever since I watched "The Blair Witch Project," I've experienced a few sleepless nights. I don't particularly like being scared of the shadows in my room, late at night. However, I know it won't prevent me from watching or reading "scary" stories. I think horror films and novels draw people in because they fulfill certain needs and desires. Some examples are the need to be distracted from the realities of life, the desire to see villains in action, and the need to confront, in a controlled situation, the horrible and the terrible. They also fill the need to have shared experiences with others. Some people may not necessarily like frightening stories, but they might enjoy other aspects of the experience. For instance, some may like embracing a loved one to feel a sense of security during a horror flick. Some people may enjoy discussing or describing the stories to others.

Horror films and novels also contain many universal themes, such as darkness, mutilation, ghosts, and Satan. They consist of many other terror inflicting themes, yet people stand in line at bookstores and movie theaters. They basically pay to be frightened. This fascinates me because I am one of those people.

I think the target audience will be interested in this feature report because the Blair Witch myth will pique their curiosity. They will also be able to relate to the moviegoers. I believe the interviews will help lighten the mood of the piece. I often wonder why I keep subjecting myself to nightmares and the uncomfortable emotion of fear. Therefore, I hope the report will make people think about it, too.

A report of a very different kind was developed around a single incident at a record production studio.

FIND OF THE CENTURY
By David Jorgensen*

VIDEO	AUDIO
	MUSIC: "Green Onions"—Booker T & The MGs—IN & UNDER
WS OF OUTSIDE STAX STUDIOS	DAVID: Stax Records was one of the most unusual and important record companies in history.
	Along with Motown, it represented one of two main streams of Black American music in the 1960s, namely that of the newly emergent sounds of Southern soul music.
MS WHERE MAIN STUDIO ONCE WAS	At one time this room was the studio where artists such as Booker T and the MGs, Otis Redding, and Albert King laid the foundation of what would later become soul, funk, and rock n' roll music.
MCU OF DAVID JORGENSEN IN AWARDS AT STAX MUSEUM	These gold records surrounding me are the result of years and years of incredible recordings at Stax. "The Dock Of The Bay," "Green Onions," and "Walkin' the Dog" are among the many recordings which put Stax at the top of the industry.
SUPER: DAVID JORGENSEN	
WS OF FANTASY STUDIOS IN BERKELEY	Today, Stax is owned by Fantasy Records of Berkeley, California. They purchased the company in 1977 and continue to distribute Stax material through an active reissue program,
PAN OF ARCHIVE ROOM	Down these aisles are where hundreds of hours of master tapes are stored. These tapes, from the original Stax

	sessions, were transported here to Berkeley when Fantasy bought the company in '77.
CU: BOBBY O'BRIEN AT HIS INTERN DESK SUPER: BOBBY O'BRIEN FANTASY STUDIOS	Yesterday, 20-year-old Bobby O'Brien, an intern at Fantasy Records, stumbled upon what music historians have called the "Find of the Century".
	MUSIC: "'The Dock Of The Bay"—Otis Redding
WS OF BOBBY O'BRIEN SWEEPING THE ARCHIVE ROOM	Last night young Bobby O'Brien of Daly City was going about his business as he always does on a Friday night, sweeping the floor and dusting the reels of Fantasy Studios.
XCU OF A TAPE	These are the tapes Bobby dusts every week.
STORAGE SHELF	Most of these reels have detailed labels to give producers here at Fantasy Studios easy accessibility to the audio they need.
CU OF BOBBY O'BRIEN	BITE: "I'm a huge fan of Stax Music and soul music in general. when I'm cleaning up at night I enjoy racking up some of these old reels and playing them while I'm sweeping. Last night I grabbed a reel labeled "Albert 9-6-68." I figured it was just Albert King and his band in a studio session."
	MUSIC: "Born Under A Bad Sign"—Albert King.
CU OF REEL AND ITS CUE SHEET	DAVID: At the end of this 1968 Albert King studio session, young Bobby O'Brien ran across fifteen minutes of some of the greatest music ever laid to tape. Following the session and three minutes of blank tape, lies one of the greatest jam sessions of all time.

MS DAVID HOLDING TAPE	On this tape Albert is joined by none other than Otis Redding and the
STILLS OF ALBERT, REDDING, AND HENDRIX	legendary Jimi Hendrix. Together the three recorded "Born Under A Bad Sign", "Respect" and "Red House."
	Stax cofounder Jim Stewart:
CU OF JIM STEWART CO-FOUNDER OF STAX RECORDS	BITE: "Albert and Otis had keys to the place. They were free to come and go when they pleased. Many times Albert or Otis would stay hours after everyone else left to lay down tracks. They knew they weren't supposed have guests though. I'm sure that's why Albert never brought this recording to my attention."
MS OF BILL SMITH	Bill Smith is the man who bought Stax records eleven years ago.
SUPER: BILL SMITH FANTASY RECORDS	BITE: "This is truly the find of the century. We're already in the process of remastering this session and making it available to the public. It is a recording every music lover has got to hear."
WS OF DAVID JORGENSEN IN FRONT OF FANTASY STUDIOS	I have heard it, and in my opinion if is possibly the best thing I've ever heard.
	When will it hit record stores, you might be asking? Fantasy hopes the recording will be in stores by the end of the month with experts forecasting sales in the millions. And what might happen to the young intern who stumbled upon this pot of gold?
XCU OF A SMILING BOBBY O'BRIEN	BITE: "A full-time position would be nice."

Bob Davy, whose report on the killer whale Keiko opened this chapter, now concludes it with four brief pieces that show the diversity of locations he seeks out for potential stories.[15] Where some see the sound-only nature of radio as a limitation, Davy see it as an opportunity to explore themes and subjects in unique ways. Topics that would be inappropriate or too costly to produce for television find a welcome home on radio. Much as the makers of presound motion pictures became adept at telling stories in pictures only, radio artists should become equally inventive in telling stories with sounds alone.

One of Bob's features, *Queen Mary,* came together in an unusual manner, which he describes in these paragraphs:

THE OUEEN MARY FEATURE: A LEARNING EXPERIENCE

At first it seemed that producing a radio feature about the romantic old ship parked in Long Beach harbor would be a snap. That's what I thought until I got into it.

The old hulk sits there, dead in the water. . . . the only sounds it makes these days are the horn and an air conditioner fan here and there. . . . along with a few wandering musical groups. Of course there are the tour guides, but their material seems a bit secondhand. The life of the ship is history. . . . how does one bring HISTORY alive?

I heard about TOUR TAPES, and asked the Queen Mary Marketing Director to provide me one—and, she did. I also asked permission to use this material. The tape contained a wealth of music, stories told by former captains, waiters, passengers, as well as a neat ballad recorded in the '30s on the ship. It brought the piece alive. Also, I heard that Bob Hope had recently put out a video telling about his WW II days. I called his office in Burbank and they sent me a copy—again at no cost. It contained delightful stuff of Hope telling about when he was asked to entertain passengers the day after war broke out in Europe. . . . the *Queen Mary* had just sailed from Britain and the passengers were petrified at the prospect of a German sub attack. As Hope says in the piece: "that's not my warmup. . . . people crying and praying. . . . NOT my warmup. . . ." Another rich addition to the piece.

Then as I was having lunch with Bob Mott, my former boss and still-friend at WSU, now living in San Diego, he told me about *his* experience aboard the *Queen Mary* as his army unit shipped out for Europe. I had him record his memories at the PBS radio station in San Diego and send me the cassette. Another nice addition.

So I was able to go from a dearth of material to a wealth that made the piece quite listenable.

When a producer hears little voices in the back of his or her head that say "this is dull—there's something missing" they'd better be listened to. Their comments can lead you to further inquiries and probing—like to the Marketing Director of the *Queen Mary.* Their job is to help you get answers to these questions.

I think one of the lessons here is that production and writing are intertwined in radio features. This seems to make it a one person enterprise. And I think it helps if that one person is pretty creative—a "non-linear" thinker. However, the final script needs to be quite linear in its idea development: one idea leading clearly to the next.

THE QUEEN MARY[16]
AS BROADCAST ON MONITOR RADIO NETWORK

HOST:
Sixty years ago, the *Queen Mary,* the largest ocean luxury liner ever built, and probably the most glamorous, was launched at Clyde Bank, Scotland, now listed in the National Registry of Historic Places. The ship is permanently docked at Long Beach, California, hosting thousands of visitors yearly. Bob Davy took a tour of the venerable old ship recently and has this story.

(SOUND: SEA GULLS FOLLOWED BY SHIP'S HORN BELLOWING)

NARRATOR (DAVY):
They called her "QUEEN OF THE ATLANTIC," a floating city awash in elegance. Press releases described her unmatched grace and peerless power—nothing less than a "floating miracle"—longer than three football fields, over a thousand feet. English actress and comedian Beatrice Lillie once asked: "When does this *place* get to New York?"

SOUND: SHIP'S HORN WITH BIG BLAST PUNCTUATING THE JOKE)

NARRATOR:
The *Queen Mary* was launched at Clyde Bank, Scotland, in September 1934. King George the Fifth and his wife, Queen Mary, were there for the ceremony.

ACTUALITY: KING GEORGE
AS A SAILOR, I HAVE DEEP PLEASURE IN COMING HERE TODAY TO WATCH THE LAUNCHING BY THE QUEEN OF THIS GREAT AND BEAUTIFUL SHIP.

ANNOUNCER VOICE:
HER MAJESTY, QUEEN MARY.

ACTUALITY: QUEEN MARY
I AM HAPPY TO NAME THIS SHIP THE QUEEN MARY.

(SOUND: CHILD VOICE SAYS: HEYYYYYYYYY)

NARRATOR:
As we walk the decks of the grand old ship today, we hear music everywhere, small groups that help create the ambience of the original *Queen Mary.*

(SMALL DECK BAND—ESTAB THEN UNDER)

NARRATOR:
On the *Queen Mary* Tour Tape, chefs and waiters tell about the elaborate food service.

(MUSIC GROUP FROM ABOVE CONTINUES BEHIND)

WAITER:
THE GLASS WAS BEAUTIFUL—CRYSTAL GLASS. AND THE MENUS WERE ALL ESPECIALLY PRINTED AND IT REALLY DID LOOK ABSOLUTELY SUPERB.

PASSENGER:
THEY WOULD BRING YOU A MENU WHICH WAS SEVERAL YARDS LONG.

CHEF:
YOU COULD DO ANY KIND OF MEALS THERE BECAUSE OUR CHEFS WERE FIRST CLASS. I USED TO DO THE CREPE SUZETTE AND THE CHERRIES JUBILEE, STEAKS DIANE, CAVIAR AU BLINI . . . .

NARRATOR:
Between sumptuous meals there was plenty for passengers to do. On the tour tape, former passengers run down the list.

(AMBIENT DANCE MUSIC BEHIND THE FOLLOWING)

PASSENGERS (INTERCHANGEABLY):
ANYTHING WE WANT TO DO OUTSIDE OF HORSEBACK RIDING. FREE DANCING LESSONS. LATIN AMERICAN DANCING. BOWLING ALLEY. (SOUND OF BOWLING ALLEY IN BACKGROUND) HORSE RACING MACHINE. FIVE ORCHESTRAS ABOARD. DANCING. JUKE BOXES. COMEDIANS. SINGERS. ENTERTAINERS. TOP QUALITY.

(MUSIC ENDS, FOLLOWED BY APPLAUSE)

NARRATOR:
In 1939, clouds of war loomed over Europe. The Queen Mary left England on August 30 with a huge number of passengers anxious to leave for America.

Two days later, war broke out on the Continent. Jittery passengers thought they were aboard a likely target for German U-Boats.

Comedian Bob Hope and his wife, Dolores, were passengers on that trip. Hope was asked to do a show to help calm the passengers. On a video, the comedian recalls his first reaction to this request.

HOPE (FROM MEMOIR VIDEOTAPE):
I SAID, "NO WAY." THE PEOPLE WERE CRYING. THEY, YA KNOW, KNEW WE WERE IN TROUBLE AND THEY WERE ALL PRAYING AND CRYING AND I SAID "THIS IS NOT MY WARMUP FOR AN AUDIENCE FOR ME, YOU KNOW" AND HARRY WARNER WAS ON THE SHIP AND HE SAID: "THIS IS THE TIME TO DO IT, BOB. YOU'VE GOTTA DO IT." AND HE AND THE CAPTAIN TALKED ME INTO DOING IT.

NARRATOR:
The Queen Mary had a top speed of about twenty-nine knots, the fastest large ship afloat at that time. This speed enabled her to avoid German submarines, which could average only about 10 knots. During the following months, the Queen Mary was converted into a troop ship, now called "the grey ghost." Bob Mott, a young first

lieutenant in the U.S. Army in 1944, describes how they were packed into the once-luxurious *Queen Mary.*

MOTT:
THE SLEEPING QUARTERS WERE EXTREMELY CRAMPED. I WAS IN A SMALL INTERIOR ROOM WITH NO PORTHOLES. . . . EIGHT PEOPLE INCLUDING MYSELF. THERE WERE FOUR OF US ON ONE SIDE OF THE ROOM IN TIERS OF BUNKS AND I WAS IN THE TOP BUNK IN ONE OF THOSE TIERS. I HAD ABOUT A FOOT OF HEAD SPACE BETWEEN MY HEAD AND THE TOP OF THE BULKHEAD.

NARRATOR:
When the war ended, the *Queen Mary* brought war brides and their children to the U.S. from Britain. By the summer of 1947, the ship had again been refitted as a luxury liner for Atlantic crossings. But by the 1960s, airliners could carry passengers across the Atlantic in hours instead of days at a lower ticket price. Ocean liners had become obsolete. The *Queen Mary* was put up for sale and purchased by the City of Long Beach, where it arrived December 9, 1957. Since that time, hundred of thousands of visitors have walked its decks, reliving the luxury crossing days of old.

(AMBIENT SOUND: SINGER FROM TOUR TAPE: ESTAB THEN FADE UNDER)

SINGER: ". . . AND ME, . . ."

NARRATOR:
For the *Christian Science Monitor,* I'm Bob Davy on the *Queen Mary* in Long Beach, California.

SINGER: ". . . WON'T YOU BE, ANSWER MY PLEA, SOMEWHERE AT SEA . . ."

(MUSIC UP FULL TO END OF VERSE THEN OUT)

Another feature from Bob Davy brings us a remarkable story of an elementary school producing a musical for a paying audience. It's fun to read the script, but as is true of all reports that make creative use of radio's unique potential, the story must be heard to be fully appreciated.

FEATURE FROM THE JEFFERSON DAILY,
JEFFERSON PUBLIC RADIO, MAY 4, 2001
PRODUCED BY BOB DAVY.

GUYS AND DOLLS PERFORMED BY ST. JOSEPH'S ELEMENTARY
SCHOOL, REDDING, CALIFORNIA

HOST INTRO:
Elementary students in Redding this week are putting on a performance of the Broadway musical *Guys and Dolls.* Arts Reporter Bob Davy has the story.

MUSIC FROM SHOW. ESTABLISH, THEN UNDER

DAVY:
These voices are all of students at St. Joseph's Elementary School in Redding. Eighty-seven kindergarten through fifth graders fill the gymnasium stage in their current production of *Guys and Dolls.*

SAME MUSIC UP FULL BRIEFLY THEN DOWN UNDER

DAVY:
Music teacher Joyce Summers says their production is the so-called Broadway Jr., a shortened version edited to be age-appropriate. Summers says the junior versions work well for elementary students and for the audience.

SUMMERS:
THEY EDIT THE FULL PRODUCTION TO FIT THE AGE LEVEL—PROBABLY K THRU 9TH GRADE. THEY CUT OUT SOME OF THE SONGS, EDIT SOME OF THE MUSIC, AND ACTUALLY TAKE OUT SOME OF THE SCENES SO WE END UP WITH A PRODUCTION THAT IS ABOUT 75 MINS LONG RATHER THAN TWO AND A HALF HOURS.

DAVY:
Guys and Dolls is a jazzy musical with a cast of street-wise Manhattan gamblers, night-club performers, and inner-city salvation mission workers. Summers says that some things had to be translated for the young performers.

SUMMERS:
WE CHOSE *GUYS AND DOLLS* BECAUSE THE MUSIC IS SO CATCHY AND SO MUCH FUN. AND THERE ARE THINGS ABOUT IT THAT ARE A LOT OF FUN TO DO. ESPECIALLY THE MISSION BAND AND ADELAIDE'S PART . . . AND THE CRAPSHOOTERS. WE HAVE YOUNG GUYS AND YOUNG DOLLS AS WELL AS THE GUYS AND DOLLS AND THE FARMERETTES AND THE HOT BOX GIRLS.

DAVY:
ARE THESE IN COSTUME?

SUMMERS:
YES. ALL THE GUYS ARE DRESSED IN DOUBLE-BREASTED SUITS OR VESTS AND THEY HAVE THEIR HATS ON LIKE THE GAMBLERS WOULD HAVE. IT'S VERY ADAPTABLE TO YOUNG CHILDREN AND YOU KNOW WE HAD TO EXPLAIN A FEW THINGS. LIKE WHAT "CRAPS" ARE AT THE BEGINNING BECAUSE TO THEM THAT WAS A NAUGHTY WORD. WE EXPLAINED TO THEM WHAT THAT MEANT.

DAVY:
DO THEY DO IT WITH AN ACCENT?

SUMMERS:
YES, ESPECIALLY ADELAIDE. SHE'S A FABULOUS FIFTH-GRADE GIRL. SHE'S SINGING "A BUSHEL AND A PECK" SOLO FIRST.

MUSIC: " A BUSHEL AND A PECK" (ADELAIDE). AFTER CHORUS FADE UNDER

DAVY:
Guys and Dolls, performed by St. Joseph's Elementary School in Redding. The two remaining performances are sold out. For Jefferson Public Radio, I'm Bob Davy.

MUSIC: SAME SONG UP FULL TO END, THEN FADE OUT

SOUND PORTRAITS

Bob Davy's next two features are classified as sound portraits. The characteristic that makes these reports *sound portraits* is that they're made up entirely of actualities—edited statements made by persons other than broadcast personnel—and are entirely without narration or commentary. Sound portraits are short pieces that use only a lead-in or introduction by a host, followed by actualities and sound.

The portrait that follows is an excellent example of this type of report. It has tongue-in-cheek humor, it moves rapidly from one point to another, and was produced easily and inexpensively. Bob Davy, who produced this piece for Monitor Radio, says "It's an excellent example of the audio you can find at a location if you keep your mind open—and your recorder at the ready. Finding material for sound portraits is easy if you keep your imagination open—good raw material is everywhere!"[17]

BOB DAY
A sound portrait by Bob Davy

ANNCR: A "Bob" by any other name would sound as sweet. But, why bother using any other name when "Bob" serves so many, so well? To celebrate the people who bear the name, the small Southern Oregon town of Talent recently held a "Bob Day." All the world's Bobs were welcome. There were contests for the tallest Bob, the most talented Bob and, of course, the "Thing-a-ma-Bob" contest. There was also a "Bob-e-que," organized by the Volunteer Fire Department. From Talent, Oregon, Bob Davy filed this sound portrait of "Bob Day."

SFX: CROWD SOUNDS, IN AND UNDER

CHEER: (MALE VOICES) BEE! OHHHH! BEE! (PAUSE) Bob!!!!!

JUDY: I'm Judy Bunch, and I'm the "Bob Day" coordinator. And, we're having a great time out here today. We've got more Bobs here than I ever expected to see . . .

MUSIC: (FEMALE VOICES SINGING "IT'S A SMALL WORLD AFTER ALL") "Though a man is handsome and rich and smart, he won't light my fire if his name is Bart . . ." (SINGING UNDER)

JUDY: We're the Decibelle Singers from Grants Pass, Oregon, and we'd like to present "It's a Bob World," for all the Bobs we know and love. (SINGING UP) "It's a Bob World after all, It's a Bob World after all, It's a Bob World after all." (UNDER)

BOB KAY: I'm Bob Kay. I'm Jackson County's Justice of the Peace, and I've been retained to perform a wedding here at today's festivities. Bobism is an important part of my life, being one of the many . . . and, we all come from families that obviously have no real imagination going for them, 'cause we all end up being Bob after Bob after Bob. I don't see near as many Mikes stacked up like that.

BOB S: My name is Bob Sullivan. I'm from Medford . . . and, I'm a Bob, so I like to be where Bobs are at! (LAUGHS)

BOB J: I'm Bob Johns, from Junction City, Oregon. I heard about it at the newspaper, the *Register Guardian* at Eugene. And, I think it's about time we're recognized for who we really are. Bob! I've waited years for this. Haven't you, Bob?

BOB: You bet!

BOB J: How about you, Bob?

BOB K: Well, my name is Bob Koash, and I'm from Medford. The name of Bob goes back to the 14th century. Ghengis Khan had a whole battalion of Bobs. "Bob-arians."

BOB S: My name is Bob Seaton. I live in Phoenix, Oregon. If you're a Bob, you've got it! Ever'body else is just tryin'.

BOB K: I'm Bob Kearns from Jacksonville, Oregon. And . . . it's . . . it's awe inspiring. Ah, it almost brings tears to your eyes. All the Bobs together in one place—it just reminds you of Heaven a little bit!

BOB C: Bob Carrie, from Medford, Oregon. And, I think this is great . . . A little weird, but it's great!

MUSIC: (THE DECIBELLES, UP TO END) "It's a whole world to me, it's a Bob world after all."

SFX: CROWD CHEERING. FADE OUT

ANNCR: Bob Davy, in Talent, Oregon.

SF ZOO
SOUND PORTRAIT
BOB DAVY FOR MONITOR RADIO
PRODUCED BY BOB DAVY

(MUSIC: SIMON & GARFUNKEL)
SOMEONE TOLD ME
IT'S ALL HAPPENING AT THE ZOO
I DO BELIEVE IT
I DO BELIEVE IT'S TRUE (MUSIC UNDER)

HOST INTRO:
Translating discourse between the animal and human worlds presents a dilemma.
People see and hear animals communicating amongst themselves but it's hard to
know what's being said. Producer Bob Davy visited the San Francisco Zoo recently
to listen to the animals as interpreted by their keepers.

(MUSIC OUT)

(SOUND: LION ROAR)

LION KEEPER:
THAT SOUND YOU'RE HEARING, THE ROAR OF THE LION, IN HIS COMPETI-
TIVE ENVIRONMENT, CAN BE HEARD FOR ABOUT FIVE MILES. IT CAN MEAN
TERRITORIAL POSSESSION OR IT CAN MEAN CALLING—THEY'RE CALLING
OTHER LIONS IN THE VICINITY TO FEED BECAUSE THEY'VE GOT THE KILL.
AND IT ALSO CAN WARN OTHER PREDATORS AWAY FROM THAT AREA OF
THE KILL.

(KOOKABURRA SOUND UP BRIEFLY THEN DOWN UNDER)

KOOKABURRA KEEPER:
THE KOOKABURRA MAKES SEVERAL NOISES. ONE CALL IS A VERY LOW
GUTTURAL NOISE THAT CAN ONLY BE HEARD AT SHORT RANGE. SO THE
BIRDS TALK TO EACH OTHER IN SORT OF A SOFT VOICE WHEN THEY'RE
NEAR EACH OTHER. BUT THEY ALSO DO A VERY LOUD TERRITORIAL CALL,
THAT CHARACTERISTIC JUNGLE NOISE YOU ALWAYS HEAR. AND THAT'S A
BONDING NOISE THAT BONDS ALL THE MEMBERS OF THE CLAN TOGETHER.
IT ALSO LETS OTHER CLANS KNOW THEY MAY BE APPROACHING THE
TERRITORY OF THE CLAN THAT IS CALLING.

(SAME SOUND AS ABOVE BRIEFLY THEN CROSS-FADE TO EAGLE SOUND . . . ESTAB THEN FADE UNDER)

EAGLE KEEPER:
THE FEMALE BALD EAGLE IS MUCH LARGER THAN THE MALE, SO SHE'S DEFINITELY A DOMINANT BIRD. THE MALE IS A MUCH SMALLER BIRD. THE MALE BALD EAGLE IS GIVING A TERRITORIAL CALL TRYING TO SCARE US OUT OF HIS AREA. MALES HAVE A LOWER TONE THAN THE FEMALES BUT THEY BOTH GIVE A REAL BASIC KIND OF SCREAM.

(SOUND: MORE EAGLES BRIEFLY THEN FADE UNDER)

KOALA KEEPER:
KOALAS ARE MARSUPIALS. THEY ARE NOT BEARS. THEY'RE RELATED TO KANGAROOS, AND THEY HAVE A POUCH. AND THEY LIVE UP IN EUCALYP-TUS TREES AND THEY EAT EUCALYPTUS LEAVES. THEY'RE A VERY SLOW, SLEEPY ANIMAL AND THEY SLEEP ABOUT 20 HOURS A DAY.

(SOUND: INTRODUCE KOALA SOUND BRIEFLY THEN DOWN UNDER)

KOALA-KEEPER CONTINUES:
THEY'RE USUALLY ALONE IN A TREE. THEY HAVE TO HAVE A VERY LARGE BELLOW TO COMMUNICATE WITH THE OTHER KOALAS TO FIND A MATE. WHEN THE MALES VOCALIZE, IT'S VERY LOUD. AND IT TRAVELS FOR MILES. AND A FEMALE WHO WANTS A DATE WILL HEAR IT.

(SOUND: TYPE OF SIAMANG APE)

KEEPER OF APE:
WHAT YOU ARE HEARING NOW IS THE SIAMANG VOCALIZATION. LIKE CHIMPS, THEY'RE A SOCIAL APE. THEY'RE A DIFFERENT GROUP. THEY ARE A LESSER APE VERSUS CHIMPS, WHICH ARE GREAT APES. THEY'RE A SMALLER ANIMAL. THEY ARE STRICTLY A MONOGAMOUS ANIMAL, MUCH MORE TERRITORIAL THAN ARE CHIMPS. THEY DO A VOCALIZATION WHICH IS A TERRITORIAL CALL AND THERE'S A DISTINCTION BETWEEN THE MALE VERSUS THE FEMALE CALL. IT'S CALLED "DUETING." WHEN THEY'RE DOING THE CALL, THE MALE AND THE FEMALE ARE THE BASIS OF IT AND THEIR OFFSPRING WILL JOIN IN THE CALLING.

(SOUND: SAME AS ABOVE REPEATED—UP BRIEFLY THEN UNDER)

HOST:
Animals and their keepers . . . at the San Francisco Zoo.

(SAME SOUND UP BRIEFLY THEN FADE)

INFORMATIONAL COMMUNICATIONS: INDUSTRIALS

Industrials, is an umbrella term for information productions made or commissioned by companies, corporations, government agencies, schools, hospitals, and other organizations wishing to reach selected audiences with highly specific messages. The term itself is potentially misleading because the range of productions encompassed is far greater than those created for industries. Because the term is established and widely understood, it is used here.

Scripts written by or for companies and agencies are created for a variety of purposes, among them:

- to attract potential employees and invite them to apply for open positions;
- to welcome new employees;
- to provide orientation to basic company policies, practices, and values for new employees;
- to keep staff aware, through in-house reports, of news and developments that affect them;
- to provide training resources (most often videos) for employees, including those working away from company headquarters;
- to provide informational and training materials for use by noncompany personnel who use the equipment or services of the sponsoring company; and
- to create stories about company involvement in worthwhile causes that are likely to promote goodwill in the community.

Creating an industrial script is similar in process to conceiving and writing public service programs for nonprofit organizations. That process is described at the outset of Chapter Eleven, "From Theories to Practice," and is repeated here with appropriate modifications.

When a client or sponsor engages a writer to create an informational piece, these key questions demand precise answers:

What, specifically, is the purpose of the sponsoring unit's program?

What are the characteristics of those who make up the intended audience?

What information will be needed to develop an accurate—and in many instances, highly technical—message?

How will those who respond to the production benefit?

Most industrials are produced as videos, and many major corporations have in-house media departments to create them. A typical corporate arrangement sees a media department "commissioned" by a unit within the larger company to produce an instructional or informational piece to meet clearly defined objectives. The media department receives its funding through a transfer of funds from the commissioning unit. A commissioning unit supplies factual information for inclusion in the piece.

Sometimes independent companies produce industrials, either under contract to businesses lacking their own production units or on speculation. Dave Parker operates his independent production company and serves as writer, producer, camera and sound recorder, editor, and voice-over narrator. He's made informational programs for school districts, museums, small businesses, utilities companies, the military, and many others in need of professionally produced information pieces.

Dave Parker's production *The Fatal Stop* was created on speculation. The National Traffic Safety Administration had allocated a large sum of money to support school bus driver training, so Dave spent several days researching school buses, bus drivers, bus accidents, and safety equipment carried on school busses and interviewing school bus drivers and school administrators. He consulted with the State Department of Pupil Transportation and the Director of Public Transportation in Napa, where the show was shot.

Dave has this to say about his approach to this production and about the school bus drivers' reaction when they saw the tape:

> They [The National Traffic Safety Administration] said they didn't want anything with "scare tactics," but of course they really DID! And for sure we gave it to them in this little piece. The country's school bus drivers hated the title, but they loved the show which told a story. They talked about it with one another, and the general reaction was, "Yeah, we had a guy just like that Shilling guy." In fact, all of our [safety] films/videos "told a story," always built around someone who screwed up with lethal consequences.
>
> As I look back on it, practically all our shows had some kind of story line. Kind of INVENT A CHARACTER; GIVE HIM/HER SOME ON-THE-JOB PROBLEM, and show how he/she messed up because of a bad attitude . . . and then picture the (usually bloody) consequences.[18]

THE FATAL STOP!

A story of pre-trip inspections—and why they MUST be done.
Written and Produced by Dave Parker
Parker Productions, Inc.

VIDEO	AUDIO
FADE IN: NIGHT BUS CRASH	SOUND: POLICE RADIO. SHOUTS. SIRENS, ETC.
POLICE, AMBULANCES, ARRIVING	NARR: Portrait of a school bus crash; that catastrophic event which happens so seldom—but with such horrifying results.

This *particular* school bus crash happened 25 minutes ago, and because it's night, and the police and ambulances are still arriving, no one knows at just this moment how many of Bus number 124's passengers are injured. But it's already abundantly clear that there ARE some fatalities.

VOICE:
(SHOUTING OFF CAMERA) Where's the driver?

CUT TO: DRIVER (IN SHOCK, BUT NOT HURT)	NARR: There's the driver. Unhurt—helping the best he can, but burdened with the mind-sickening knowledge that very probably the responsibility for this scene was his. Tomorrow the newspapers will describe this tragedy in detail. Tonight, the details *need* no describing.
CUT TO: FULL SHOT SUPER: TITLES SUPER OUT FADE OUT	SOUND: UP FULL
FADE IN: CHARLEY SITTING IN CHAIR, WATCHING TV	SOUND:FADES SOUND: TV SET IN BG NARR: Portrait of a school bus driver—on his day off. His name is Charley Shilling; and he's been driving for 16 years without even "scratching the paint" as they say in his District.
WEARING BATHROBE, SIPPING HOT TEA PILL BOTTLES ON TABLE NEXT TO HIM. TAKES PILL, WASHES DOWN WITH WATER	He likes his job and he's good at it—but he's glad to have a day off because—frankly—5 days of transporting students is enough for anyone. And anyhow, Charley has a bad cold in the head.
CUT TO: CU PHONE	SOUND: PHONE RINGS NARR: But Charley Shilling's day off is about to "go down the tubes" as they say.

CHARLEY CROSSES TO PHONE, PICKS IT UP	CHARLEY: (SYNC) Hello, Oh, hi Rick. (PAUSE) Aw, come on! This is supposed to be my day off—can't someone *else* take that I trip? (PAUSE) Yeah—yeah, I guess so. In about a half hour maybe.
CUT TO: PHONE HUNG UP	SOUND: PHONE HUNG UP
	CHARLEY: (VO "STREAM OF CONSCIOUSNESS") Man—the way *I* feel, I should've told 'em "no"—straight out. Oh well, that's what I get for answering the phone. Anyhow, I can use the extra money.
CUT TO: CHAS SHAVING	NARR: And so it begins; a never-to-be-forgotten day: to be entered on the transportation schedule as FAIROAKS FOOTBALL TRIP.
CUT TO: FULL SHOT TRANS OFFICE. VERY BUSY. LOTS OF ACTIVITY	SOUND: BUSY OFFICE. PHONES, ETC.
	RICK: (SYNC) Sorry to roust you, Charley, but like I said Larry's sick.
RICK IS UNDER PRESSURE	
	CHARLEY: Yeah—so am I. So what's with this football trip?
	RICK: Got to take 'em to Fairoaks for the semifinals, and I hate to tell you, but we're already late.
	CHARLEY: (RESIGNED) OK—what bus?
	RICK: 124. And you better get a move on. The team is waiting for you out by the Gym.

CHARLEY:
OK, but I've never driven 124 before.
Never been to Fairoaks, either.

RICK:
(HURRYING HIM) Don't worry about it.
124's just like your bus—and the Coach
will tell you how to get to Fairoaks.
Now hustle, will you?

CUT TO BUS # 124   SOUND: BUSY TRANS YARD BG
IN YARD

NARR:
Portrait of a school bus; an immensely
complicated piece of equipment in which
thousands of parts must work together
correctly if the bus is to provide reliable
and SAFE transportation.

OTHER BUS DRIVES
PAST   SOUND: BUS PASSES BY

NARR:
CUT TO: CU ITEMS   But school buses get a lot of use. And
MENTIONED   use leads to wear—and wear leads to
                          "worn out," a condition that faces tires,
                          brakes, headlights, and directional
                          signals—and the thousands of *other* bus
                          components.

                          MUSIC: FAINTLY OMINOUS. BG

                          NARR:
DISS TO: LEFT FRONT   Case in point—Charley Shilling's left
TIRE. SLO ZOOM   front tire—which has developed a serious
IN TO SHOW   problem on the day of the Fairoaks
BLISTER NEAR   football trip—it has reached a
FENDER   dangerous point. And when Charley
                          spots it on his pre-trip inspection, he'll
                          want it replaced—immediately.

CUT TO: OVER-THE-
HOOD SHOT; CHAS
APPROACHING

CHAS OPENS HOOD,   MUSIC: 5-JB-6. THEN BG
CHECKS WATER, OIL,

ETC.
CUT TO: XCU CHAS

Beginning before the engine is even started with an under-the-hood examination of water and oil levels, and the condition of hoses and belts, pre-trip inspection is required by regulation and common sense by every school bus operation in the land. It is, unquestionably, one of the most critical tasks that school bus drivers perform.

CHAS CONTINUES HIS
PRE-TRIP . . . GOES
INTO BUS, STARTS
ENGINE

MUSIC: 10 OK 3029

CHAS CONSULTING
CHECK SHEET

Printed on a thorough check sheet, which lists all items in sequence, pre-trip inspections may contain as many as 80 separate items—each of which must be checked before every trip on which students will be carried.

DISS TO: AIR
PRESSURE GAUGE,
THEN OTHER ITEMS
IN SEQUENCE

MUSIC: SNEAKS BG

DRIVER'S VOICE:
Brakes—

SOUND: HORN

DRIVER'S VOICE:
Horn—
Defroster—heater—windshield wipers—dome lights—stepwell light—emergency door—4-way flashers—return signals—brake lights . . .

VOICE FADES TO BG BUT
CONTINUES

NARR:
And the list continues—itemizing every bus component, the proper condition and functioning of which is essential to bus SAFETY.

DISS TO: CHAS
CHECKING RIGHT
FRONT TIRE
CHAS MOVES AROUND

But no list, however comprehensive and well-devised is any better than the driver

BUS TO CHECK LEFT
FRONT TIRE

CHAS STARTS TO
CHECK LEFT FRONT
TIRES, WHEN HE'S
INTERRUPTED BY
RICK'S VOICE

who uses it—and if just one item is
overlooked the consequences can be
catastrophic. . . .

RICK:
(SYNC. SHOUTING) Hey, Charley—
move it, will yuh? Principal's on the
phone and says the Coach is getting
sore.

CUT TO: CHARLEY

CHARLEY:
(SYNC) Tell the Coach he can . . . all
right, all right, I'm coming.

CHAS CONTINUES HIS
CHECKS IN HASTE,
BUT DOESN'T CHECK
THE TIRE

MUSIC: SF-1046-B

CHARLEY:
(STREAM OF CONSCIOUSNESS)
What's the Coach and teachers know
about driving a bus anyhow? Takes time
to do this stuff right . . .

MUSIC: WIPES OUT CHARLEY'S
VOICE

CUT TO: CU BAD TIRE

NARR:
And so, Charlie Shilling continues his
already flawed pretrip inspection . . .
And Bus 124 leaves the transportation
yard for the last time.

DISS TO: BUS LEAVING
CUT TO: REVERSE
ANGLE. SUPER:
QUESTION

Oh. incidentally—observing as you have
been, what's happened so far. What
comments do you have about this
football trip to Fairoaks?

MUSIC: TO TAG

STOP PRESENTATION FOR
DISCUSSION

FADE IN: COACH & TEAM. CHEER GIRLS, WAITING FOR BUS	SOUND: GENERAL EXCITED AD-LIB BG [IN BACKGROUND]
CUT TO: COACH:	COACH: (SYNC) All right over there—save it for the game will yuh? (ETC.)
CUT TO: EXCITED KIDS	NARR: Portrait of the passengers; excited, impatient, anxious, worried about the game ahead. Altogether, a fairly typical football team an the way to an important game.
CUT TO: BUS ARRIVING, STOPS, DOOR OPENS	
CUT TO: TEAM LOADING	ATHLETES: Yeahhhhhhhhhh!(CHEER) AD LIB EXCITED LOADING . . .
CUT TO: CU CHARLEY	CHARLEY: (SYNC) Come on you guys—settle down. I'll get you there and back. But let's start this thing off right . . . OK?
CUT TO: NOISEMAKER DISS TO: BUS ON ROAD	SOUND: NOISEMAKER SOUND: AIRHORN
	MUSIC: SNEAKS BG
CUT TO: PASSENGERS IN SEATS	NARR: Passengers in their seats—bus on the road. But today its thousands of parts AREN'T working together correctly to provide safe transportation. And later, when the question is asked, "who could have prevented the tragedy?" the answer on many lips will be—
CU: CHARLEY	Charley Shilling.

CUT TO: LEFT FRONT WHEEL (AT HIGHWAY SPEED)	MUSIC: 8 OK 302,7N BG
(MATCH) DISS TO: SIMILAR WHEEL ON STATIONARY BUS.	Which introduces the all-important subject of "driver responsibility"— including the professional responsibility for a scrupulous pre-trip inspection; performed just as thoroughly the 1,000th time as the first . . . in order to find the one or more parts that might not be functioning properly. But not all drivers ARE responsible. (SYNC) It was OK yesterday—
A DRIVER IS CHECK-ING IT. THEN CONTINUES WITH REST OF CHECKS	
DISS TO: DRIVER # 1	DRIVER # 1: (SYNC) Nothing's EVER wrong with MY bus.
CUT TO: DRIVER # 2	DRIVER # 2: (SYNC) It just came out of the shop.
CUT TO: DRIVER # 3	DRIVER # 3: (SYNC) Marian checked it this morning.
CUT TO: DRIVER # 4	DRIVER # 4 (SYNC) I was in a hurry . . .
	MUSIC: 6 EM 1361
DISS TO: NEW BUS BEING PRE-TRIPPED	NARR: Excuses—yes, in fact, words to crash by. Even a factory fresh bus should be pre-tripped before it carries passengers, because even new parts can malfunction and only one malfunction can cause a tragedy. To many drivers, it isn't just a question of whether or not a directional signal is working; but what might happen if it ISN'T working. And at the risk of being thought "overly dramatic," we suggest that each and every item on the pre-trip check list be thought of in terms of CONSEQUENCES: the frightening list of "what could happen if that particular item failed or malfunctioned."
DISS TO: OTHER PRE-TRIP SCENES	

DISS TO: BUS GOING THRU HEAVY CONSTRUCTION ZONE (VERY NOISY)	SOUND: AIR HAMMERS. ETC.
	DRIVER # 1: (VO) We had a bus with a blown emergency door warning light. But the buzzer still worked, so the driver thought she'd take it anyhow. Problem was, she couldn't HEAR the buzzer—and a kid fell out and almost killed himself.
	MUSIC: 7-LM
DISS TO: RAIN STORY	DRIVER # 2: I knew the windshield wipers didn't work on my bus, but—but it hadn't rained for a while so I figured "no problem." Well, of course it DID rain . . . and I have to tell you that there's NO WAY you can drive in a cloudburst without wipers.
DISS TO: FUEL STORY	DRIVER # 3: Kind of embarrassing—what happened to me, I didn't check the gas gauge quantity—and actually ran out of gas with a full bus—on a rainy day in the middle of nowhere!
DISS TO: SEAT STORY	DRIVER # 4: One of our buses had a loose seat—nothing that seemed urgent to fix or anything—but I had to make a panic stop—and a little girl broke her nose.
DISS TO: SIGNAL STORY	DRIVER # 5: A broken right-turn signal cost us a few thousand dollars and a law suit. Driver of the other car couldn't tell I was going to turn right, and before the whole thing was over the other driver spent some time in the hospital, and I almost lost my job. Whole thing happened because of an inexpensive little light bulb. Taught me a lesson I'll never forget.
DISS TO: SEAT BELT STORY	DRIVER # 6 (MIDDLE-AGED MALE): I always had the idea that checking and

using my seat belt wasn't all that important. I mean I don't always use the seat belt in my car, and I've never had a problem.

But, on this one trip, I had to swerve to miss a car—hit a soft shoulder and got tossed into the step well.

DISS TO: WHEEL STORY	**DRIVER # 7:** There was this one day I forgot to check the lug nuts on the front wheel . . . and before I got out of the yard the wheel fell OFF. Some kids figured loosening the nuts would be a slick Halloween trick. Funny, right? MUSIC: 15 LM 319 N BG
DISS TO: BROKEN WINDOWS, SLASHED SEATS, EMPTY FIRST AID KIT, EMPTY REFLECTOR BOX CUT TO: SUGAR IN TANK, NAILS IN TIRE	**NARR:** Which introduces the subject of vandalism—a costly and dangerous practice which increasingly plagues a lot of bus operations. Broken windows—slashed seat cushions—spray paint on the seats—dangerous fun with a fire extinguisher? Yes, you *know* they happen But also sugar in the gas tank—and nails in the tires. How would you like to miss THAT little booby trap on a pre-trip inspection? If you'd like a personal anecdote, listen to the driver who had his *brake* lines cut by vandals. MUSIC: 10-LM-3
DISS TO: BRAKE STORY	**DRIVER # 8 (YOUNG GUY):** I was in a hurry to leave the yard and I didn't check anything very well. And when I tried to stop I sailed right out into the street and up the driveway across it.
DISS TO: CONTINUATION OF STORY	**NARR:** So—he returned for *another* bus, which had the same *problem!* And as he sailed through the same stop sign for the 2nd

time he became convinced that a complete pre-trip inspection should include a thorough brake test.

MUSIC: 4-LM 20

DISS TO: MIRROR
STORY

DRIVER #9 (WOMAN):
A really tragic thing happened in the district across the river from us. One of the drivers was in a hurry, I guess, and she forgot to adjust her crossover mirror. So—she couldn't see little girl getting her lunch box from in front of the bus.

NARR:
You see—the school bus driving profession allows NO MISTAKES. None! And the 1st place to prevent on-the-road problems is that all-important pre-trip inspection . . . as Charley Shilling has been trained to do.

CUT TO: FULL SHOT,
WHEEL

CUT TO: CHARLEY
DRIVING.
CUT TO: BUS PASSBY
CUT TO: REVERSE ANGLE
SUPER: QUESTION

SOUND: BUS PASSBY

Well, you've heard our drivers talk about some consequences of sloppy pre-trip inspections but what are some consequences?
And—what constitutes a good pre-trip examination?

OTHER FADE OUT

STOP SHOWING TO ALLOW PARTICIPANTS TO DISCUSS AND ANSWER THESE QUESTIONS.

NARR:
Bus at Fairoaks and excitement in the air. This is the day—the day they worked hard for and plan to remember always for fun and football.
It's a day they WILL remember for a school bus and its driver; their friend Charley Shilling.

FADE IN: STUDENTS
UNLOADING AT
FAIROAKS
CUT TO: CHARLEY
MANAGING KIDS . . .
FEELING IS GOOD-
NATURED

CUT TO: CHEER GIRL	GIRL: (SYNC) Going to cheer for us, Mr. Shilling?
	CHARLEY: You bet Joanie. Be over soon as I secure this bus.
CUT TO: ECU CHAS	CHARLEY: (VO STREAM OF CONSCIOUSNESS) What a bunch of really great kids . . . you can't help but hope that they'll be this happy when they grow up . . .
	MUSIC: SNEAKS BG
	NARR: And so—miles from home—Charley finishes securing his bus—confident in the knowledge that everything is A-OK.
CUT TO: CU BAD TIRE	But everything ISN'T A-OK—and this is the day that Charley Shilling will "scratch the paint."
	MUSIC: 10-OK 3029
	NARR: One of the best ways known to bus drivers NOT to "scratch the paint" is that all-important pre-trip inspection.
DISS TO: EMERGENCY DOORS BEING CHECKED	Emergency exits—check for proper operation in opening and closing . . .
DISS TO: AIR BRAKE TEST	DRIVER # 13: Check vacuum tanks.
DISS TO: TURN SIGNAL CHECK	DRIVER # 14: Check turn signals—right and left—front & rear . . .
DISS TO: TIRE CHECK	DRIVER # 15: Check tires for condition and pressure . . .
	MUSIC: FULL THEN BG
	NARR: And the check list continues, because

the pre-trip ritual can never be left to *chance*—whether the inspection takes place in the bus yard or at home.

But isn't the responsibility for putting safe buses on the road a "team" operation; involving manufacturers, mechanics, and transportation supervisors—as well as drivers? Yes, it is.

DISS TO: MANUFACTURER	MANUFACTURER: [(SYNC) BRIEF STATEMENT RE HOW HIS (UN-NAMED) COMPANY ALWAYS MEETS OR EXCEEDS FEDERAL SAFETY STANDARDS . . .]
DISS TO: MECHANIC IN SHOP	MECHANIC: [(SYNC) BRIEF STATEMENT RE HIS RESPONSIBILITY. MAY SAY THAT HE'S NEVER AFRAID TO SPEAK OUT AND "GO ON THE RECORD" ABOUT AN UNSAFE BUS . . . IN SPITE OF THE PRESSURES HE (SOMETIMES) GETS FROM THE DISPATCHER . . .]
DISS TO: MECHANIC RIDING WITH DRIVER	ANDY: SC 30 I OFTEN RIDE WITH THE DRIVERS TO PERSONALLY SEE WHAT THEIR PROBLEMS ARE, BECAUSE I'M NEVER GOING TO OK A BUS UNLESS I'D BE WILLING TO HAVE MY OWN CHILDREN RIDE IN IT.
DISS TO: DISPATCHER IN OFFICE	DISPATCHER: [(SYNC) BRIEF STATEMENT, RE HIS RESPONSIBILITIES FOR SAFE BUSES. MAY MENTION HIS "PRESSURES" BUT SAYS NOTHING IS WORTH PUTTING AN UNSAFE BUS . . . OR BUS DRIVER (MAY ADD A COMMENT ABOUT HIS PERSONAL DAILY CONTACT WITH THE DRIVERS, AND HOW HE EXAMINES *THEM* TOO . . . FOR FITNESS).]
DISS TO: SUPERVISOR	SUPERVISOR: [(SYNC) TELLS US ABOUT HIS

RESPONSIBILITIES . . . THE "FINAL SAY SO" IS HIS . . . AND HE'S THE ONE WHO HAS TO FACE THE PARENTS (AND SCHOOL BOARD) . . . SAFETY IS PARAMOUNT . . . "YOU HAVE TO SLEEP AT NIGHT."]

MUSIC: 4-JB-5

DISS TO: DRIVER

NARR:
But while the "team" is behind the wrench, or the phone, or the desk—it's the *driver* who ends up behind the wheel, and if there's trouble or tragedy—it's the driver who is there when it happens. . . .

DRIVER # 1:
[(SYNC) AGREES. TELLS HOW ALL OF THEM HAVE A DAILY REPORT FORM—A "GRIPE SHEET" . . . AND THEY'RE NOT AFRAID TO USE IT.]

DISS TO: OTHER DRIVER

DRIVER # 2:
[(SYNC) ADDS THAT IN HIS (HER) DISTRICT THEY DON'T JUST STICK WITH THE GRIPE SHEET EITHER: THEY ARE ENCOURAGED TO ADD THEIR OWN COMMENTS.]

DISS TO: OTHER DRIVER

DRIVER # 3:
[(SYNC) THERE'S ONE OTHER THING ALL OF US THINK IS IMPORTANT BECAUSE WHILE IT'S ABSOLUTELY NECESSARY FOR OUR BUSES TO BE READY FOR THE ROAD, IT' S IMPORTANT FOR *US* TO BE READY TOO.]

MUSIC: SNEAKS BG

DISS TO: DRIVERS IN VARIED SITUATIONS. SOME IN LOUNGES, SOME WITH SUPES, DRIVING

NARR:
A pre-trip inspection for drivers too? A kind of self-inspection to answer the question "Am I ready to get behind the wheel?" Yes, because the driver is an even more complicated piece of

equipment than the bus, and good as the bus may be—it's no better than its driver is—today.

DRIVER # 16:
(SYNC OR VO) I don't get sick very often, but when it *happens,* I *always* tell my boss if I don't think I'm up to driving safely. I never take *advantage* of that, but he wants us to tell him—and we *do* tell him.

DRIVER # 17:
Being ready to drive has to do with taking *medication,* too. Almost everyone knows that some medications make driving unsafe . . . and if my doctor prescribes something that might make me unsafe behind the wheel of my bus . . . no way am I going to take that chance.

DRIVER # 18:
Being specially emotional—angry or upset—can affect driving ability too. It may be a sort of "human tendency" to try and *hide* their problems.

NARR:
Now for the ride home. Passengers in their seats—bus on the road. But tonight the mood is different because the "Number One Team" is enjoying the right of football teams everywhere to be excited about its most important victory. And it's hard to blame a "number one team" for celebrating a victory even on a school bus. Tonight they'll tell their parents—tomorrow the whole school will know what happened in Fairoaks.

SOUND: BUS UP FULL

NARR:
CUT TO: CU TIRE   On the left front wheel—an UNcharacteristic condition—approaching

	the kind of consequence that will affect the lives of everyone on board.
	SOUND: BUS BG
CUT TO: CHARLEY	CHARLEY: (SYNC) OK you guys—set down back there and let's go. (TO COACH) Jim, can't you get those kids shaped up?
	COACH: But they WON Charley—what you want me to do?
CUT TO: CHEER GIRL	CHEER GIRL: (SYNC) Let's hear one more cheer for OUR team.
	ALL: YEAHHHHHHHHHHHHH!
CUT TO: CHARLEY	CHARLEY: (GIVING IN WITH A GRIN) OK, OK—
	SOUND: BUS PULLING OUT
	NARR: Almost home—and with only a few miles left to go it finally happens. That tire with the blister finally blows out.
TIRE BLOWS OUT	SOUND: BANG
CUT TO: CHAS FIGHTING THE WHEEL	MUSIC: STING & PUNCTUATE BG
CUT TO: BUS SWERVING	SOUND: KIDS YELLING IN FRIGHT
CUT TO: FRIGHTENED KIDS	SOUND: BUS SKIDDING
CUT TO: TIRE	
CUT TO: BUS HEADING FOR DITCH	

CUT TO: CHARLEY
BRINGING BUS
UNDER CONTROL

CUT TO: BUS COMES TO STOP

MUSIC: TAGS

CUT TO: INTERIOR

COACH:
(SYNC) Geez Charley—what happened?

CHARLEY:
Tire blew—man that was close . . .

COACH:
(AGREEING WEAKLY) Yeah—yeah it
was.

CHARLEY:
Well, can't move this thing—that's for
sure. Better put out the reflectors.

CUT TO: CHAS ENTERS
SHOT AND STARTS TO
OPEN REFLECTOR BOX

NARR:
So often it's a combination of things that
make the difference. Like right now, with
Bus 124 stopped on a curve at night—
Charley Shilling faces the FINAL
consequence of a sloppy pre-trip
inspection when he opens the cover of
his "reflector box" . . .

CUT TO: CU FLARE
BOX IS EMPTY

CHARLEY:
(SYNC) Oh no!

COACH:
What's wrong now?

CHARLEY:
Looks like somebody ripped off my
reflectors.

CUT TO: CHAS EXITING BUS

NARR:
Well, as they say—"that's it." A set-up
for catastrophe, which will involve
everyone connected with Bus # 124.
And the driver of that big interstate rig;
just now closing the gap down the
highway . . .

CUT TO: PETERBILT DRIVER

SOUND: AIR HORN (OF TRUCK)

FLURRY OF CUTTING
ECU TRUCK DRIVER;
SHOCK ZOOM TO BUS;
CUT TO: CHARLEY
CUT TO: RADIATOR
OF TRUCK (SHOCK ZOOM)

SOUND: CRASH

SLO DISS TO:
AFTERMATH

MUSIC: 7-JB 33

CHARLEY RUNNING
TO WRECKAGE,
TRYING TO GET
INSIDE TO HELP

NARR:
Not much else to say. At just this
moment, Charley Shilling is the only one
at the scene who could even describe
what happened. But later an awful lot of
questions will be asked about that
FAIROAKS FOOTBALL TRIP

. . . AND the reasons it never returned
home. When the National Transportation
Safety Board investigates the crash,
they'll fill out a lot of forms having to do
with the driver, the vehicle—and the
environment.
If YOU had to fill out those forms, what
things would YOU say caused that
crash?

FADE IN: CRASH AS
AT BEGINNING

SOUND: SIRENS, ETC.

SUPER CREDITS
FADE OUT

SOUND: FADES OUT.

QUESTIONS

1. In the story of Keiko (*Free Willy*) identify the specific statements that you feel arouse the greatest audience interest, and those at or near the end that bring closure and reward viewers for following the story from beginning to end.

2. How does Wayne Freedman establish the mood of his piece, *Route 66,* other than with spoken dialogue? Be specific.

3. Richard Rodriguez's *The Death of a Church* is a moving depiction of the closing of a sanctuary and monument to the faith of elderly people. The church members who asked Mr. Rodriguez to be present for the closing believed that the church would always be there to provide comfort, reassurance, and an avenue connecting them to a Higher Power. Describe your feelings, especially those you may have felt during the

closing moments. Referring back to the concept of catharsis, did you share with the worshipers and Rodriguez the high emotional impact of this story?

4. *Fear Equals Fun* is followed by an analysis by its author, Sharon Yamane. Analyze *her* analysis. Do you agree with the points she makes? Is there anything you would change? Anything you would add? Review the material in universal themes (Chapter 4 and Appendix B) and find themes not identified by Yamane.

NOTES

1. From a personal letter from Bob Davy to author, April 7, 2000.
2. Courtesy of Bob Davy.
3. Telephone interview with Richard Rodriguez, September 14, 2001.
4. Reprinted by permission of the author and Georges Borchardt, Inc.
5. Wayne Freedman, telephone conversation, November 21, 2001.
6. From personal discussions, December, 2000.
7. Courtesy of Wayne Freedman.
8. You can access Garfield's analyses of commercials at: http://www.adreview.com
9. From dust jacket of "Waking Up . . ."
10. Bob Garfield, *Waking Up Screaming from the American Dream* (New York: Scribner, 1997), 248ff. Reprinted by permission of the author.
11. Another of Garfield's PBS reports, "As the Worm Turns," may be found in "Waking Up . . . ," p. 138 ff.
12. Bob MacKenzie has received thirteen Emmys, a National Headliners award, membership in the Television Academy's Silver Circle, and numerous other professional honors.
13. Reprinted by permission of Bob Mackenzie, KTUV, Oakland, California.
14. Reprinted by permission of the author and Georges Borchardt, Inc.
15. Bob Davy, whose career includes eight years in commercial television, three years in marketing, and fifteen years in Maryland public television, is the recipient of many awards, including three from The Ohio State University, and one from San Francisco State University, as well as awards from The Freedoms Foundation, American Bar Association, the Birmingham Film Festival, and an Emmy from the Academy of Television Arts and Sciences.
16. The "Queen Mary" and the next three features— "Guys and Dolls," "Bob Day," and "San Francisco Zoo," reprinted courtesy of Bob Davy.
17. From letter by Bob Davy to author, March 7, 1996.
18. From a letter from Dave Parker to the author, October 1, 2001.

CHAPTER SIXTEEN

WRITING COMEDY

Chapter 16 connects comic theories discussed in Chapter 8, "The Anatomy of Comedy," to writing challenges in the present. Comic sketches and jokes are analyzed to reveal comic techniques that underlie their effectiveness. *Attitude* is described as an important basis for comic conception and writing. Examples from several comic tales, ancient and modern, illustrate how a writer's attitude toward characters and situations helps identify fruitful subject matter and determine an appropriate degree of disapproval.

As you read Chapter 8, "The Anatomy of Comedy," you may have wondered how comic theory could possibly be put to use, how it could help you be "funny." In this chapter, the connection between comic theory and practice should become clear.

If you want to write comedy, the worst thing you can do is to set out determined to be funny! As contradictory as this may sound, it's true. Good comedy doesn't come on demand, and it can't be ordered to spring effortlessly from a writer whose sole motivation is to come up with something "funny." You may remember the line, "Fred, meet Maria. Fred's really funny. Say something funny, Fred." The joke here is that its almost impossible to be funny under pressure!

ATTITUDES

There's a precondition that makes comic writing easier and more likely to succeed that's best summed up as the possession of an *attitude.* An attitude (which Freud called a *tendency*) underlies nearly every successful joke, sketch, or comic drama. Attitudes are of many kinds and degrees, and illustrating the range of possibilities will clarify this point.

Scripts written by college students for a class in writing for the electronic media are identified by an asterisk (*) appearing after the author's name.

Attitudes vary from delight to rage, with many gradations between. Here are some readily recognized attitudes toward the characters' appearance, actions, or viewpoints in comic dramas, and toward anything else that can bring about an attitude:

delight with a nonthreatening deviant from the norm;

amusement at a person's or a group's deviant behavior;

annoyance over the conduct of a person or a group;

anger at some practices or miscarriages of justice;

hatred toward a person, condition, or group; and

rage that's out of control—or nearly so—usually toward a person or group that is both powerful and dangerous.

To better understand this concept, we can turn to dramatists and their plays, past and present. Here are examples from several successful comic playwrights, including brief comments about the attitudes behind some of their best comic moments. They're presented in logical, rather than chronological order—from amusement to annoyance to anger.

Delight.   Eugene O'Neill (1888–1953) wrote but one comedy, *Ah, Wilderness,* a nostalgic semiautobiographical view of family life during O'Neill's adolescent years. Written in 1933, it's a gentle comedy, as it "recreates with tenderness and sympathy the almost forgotten world of 1906, when O'Neill was about the same age as Richard Miller of his play."[1]

Comic laughter arises from complications in Richard's life (a night at a road house, a rocky romance with his girlfriend, and a crisis in relations with his parents). Much of the comedy arises from his Uncle Sid's drinking bouts, as seen in this incident:

(Richard's father and his Uncle Sid have returned late from a picnic. Sid is somewhat drunk—the stage direction reads, "He is in a condition that can best be described as blurry." They sit down for dinner and, after much by-play, Sid's sister has had enough.)

Mrs. Miller: *Will* you go to bed, you idiot?

Sid: (*mutters graciously*). Immediately—if not sooner! (*He turns to pass behind* LILY, *then stops staring down at her*) But wait. There is still a duty I must perform. No day is complete without it. Lily, answer me once and for all, will you marry me

Lily: (*with a hysterical giggle*). No I won't—never!

Sid: (*NODDING HIS HEAD*). Right! And perhaps it's all for the best. For how could I forget the pre—precepts taught me at my mother's dying knee. "Sidney," she said, "never marry a woman who drinks! Lips that touch liquor shall never touch yours!" (*Gazing at Lily mournfully*) Too bad! So fine a woman once—and now such a slave to rum! (*Turning to* NAT) What can we do to save her, Nat? (*In a hoarse, confident whisper*) Better put her in an institution where she'll be removed from temptation! The mere smell of it seems to drive her frantic![2]

From this exchange, it can be seen that O'Neill's feeling (his *attitude*) toward his extended family was one of nostalgic amusement. This comic masterpiece can best be compared to the Andy Hardy movies that began with *A Family Affair* in 1937, and ended sixteen films later with *Andy Hardy Comes Home* in 1958. (These movies may be found in rental stores, or in college AV departments.) Television counterparts of the past include *Father Knows Best, Leave It to Beaver, The Partridge Family,* and *Mayberry R.F.D.*

Amusement. William Shakespeare (1564–1616) inserted many comic scenes in plays classified as histories and comedies. Among the memorable comic characters he created are the uneducated workmen in *A Midsummer Night's Dream,* including Bottom (a Weaver), Quince (a carpenter), and Snout (a tinker). These rustics rehearse and perform a play in honor of the marriage of Theseus and Hippolyta (Theseus is Duke of Athens; Hippolyta is queen of the Amazons), and the resulting performance is ripe with comic of speech, comic pantomimic movement, comic of the naive, comic of the unexpected, and caricature. The nobles and fairies who constitute the audience are amused at the clumsy efforts of the semiliterate tradesmen, but there is a note of endearment in their whispered comments to one another.

For his history plays about Prince Hal (later crowned Henry V), Shakespeare invented Sir John Falstaff, ". . . a liar, a sot, a coward, and a whoremonger," but nevertheless, "almost all conclude that Falstaff is essentially a poetic creation . . . a thing of beauty."[3]

The nature of those on the receiving end of comic barbs in these two plays show that Shakespeare was more amused than angered by behavior that was out of the norm—so long as it was not harmful to others. Compared with *Ah, Wilderness,* these comic creations of Shakespeare's are just one step "cranked up" in the direction of annoyance from the attitude level shown by O'Neill.

Amusement, with Some Annoyance. George S. Kaufman and Moss Hart wrote the Pulitzer Prize-winning play, *The Man Who Came to Dinner,* in 1939. The lead character, Sheridan Whiteside, was a caricature of Alexander Woollcott, a famous wit, cynic, and close friend of the playwrights. Whiteside's sharp tongue and self-centered nature are responsible for nearly all of the comic moments in the play. In this brief exchange, he shows his aversion to his nurse, Miss Preen:

Miss Preen: Oh, my! You mustn't eat candy, Mr. Whiteside. It's very bad for you.

Whiteside: My great-aunt Jennifer ate a whole box of candy every day of her life. She lived to be a hundred and two, and when she had been dead three days she looked better than you do now.[4]

As Act Three opens, Whiteside, bellows for his nurse:

Whiteside: Miss Preen! Miss Preen!

Miss Preen: (*Nervously*). Yes, sir. Yes, sir.

Whiteside: Where do you disappear to all the time, My Lady nausea?

Miss Preen: (*Firmly*). Mr. Whiteside, I can only be in one place at a time.

Whiteside: That is very fortunate for this community.[5]

In Whiteside, Kaufman and Hart portrayed a highly amusing deviant, one whose acid tongue could wound a hapless victim at twenty paces. The trick was to make this outrageous character somehow acceptable—even endearing—and this they accomplished. In the play, nearly all hostile wit is initiated by Whiteside, and to make this palatable, the targets of his scorn are, with few exceptions, wimps and incompetents. *The Man Who Came to Dinner* shows us a stronger "bite" than either *Ah, Wilderness,* or the comic figures in *A Midsummer Night's Dream,* but it works because its authors clearly show that they're more amused than annoyed by Whiteside's idiosyncrasies. As if to prove this, Kaufman and Hart wrote this dedication to the man who inspired the Sheridan Whiteside character:

TO ALEXANDER WOOLLCOTT
For reasons that are nobody's business.
THE AUTHORS

Anger, Moderate.   George Bernard Shaw (1856–1950) is considered one of the greatest playwrights of the late nineteenth–early twentieth centuries. Among his comedies are: *Mrs. Warren's Profession,* an exposé of the economic basis of prostitution; *Major Barbara,* a clinical (and cynical) analysis of poverty; and *The Doctor's Dilemma,* a caustic treatment of the medical profession.

Shaw was incensed by injustice and by what he considered stupidity on the part of national leaders, and he lashed out with comic sarcasm at the objects of his displeasure; at the same time, he was a utopian who felt that society was redeemable, and it was in this spirit that he wrote most of his comedies. He had anger in him, but as it was reflected in his plays, it was more like a 6 on scale of 1 to 10.

Anger.   Aristophanes, the greatest of all Greek comic playwrights, lived from ca 445–388 B.C. Eleven of his forty-four plays have survived. The one element that characterizes all of his plays is his anger (attitude) toward persons, ideas, or activities that he found offensive. To select a few plays at random, his *Acharnians* attacked the war party in Athens; the *Knights* was an attack on Cleon, head of the war party; *Lysistrata* was another diatribe against the war that had brought Athens to exhaustion and despair; *Clouds* was a devastating attack on Socrates and Greek education; and the *Wasps* criticized the perversion of judicial power. Every one of Aristophanes' plays has as its central thrust, something or someone that he saw as being unacceptable, stupid, or dangerous. His chief weapon was hostile wit, but to achieve his goal of ridiculing those he found absurd, he also used the devices of obscene wit, caricature, comic of motion, comic of speech, and deflation of authority figures. His attitude was high on the scale of anger.

Anger, Extreme.   Ben Jonson (1573–1637), friend and drinking buddy of William Shakespeare, wrote his masterpiece, *Volpone,* in 1605 as a biting satire against human greed. His *Sejanus* (1603) was an exposé of dictators, and was a commentary on increasing repression in England during the declining years of the reign of Elizabeth I. Ben Jonson was a very angry man, and his cynicism toward what he perceived as the baseness of human nature made the anger in his writings more extreme than that of Aristophanes. His anger would rate a 9 on a scale of 1 to 10, approaching outright hatred.

Mix of Attitudes.   Neil Simon is a hugely successful comic playwright of our own time. Among his successes are *The Odd Couple, The Goodbye Girl, California Suite,* and *Barefoot in the Park.* Simon is considered last in this sampler of comic attitudes because his comedy is more far-ranging than that of most other playwrights. Each of his plays is funny, of course, but his plays also demonstrate a greater range of attitudes that underlie comedy than do the plays of other authors examined here. Simon's plays feature two major themes: friends who are in constant conflict, as in *The Odd Couple* and *The Sunshine Boys,* and autobiographical family stresses and strained relationships seen in the "Brighton Beach" trilogy—*Brighton Beach Memoirs, Biloxi Blues,* and *Broadway Bound.*

In The Odd Couple, Simon makes fun of the prissy perfectionist Felix, and the messy, easygoing slob, Oscar, but Simon's treatment reveals a definite affection for both comic deviants.

In his autobiographical trilogy, "Brighton Beach" Simon shows anger toward his mother's cooking (relatively indulgent), the overabundance of close relatives who've moved in with his immediate family (stronger resentment), the domineering attitudes of his parents (stronger still), and the U.S. Army (outright hatred). Because Simon himself is the central figure in these plays, they include heavy doses of humor—comic laughter by which he produces laughs based on his own shortcomings or misfortunes, including events that were anything but funny to him at the time. Neil Simon's comedies illustrate every technique described by Freud, from the eight categories of the comic to humor and both hostile and obscene wit.

Rage.   Extreme anger is seldom found in comedies. A level of hostility lower than all-out rage is found in most comic stories of merit, but taken to the extreme of rage, comedy loses its capacity for pleasurable audience experiences.

There's a role in the public arts for stories marked by rage, because rage is a justifiable human reaction to events, practices, or individuals seen as unacceptable, or even as evil. While audiences generally prefer pleasant—or at least balanced—stories, many works written with unmasked outrage have made important contributions to the arts. *Uncle Tom's Cabin* (1852) attacking the evils of slavery was written by a very distressed Harriet Beecher Stowe; the documentary, *Land Without Bread* (1932) by the Spanish filmmaker Luis Buñuel, dwelled on the impoverished and dehumanized people in the Las Hurdes region of Spain; Barry McGuire's fierce antiwar song *Eve of Destruction* (1965) is considered the first and angriest anti-Vietnam War protest song; and John Steinbeck's *Grapes of Wrath* (1939) about the suffering of victims in the 1930s dust bowl is only slightly less angry. A work written in great anger nearly always carries with it an implicit demand for change.

Freud's concept that hostile wit fails when the disguise doesn't mask the vitriol behind an attack helps explain why writer's with angry messages are better served by modes or genres other than the comic.

Each of the playwrights briefly mentioned employs at least some of the standard techniques of the comic: the naive, motion, speech, the unexpected, incongruity, unmasking (deflation of authority figures), caricature, the mechanistic, and inadequacy. Undergirding all, however, are varying degrees of what Freud called tendency wit. The lesson to be learned from all this is that a comic script will likely succeed if it arises from an *attitude*. The magic common motivator is an attitude, reflecting a degree of emotion toward the portrayed subject(s).

A general truth is that comedy, when it's at an extreme of delight or of rage, tends to be less funny—and therefore less successful—than when it ranges from mild annoyance to moderate anger. That doesn't mean that delight or rage are inappropriate to the telling of a good story; it simply means that a story sacrifices comic laughter. *Josie,* by Mari-Ela David (found later in this chapter), is a fine example of a sketch that has some laughs in it, but the depiction of character and the exploration of a family's tenuous relationships takes center stage.

Comic stage plays can run in length from two to three hours, so careful plotting is essential for their successes. You can't sustain a single joke or comic encounter for an entire evening. A solid comedy, such as *The Man Who Came to Dinner,* has a basic idea, an idea that sets the stage for the outrageous events that follow. That idea, placing a world-famous, arrogant, sharp-tongued conniver into the home of a colorless, humorless Midwestern doctor and his family, is based on *incongruity.* Beyond that basic concept, Kaufman and Hart use all other techniques of comedy to create a succession of plot reversals—unexpected shifts in the story line that reinvigorate interest and sustain the audience's interest.

THE INITIAL CONCEPT

Aside from having an attitude, a writer must invent a situation or a set of circumstances that provide fertile ground for the comic actions of the story. In *A Midsummer Night's Dream,* as indicated earlier, Shakespeare came up with the idea of having a group of well-meaning but semiliterate men of the working class rehearse and perform a classic tragedy, *Pyramus and Thisby,* before the nobles of Athens. From this concept, much comic of naivete, of speech, and of movement; incongruity; the unexpected; and caricature follow. It's no exaggeration to say that the initial concept is a major factor in determining the outcome of this extended scene.

To use another example, the film *Shakespeare in Love* stems from the idea that young William Shakespeare has writer's block. He's been struggling some time with the writing of a play, *Romeo and Ethel, The Pirate's Daughter,* but nothing works for him. He then sees and falls in love with a charming and beautiful woman, and in no time at all he's back on track, eventually turning his intended comedy into one of the greatest love stories of all time, *Romeo and Juliet.* There's much, much more to *Shakespeare in Love,* but the initial concept triggered much of what became superb comic moments and compelling drama. Neil Simon's *The Odd Couple* bases its comic conflicts on two adult male roommates, as unlike as two men can be: Felix is effete, loves classical music, is meticulous in his grooming, and demands quality food and a neat apartment. Oscar, a sports writer, is a slob, will eat anything that isn't crawling, loves to play poker, doesn't pick up after himself, and is generally unkempt. If you try, you can undoubtedly come up with several of examples of basic concepts that are the motivating forces in film and television comedies.

PLOTTING COMIC DRAMAS

According to Aristotle, a play is made up of six parts, arranged in order of importance (see Chapter 5, "Form in the Arts"). The first and most important part is plot—another word for form or structure. This statement applies equally to shorter stories, including jokes. A brief, uncomplicated joke will fail unless it builds expectation and culminates in a good "punch line." Here's a joke that's short and gets to the point economically, with the laughter occurring only at the very end of the joke:

Tina and Ole are talking:

Tina: I yust vent to Yay See Penney, and got a brassiere on sale.

Ole: Vat for? Yew got nothin' to put in it!

Tina: Vell, yew vear Yockey Shorts, don't yew?

This ethnic joke involves several themes and comic techniques: battle of the sexes, obscene wit, hostile wit, comic of expectation, comic of speech, naivete, and deflation. The success of the joke depends entirely on the punch line.

Here's a joke that's longer, and may bring smiles or even laughter before the punch line is reached. Said to be Ronald Reagan's favorite Russian joke, it isn't as funny now as it was during the cold war—an example of how decreased fear or removal of a perceived threat can make hostile wit lose its punch.

Dmitri saves enough money to buy a car. He goes to the Bureau of Automotive Transportation, picks out his model from an illustrated catalog, and produces his money.

Dmitri: [*Putting down a sack of money*] Here, Comrade Commissar Petrov— I've saved every kopek for seven years, and now I have enough rubles to buy a Yugo, the great import from our brother and sister workers of the Democratic Republic of Yugoslavia.

Petrov: Very good, comrade. Let me see . . . (*Looking through a large file, he mumbles for a time as he scans the pages; then, he makes a pencil check on his master sheet and speaks.*) Congratulations! You can pick up your car on September 18, exactly ten years from today, Comrade!

Dmitri: Great! (*He starts to leave, remembers something, returns and sits again.*) Comrade Commissar, one question: In the morning or the afternoon?

Petrov: In ten years, what difference will it make?

Dmitri: Well, Comrade, the plumber is coming in the morning.

So, even in a joke, plotting—the arrangement of the parts of the story—is crucial to its success.

COMIC SKETCHES

In contrast with comic dramas that run from thirty to sixty minutes (with time subtracted for commercials), comic sketches, such as those featured on *Saturday Night Live* and *Mad TV*, generally run from three to six minutes and are independent of other segments of the programs in which they appear. Examples of sketches are recurring episodes of "Hans and Franz" and "The Coneheads," and topical parodies of people in the news on *Saturday Night Live*. *Mad TV* also features sketches of a topical nature—during the long ordeal of the impeachment hearings involving President Clinton, sketches featured satiric portrayals of Kenneth Starr, Linda Tripp, Monica Lewinski, and President Clinton.

The key to writing funny sketches is to begin with a subject about which you have a feeling, an attitude. Perhaps the best way I can make this point is by citing my own experiences as a sketch writer.

As an undergraduate drama major, I wrote several short comic sketches that were performed in a workshop before an audience of fellow drama majors and our instructors. One sketch in particular was well received. In it, I had each character speak lines as if a specific playwright—Shakespeare, Ibsen, Tolstoy, Clifford Odets, Eugene O'Neill, and so on—had written them. The director had each actor imitate the acting style of a particular student in the department, matching the performance to that actor's work in a play by the author being parodied. So, this was a double-satire: first, a parody of lines by famous playwrights; second, a caricature of several students in the drama department.

At another school, as a graduate student, I wrote sketches for an annual revue, performed the week before that school's final football game of the season, the so-called Big Game. The most successful of these sketches portrayed well-known administrators, and satirized the behavior of both undergraduate and graduate students.

I later realized the success of these sketches at both schools was mainly due to my reflection of low-level hostility toward the behavior or traits of classmates, overblown rhetoric in dramas by famous playwrights, university red tape, childish antics of spoiled-brat freshmen, hulking athletes whose only interests were in getting high-paying jobs in professional sports, and gross food served in the student union—these were the sources of annoyance that fueled my comic writing.

Years later, after I'd been away from both campuses for several years, I was asked to write a comic sketch for the annual Big Game variety show. I was flattered, thanked the person who asked, and started to work. And, then? Nothing! I tried and tried, and simply couldn't be funny! What was wrong? After thinking it over, the answer came to me, and it was quite simple: Being away from the school for about five years, I'd (1) lost touch with what currently was going on there, what the hot issues were; and, (2) lost my low-level feeling of hostility toward the institution and its students and staff. In other words, I lacked timely and relevant information and whatever attitude I'd once had.

Some comic sketches are short on hostility and long on incongruity. A sketch that depicts *Gone with the Wind* as it might have been written by Leo Tolstoy about the Russian Revolution and the freeing of the serfs, for instance, could use all sorts of juxtapositions to satirize the Antebellum South as well as Bolshevik revolutionists.

Here's a comic television sketch written by Michelle Ryan. Once Michelle had conceived the idea of writing a parody of the film *Boys 'N the Hood,* featuring dogs as the agents and a dog pound as the scene, the rest flowed rather smoothly.

Dogz 'N the Pound
by Michelle Ryan*

VIDEO	AUDIO
ELS—INSIDE OF A DOG POUND. A SMALL TERRIER IS BEING BROUGHT IN, DOGS ARE HECKLING HIM. MANY DOGS WEAR EITHER BLUE OR RED BANDANAS.	MUSIC: RAP
MS—T-BONE, A GERMAN SHEPHERD WEARING A BLUE BANDANA	T-BONE: (TO TERRIER) Don't worry. Just try to be hard.
A LITTLE CHIHUAHUA BIGGEE DOG) WITH A BLUE BANDANA WALKS UP	BIGGEE DOG: Yo, Toto, Where's Dorothy? Look—we ain't no pound puppies in here and this ain't Oz. This here is the pound. Watch your tail.
BIGGIE NODS AT T-BONE	BIGGIE DOG: Yo dog, what's up? Peace out.
T-BONE NODS BACK	T-BONE: Peace out dog.
BIGGIE WALKS OFF CU T-BONE AND TERRIER	T-BONE: That's Biggie Dog. On the streets he ran the 48th Street fire hydrant to the 57th. In here he heads the Blue Ticks. The Black Lab over there—he's head of the Bloodhounds. He goes by 2Bones4Sure. Don't mess with him. He comes sniffin' In your

yard, he gonna get himself two bones for sure. Over there, the pitbull, that's Ice P. He's in for biting two mailmen. That dog drew blood!

A COCKER SPANIEL WALKS UP

SPANIEL: Got any bones?

T-BONE: How many you want?

SPANIEL: Let's see what you got.

T-BONE BRINGS OUT A STASH OF BONES FROM UNDER HIS BED.

T-BONE: And these ain't no pork chops. This is top sirloin.

SPANIEL: How 'bout crack bone? You got any crack bone?

T-BONE BRINGS OUT ANOTHER STASH

T-BONE: Check it out. Cracked so you can get right to the marrow. Real tasty.

SPANIEL: How much?

T-BONE: Five Scooby snacks. The slop they give us in here tastes like dog breath. And yo, eat some milk bones. Your breath smells like the back end of a garbage truck.

THEY EXCHANGE AND THE SPANIEL WALKS AWAY

T-BONE: Oh oh. Here comes 2Bones4Sure. Act cool.

2BONES4SURE WALKS UP TO TERRIER

2BONES4SURE: You mess with me and one thing's for sure—that bitch Lassie ain't gonna be here to save your tail.

2BONES LOOKS AT GOLD TAGS AROUND TERRIER'S NECK

2BONES4SURE: Hey . . . nice chain. Give it to me.

T-BONE: Wait a minute. That ain't yours.

2BONES4SURE: Step back with you and your funky blue bandanna. The Blood-hounds are here to stay.

ALL DOGS WITH BLUE
BANDANNAS GO BEHIND
T-BONE AND DOGS WITH
RED BACK UP 2BONES.

CUT BONE

T-BONE: Look at us—all trying to see who's hardest. We're acting more like humans. My owner left me to rot in here. After years of faithful devotion and what do we get? They move away and leave us behind.

CU COCKER SPANIEL

SPANIEL: You think your owner was bad. Mine dressed me up in clothes! And if that wasn't bad enough, she wheeled me around in a carriage for all of the neighbor dogs to see.

FLASHBACK OF SPANIEL BEING
PUSHED IN BABY CARRIAGE BY
A LITTLE GIRL. ANOTHER DOG,
HIS BUDDY, WALKS UP AND
STARES AT HIM TILTING HIS
HEAD TO THE SIDE CONFUSED.

SPANIEL'S BUDDY: Yo, Lucky—what happened to you? You be toe up from the flo' up.

CU POODLE

POODLE: Look at me—my owner gave me this funky haircut.

CU BIGGIE DOG

BIGGIE: Mine made me do tricks just to get something to eat.

CU 2BONES4SURE

2BONES: Mine made me stay out all day long.

CU TERRIER

TERRIER: Mine gave me a bath every week!

LS ALL DOGS SHAKING
WITH EYES OPEN WIDE

ALL DOGS: Whoa . . . That's terrible!

CU POODLE

POODLE: Humans can be such animals!

GUARD WALKS IN

2BONES: Here comes a human now . . .

GUARD OPENS CAGE

Let's break out of here!

DOGS START GROWLING AND
GUARD BACKS OFF. THEY ALL
RUN SAFELY OUT. FREEZE SHOT
ON BACK OF DOGS AS THEY
RUN FREE.

STILL SHOT CU 2BONES	NARR VO: 2Bone4 Sure went on to graduate with honors from the Seeing Eye Dog Academy.
STILL SHOT CU BIGGIE DOG	NARR VO: Biggie Dog went on to star in a line of Taco Bell commercials and became quite famous.
STILL SHOT CU TERRIER	NARR VO: The terrier realized that baths weren't so bad after all and went home to his master.
STILL SHOT CU T-BONE	NARR VO: T-Bone became top dog in the NYPD K-9 unit.

"Dogz 'N the Pound" uses these comic techniques: incongruity, comic of speech, the unexpected, deflation of authority figures (some dog owners, the pound keeper), caricature, and comic of motion. It includes the universal theme of animals acting like humans. With a slight change, comic of the naive could have been added; it would require adding another dog, one whose innocence would be the basis of the comic naivete. Note the closing comments over still shots, a take-off of the ending of *American Graffiti*.

Commercials often use a comic approach to attract, hold, amuse, and eventually sell a product or service. As with the comic sketch "Dogs 'N the Pound," this commercial by Eric Poole was destined for success the minute Eric came up with the incongruous concept that supports it. Once the idea of using the creation of a famous painting to set the scene, the "cast," and the context, everything else fell into place.

AGENCY: ERIC POOLE, SPLASH RADIO[6]
CLIENT: NORTHWEST DENTAL COOPERATIVE
PRODUCT: CHECK-UPS
"Mona Lisa" AS PRODUCED

MUSIC: ITALIAN CLASSICAL THEME UNDER

MONA: Gee, Leonardo, I'm really excited about you painting my portrait.

LEONARDO: So am I, Mona, you're gonna make me famous.

MONA:	Ah, you DaVinci boys, such flatterers.
LEONARDO:	Okay, sit down on this marble slab and smile.
MONA:	Okay.
LEONARDO:	(A BEAT) Mona . . .
MONA:	Yeah?
LEONARDO:	You're not smiling.
MONA:	I know.
LEONARDO:	I can't paint a world-famous portrait that'll hang in the Louvre if you don't put on a happy face.
MONA:	This is as happy as it gets.
LEONARDO:	Look, just say "cheese."
MONA:	I can't.
LEONARDO:	What do you mean, you can't? I got a career riding on this picture.
MONA:	It's my teeth.
LEONARDO:	Your teeth?
MONA:	I didn't get regular checkups as a kid, so now I'm paying for it.
LEONARDO:	Let me see.
MONA:	No!
LEONARDO:	Open your mouth.
MONA:	Lay off, DaVinci, or I'm calling Mister Lisa.
LEONARDO:	Maybe you oughta call a dentist.
MONA:	Maybe I oughta call Van Gogh.
LEONARDO:	Not with those ears.
ANNCR:	Today's dentistry is more than just filling cavities. Your regular dentist cares about your teeth for the long-term, too. And keeping your teeth healthy now can save you lots of money down the road. Get the picture?
MONA:	Can't you just pretend I'm smiling and draw in some teeth later?
LEONARDO:	Oh, forget it. Just sit there with that dumb blank expression.
MONA:	It's mysterious.

LEONARDO: Yeah, who's gonna buy that?

ANNCR: Call your regular dentist for your six-month checkup now.
A reminder from the Northwest Dental Cooperative. And smile.

Some sketches are mainly applications of a single comic device, as deflation of authority in a satire on a prominent politician; others are techniques used within a sketch: Woody in *Cheers* was characterized by comic of the naive. The Tramp in *City Lights* uses much comic pantomime (motion); Dana Carvey as Ross Perot is long on caricature; In a *Mad TV* sketch of Independent Counsel Kenneth Starr's investigation, he's shown as a bumbling, vengeful, idiot—emphasizing unmasking, or deflation of authority figures. He also is the target of hostile wit. Comic of speech is important in most sketches. Inadequacy is seldom used, but can be a brief moment in nearly any sort of sketch.

The intent of this chapter is to show how comedy techniques and categories work in actual practice. Theory's a good foundation for comedic writing. It's not essential—skilled comic writers know their craft, and few analyze what they do—but, unless you have the time and patience to learn to be funny through years of trial and error before an audience, using comic theory to conceive your sketches will give you a head start.

Here is another comic sketch, this one a parody of a parody—*Saturday Night Live*.

TITLE: THE LATE NEWS
CLIENT: THE COMEDY CHANNEL
BY: Voltaire Villanueva*

VIDEO	AUDIO
MCU OF KEVIN	KEVIN: Welcome to the Late News, I'm Kevin Plummer.
MLS, KEVIN, SADDAM CHROMAKEYED BEHIND	This morning, Iraqi President Saddam Hussein suggested that a compromise be made over the current situation plaguing the U.S. and Iraq. Hussein suggested that he would allow Americans from UN inspection teams to survey his bombs, only if they pinkie swore and didn't tell anyone that the bombs were illegal.
MS KEVIN, CASTRO AND ZEMIN	Hussein purchased the American made bombs from wegotbombs.com after Cuba's Fidel Castro e-mailed him about the dirt-cheap prices they were offering

on bombs. This was after China's President Jiang Zemin bought over half a million dollars worth of bombs from the Democratic National Convention. Jiang had a hissy-fit when he found out that President Clinton was ripping everyone off and embezzling the funds to pay his small army of lawyers.

MS KEVIN AND NEWSPAPER ARTICLE

Also in the news, President Clinton played dad this weekend during his brief visit to California. The Associated Press reported that Clinton's aspiration of being a movie star was achieved when he played a lover for the Democratic National Convention's feature film, "When You See the White House Rockin', Don't Come a Knockin.'" Most of the footage was filmed in the White House by the same crew that taped the infamous White House coffee functions. The movie is due to be released in time for Valentine's Day, and can only be viewed by those offering a large donation.

MS KEVIN. KEY IN HILLARY BEHIND

A White House aide, speaking on condition of anonymity, said the DNC is expecting over $5 million dollars worth of donations from the movie, and expects twice the amount when First Lady Hillary Rodham Clinton releases her debut film entitled, "Boogie Flights on Air Force One."

CU NEWT GINGRICH

Speaker Newt Gingrich admitted today that he had legally changed his name, but denied that his parents had him Christened "Gecko." He added that, while he liked the alliterative sound, "Gecko Gingrich," he felt that "Newt" was the more dignified of the two names, assuming that his choices were limited to members of the salamander family.

MS KEVIN HOLDING NEWSPAPER

In other parts of the country, a town in south Georgia forgot to hold local elections last Tuesday. Sixteen-term Mayor Tommy John Frickert of Rebelle, Georgia, apologized for the mess-up since, "in little, itty, bitty, towns like ours, things get dropped into the cracks." Citizens were appeased, even though they pointed out that this was the eighth consecutive time this had happened.

MS KEVIN, HOGS CHROMAKEYED BEHIND

Residents in Milford, Utah, say that "hog farms are turning parts of Utah into a sewer." Spayed Farms, the largest hog-farming operation in the country, has over 600,000 hogs on the site, which produce the yearly equivalent of waste from 1.8 million people. A citizen's committee petitioned the mayor to cancel the hog farmer's permit, but the Mayor angrily said, and I quote, "They can't shove that mess down my throat!"

Resident Allen Mayer says that he's almost gagged inside his very own home because of this. While some want the farm to leave town and never look back, others see them as a blessing to the community since they also operate the local tourist attraction, Hog City Mud Baths.

MS KEVIN. NEWSPAPER ARTICLE KEYED IN BEHIND

In Texas, an accused serial killer said he'd left Louisiana to escape high crime. Police say Daniel J. Meaney told them that he was a serial killer who stabbed and shot six people to pay for his gambling debts. Folks in the piney woods town of Onalaska, Texas, say Meaney told them he'd moved there last summer to get himself, his wife and their four kids away from crime.

MS KEVIN. PHOTO OF TEACHER KEYED IN BEHIND

A former elementary school teacher who bore the child of her 14-year-old student was sentenced to six months in jail Friday by a judge who rejected prosecution pleas for a harsher prison term. Mary LeTeenager [luh-TEEN-uh- jer] first met the boy when he was in her second-grade class. Their relationship turned sexual after LeTeenager became a sixth-grade teacher and the school's sex education counselor. As one student said, "a lot of the guys liked her class because you got to practice what she taught every day."

MS KEVIN, KACZYNSKI KEYED
IN BEHIND

And finally tonight, Unabomber suspect Ted Kaczynski was caught smiling and laughing in Court after his attorney, Quin Denvir, began to question several potential jurors for the trial. Some questions asked included current occupation, average family income, if they owned a computer, and their exact street address.

MS KEVIN

That's all the news tonight. We hope you'll join us again tomorrow for more of the Late News.

ANALYSIS

This comedy sketch takes the form of a televised newscast and pokes fun at current events. It's similar to what *Saturday Night Live* does with the "Weekend Update," where they take the news and twist it just a little to get some laughs. The target audience for my program are those approximately between the ages of seventeen and forty, or basically anyone who has an idea about politics and political leaders. I use this type of television genre since nearly everyone has a need to feel informed.

The first technique I employ, and a major one in my comedy sketch, is the deflation of authority figures. I use this technique early in my sketch with Saddam Hussein, and later with the Clintons. I probably found unmasking the easiest to accomplish simply because we all have a need to see authority figures deflated. I mock the political leaders in several ways. One way was to portray them making mistakes (the desire to see others make mistakes), another was to use obscene wit by portraying them as adult movie stars (the desire to find outlets for the sex drive in a guilt free context). Obscene wit certainly played an important role in my sketch. Whether it was the hog or the LeTeen piece, this type of wit certainly helped me write this parody.

Another device I used extensively was incongruity. It was used in several pieces like the accused serial killer leaving Louisiana to get away from crime, or the one with the teacher engaging in sex with a student. These were actual stories, and I included them because they were odd and had conflicting ideas

CHARACTER AND DIALOGUE

Brief comic sketches have little need to provide three-dimensional characters or to invent dialogue that shows character development. Longer comedies, however, need to have more depth. The sketch *Josie* is a story that reveals to us the personalities and relationships of its agents. It isn't hilariously funny, but the story is more honest than most television comedies in dealing with human emotions, frailties, and the possibility of change.

JOSIE
COMEDY SKETCH—TV
BY: Mari-Ela David*

1 INT. CASTRO KITCHEN

Kitchen is large, with room for stove, sink, cupboards, and a large table where most informal meals are served family style. EVA CASTRO, mother of the three Castro children, is 40-ish, attractive, and is the stable parent in the household. Her husband, VINCE, is known for his thrifty ways and lack of sentiment. Children include JOSIE, a 17-year-old high school senior, and her brother, JEREMY, age 19.

As scene opens, Eva is standing by the sink, pouring noodles into a strainer. Son Jeremy is sitting at the kitchen table, reading *The Sporting News*.

VINCE

(ENTERS AND WALKS TO STOVE) MMM! What's that smell? (OPENING POT ON THE STOVE)

EVA

(POURING NOODLES IN A STRAINER) My natural, womanly scent.

VINCE

(TEASES) Ah, no wonder I sense the aroma of eau de garlique! (KISSES EVE ON CHEEK)

EVA

(SMILING) You're so funny, I forgot to laugh.

(VINCE PICKS UP BROOM AND STARTS SWEEPING KITCHEN FLOOR)

                              VINCE

Jer! Can you get the pan for me?

                             JEREMY

(WITHOUT LOOKING UP) Dad, why don't you just vacuum the floor. It's easier.

                              VINCE

Vacuum? That's a waste of electricity! Besides, I invested three dollars and twenty-
eight cents in this broom, and I intend to take full advantage of it. Y'know, Jer, when
I was a kid, we didn't even have a vacuum!

                             JEREMY

I know—nature and Castros abhor a vacuum . . .

                              VINCE

Huh? What was that?

                             JEREMY

(RESIGNEDLY—HE'S USED TO SAYING THINGS THAT GO OVER HIS DAD'S
HEAD) I'll get the pan. (RISES, GOES TO CABINET, REMOVES PAN AND TAKES
IT TO HIS FATHER)

                               EVA

(RINSING NOODLES IN SINK, RAISES VOICE) Josie! Will you please come down
and set the table?

                              JOSIE

(CALLING FROM UPSTAIRS) Kay! Just a minute!

2 JOSIE'S BEDROOM

(JOSIE, LYING ON BED, IS ON PHONE TO HER SERIOUS BOYFRIEND,
ROBERT)

                              JOSIE

Sorry, that's my mom. I gotta go. We're about to eat dinner.

                             ROBERT

(ON FILTER MIC) Are you gonna ask them?

                              JOSIE

Yeah, but I bet you anything they're gonna say no. You know how strict they can be.
Plus, my Dad's a bird.

ROBERT

A bird?

JOSIE

Yeah, you know, he's "CHEEP CHEEP CHEEP!"

ROBERT

(LAUGHING) Well, if they say no, you know you can always depend on me.

JOSIE

(SMILING) I know. I'll call you back and let you know what happens, yeah?

ROBERT

Kay. Love ya.

JOSIE

(BLUSHING) Right back at ya, two times over. Bye. (HANGS UP PHONE)

3 CASTRO KITCHEN

EVA

(RAISING VOICE AGAIN) Josie!!!

JOSIE

(RUNS DOWN THE STAIRS) Coming!!! (ENTERS, WALKS TO KITCHEN, OPENS DRAWER AND PULLS OUT PLATES) Wow, Mom, it sure smells good in here!

EVA

(JOKES) I know, it's my natural sc—-

VINCE

(INTERRUPTS)—odor.

EVA

(MAKES A FACE AT HER HUSBAND)

JOSIE

(SITTING AT TABLE, NERVOUS) Hey, you know Melissa got her license yesterday.

JEREMY

From the Humane Society? Did she have all her shots?

JOSIE

Jeremy, if you don't get your hair cut, you'll be picked up by the dog catcher, y'know.

EVA

(IGNORES THE FAMILIAR SIBLING RIVALRY, CARRIES PLATE OF NOODLES TO THE TABLE) That's nice, Josie. Melissa must be very happy.

JOSIE

Yeah, and Ariel's parents bought her a car.

JEREMY

(SITS AT THE TABLE) What kind?

JOSIE

A Nissan 240SX . . . Black.

VINCE

(PUTS AWAY BROOM, SITS AT THE TABLE) She should've just bought the Nissan Altima. It's got the same engine, but it's cheaper.

JOSIE

(UPON HEARING HER DAD SAY CHEAPER, JOSIE ACCIDENTALLY DROPS A FORK. PERPLEXED, SHE PICKS IT UP, LOOKS AT IT, SHRUGS, AND GOES BACK TO USING IT) The five-second rule!

VINCE

The what?

JOSIE

(IGNORING HER DAD) Well, it's a nicer car. (SITS AT THE TABLE) It has automatic door locks and window. . . . Anyway, I was thinking, I'm already 17, turning 18 pretty soon. And now that I have a job, and with school and my extracurricular activities and everything, it's getting really hard depending on other people for rides, and so . . . (MUMBLES FAST) I think it's about time I get my license.

EVA

(BRINGS PASTA SAUCE TO TABLE, SITS DOWN) You're too young.

JOSIE

The legal driving age is 16.

EVA

It's too dangerous.

JOSIE

All my friends drive. Their parents let them, why can't you?

VINCE

Insurance—too expensive. Plus, we'd have to pay for driver's school, then a car . . . and don't even get me started on gas! Y'a know, when I was your age, I rode my bike—to school, and all over town. Good and cheap transportation.

JOSIE

I'll help pay for it.

EVA

You don't need to drive yet. You have the school bus, the city bus . . .

JEREMY

You mean the shame train?

EVA

(IGNORES JEREMY'S SARCASM) . . . You have your friends and your Dad and me to take you around.

JOSIE

Yeah, and boy is it embarrassing when you let me out at school with all my friends watching. . . . And, Mom, everyone else drives but me!

EVE

You can't always be like everyone else. Right now, you don't need to drive. You're just gonna have to wait until we feel you're ready.

JOSIE

But Mom!

EVE

(FIRMLY) I said no, Josie.

VINCE

Josie, I remember when I was. . . .

JOSIE

(ANGRILY) Not now, Dad!

EVE

Josie, let's just drop it. (DEFEATED, JOSIE TURNS SULLEN, AND EATS SI-LENTLY)

4 EXT JOSIE'S HIGH SCHOOL.

(JOSIE AND ROBERT WALK ACROSS LAWN AFTER SCHOOL TOWARD ROBERT'S CAR. THEY ENTER CAR AND DRIVE OFF)

5 INT ROBERT'S CAR

ROBERT

They said no, huh?

JOSIE:

(LOOKS OUT THE WINDOW, DEPRESSED) Yeah.

ROBERT

Well, if you ever need a ride, you can always (STARTS TO SING WHITNEY HOUSTON'S SONG, "COUNT ON ME" TO CHEER JOSIE UP) "Count on me through thick and thin, my love for you will never end, when you are weak I will be strong . . ."

JOSIE

(PLUGS HER EARS, GRIMACES TEASINGLY) Great! My headache just arrived on schedule!

ROBERT

I'll sing even louder if you don't smile!

JOSIE

(FORCES A WEAK SMILE)

ROBERT

(SYMPATHETICALLY) You know, your parents are just trying to look out for their baby daughter.

JOSIE

I'm not a baby!

ROBERT:

Okay . . . their little girl trapped in a teenage body.

JOSIE

I'm not a little girl, either.

ROBERT:

(LAUGHS) Okay, okay. Seriously, though, I'm sure they don't mean to stick a ball and chain on your leg. They're probably just in denial. They don't want to admit you're growing up, and driving is definitely a sign of adulthood.

JOSIE

(ROLLS WINDOW DOWN, OPENS A SODA CAN) I know. But, I just want that freedom of driving wherever I want. If I had a car, I wouldn't have to depend on anybody for a ride. (TAKES A SIP OF HER SODA) And I hate waiting around for the bus!

ROBERT

(TENDERLY) Well, if you want, I can teach you how to drive my car.

JOSIE

Nah, yours is stick shift. I'd rather learn automatic first.

ROBERT:

Oh, that's right. You wouldn't be able to handle a manual car cause you're such a klutz.

JOSIE

What was that?!

ROBERT

I said you wouldn't be able to handle a manual car 'cause of the clutch!

JOSIE

That's not what you said! I heard you! (PUNCHES ROB)

ROBERT

(LAUGHING) Ow!

6 JOSIE'S ROOM

(JOSIE SULKS. WE SEE HER IMAGINING HERSELF DRIVING, AND SMILES AT THE THOUGHT OF THE FREEDOM. SHE TUNES BACK INTO REALITY, AND GETS FRUSTRATED. SOON SHE THINKS OF A PLAN)

7 PARENT'S BEDROOM

(JOSIE GOES INTO HER PARENTS ROOM AND TAKES THE VAN KEYS. SHE GOES OUTSIDE TO WHERE THE VAN IS PARKED, CLIMBS IN THE DRIVER'S SIDE OF THE VAN AND STARTS THE ENGINE)

JOSIE

(ENGINE RUNNING) (WE HEAR HER THOUGHTS, VO) I may not get my license yet, but at least I can practice driving. Let's see, it's 3:30, Mom and Dad won't be home until 6. Perfect! I can drive around for about an hour or so.

8 INSIDE VAN

(JOSIE DRIVING AROUND NEIGHBORHOOD, VERY SLOWLY AND CARE-FULLY. CU DASHBOARD CLOCK, MOVING FROM 3:30 to 4:30)

JOSIE

(DRIVING TOWARD HER HOUSE)

JOSIE

(WE HEAR HER THOUGHTS) Whew! I did it! All I have to do now is park this baby back where it was before. Parking should be easy. (JOSIE TURNS INTO HER BLOCK, ONLY TO SEE A POLICE CAR PARKED IN FRONT OF HER HOUSE)

(ALOUD) OH MY GOD! What's a policeman doing here? (TO HERSELF) Who could have told on me?! Lordy, what do I do? If he sees me driving without a license, I'm dead! Then I'll never be able to drive! Ew, Josie, you've really done it this time! (SHE TURNS INTO ANOTHER STREET) Think, Josie, think.

(JOSIE EXITS CAR AND RUNS TO HER HOUSE)

9 FRONT STEPS OF CASTRO HOME

(THE POLICE OFFICER HAS JUST RUNG THE CHIMES)

JOSIE

Hey officer! What seems to be the problem?

POLICEMAN

Looks like your van got stolen. A neighbor saw it being driven away by someone who looked suspicious.

                                JOSIE

Stolen? (JOSIE ACCIDENTALLY DROPS VAN KEYS. SOUND: KEYS CLINK ON
PAVEMENT. POLICEMAN TURNS AROUND, BUT JOSIE GRABS THE KEYS IN
TIME AND HIDES THEM IN HER POCKET. SHE SMILES FOOLISHLY AT THE
OFFICER)

                              POLICEMAN

There's no sign of forced entry anywhere . . . no broken glass. Do you know anything
about the van, Miss?

                                JOSIE

(STUTTERS) Who me? No, I wouldn't know where it would be. (JOSIE'S FACE
LIGHTS UP) Oh wait! Yes! My brother may have taken it. He drives it sometimes.

                              POLICEMAN

Are you sure? (HE EYES JOSIE SUSPICIOUSLY)

                                JOSIE

(SHRINKS AT HIS SIGHT, INTIMIDATED) Nooo.

                              POLICEMAN

Well, Miss, do you know where your parents keep the van keys?

                                JOSIE

(NERVOUS) Yes.

                              POLICEMAN

Well, why don't we check to see if they're there. If they're not, then we can assume
that your brother did take the van.

                                JOSIE

(FEELS THE KEYS IN HER POCKET) Kay!

10 PARENTS' BEDROOM

(JOSIE AND POLICEMAN ENTER. JOSIE OPENS HER PARENTS' DRESSER
DRAWER. POLICEMAN SEES THAT THE KEYS AREN'T THERE)

                              POLICEMAN

Hmmm, they're not there. Well, before I file a report, I think you should find out for
sure whether your brother did take the van. If I file one now an officer might see the

van, and think your brother stole it. So, let's save him some embarrassment. Tell your parents to call me as soon as your brother comes home.

JOSIE

(RELIEVED) 10-4, I copy. (OFFICER LEAVES)

11 PARKED VAN

(JOSIE GOES TO VAN, ENTERS IT, AND PARKS IT IN FRONT OF CASTRO HOUSE)

12 KITCHEN

(JOSIE SEATED AT TABLE. JEREMY ENTERS)

JEREMY

Hi, turkey breath!

JOSIE

No jokes, Jer. I'm in deep doo-doo!

JEREMY

(TAKEN ABACK, GETS SERIOUS AND SITS) Well?

JOSIE

I took the van for a joyride—only it doesn't seem very joyful right now . . .

(PARENTS ENTER IN AGITATED STATE)

EVE

Josie Castro! Tell me it isn't true!

JOSIE

(FEIGNING INNOCENCE) What isn't true. . . .?

VINCE

Can that! I had a call from the police.

JOSIE

Look, Dad, Mom, I'm sorry, I don't know what came over me.

VINCE

How long were you gone driving?

JOSIE

About an hour or so.

VINCE

An hour? Well, you're going to have to pay for the gas you used!

JOSIE

Yes, sir.

EVE

Do you know what you could've gotten yourself into? A police officer for goodness sake!!

VINCE

And what if you got into an accident? What then? Do you know how high our insurance will go up?

JOSIE

I know, Dad, I'm sorry.

EVE

You know we're going to have to ground you, right?

JOSIE

Yes.

EVE

And you know we're going to have to lie to the police, right?

JOSIE

Yes, ma'am.

VINCE

And you know you parked that van better than I do, right?

JOSIE

(SMILES) Really?

JEREMY

That confession ranks up there with the ten best mea culpas of all time!

EVE

(SMILES) Really. I'm pretty impressed. Maybe you are ready to drive after all.

JOSIE

(EYES LIGHTS UP) NO KIDDING!

VINCE

Josie, let me tell you something. When I. . . .

EVE, JEREMY, AND JOSIE

(IN CHORUS) . . . was your age, I . . .

VINCE

(LOOKS STARTLED AT FIRST, THEN HE LOWERS HIS GAZE, HOLDS UP A HAND, AND THE LAUGHTER STOPS. AFTER A PAUSE, HE LOOKS UP AND SPEAKS QUIETLY) That's not what I was going to say . . . . Josie, when I was your age, I wanted the same things you do. I wanted to drive so bad it hurt. I was afraid to ask girls out because I didn't have a car. Dad would say, "Vince, you don't need it," or "you're too young." It was like he was on a different planet.

It's only been the last day or so that I really came to understand my Dad. He heard me, all right. But I see now he just couldn't admit we were too poor for him to give me the things I wanted. Well, I'm not *my* dad—I'm *your* Dad. Josie, I don't have the money to buy you a car, either. But, I do have a job, and so do you. What say we both start putting money aside every week? Maybe, by graduation day, we'll have enough for a down payment on a good used car—maybe even a Nissan . . .

JEREMY

(JEREMY HAS A GLAZED, AWED, EXPRESSION)

(SLOWLY, ALMOST IN A WHISPER) Maybe a 240SX . . . Black.

JOSIE

(OVERCOME WITH EMOTION, SHE GOES TO VINCE, AND PUTS HER ARMS AWKWARDLY AROUND HIM . VINCE GRABS HER IN A BEAR HUG, AND KISSES HER ON THE FOREHEAD. EVE TRIES TO HOLD BACK A TEAR. VINCE CLENCHES HIS TEETH, TRYING HIS BEST TO REMAIN STOIC.)

FADE TO BLACK

Theories of comedy are illustrated throughout this text, particularly in Chapter 8, "The Anatomy of Comedy." Many examples of comic writing are found in Chapter 13, "Radio and Television Commercials," and Chapter 17, "Media in Community Service."

You can find an immense supply of television comedy scripts on the Internet. Select Yahoo! or other search engine, click on or enter "TV," enter "Drew's Script-O-Rama." You'll find hundreds of scripts for *Seinfeld, Friends, Beavis and Butthead, Northern Exposure, Eastenders,* and many other television comedies. Another source is the "Television Transcript Project." There you'll find partial and complete scripts of *Home Improvement, Fawlty Towers, The Simpsons, Married . . . With Children, Bewitched* and many others. Note, however, that most of these scripts are *not* presented in television script format. In fact, the layout used is a modified radio format. So, while you can examine many examples of comic dialogue, you should not use them as models of acceptable formatting.

QUESTIONS

1. Select two commercials from Chapter 13 that you consider good examples of comic writing. Analyze them in terms of their use of the various categories of the comic, as well as humor and wit.

2. Watch (and preferably record so you can review as many times as you like) an episode of one of your favorite continuing comedies. Analyze it to identify the following: comic of speech; comic of the naive; comic of motion; hostile wit; and obscene wit.

3. The production scripts *Bob Day* (Chapter 15) and *Annoying Ads Make You Want to Shout* (Chapter 14) reflect two extremes of comedy. The first is very subtle, the second is the opposite. Analyze both of these, looking for what makes each funny.

4. Most newspapers provide daily or weekly announcements of events scheduled for the upcoming week. Find and read a current list of coming attractions as listed in your local newspaper. See if you can spot events that might make offbeat or bizarre stories that you feel could be researched and turned into comic essays or feature reports.

5. Review *Josie* and locate the exact lines through which: Vince's character is first revealed; lines that establish a teasing/loving relationship between Eva and Vince; lines that show Josie as a rather spoiled—but not hostile—daughter; find every line that reveals a tendency toward low-level hostility.

NOTES

1. Harlan Hatcher, ed., *A Modern Repertory* (New York: Harcourt, Brace, 1953), 146.
2. Eugene O'Neill, *Ah Wilderness!* in *Sixteen Famous American Plays,* ed. by Bennett A. Cerf and Van H. Cartmell. (New York: The Modern Library, 1941), 311.
3. Comment by J. D. Wilson in *The Essential Shakespeare,* quoted in Otis and Needleman, *Outline History of English Literature,* Vol. 1 (New York: Barnes & Noble, 1939), 182.
4. George S. Kaufman and Moss Hart, *The Man Who Came to Dinner* (New York: Random House, 1939), 35.
5. Ibid., 151–152.
6. Courtesy of Eric Poole, Slash Radio, Los Angeles.

CHAPTER SEVENTEEN

MEDIA IN COMMUNITY SERVICE

This chapter explores scripts written to support the work of nonprofit organizations. Most such work is pro bono—time and talent are contributed, but no salary is expected or received. Incidental expenses are, in most instances, provided by the nonprofit agency. This chapter examines two types of public service productions: presentations aimed at limited audiences for informational or fundraising purposes; and public service announcements, brief (ten–sixty seconds) messages intended to reach large audiences through broadcast or cable access radio and television. Print media, including magazine and outdoor advertising, while important, are not discussed here.

One of the most satisfying arenas media writers can enter is that of community service. It's no surprise that in this age of media dominance, agencies engaged in not-for-profit services make extensive and effective use of the electronic media to survive and prosper. Those equipped with the skills and knowledge to create convincing communications through the electronic media who feel a need to serve causes they want to support, will find no end of challenges—as well as the satisfaction that comes from being an important part of a service agency's outreach.

Scripts for community agencies generally fall into one of two areas: brief public service announcements (PSAs); and five- to fifteen-minute productions that may take the form of audio or video recordings, or slide presentations. PSAs make up the latter part of this chapter, longer media presentations are considered first.

Chapter 11, "From Theories to Practice," describes a public service campaign from the initial challenge to its completion. In reading that case history you may have noticed that most of the PSAs that emerged told the story of AAU swimming in the words of its participants or their parents. This is an example of how a story, at times, is best served when its creator stays out of it. In such a capacity, the writer serves in every scriptwriting capacity

Scripts written by college students for a class in writing for the electronic media are identified by an asterisk (*) appearing after the author's name.

except one: and that is the *writing* of a script! All other tasks are pursued as though the outcome will be a written script, but the final "script" is actually a compilation of edited and arranged statements made by the subjects of the story.

To produce such stories, writers perform very much like architects. First comes an understanding of the challenge, followed by a vision that includes mood and purpose. Elements of the story structure are sought and gathered—in the case of a story, by interviewing and recording statements made by those closest to it. Once the raw material has been gathered, it must be reviewed, decisions made as to what to retain and what to omit and the sequence in which the elements will be arranged. The last step is writing a bare minimum of connective narration. This process was followed in the productions of the two slide presentations featured in this chapter.

The AAU public service campaign resulted in several brief announcements destined for broadcast and designed to reach large heterogeneous audiences. By contrast, productions such as those for Amigos de las Americas and Friends Outside are targeted to smaller, more focused audiences. Despite these differences, both begin by asking the same questions:

What, specifically, are the agency's needs?

Who makes up the potential audience for the production?

If the production is successful in achieving the agency's objectives, what will have changed?

What motivational devices will be appropriate for this cause?

How will those who respond to the production benefit?

How will the agency be better off than before?

Who will have been helped, and in what ways?

After pondering these questions, decide on the preferred medium. Considerations would include:

- amount of funds available
- location of potential audiences
- availability of equipment for the production
- availability of equipment for dissemination to audiences
- appropriateness of a medium to the specific story to be told

A presentation for a community theatre or ballet company might best be told by video, while an appeal for funds for a childrens' "art in the schools" program may well be told with still photos and a recorded narrative (slide-audio presentation).

Assuming that your production will not be broadcast on radio or television—although a video production may very well find a place on a cable access station—you're freed from attempting to meet broadcast-quality standards.

After being satisfied that you're at least tentatively knowledgeable with cause and purpose, it's time to start planning.

TWO CASE HISTORIES

The histories that follow were designed for two very different organizations and causes. The first is a slide-tape presentation to local community groups—Kiwanis, Rotary, Lions, the chamber of commerce, and religious groups—to enlist goodwill and financial support for Friends Outside, a nonprofit organization that maintains a hospitality center for families visiting husbands, fathers, brothers, and other men incarcerated in Soledad State prison.

The first step in the actual production was on-site visitations to the agency's headquarters in Salinas and to the center just outside the prison's walls, several miles away. Interviews with staff and volunteers of Friends Outside were recorded at headquarters, while wives and mothers of inmates were recorded at the small center just outside the prison. The inmate who agreed to participate was released on a Temporary Community Release (TCP) by prison officials, who were eager to cooperate with the project.

The interviews were later edited, arranged in an effective sequence, and supplied with just enough narration to hold the story together. Because of the unavailability of significant funds, and without film or video playback equipment, the script's producers decided that the only practicable medium was slides with audio. Microsoft PowerPoint, a convenient software for creating slide shows, was not available. Had it been, the entire project would have required far less effort. If you work with a not-for-profit organization your first question may well be to determine if PowerPoint is available.[1]

Friends Outside

The script that follows presents the audio-only portion of the production. You can most likely visualize the slides as you read this script because the photos were shot and coordinated to match what was being said on the tape. Photos of interviewees were made during their interviews; all other shots were taken after completing the audio so as to match the content.

SCRIPT FOR FRIENDS OUTSIDE, MONTEREY COUNTY
SLIDE/TAPE PRESENTATION

BLACK SLIDE

SLOW GUITAR MUSIC BEGINS SHOW—PUNCH UP SLIDE #1

VOICE OF INMATE POET OVER MUSIC:

LONELINESS, WITHOUT A LAMP TO SEE THE WAY,
FRUSTRATION FROM RUST OF DEPARTMENT.
OUR WORLD IS SUCH A BEAUTIFUL SPHERE TO BE BORN INTO
IF YOU DON'T MIND A FEW DEAD MINDS IN HIGHER PLANES,
RESTRICTING.
SCREAMING FOR RAIN, FOREST, WIND, SEASONS,
STRONG PEOPLE, LONGING TO BE FREE.
VISITS FROM HOME. . . . (FADE OUT VOICE)

(GUITAR MUSIC TO END OF SEGMENT)

INMATE:
What does a visit mean? It means a lot. It means almost everything. When my wife comes to see me, it reminds me that I've got someone to go back to. That someone out there cares. A visit keeps me going. For a little while, I can shut out the madness of this place. I remember that I'm a human being. I come back from a visit knowing that I can get through another month.

HETTY:
WHAT A VISIT MEANS TO ME. I GO . . . UP TO SEE MY HUSBAND. WHEN HE COMES THROUGH, I KNOW HE'S OK. I KNOW HE CAN HANDLE HIMSELF IN THERE AND ALL, BUT . . . YOU WORRY. WHEN I SEE HIM, I CAN RELAX . . . BECAUSE I'M WITH HIM. WHEN HE KISSES ME, EVERYTHING JUST DISAP-PEARS.

WE VERY SELDOM TALK ABOUT WHAT GOES ON IN THE PRISON, WE JUST TALK ABOUT WHAT IT'S GOING TO BE LIKE WHEN HE COMES HOME. AND THAT'S WHAT'S IMPORTANT—WHEN HE COMES HOME.

NARR:
Family visits are supported by the prison because they give inmates an incentive to prepare for their eventual release. A hopeless prisoner is of no value to himself, his family, or to the society to which he will someday return.

OFFICER HIGGINS:
I'VE BEEN A CORRECTIONAL COUNSELOR IN THE CALIFORNIA DEPART-MENT OF CORRECTIONS FOR OVER THIRTEEN YEARS AND IN OTHER AREAS OF CRIMINAL JUSTICE, AND I KNOW THAT FAMILY TIES ARE VERY IMPORTANT. IT'S WELL DOCUMENTED THAT THE MAN WHO HAS GOOD STRONG FAMILIES AND VISITING FROM THOSE FAMILY MEMBERS, MAKES A BETTER AND MORE SUCCESSFUL RE-ENTRY INTO THE COMMUNITY WHEN HE'S RELEASED.

NARR:
Despite institutional approval of family visits, the only support actually provided is that of providing visiting rooms. Visitors must make it to the prison on their own, and must provide their own transportation, meals, and lodging.

TAWANA:
WHEN I FIRST CAME DOWN, I DIDN'T KNOW ABOUT THE HOSPITALITY HOUSE. I LANDED IN SOLEDAD . . . IN THE TOWN. I DIDN'T KNOW ANYBODY. I DIDN'T KNOW WHERE TO GO. I WENT UP TO THE PRISON. I WAS FRANTIC AND CRYING. ONE OF THE OFFICERS TOLD ME TO CALL THE HOSPITALITY HOUSE, ASK FOR JOANNE. I CALLED JOANNE—I WAS CRYING, HYSTERI-CAL—SHE TOLD ME TO CALM DOWN, SHE WOULD GET ME A RIDE UP HERE. I CAME IN, JOANNE HUGGED ME. THERE WAS SOMEBODY . . . THAT CARED.

JOANNE:
WE'RE HERE TO HELP WITH SOME OF THE MATERIAL THINGS THAT THEY NEED. WE'RE HERE TO SUPPORT THEM. AND, WE'RE HERE SO THAT WHEN THEY GET DISCOURAGED, TO SAY, HEY—IT'S OK. THERE'S SOMEBODY HERE WHO REALLY CARES.

NARR:
The visitor center, just outside the walls of Soledad State Prison, is staffed mainly by volunteers. They've opted to serve several hours each week because they know they make a difference—a very poignant difference.

SHELLY:
I SPEND ABOUT FIFTEEN HOURS A WEEK HERE AT THE CENTER. IF WE DIDN'T HAVE THIS CENTER, A LOT OF LADIES WOULD BE IN TROUBLE. THEY NEED RIDES . . . THEY NEED HELP WITH LODGING . . . THEIR CARS BREAK DOWN . . . WHAT HAVE YOU. SOMETIMES THEY COME UP WITH JUST A ONE-WAY TICKET, JUST TO COME UP, TO BE ABLE TO COME UP AND SEE HIM—AND, DON'T HAVE A WAY TO GET BACK OR NO PLACE TO STAY. THEY DON'T KNOW ANYBODY. AND, SOLEDAD IS OUT OF THE WAY, ANYWAY. IF YOU GET DROPPED OFF OUT HERE WITH THE GREYHOUND, YOU'RE STRANDED.

NARR:
Amanda sees the Visitor Center as an island of hope in a sea of frustration. Her first experience was as a visitor. Years later, reunited with her husband and their son, she finds many reasons for volunteering her time.

AMANDA:
IF THIS PLACE DIDN'T EXIST, IT WOULD BE A REAL BURDEN, Y'KNOW, TO THE PEOPLE THAT COME UP HERE TO VISIT THEIR HUSBANDS. BECAUSE, THIS IS A PLACE WHERE YOU CAN GO, IT'S LIKE A RESCUE POINT.

THE VISITOR'S CENTER IS THE FIRST THING I WAS EVER INVOLVED IN. MY SON WOULD STAY THERE WHILE I WAS VISITING WITH MY HUSBAND, WHICH WAS GREAT BECAUSE I WOULDN'T HAVE HIM ON MY ARM ALL THE TIME, AND I COULD HAVE A REAL CONVERSATION WITH MY HUSBAND. AND A LOT OF PEOPLE WHO COME HERE WOULDN'T EVEN COME IF IT WASN'T FOR THIS PLACE. 'CAUSE, THEY'D HAVE TO GO TO A MOTEL BY THEMSELVES. AND, THAT'S WHAT THEY USED TO DO. THEY'D GO AND LOCK THEMSELVES IN A MOTEL DOWN IN SOLEDAD, AND IT WAS JUST TERRIBLE. I KNOW, BECAUSE I DID THAT A COUPLE OF TIMES MYSELF BEFORE I FOUND THE CENTER. AND IT WAS BAD. YOU HATED TO EVEN COME, BECAUSE OF THAT.

NARR:
The Friends Outside staff, including volunteers, understands the price families pay when a husband disappears behind prison walls for up to a dozen years. Jackie, who's worked as a volunteer for five years, sees the entire picture:

JACKIE:
WHEN THE HUSBAND GOES TO PRISON, THE WOMAN AND THE CHILDREN ARE IN JUST AS BAD A POSITION AS THE MEN ARE. THEY'RE OUT ON THE STREETS, BUT THEIR, Y'KNOW, THEIR MEANS OF SUPPORT MOST OF THE TIME HAS BEEN TAKEN AWAY FROM THEM. THEY'VE GOT TO SPEND THEIR RENT MONEY OR THEIR P.G.&E. MONEY, OR WHATEVER MONEY THEY USE FOR FOOD TO COME UP HERE TO SEE THEIR HUSBANDS. AND, THEY FIGURE THAT IT'S WORTH IT BECAUSE THEY CAN'T SEE HIM UNLESS THEY DO THAT. SO, THEY'VE GOT TO HAVE A WAY TO GET TO SEE THEIR HUS-BANDS. AND, THIS PLACE HELPS THEM DO THAT.

NARR:
Services provided by the Hospitality House were developed and adjusted over the years according to experience and changing needs. Joanne, Director of Friends Outside, describes its current priorities.

JOANNE:
THE SERVICES THAT WE HAVE AT THE HOSPITALITY HOUSE INCLUDE OVERNIGHT STAYS FOR WOMEN AND CHILDREN. IT INCLUDES AN EVENING MEAL FOR THEM FOR A SMALL DONATION. WE PROVIDE TRANSPORTATION BETWEEN THE HOSPITALITY HOUSE AND THE VISITOR'S CENTER ON GROUNDS AT SOLEDAD PRISON.

AT THE VISITOR'S CENTER, ONE OF OUR MAJOR SERVICES IS CHILD CARE. THE VISITING ROOMS ARE VERY SMALL, AND OFTENTIMES CROWDED. THERE ISN'T MUCH THAT THE CHILDREN CAN DO, AND THEY'RE NOT ALLOWED TO TAKE IN TOYS. WE GO AND PICK THEM UP, TAKE THEM OUT, AND HAVE ALL SORTS OF ART PROJECTS, AS WELL AS A NICE YARD FOR THEM TO PLAY IN ON SUNNY SUMMER DAYS. WE GIVE THEM A SMALL LUNCH OR A SNACK, AND RETURN THEM TO THEIR PARENTS AT THE END OF THE DAY.

NARR:
Amanda, a volunteer for the last five years, is equally aware of the pressing needs of the Hospitality Center.

AMANDA:
BOTH AT THE VISITOR CENTER AND THE HOSPITALITY HOUSE WE HAVE A MULTITUDE OF NEEDS. WE CAN USE ALMOST ANYTHING THAT YOU HAVE.

WE NEED, UH, EMERGENCY FOOD—BIG PROBLEM. WE NEED . . . WE NEED TOYS. WE NEED TOYS THAT THE KIDS CAN REALLY USE AND LEARN FROM. LIKE BUILDING TOYS, NOT STUFFED ANIMALS. WE NEED TOYS WHERE THESE KIDS CAN SIT DOWN AT A TABLE AND LEARN SOMETHING . . . WE NEED MONEY.

NARR:
Volunteer Jackie provides a discouraging view of the present status of the toy inventory.

JACKIE:
TOY SITUATION OUT HERE. WELL, THE LAST TIME WE WERE ABLE TO GET SOME TOYS—NOT WHAT WE WANTED, BUT SOME OF IT ANYWAY—WAS ABOUT A YEAR AGO. EVER SINCE THEN, WE HAVEN'T HAD THE MONEY TO GET NEW TOYS. MOST OF THE TOYS IN HERE ARE IN PRETTY ROUGH SHAPE. A LOT OF IT IS LOST, PUZZLES—MOST OF THE PUZZLE PIECES ARE LOST, AND WE CAN'T REPLACE THEM. THINGS NEED FIXING . . . DESPERATELY.

JOANNE:
WHY SHOULD PEOPLE IN MONTEREY COUNTY CARE? WHEN WE CONSIDER MONTEREY COUNTY, WE CONSIDER ALL THE RESIDENTS OF THE COUNTY. WE DON'T ASK PEOPLE, "HAVE YOU LIVED IN MONTEREY COUNTY ALL YOUR LIFE? DID YOUR GRANDFATHER GROW UP HERE?" WE SAY THAT MONTEREY COUNTY ENCOMPASSES ALL OF THE PEOPLE WHO LIVE HERE. THESE INMATES ARE PART OF OUR COMMUNITY. SOME OF THEM ARE HERE FOR THIRTEEN YEARS, SOME ARE HERE FOR TWO YEARS. THEY ARE PART OF US. ONE OF MY FEELINGS IS THAT WE CAN'T DIFFERENTIATE BETWEEN WHO *WE* ARE AND WHO *THEY* ARE. "THEY" CAN BE INMATES, "THEY" CAN BE VISITORS. " THEY" CAN BE WHOEVER WE DON'T WANT TO ASSOCIATE WITH. MY FEELING IS THAT IN OUR COMMUNITIES, *WE* ARE US, AND *US* INCLUDES EVERYONE.

NARR:
A recent visitor shares her feelings about the house as a place for wives to be among friends who face the same obstacles in their lonely lives.

MARIA:
IT'S LIKE—THE HOSPITALITY HOUSE, 'CAUSE I'VE TALKED TO A LOT OF THE GIRLS—IT'S LIKE YOU'RE GOING DOWN THE FREEWAY, YOU'RE SCARED. IT'S DARK AND THERE'S NOBODY AROUND, BUT YOU SEE THIS LITTLE LIGHT, AND YOU KNOW WHEN YOU GET THERE YOU'RE GONNA BE SAFE. YOU'RE GONNA BE ALL RIGHT. THERE'S OTHER GIRLS HERE GOING THROUGH THE SAME THING YOU ARE. YOU CAN TALK. YOU CAN RELATE TO THEM. THERE'S LOVE HERE. THERE'S UNDERSTANDING. AND, I LOVE IT.

(GUITAR MUSIC)

VOICE OF INMATE POET OVER MUSIC:
LONELINESS, WITHOUT A LAMP TO SEE THE WAY,

FRUSTRATION FROM RUST OF DEPARTMENT.
OUR WORLD IS SUCH A BEAUTIFUL SPHERE TO BE BORN INTO

IF YOU DON'T MIND A FEW DEAD MINDS IN HIGHER PLANES,
RESTRICTING.

SCREAMING FOR RAIN, FOREST, WIND, SEASONS.
STRONG PEOPLE, LONGING TO BE FREE.
VISITS FROM HOME . . . (FADE OUT MUSIC)

(GUITAR MUSIC TO END)

(CREDIT SLIDE # 1)   HOSPITALITY HOUSE—VISITOR'S CENTER

(CREDIT SLIDE # 2)   OPERATED BY FRIENDS OUTSIDE, MONTEREY
                      COUNTY

(CREDIT SLIDE # 3)   A MEMBER OF THE CENTERFORCE NETWORK

Amigos de las Americas

The second history is another slide-tape production, done in support of Amigos de las
Americas. Amigos is an unusual program, basically for high school students. It provides
paramedic assistance to people in rural areas of Latin America. Most of the hard facts are
implicit or explicit in the completed slide-tape presentation. Please note that this production
was done a few years ago, and statistics and other details have changed.

AMIGOS DE LAS AMERICAS
SLIDE/TAPE PRESENTATION

(MUSIC: SOFT GUITAR PLAYING LA GOLONDRINA, UP AND UNDER)

JENNY:
WHEN I THINK OF AMIGOS, WHAT COMES TO MIND? THE SEVEN MONTHS
OF TRAINING? SPANISH LESSONS? STUDYING THE MANUAL. . . . OR IS IT
THE FUND-RAISING? WORK-A-THONS, RUMMAGE SALES . . . AUCTIONS?
YES, I THINK ABOUT THESE THINGS SOMETIMES BECAUSE THEY'RE PART
OF THE COMPLETE REALITY. BUT, MOST OF THE TIME I THINK OF MY
VILLAGE. I THINK OF MY FAMILY. OF THE CHILDREN I MET AND WAS ABLE
TO HELP. WHEN I THINK OF AMIGOS, I THINK OF PEOPLE, BECAUSE PEOPLE
ARE WHAT AMIGOS DE LAS AMERICAS IS ALL ABOUT.

NARRATOR:
The Amigos experience. It's unique. How can it be explained? What you'll will see
and hear in the next few minutes are some of the recollections of Amigos volunteers.
You'll learn of their feelings, their experiences, and their memories. This is a very
personal view of Amigos de las Americas. Perhaps through their words and pictures,
you'll come to understand what this program is all about . . . what the Amigos
contribute, and what the volunteers gain from the program.

CATHY:
I COULDN'T SLEEP THE NIGHT BEFORE I LEFT. THOUGHTS ABOUT GOING TO MEXICO TO WORK IN THE DENTAL PROGRAM WERE TURNING THEM-SELVES OVER IN MY MIND. BUT, MAINLY I COULDN'T SLEEP BECAUSE I WAS TERRIFIED. WHAT KIND OF PEOPLE WAS I GOING TO SPEND MY SUMMER WITH? COULD I HANDLE BEING INDEPENDENT, RESPONSIBLE FOR MYSELF AND MY WORK? WAS I GOING TO ENJOY THE AMIGOS FIELD PROGRAM?

WELL, NONE OF MY FEARS WERE JUSTIFIED. MY EXPERIENCE LAST SUM-MER WAS EVEN BETTER THAN I DARED HOPE IT WOULD BE. NOT ONLY DID I LOVE THE MEXICANS, BUT I ALSO FELT THAT FOR THE FIRST TIME IN MY LIFE I'D ACTUALLY DONE SOMETHING VERY IMPORTANT IN HELPING OTH-ERS. I LOVED EVERY MINUTE I SPENT IN MEXICO.

THE LAST THREE DAYS I SPENT THERE I DIDN'T SLEEP, BECAUSE I DIDN'T WANT TO MISS OUT ON ANYTHING. LITTLE AS I WANTED TO, I HAD TO GO HOME. BUT, COMING HOME, I BROUGHT SOME THINGS WITH ME. THESE INCLUDED MEMORIES OF FRIENDS, FUN, THE KNOWLEDGE OF ANOTHER CULTURE, A BETTER UNDERSTANDING OF MYSELF. . . . AND, A SENSE OF ACCOMPLISHMENT.

NARRATOR:
When Amigo volunteers go to Latin America, they're *not* on vacation. They go to their assignments to work, and to bring their skills and knowledge to bear on serious medical problems. They measure their success by the number of people they've helped, and by the quality of their service

Amigos began in 1965, as a program to inoculate Latin Americans against a variety of diseases. Since that year, more than five million people have been inoculated against diphtheria, typhoid, pertussis, tetanus, polio, and measles. In 1969, Amigos were credited with ending a polio epidemic in their region of Honduras.

MARCO:
IN THE DOMINICAN REPUBLIC WE DID VACCINATIONS HOUSE TO HOUSE. WE'D WALK IN ON THESE FAMILIES DURING LUNCH OR BREAKFAST OR WHILE THEY WERE DOING THE WASH, AND SAY WHAT WE WERE ABOUT, AND TRY TO EXPLAIN TO THEM WHY THEY NEEDED SHOTS.

AND, IT WAS REALLY A NEAT THING THAT WE GOT TO WALK IN ON THESE FAMILIES RIGHT IN THE MIDDLE OF THEIR LIVES, AND MEET THEM IN A SITUATION WHERE YOU HAVE TO BE FRIENDS. WE WEREN'T IN A CLINIC, WHERE IT'S AN ORGANIZED LINE—YOU KNOW WHERE YOU GRABBED AN ARM, GAVE THEM THE COUNTER-INDICATIONS, AND THE REACTION TO THE SHOT AND EVERYTHING, AND PLUGGED THEM. WE HAD TO *SELL*.

YOU'D ENTER THE HOUSE, AND THE KID WOULD BE UNDER THE BED, AND THE MOM WOULD BE LOOKING WORRIED, AND YOU'D SIT DOWN AND TALK

TO THE DAD WHO DIDN'T BELIEVE IN SHOTS, AND EXPLAIN TO HIM WHAT WE WERE ABOUT, AND WHY WE WERE DOING THIS. AFTER FINISHING THE AMIGOS BUSINESS—THE SHOTS—WE HAD A GREAT OPPORTUNITY TO SIT DOWN AND TALK. AND, IT WAS REALLY ENJOYABLE, TO DO YOUR JOB, AND THEN SIT DOWN AND JUST BE FRIENDS. AND LEAVE, HAVING RECOGNIZED EACH OTHER AS *PEOPLE*.

NARRATOR:

Every day in Latin America, 30,000 people die of diseases related to contaminated drinking water. One-half are children. In 1979, Amigos began a latrine-building program and to date have overseen the construction of over a thousand latrines. More important, they've taught sanitation and encouraged Latin Americans to undertake their own community sanitation projects.

BRIAN:

I WENT TO OAXACA, MEXICO, AND I HAD A GREAT TIME DOWN THERE. WE WORKED IN THE LATRINE PROGRAM IN THE TOWN OF SAN FILIPE AND THE PEOPLE WERE REALLY FRIENDLY. . . . AND THEY WERE REALLY HELPFUL, AND EAGER. THEY WERE REALLY EAGER ABOUT LATRINES. THEY WANTED A LATRINE IN THEIR BACKYARD. THEY COULD DIG PERFECT HOLES, SO WE DIDN'T HAVE ANY REAL MANUAL LABOR AS FAR AS DIGGING AND BUILDING THE LATRINES. WE JUST GOT OUT THERE AND SHOWED THEM THE BLUE-PRINTS GIVEN US BY AMIGOS, AND THEY FIGURED OUT HOW TO DO IT. WE HAD A LITTLE DIFFICULTY GETTING OUR IDEAS ACROSS, 'CAUSE OUR SPANISH WASN'T THAT FLUENT—BUT WE WORKED IT OUT. THE LATRINE PROGRAM WAS REALLY DIFFERENT, 'CAUSE AT FIRST THEY SAW A LOT OF WORK, AND THE PRESIDENTE KIND OF GAVE THEM THE IDEA WE WERE GOING TO DO ALL THE WORK, BUT AS SOON AS THEY SAW THAT WE WOULD WORK SIDE-BY-SIDE WITH THEM, THEY WERE REALLY EAGER TO BUILD THE LATRINES.

NARRATOR:

The Amigos eyeglass-fitting program is in great demand in Latin America. Amigos work with used, donated prescription eyeglasses. These have been evaluated by optometrists, and ratings have been assigned to each pair. Working with vision charts and rating sheets, Amigos—few of whom have had formal training in optometry—are able to find eyeglasses for nearly everyone. To date, Amigos volunteers have tested tens of thousands of people, and have fitted more than 30,000 Latin Americans with eyeglasses.

MARIKO:

I WORKED WITH THE EYEGLASS PROGRAM THAT WAS THERE. AND THAT WAS REALLY NICE TO BE ABLE TO HELP SOME PEOPLE. . . . SOME CHIL-DREN, WHO'D NEVER BEEN ABLE TO READ. OR, CHILDREN WHO'D NEVER BEEN ABLE TO SEE FAR AWAY. AND, YOU'D JUST GIVE THEM THESE

GLASSES, AND ALL OF A SUDDEN, FOR THE FIRST TIME IN YEARS, THINGS THAT WERE FAR AWAY WOULDN'T BE BLURRY.

AND, I KNOW MYSELF, I WEAR GLASSES, AND WITHOUT THEM I CAN'T SEE MORE THAN FOUR INCHES IN FRONT OF MY FACE. AND, TO SEE THE SMILES . . . THE FACES THAT LIT UP . . . FROM BEING ABLE TO SEE CLEARLY, IT WAS JUST WONDERFUL. AND OLD PEOPLE WHO HADN'T BEEN ABLE TO READ THE NEWSPAPER OR DO THEIR EMBROIDERY IN YEARS . . . JUST BE ABLE TO DO IT AGAIN. AND THAT WAS A REALLY SATISFYING PROGRAM—TO BE ABLE TO JUST SEE PEOPLE'S EXPRESSIONS WHEN THEY COULD SEE AGAIN.

NARRATOR:
Tuberculosis once ravaged the Ecuadoran lowlands. In 1980, Amigos was invited by the Ministry of Public Health to conduct surveys throughout Esmeraldas Province, and to help detect active cases of tuberculosis. During the two next two summers, Amigos volunteers tested over 35,000 people. They traveled from village to village by dugout canoe, and they and their local guides made their way through the equatorial jungle with machetes. No, Amigos de las Americas did not wipe out tuberculosis in Ecuador. But their survey showed that the disease is at last under control.

ALLISON:
DEAR MOM AND DAD,
WELL, I'VE MOVED MY LOCATION AGAIN AND THOUGHT YOU MIGHT BE INTERESTED IN WHAT I'M DOING. LEFT ZAPALLO GRANDE YESTERDAY AFTER TEN DAYS OF TB SCREENING. UP UNTIL NOW, OUR ROUTE (9 PEOPLE) AND ROUTE LEADER WERE TOGETHER. NOW I'M ALONE WITH MY PARTNER—SUSAN FROM CHICAGO. SHE'S NICE AND INTELLIGENT.

ANYWAY, WE ARRIVED, BY CANOE OF COURSE, IN THE TOWN OF MAL-DONADO. THERE ARE APPROXIMATELY 1,5OO PEOPLE, BUT IT'S VERY UNDERDEVELOPED AND SPREAD OUT, GIVING THE APPEARANCE OF A SMALL TOWN. IT WAS GETTING DARK AND RAINING WHEN WE GOT HERE, AND IN THE CONFUSION OF DISEMBARKING, WE FORGOT OUR SUPPLIES. HECTOR, THE ROUTE LEADER, WILL BE BACK THIS WAY TONIGHT, BUT TODAY WE'RE DOING NOTHING.

OH, I DIDN'T TELL YOU ABOUT MY LITTLE EXCURSION, DID I? A FEW DAYS AGO MY PARTNER SUSAN AND HECTOR THE ROUTE LEADER AND I WENT ON AN OVERNIGHT TRIP UPRIVER TO TWO SMALL MORENO TOWNS. WHAT WE WERE TOLD WAS GOING TO BE A FOUR-HOUR HIKE ON A DRY RIVER BED TURNED OUT TO BE A BACK-BREAKING FIVE-HOUR CLIMB OVER MANY HILLS—IN THE DEEPEST PART OF THE JUNGLE. MOST OF THE TIME WE WERE KNEE-DEEP IN MUD. I HAD ON HEAVY PANTS AND THOSE COMBAT BOOTS AND CARRIED A VERY HEAVY BACKPACK.

ANYWAY, I SUPPOSE THE JOURNEY WAS WORTH IT, BECAUSE WE FOUND A CASE OF TB. SO FAR, COLLECTIVELY, OUR GROUP HAS ONLY FOUND 5 CASES OUT OF HUNDREDS OF SAMPLES.

NARRATOR:
Over three hundred thousand Latin American children have taken part in the Amigos dental hygiene program. Children are taught proper tooth-brushing, are given toothbrushes, and are also are given fluoride treatments. For many of these children, it's the first time they've seen or owned a toothbrush.

SERENA:
THE DENTAL PROGRAM. WE'D GO TO SCHOOLS AND TEACH THE KIDS AT THE SCHOOLS GRADE BY GRADE, HOW TO BRUSH THEIR TEETH—WHY IT'S IMPORTANT TO BRUSH THEIR TEETH—AND WE DISPENSED TOOTH-BRUSHES. WE'D ALL GO THROUGH THE MOTIONS OF BRUSHING OUR TEETH TOGETHER. AND HOPEFULLY, ONCE WE'RE GONE FROM SOUTH AMERICA, THE TEACHERS WILL CONTINUE WITH THE KIDS EVERY MORN-ING BRUSHING THEIR TEETH.

ALSO, WE'D GIVE A FLUORIDE APPLICATION AND WE'D DO THAT TWICE — ONCE AT THE BEGINNING OF THE MONTH, AND ONCE AT THE END OF THE MONTH. AND, THIS IS SHORT-TERM PROTECTION—LIKE MAYBE A YEAR, BUT IT HELPS. ALSO, AFTER THE FLUORIDE TREATMENTS THE KIDS CAN'T EAT OR DRINK ANYTHING FOR A HALF-HOUR, SO WE'D HAVE TIME TO KEEP AN EYE ON THEM, AND WE'D PLAY FRISBEE OR BASKETBALL—WE'D RE-ALLY HAVE A VERY FUN TIME, 'CAUSE LATIN AMERICAN KIDS ARE VERY COOPERATIVE AND RESPECTFUL, AND THEY LOVED THE GRINGOS. SO, IT'S FUN.

NARRATOR:
Aside from the primary purpose of bringing medical, paramedical, and sanitation programs to Latin America, what else is accomplished by the program?

First of all, Amigos Is a character-building program. Young Americans, most of whom have never been overseas, must adjust to a different climate, a different language, and a different way of life. Amigos quickly learn that the values they've grown up with are not necessarily the only or the best values.

JENNIFER:
ONE OF THE THINGS I LEARNED IN THE DOMINICAN REPUBLIC WAS HOW TO SHARE. THE FIRST COUPLE DAYS COMING HOME FROM VACCINATING, I'D FIND A SISTER IN MY SHOES, MAYBE A BROTHER IN A SHIRT OR SHORTS, AND MAYBE MY SHAMPOO IN THE SHOWER HAVING BEEN USED. AND, MY FIRST REACTION WAS, "YA'KNOW, THIS IS MY STUFF! THIS IS MINE—WHY ARE THESE PEOPLE USING IT? WITHOUT ASKING ME?" AND THEN, THROUGH THE COURSE OF THE SUMMER, I REALIZED, AND I SHARED EVERYTHING. IT WAS A SITUATION WHERE EVERYTHING WAS EVERY-

ONE'S, BECAUSE OF WHAT LITTLE WE HAD. Y'KNOW, THEY WOULD SHARE THEIR FOOD WITH ME, AND I WOULD SHARE WHAT I HAD WITH THEM. AND, IT ESSENTIALLY DEVALUED WHAT I HAD—MY MATERIAL POSSESSIONS. COMING HOME, THINGS I HAVE I SEE AS MORE EVERYBODY'S NOW.

NARRATOR:
What else does the Amigos program accomplish? Well, Amigos represent you and me—in an area of the world where our nation has not always been well thought of. Many believe that the Amigos are the best representatives our country has.

MICKY:
THE THING THAT REALLY IMPRESSED ME A LOT WAS THE QUALITY OF THE PEOPLE THAT DO AMIGOS. THE STAFF AND ALL THE VOLUNTEERS ARE REALLY SPECIAL. AND, EACH PERSON IS SO UNIQUE AND SO MOTIVATED . . . AND THEY'RE ALL GOING SOMEWHERE. SOME OF THE PEOPLE DOWN THERE RESENT THE UNITED STATES, AND I THINK THAT AMIGOS IS ONE OF THE PROGRAMS THAT CAN DO A LOT TO CHANGE THE IMAGE OF THE UNITED STATES, AND A LOT OF PEOPLE IN LATIN AMERICA WERE JUST GLAD THAT WE WERE THERE SO THAT WE WOULD DISPEL THE PROPAGANDA IMAGE. WE COULD SHOW THAT UNITED STATES CITIZENS REALLY CARE ABOUT WHAT GOES ON IN LATIN AMERICA.

NARRATOR:
Amigos bring back memories of exotic lands. They remember the incredible beauty of mountain ranges, volcanoes, tropical storms, and the mystery of the equatorial Jungles.

But, most of all, Amigos bring back memories of people. The families they lived with, the friends they made, the people they helped, and who helped them. All Amigos are deeply touched by their experiences in Latin America. In remote areas, they find a level of poverty that's almost incomprehensible. But, they also see the incredible strength of a brave people, who not only have learned to cope, but who actually have risen above a concern for material things.

Amigos return with new attitudes toward spiritual and moral values.

MARIA:
MY PARTNER AND I LIVED IN ABOUT THE SMALLEST STORAGE SHED I'VE EVER SEEN IN MY LIFE. WHICH WAS THE BEST THING THAT HAPPENED TO US—FOR ME AT LEAST—BECAUSE IT MEANT THAT I HAD A FAMILY OF TEN OR TWELVE FAMILIES. AND I REALLY GOT TO KNOW THE PEOPLE IN MY TOWN. I TRIED TO IMMERSE MYSELF IN THEIR LIVES, AND BECOME ONE OF THE FAMILY. WE HAD A REALLY SMALL TOWN—ABOUT 150 PEOPLE—AND EVERYONE WAS RELATED, AND BY THE TIME I LEFT I FELT I WAS RELATED TOO.

AS FOR THE PEOPLE—I HAVE TO SAY THAT THE MEN, WOMEN, AND CHIL-
DREN ARE THE HARDEST WORKING PEOPLE I'VE EVER MET. WHERE I
COME FROM, THERE'S A LOT OF UNJUSTIFIED FEELINGS TOWARD LATIN
AMERICAN PEOPLE THAT I THINK AMIGOS CAN DO SOMETHING ABOUT.
'CAUSE MY EXPERIENCES PROVED THAT SOME OF THE POOREST PEOPLE
I'VE EVER MET ARE THE RICHEST. YOUR RICHNESS IS NOT HOW MUCH
MONEY YOU HAVE IN THE BANK. IT'S TO SEE THEIR CHILDREN SO HAPPY,
AND TO WORK REALLY HARD FOR EVERYTHING THEY EAT. AND TO BE SO
GENEROUS TO PEOPLE THEY DON'T EVEN KNOW, WHO MATERIALLY HAVE
MUCH MORE THAN THEY DO, BUT WHEN YOU GET RIGHT DOWN TO IT ARE
PROBABLY A LOT POORER.

(MUSIC: SOFT GUITAR, SAME AS OPENING. UP AND UNDER)

NARRATOR:
Over the years, Amigos volunteers have numbered ten thousand. Amigos have
rendered over six million public health services. Millions of Latin Americans have
seen the United States in the dedication and the character of the young men and
women of Amigos de las Americas.

And, Amigos have seen the heart and soul of Latin America. Do I have to tell you
why the young people whose voices you've just heard are proud to be Amigos?

(MUSIC: UP TO CLOSE)

PUBLIC SERVICE ANNOUNCEMENTS (PSAs)

From the early days of radio broadcasting in the United States, broadcasters were required
to meet specified criteria in order to receive and renew broadcast licenses. Among other
regulations, the Federal Communications Commission (FCC) required station licensees to
make regular ascertainments of community needs and to document the specific ways in
which those needs were being addressed. Two categories of public service broadcasts
were recognized: unsponsored programs serving the public interest and public-service
announcements (PSAs).

Deregulation, which began in the 1970s and continued through the early 1990s, freed
broadcasters from most public service requirements, and public affairs programs have all
but disappeared from American radio and television.

On the other hand, despite governmental indifference, nearly all commercial broadcast
stations continue to provide air time for PSAs, roughly defined as brief messages promoting
charities, governmental agencies, or similar not-for-profit causes.

PSAs and commercials have much in common, but there are some differences: PSAs
usually are shorter, some being only brief notices on a community billboard; and PSAs
seldom use elaborate production techniques, such as music and sound effects.

More important differences lie in the objectives and in the motivational devices of
PSAs. Some commercials present rational arguments to sell a product or a service, such as

a spot for a supermarket that lists weekend specials. And some commercials simply try to make you feel favorable toward the product advertised. But other commercials attempt to arouse fear, greed, or insecurity. Public service announcements should avoid such tactics. Fear, greed, and insecurity are basic human emotions that are rather easy to exploit. A campaign for famine relief or to "save the whales" certainly appeals to basic human emotions, but producers of PSAs for such causes traditionally avoid emotional overkill.

Examples might help clarify this point. Below are listed some conventional target audiences, together with examples of PSAs that might attract each:

The young—city park department with schedule of activities

The elderly—a senior center with hot lunch notice

Young adult to middle-aged—blood donation drives

All ages—antismoking campaigns

Ethnic groups—sickle-cell anemia checkups; Tay-Sachs checkups (people of certain ethnicities are especially vulnerable to these diseases)

Gender—women's resource center; spousal abuse control programs, battered women shelters

Economic group—job-training opportunities

Common-interest support programs—Alcoholics Anonymous, Alano, Alanon, Cocaine Anonymous

Religion-sponsored activities: Jewish community centers; various singles groups

Special services for the handicapped; home food delivery to the infirm, the elderly, and AIDS sufferers.

There are, of course, many possible refinements of this list, but the general idea of determining target audience is clear.

When possible, it's good practice to use the voices of those served by, or otherwise involved in, the nonprofit organization for whom the spot is made. There's a note of authenticity in the words chosen and the style of delivery of one who's personally affected by the services offered. Here are two PSAs: in the first, a staff writer on assignment wrote a spot for a senior center, and a professional announcer performed it. In the second, an inmate of a state prison wrote and delivered a spot for a hospitality center outside the prison's walls. Can you see (feel) the difference between the two?

AGENCY: San Francisco Senior Center
LENGTH: :60
MUSIC: INSTRUMENTAL, SLOW AND MELANCHOLY

ANNCR: Few people stop to think that they will one day grow old. When they wake up to this fact, they see it as being the end of the world. Getting old has become synonymous with becoming "inactive."

This is not necessarily so. There are people out there trying to make life a little easier for the elderly to live full lives. The Austin Senior Center is one such group of people that cares. The Downtown Branch is involved in a number of activities geared to the elderly. Services offered include legal assistance, educational opportunities, such as painting, dancing, music, and so on, social activities, luncheons and more. These activities are offered at relatively no expense to the elderly. The Austin Senior Center.

MUSIC: UP TO CLOSE

AGENCY: The House at San Quentin
LENGTH: :60

INMATE: I'm a convict, and I want to tell you that from my own personal experience, The House at San Quentin State Prison has proven to be a genuinely valuable service to inmate's visitors. My daughter, Lisa, whom I have never seen, and who is 17 years old, and attending High School, was offered the opportunity by one of the ladies at The House to stay at her own personal home for whatever weekend she might want to come to visit me. I like that gesture! It gave me a profound sense of comfort to know of my daughter's security. The House really helped me and my daughter. And, you know what? You can help The House. Please contact them at No. 2 Main Street, San Quentin. Or, call 555-4200. The house is a nonprofit visitor's center, sponsored by Catholic Social Services of Marin County. This message was produced by the Broadcasting Class at San Quentin State Prison.

A CASE HISTORY: PRODUCING A PSA

Some effective PSAs use edited statements made by two or more people involved in the organization they are promoting. The following example illustrates how a PSA for radio was recorded, edited, and assembled. The spot was created for Amigos de Las Americas. You've seen the slide-tape script for an Amigos de las Americas presentation before community groups. Here's a PSA for the same organization produced for broadcast on local radio stations.

After getting authorization to produce the spot, the producer took a battery-operated cassette recorder to one of the weekly meetings and during a fifteen-minute break, recorded interviews with several students who'd spent the previous summer in Latin America. Later, the producer reviewed their brief statements and edited usable parts onto a second assembly tape. The next step was to arrange the sound bites in sequence; the final step was to write and record narration. One of the high school Amigos veterans was the narrator. The final step was the mixing of bites and the narration.

Here are transcripts of the initial interviews, recorded in the school library. ("Q" means "question," and "A," means "answer.") Underlined words are those used in the final version of the spot. The order in which they were assembled is given before each excerpt, as in (1).

Q: Okay. Tell me about Amigos quickly in thirty seconds.

A: Amigos is an excellent program for youth. It's a great way to grow up really fast. It's a great way to see how another culture lives, and live with them.

Q: Where did you go last year, Jenny?

A: I went to Honduras.

Q: What did you do in Honduras?

A: I worked with cows. I was testing them for brucellosis and tuberculosis.

Q: Was it rewarding? Did you learn anything?

A: (4) Oh, it was definitely rewarding. I learned an incredible amount. I learned so much I can't believe how much.

Q: What's your name?

A: My name is Kimberly Burke—

Q: OK, Kimberly. And, where did you go last year?

A: I went to Ecuador.

Q: Did you have a good time, or was it all work?

A: I had a fantastic time. Practically all of it was work, but I still had a fantastic time.

Q: And, what did you do in Ecuador?

A: (2) I was in the immunization program, and I gave shots to children, mostly from the age of three months to five years.

Q: About how many children do you think you inoculated?

A: (5) My partner and I, Jill, gave nine hundred and fifty shots.

Q: What kind of shots?

A: We administered vaccine against four different diseases—actually seven different diseases, four different shots. Polio, measles, tuberculosis, and one DPT covered diphtheria, tetanus, and whooping cough.

Q: Were you welcomed by the people there?

A: We were in our village. We were greatly welcomed there. There were a few problems, political problems. It was the first time it happened in the whole program, but we seemed to work them out all right and we're hoping to go back there again.

Q: Thank you.

Q: Your name, please?

A: I'm Brian Sarasay.

Q: Where are did you go last year with Amigos?

A: (1) <u>Last year I went to Ecuador, in Los Rios Province.</u>

Q: And, what did you do down there?

A: (3) <u>I was in the vaccination program, vaccinating children from the age of one day to 19 years old.</u> In schools and in houses and clinics.

Q: Why was it valuable?

A: Well, I learned a lot about the people and the way of life down there. A totally different experience in life. I had a rewarding experience knowing . . . people . . . people being prevented . . .

Q: OK. Are you looking forward to going back again?

A: Yeah I'm looking forward to going back again—I'd really like to do it. A different country and to see a totally different life.

After editing and assembling the actualities in a sequence, the producers wrote and recorded the narration and assembled the final version of the spot. Here's the one-minute PSA that resulted. (Narrator's words in boldface.)

VOICE 1:   LAST YEAR I WENT TO ECUADOR, IN LOS RIOS PROVINCE.

NARR: Last summer while most of their friends were relaxing, these
             high school students were working in South America for
             no pay.

VOICE 1:   I WAS IN THE IMMUNIZATION PROGRAM, AND I GAVE SHOTS
             TO CHILDREN, MOSTLY FROM THE AGE OF THREE MONTHS
             TO FIVE YEARS.

NARR: They were in a program called Amigos de las Americas.

VOICE 2:   I WAS IN THE VACCINATION PROGRAM, VACCINATING
             CHILDREN FROM THE AGE OF 1 DAY TO 19 YEARS OLD.

NARR: These young people worked hard to prepare for their trips.
             They learned Spanish, medicine, hygiene, veterinary medicine
             and other skills that made them helpful where they went. They
             paid their own way, too, earning money through jobs, rummage
             sales, auctions, and other fund-raising events.

VOICE 3:   OH, IT WAS DEFINITELY REWARDING. I LEARNED AN
             INCREDIBLE AMOUNT. I LEARNED SO MUCH I CAN'T BELIEVE
             HOW MUCH.

NARR: The time they spent In the Amigos program has broadened
             them immeasurably, and has given them an experience they
             won't forget.

VOICE 4: MY PARTNER AND I, JILL, GAVE NINE HUNDRED AND FIFTY SHOTS.

NARR: If you're a high school student, and you're interested in the Amigos program, ask your counselor. It'll be the best experience you've ever had.

THE ADVERTISING COUNCIL

The Ad Council began as The War Advertising Council in 1942 to rally support for World War II–related efforts. It continued after the war as The Advertising Council, and every year since it's used radio, television, outdoor advertising, and other print media to spread its messages. It relies on volunteer efforts by advertising agency personnel for the actual creation of its PSAs, while marketing executives help guide the activities and placement of its productions. The Ad Council created Smokey the Bear and the slogan, "Only you can prevent forest fires," as well as McGruff the Crime Dog ("Take a bite out of crime"). Its "Friends don't let friends drive drunk" is credited with saving many lives.

A Sampler of PSAs from The Advertising Council

The Ad Council domestic violence campaign included an unusually effective sixty-second television spot. As is true of most Ad Council spots, it was created by volunteers at Altschiller & Company Advertising Agency, and directed by a professional from AT&T. Faced with the challenge of confronting the ugliness of domestic violence without becoming too visually shocking, the approach focused not on the husband and wife but on their child.[2]

VIDEO	AUDIO
	(Note: Man and woman are voice-over throughout.)
CU OF FRAMED PHOTOS, PROMINENT IS PHOTO OF SMILING BOY ABOUT 3 YEARS OF AGE	MAN: Where, where's dinner? WOMAN: Well, I thought you'd be home a couple of hours ago.
FRAMED PHOTOS NOW MOVE TO INCLUDE YOUNG COUPLE DANCING IN WEDDING CLOTHES	WOMAN: And I put everything away, so I— MAN: What is this? Pizza? What do I have—Pizza?
SHOT OF STAIRS, WITH BOY'S SHADOW	WOMAN: Well, if you'd have just called me, I'd—
	MAN: Dinner ready: it's pizza.

BOY MOVING DOWN STAIRS HOLDING A SMALL TOY. HE'S WEARING PAJAMAS	WOMAN: I didn't know you'd be so late. MAN: Let me ask you something— is it too much to have dinner waiting when I get home?
BOY SITS ON STAIRS	WOMAN: Please don't be so loud.
MCU OF BOY FROM BEHIND	MAN: Don't tell me what to do. You shut up.
	WOMAN: I thought you'd be home—
	MAN: I can get pizza at work.
BOY LOOKS DOWN AT TOY	WOMAN: I'm sorry. I'm sorry. I'll fix you something better. Let go of me.
CU OF BOY	MAN: Get in the kitchen. (SFX: SLAP)
	WOMAN: No, no; that hurts.
	MAN: Oh, it hurts? You want to see what hurts?
MLS OF BOY FROM REAR, TRYING TO SEE WHAT IS HAPPENING	That's what hurts (SFX: SLAP) That's what hurts. (WOMAN SOBBING) Now, get up. Clean up this mess. Shut up.
XCU OF BOY PEERING BETWEEN DOWELS	WOMAN: I'll be quiet. I'll be quiet. (SFX: SLAP) Oh please.

TO BLACK. SUPER:
CHILDREN HAVE TO SIT BY AND WATCH.
WHAT'S YOUR EXCUSE?

THERE'S NO EXCUSE
for domestic violence
1-800-END-ABUSE
Family Violence Protection Fund

The Ad Council has supported the United Negro College Fund (UNCF) since 1972. It created the slogan "A mind is a terrible thing to waste." The UNCF has raised over $1.4 billion, and helped more than 300,000 minority students attend college.

The Advertising Council, Inc.
UNITED NEGRO COLLEGE FUND

"INVESTMENT/SAMUEL L. JACKSON" :15

GRAPH SHOWS $50 IN A CIRCLE AT LEFT BOTTOM	ANNCR. $50 invested in a mutual fund twenty years ago
GRAPH NOW SHOWS CIRCLE TOP RIGHT WITH $452 IN IT.	returned $452.
CU OF MAN WITH ID BELOW' "SAMUEL L. JACKSON.	$50 in the United Negro College Fund returned an award-winning actor.
CNUF LOGO, CAPTION 800.332.UNCF UNCF.ORG	A mind is a terrible thing to waste.

UNITED NEGRO COLLEGE FUND
"TIE" :60

MLS SON & DAD CU SON	DAD: I, I think you should wear a tie.
	SON: Dad, nobody wears ties to school.
MS DAD AND SON	DAD: Tie says you're serious. It'll make a good Impression. And
CU DAD LOOKING DOWN	remember, you're there to study.
	SON: Study, to learn and to make something of myself. I got it.
HOLD SHOT	ANNCR VO: Almost half of all UNCF students are the first in their family to go to college.
CU DAD	DAD: They have some great architecture classes.
CU SON	SON: Dad, I'm not really interested in architecture.
MS OF BOTH	DAD: Well, keep your options open. And remember, no girls until you . . . .
	SON: . . . until my work is done.
	DAD: And I'd make sure that I got my . . .
CU SON	SON: Dad, Dad, you're not going, I am.
	DAD: I know.

SON: Listen, we better get going. We don't want to be late for the first day, you know.

2 SHOT, MEDIUM. DAD HAS HANDS
ON SON'S SHOULDERS

DAD: Oh yeah, yeah.

CLOSING TITLE SLIDE:
UNITED NEGRO COLLEGE FUND
A mind is a terrible thing
to waste
1 800 332 UNCF
UNCF.ORG

ANNCR VO: And when you're the first to go, you're going for a lot of people. The United Negro College Fund. A mind is a terrible thing to waste.

This spot for energy conservation is noteworthy because of its creative employment of themes and incidents that appeal to children. It features a mad genius, a monster, and the attempt to create life, all tied together with appropriate sound effects. A variation of this spot may be found in Chapter 12.

"Watts on Your Mind"

AS RECORDED RADIO TEXT—"Really Great Sound Effects" :60

SFX: (*CLASSIC MONSTER MUSICAL STING.*)

MAD: And now, Sigmund, the moment we've been waiting for.

SIGGY: We're going to the mall?

SFX: (*WE HEAR THE SOUND OF MAD PULLING OFF THE SHEET COVERING THE MONSTER'S BODY.*)

MAD: No, Sigmund, I'm going to bring this monster to life.

SIGGY: Ooo, goody. How?

MAD: To breathe life into a Monster you need two things. First, you need a powerful surge of electricity. Siggy, we must be sure we're not wasting energy *anywhere* in the castle. Now let's think . . . did we turn off the lights when we left the dungeon?

SIGGY: Yes, Master.

MAD: Did we turn off the TV when we stopped watching it?

SIGGY: Yes, Master.

SFX: (*WE HEAR THE SOUND OF A REFRIGERATOR DOOR OPENING.*)

MAD: And the VCR?

SIGGY: Yes, Master.

MAD: Sigmund, DID you decide what you wanted to eat *before* you opened the refrigerator?

SFX: (*WE HEAR THE REFRIGERATOR DOOR QUICKLY CLOSE.*)

MAD: Very good! Stand back, Siggy! It's SHOWTIME!

SIGGY: Uh but but . . . Wait! You said you needed two things to bring a Monster to life—-a powerful surge of energy is one. What's the other?

MAD: Really great sound effects.

SFX: (*WE HEAR A SWITCH BEING FLIPPED AND, OF COURSE, REALLY GREAT SOUND EFFECTS BUILDING TO A CLIMACTIC EXPLOSION.*)

ANNCR: Another sound idea brought to you by the U.S. Environmental Protection Agency, Earth Share and The Ad Council.

Here are several scripts from The Ad Council sent to radio stations for delivery by local staff announcers.

The Advertising Council
U.S. Department of Transportation

Safety Belt Education
Live Announcer Copy

:20
When you're just driving around the block or up the street, you don't need to wear a seat belt, because you know you're not going to be in a car crash, right? Wrong! Because anybody who's ever been in a car crash can tell you, they never saw it coming. So always buckle up. Always. A message brought to you by the U.S. Department of Transportation and The Ad Council.

:10
Anybody who's ever been in a car crash can tell you, they never saw it coming. So always buckle up. Always. A message brought to you by the U.S. Department of Transportation and The Ad Council.

Math is Power
Live Announcer Copy

:30

Do you want to get ahead in life, get a cool job and be in control of your future? Then you need to learn math. Algebra. Trigonometry. Calculus. Because math is power. To learn more, log on to mathispower.org or call 1-800-97NACME. This is a public service message brought to you by the National Action Council for Minorities in Engineering and The Ad Council.

:15

Want to get ahead in life? Then learn math. Because math is power. To learn more, log on to mathispower.org. This is a public service message brought to you by the National Action Council for Minorities in Engineering and The Ad Council.

"WATT"S ON YOUR MIND?"
Live Announcer Copy

"A Very Good Thing" :30

Did you know that by not wasting energy we can actually reduce air pollution? Well, until this commercial, neither did I . . . but it's true and there's something we can all do about it. By simply turning off the lights when we leave a room, by turning off the TV when we're not watching it and by deciding what we want before we open the refrigerator door, we don't waste energy which means we will burn less fossil fuels and make less of the gases that create air pollution. And that, my friends, would be a very good thing. This message brought to you by the U.S. Environmental Protection Agency, Earth Share, The Ad Council and this station.

Note how the creator of these spots varied the copy to conform to time limits of ten, twenty, and thirty seconds. It's customary for those sending copy to radio stations to offer a choice of scripts because stations don't have standardized policies for PSA selection.

Afterschool Alliance
Live Announcer Copy

:10

In afterschool programs, kids uncover hidden strengths and find the hero inside themselves. If you'd like afterschool programs in your area, call 1-800-USA-LEARN.

:20

What is a hero? Are heroes born? Or made? In afterschool programs, kids participate in a wide range of activities, discover they have the power to change their future, and find the hero inside themselves. If you'd like afterschool programs in your area, call 1-800-USA-LEARN. Afterschool programs. Helping kids find the hero within.

:30
What is a hero? Are heroes born? Or made? Inside every child is a hero waiting to be discovered. By getting kids involved in a wide range of activities, afterschool programs help them uncover hidden strengths, find the courage to try new things, and discover they have the power to change their future. All this helps kids realize they have the potential to reach further than they ever have and find the hero inside themselves. If you'd like afterschool programs in your area, call 1-800-USA-LEARN. Afterschool programs. Helping kids find the hero within.

Community Drug Prevention Campaign
Live Announcer Copy

:30
It might surprise you. But it's the simple, everyday things that can do the most to keep a kid off drugs. It's a fact. Kids who have something to do are less likely to do drugs. So whether you can drive a car, read a book, coach a team or just listen to what a kid has to say, a little of your time can help keep a kid off drugs. To find out about community drug prevention groups, call toll free 1-877-KIDS-313, 1-877-KIDS-313. A message from the Office of National Drug Control Policy, The Ad Council and this station.

.20
It's the simple, everyday things that can do the most to keep a kid off drugs. It's a fact. Kids who have something to do are less likely to do drugs. Which means a little of our time can help keep a kid off drugs. To find out about community drug prevention groups, call toll free 1-877-KIDS-313. A message from the Office of National Drug Control Policy, The Ad Council and this station.

:15
It's a fact. Kids who have something to do are less likely to do drugs. Which means a little of your time can help keep a kid off drugs. To find out how, call toll free 1-877-KIDS-313. A message from the Office of National Drug Control Policy, The Ad Council and this station.

Learning Disabilities
Live Announcer Copy

:30
Is your first grader having trouble learning to read? Or finding it hard learning to write? It could be the first sign that your child has a problem learning. Don't wait. The sooner you get help, the better it is for your kid. To find out more, call 1-888-GR8-MIND, 1-888-GR8-MIND, or visit www.aboutld.org now. Kids with learning disabilities are smart. They just learn differently. A message from The Advertising Council, the Coordinated Campaign for Learning Disabilities and this station.

:15
Trouble learning to read or write could be the first signs that your child may have a problem learning. To find out more, call 1-888-GR8-MIND, or visit www.aboutld.org now. A message from The Advertising Council, the Coordinated Campaign for Learning Disabilities and this station.

:10
Kids with learning disabilities are smart. They just learn differently. Call 1-888-GR8-MIND, or visit www.aboutld.org. A message from The Ad Council, the Coordinated Campaign for Learning Disabilities and this station.

These PSAs are representative of the efforts made by The Advertising Council on behalf of a great many not-for-profit and government causes. The Ad Council maintains a record of the dollar value of the messages that actually reach the public. In 2001, the radio, television, billboard, and other print media donated more than $1.5 billion dollars in air time and print space.

PSAs BY STUDENTS

The four PSAs making up this section were written by students taking their first class in scriptwriting for the media. Many additional student scripts may be found in Appendix A.

CLIENT: TRI-VALLEY HUMANE SOCIETY
AUTHOR: Mari-Ela David*
LENGTH: :10

ANNCR: Tri-Valley Animal Rescue is looking for volunteers. If you'd like to find homes for abandoned pets, call 555-7043, that's 555-7043.

CLIENT: TRI-VALLEY HUMANE SOCIETY
AUTHOR: Mari-Ela David*
LENGTH: :20

ANNCR: Animals in local shelters are sleeping soundly . . . but some will never wake up. They say there's no room. Our mission is to make room. But we need your help. Call Tri-Valley Humane Society, 555-7043, that's 555-7043. Make room in your heart for a lonely cat or dog. Call 555-7043.

CLIENT: TRI-VALLEY HUMANE SOCIETY
AUTHOR: Mari-Ela David*
LENGTH: :30

ANNCR: They're put behind bars. They're given a death sentence. All because they don't have a home. But you can do something about it. Volunteer at the Tri-Valley Animal Rescue Center and help keep local shelters from killing abandoned pets. Animals have the most basic right of all—the right to live. For information, please call 555-7043. That's 555-7043.

AGENCY: A.J.D. PRODUCTIONS
CLIENT: PARENTING & FAMILY SUPPORT CENTER
LENGTH: :30
AUTHOR: Ariana Deacon*

SFX: (SOUNDS OF CHILDREN ON PLAYGROUND, UNDER FOR)

CHILD: Mommy, look at this toy I just found! It's mine now.

MOM: You can't just take that—it belongs to some other child!

CHILD: A man on Crime Watch said It's OK to steal as long as you don't get caught. I saw him say it on TV. Is that true?

MOM: No Sweetie! It's definitely NOT OK to steal. Stealing is wrong. Put that back right now. Honey, did you finish your homework before we left home?

CHILD: Johnny's brother said homework's pointless and stupid, and he's in high school,

SFX OFF: SILENCE

WOMAN: Who do you want raising your child? You're the most important influence in their lives. Teach them, love them, respect them, guide them—and listen to them. Listen to them, and they'll listen to you.

   Creating public service announcements for organizations you support is good practice. Your efforts can help promote worthwhile causes, and your scripts can be examples of your work when you create your portfolio. The value of promoting a cause that helps people or animals is, to quote a current commercial, "priceless."

QUESTIONS

1. Do you feel that the poem that opens the presentation for Friends Outside is justified? Do you feel that it establishes an appropriate mood? Can you think of a better way to open the slide program?

2. After you finished reading the Friends Outside script, did your feelings about about helping the families of prisoners change? If so, in what ways?

3. Answer question one as it applies to the slide show for Amigos de las Americas.

4. What are the most apparent themes touched on in the Amigos slide presentation?

5. Choose any five public service announcements and analyze them in terms of

   - structure—Are the three parts, beginning, middle, end, appropriate and effective?
   - mood—Is the mood appropriate to the nature of the message? How is the mood established?
   - human needs—What fears, desires, concerns, etc., are evoked?

NOTES

1. To use slides with PowerPoint, you have two choices: if your project requires you to take all the photos, a digital camera will allow you to transfer the photos directly to PowerPoint through a USB port into your computer. If the visuals have been shot as 35mm slides, nearly any photo shop can digitize them to a CD with no loss of quality.

2. This and the following series of PSAs are reqprinted here courtesy of The Advertising Council.

A COMPENDIUM
OF STUDENT SCRIPTS

These scripts were written by students taking their first college course in writing for the electronic media. An assignment sheet precedes each set of scripts and, after each script the author's analysis is given. You may want to make this appendix an added learning experience by reading a particular assignment sheet and then, without looking at the scripts it generated, write your own. You may also benefit from writing an analysis of each of your script's goals: specific purpose of the script, target audience, themes employed, and needs addressed. If appropriate, you may want to include in your analysis such additional considerations as intended mood, structure, and vision.

FEATURE REPORTS

FEATURE REPORTS ASSIGNMENT SHEET

Your final writing assignment for this class is a feature report for radio or television. Select a topic you feel is: (a) an important social, political, environmental, or other issue; and is, (b) illustrative, informative, humorous, or otherwise worth investigating and developing as a feature report. Plan this far ahead of time, because it will require research, interviews (most likely), editing, and much writing and rewriting. YOUR REPORT IS TO BE 5 TO 7 MINUTES IN LENGTH.

Please pay special attention to the radio and television feature reports that are played in class, and those in your textbook; they are models, both good and bad, from which you can learn a great deal.

1. Research your topic. Read the sections of your text about feature reports. Nearly all of the information in these pages is applicable to your work.
2. Collect data. You may want to (need to) make audiotaped recordings of interviews with appropriate spokespersons. These eventually will be edited and transcribed into typescript copy.

   IMPORTANT: For a television report, you may assume (pretend?) that you have videotape of your interviews. You also may use historical film or still photos that exist or are likely to exist, as though you actually have them in hand. For example, you may safely assume that footage of President Truman meeting with Churchill and Stalin at Yalta exists and is available; you may not assume that film of President Lincoln at Gettysburg is available! For a radio report, assume that you have tape recordings of actualities you may want to include, such as a speech by MLK or JFK. Be careful to include only material that you've collected, or that is almost sure to be available.

3. Arrange your "bites" into an appropriate sequence—logical, thematic, chronological, or whatever best suits your material.

4. Write connecting narration, as appropriate. Make sure that your report has an appropriate structure, with a beginning, a middle, and an end. You may want to conclude with a summary and, as appropriate, recommendations for further action.

5. MAKE SURE YOU USE A RECOGNIZABLE SCRIPT FORMAT!!!!!

6. Include an analysis of your report.

I want to help you with this project if you so desire. If you want to "consult" with me, provide me with a statement of your topic, the objective of your report, and your bibliography. List all resources you've consulted, whether you use them in your final version or not. I'll respond with any thoughts or information that I feel may be useful to you.

FEATURE REPORT FOR RADIO
TITLE: Capoeira—Dance, Fight or Workout? Radio Feature (7:00)
BY: Katlen Schutt

SFX: SOUNDTRACK #1—FADE UP PERCUSSION AND BERIMBAU

MUSIC WITH HANDCLAPPING AND PEOPLE CHANTING, PLAY TEN SECONDS THEN FADE UNDER

NARRATOR:
People in the United States are always looking for new ways to fight fat. Recent workout trends include Kickboxing and Spinning, but the latest sport receiving attention is Capoeira (cah-po-WED-uh). What is it exactly? Capoeirista (kah-po-wehr-EES-tuh) Miguel Redar explains:

ACTUALITY (REDAR):
CAPOEIRA IS AN AFRICAN-BRAZILIAN MOVEMENT ART THAT COMBINES MARTIAL ARTS, DANCE, ACROBATICS, AND MUSIC IN ONE INTEGRATED FORM. IT'S AN IMPROVISATIONAL DANCE/FIGHT PERFORMED BY TWO PEOPLE IN THE CENTER OF A CIRCLE OF CLAPPING, SINGING, AND MUSIC-PLAYING COMRADES. SOMETIMES IT'S A BEAUTIFULLY CHOREOGRAPHED

DANCE, SOMETIMES A TOUGH FIGHT, SOMETIMES A DISPLAY OF ACRO-
BATIC SKILL, SOMETIMES A CONTEST OF BALANCE TAKING, BUT ALWAYS IT
REMAINS A GAME BETWEEN THE TWO PLAYERS.

NARRATOR:
Capoeira symbolizes many different things as Redar has explained. This dates back
to the origins of the movement. Historians of the art have traced the beginnings to
the Angolan slaves who brought the self-defense technique to Brazil in the 16th
century.

Born in the senzalas (sen-ZAH-lahs) where the slaves lived, it's a martial art based
on traditional African dances and rituals. Since the slave masters forbade the
practice of Capoeira, the slaves disguised the movement as a recreational dance.
Also called a jogo (JHO-go) or game, they practiced during their free time to develop
themselves mentally and physically for battle. Capoeira teacher Marcia Cigarra
explains:

ACTUALITY (CIGARRA):
THE GAME OF CAPOEIRA REQUIRES THE USE OF INTUITION AND FORE-
SIGHT AND DOESN'T RELY SOLELY ON THE USE OF PHYSICAL STRENGTH.
DURING THE GAME THE CAPOEIRISTAS SKILLFULLY EXPOSE THE LIMITA-
TIONS OF THEIR OPPONENTS AND ENGAGE IN PLAYFUL ATTACKS AND
COUNTERATTACKS THUS BETTER ENABLING THEMSELVES TO DISCOVER
THEIR PERSONAL POWER.

NARRATOR:
The slaves, brought by the Portuguese to Brazil, came from different parts of Africa
and arrived at three different ports: Salvador, Recife, and Rio de Janeiro. This posed
a problem in the beginning as many of the slaves belonged to different tribes who
often were enemies. Over the years, as slaves saw no end to their oppression, they
began to break out. The escaped slaves began fugitive communities in the mountain
regions. The largest of these communities, called quilombos (kee-LOWM-bos), was
Palmares. It had a population of over 20,000.

Palmares created an environment where the slaves could further develop their
Capoeira skills, and they cultivated their culture in ways they couldn't under the
former rule of their masters.

In the 1600s, the Dutch invaded Brazil. While the Portuguese were engaged in
battle, the people of Palmares took this chance to go to the plantations to free more
of the slaves. During the attacks, the Africans' main fighting tactic was Capoeira.
Having become their most important weapon, it also became their key to freedom.

Practiced in a circle called a roda (HO-dah), people watch while clapping, singing,
and playing musical instruments. In the center are two opponents. Capoeira
instructor Itabora from Santa Cruz, California tells us about the instruments played.

ACTUALITY (ITABORA):
THE LEADING INSTRUMENT IS A BERIMBAU. ALSO PLAYED IS A DRUM CALLED AN ATABAQUE AND A PANDEIRO (tambourine). A BERIMBAU IS A ONE STRINGED, BOW SHAPED INSTRUMENT WITH A GOURD ATTACHED TO ONE END TO GIVE RESONANCE. THIS CIRCLE IS THE MOST EXCITING PART OF CAPOEIRA.

SFX: SOUNDTRACK# 2—FADE UP BANDA REFLEXUS-. "FESTA DA RACA" FOR FORTY SECONDS THEN FADE DOWN

NARRATOR:
Jeff Kaliss, writer for Smithsonian Folkways, elaborates on the percussion and vocals of Capoeira music.

ACTUALITY (KALISS):
THE TOQUES, TRADITIONAL RHYTHMS ASSOCIATED WITH PARTICULAR CAPOEIRA SCHOOLS AND THE SET PROGRESSIONS OF THE JOGO, ARE REINFORCED AND ELABORATED BY WICKER RATTLES CALLED CAXIXIS PANDEIROS, DOUBLE BELLS, CALLED AN AGOGO, A NOTCHED BAMBOO SCRAPER OR RECO-RECO, AND A TALL DRUM OR ATABAQUE.

A SOLO VOCALIST, WITH SLIDES AND EMOTIONAL COLORING EVOCATIVE OF THE BLUES, INTONES LYRICS PRAISING THE GODS AND THE ANCES-TRAL MESTRES AND COMMENTING ON THE MERITS AND WEAKNESSES OF THE COMBATANTS. A CHORUS FOLLOWS THE SOLOIST IN CALL-AND-RE-SPONSE OR WITH REPEATED PHRASE.

NARRATOR:
The mestre is the senior Capoeira teacher who usually leads the roda in song and the musicians who play along, during the jogo.

Capoeira has come a long way since its roots in Africa and Brazil, and today people worldwide enjoy it for many different reasons. Mestre Camisa originally established Abada Capoeira in Rio de Janeiro in 1988. He has brought his school to Santa Cruz. In bringing Capoeira to the beachside town in California, he hopes to teach some of the positive aspects of the practice to contribute to the holistic development of his students.

ACTUALITY (CAMISA):
I SEE CAPOEIRA AS A VALUABLE CULTURAL AND SOCIAL SOURCE THAT INCORPORATES SEVERAL ELEMENTS THAT I BELIEVE WILL CONTRIBUTE TO THE FORMATION OF HUMAN AND ETHNIC VALUES.

NARRATOR:
So while exercise fanatics are looking for the latest workout trends, clearly Capoeira is more than a way to fight fat. Originally developed as a movement to empower a group of people who were enslaved, today it can be used to keep the mind, body, and soul fit in a world that becomes increasingly challenging.

SFX: SOUNDTRACK #3—FADE UP CLEMENTINA AND CLARA NUNES: "EM-BALA EU" FOR TWENTY-FIVE SECONDS THEN FADE DOWN TO SILENCE

ANALYSIS

Capoeira is an extraordinary practice, One of the appeals I am definitely using in this feature is the need to identify with a group one considers "special." Due to the nature of the history of this dance/fight art form, it certainly has a group appeal to it, By giving some of the history, including the exercise benefits and detailing the musical aspect of this, I try to emphasize how dynamic it is. Being part of a Capoeira group means being part of a subculture of people dating back to the 1600s who were seeking freedom.

In *Idea to Script,* the discussion of "growth" themes is mentioned, and another appeal I am making here relates to this: the themes of Freedom, Justice, Morality, and Spirituality are suggested in this feature if not clearly, then at least subtly. This is such a complex subject that I chose to focus on the martial arts aspect of Capoeira, but there is a connection to religion. Because Capoeira attempts to teach the players to be intuitive and holistically in touch with their minds, there is a spiritual and moral aspect to it. To be in touch with the mind means to be in touch with the god self in one way or another. To be in touch with the god self means to be seeking morality. Also, due to the predicament of the slaves, freedom and justice are themes expressed here.

FEATURE REPORT
LENGTH: 6 Minutes Radio
"A Little Piece of Heaven"
BY: John Sidhom

MUSIC: "SAN FRANCISCO," INSTRUMENTAL, VERY SLOW TEMPO. IN AND UNDER

North Beach can make your head spin.

SFX: TRAFFIC SOUNDS, BARKER YELLING ABOUT A "GIRLIE SHOW." UNDER BEHIND NARR.

Stand on the corner of Columbus and Broadway on a Friday night with sex shows in one direction and pasta and pretty people in the other, and you can feel your equilibrium go. Yet North Beach is a great love. City Lights, Vesuvio's, Viva's . . . How can you hate this place? But for some, it can be too much of a good thing and dizziness sets in.

SFX: TRAFFIC SOUNDS SEGUE INTO VERY QUIET SAXOPHONE PLAYING "SAN FRANCISCO." UNDER

But don't worry: there's a calm place in the middle of it all. Washington Square. There you're surrounded by that great heady extravaganza called North Beach, but you're no longer *in* it. Or you're so close to its center that it ceases to spin.

Washington Square is a moment's rest and a little vision of Heaven on earth. A Hindu heaven, perhaps. For it's the little "time out" before you reenter life; before you go to Tosca's for a nightcap.

MUSIC: ITALIAN OPERA ARIA, IN AND UNDER

But be aware of this: the square isn't a square; it's a trapezoid. That's because of Columbus Street.

SFX: TRAFFIC SOUNDS IN AND UNDER

Columbus Street is why you never know quite where you are in North Beach. It's not till you get out a map and study it that you realize that the streets of North Beach are not the work of a magician with mirrors; on paper, anyway, they form the conventional neighborhood grid. But you'll have to look long and hard at a map to convince yourself of this fact. Columbus is an oblique slash across the grid, causing disorientation almost everywhere. Set foot on Columbus—even catch sight of it—and instantly it's your reference. It may be its size; it's broader than Broadway. Or it may be the power of pasta and people and wine. Whatever the case, it quickly spins you 'round to its point of view.

But desert Columbus—take Stockton over to Washington Square—and you're quickly back on the grid, except for one small matter: Columbus cuts the corner of the "square," turning it into a large trapezoid and a small triangle.

SFX: DISTANT SOUNDS OF CHILDREN PLAYING

But ignore the triangle and you're at peace in this park. Have a seat on a bench with a plaque, the bench donated by some guy desperate to be remembered. Relax and don't give him a thought.

MUSIC: "I LEFT MY HEART IN SAN FRANCISCO," BEHIND NARR.

Clouds drift overhead, just like they do over Nob Hill, San Francisco's own Mount Olympus. A combination of air and moisture from the sea, the clouds are constantly drifting and changing shape. Around the edge of the park are Monterey pines fashionably trimmed like poodles. Some park barber has gone wild here.

On your bench, with a little distance between you and the great hub of Columbus, you're surrounded by other notable things.

SFX: DISTANT SOUND OF CHURCH BELLS, SOME SOUNDS OF CHILDREN PLAYING

On the north side of the park, across its rich green grass, is Saint Peter and Paul's Church. If you look to your left and then to your right, you see that its location must have once been idyllic: in a valley between Russian Hill and Telegraph Hill. In fact this used to be pasture land of a ranch owned by Senora Juana Briones, asserts an historical landmarker ignored by people but adored and adorned by pigeons.

But back to Saint Peter and Paul. Double spires stretch dramatically upwards, as though trying to snatch a little piece of Heaven. Peter and Paul's is of the Salesian order. The order was founded by Don Bosco of Becchi, a man said to have been troubled by a fiery temper in his youth. While passion still runs high in North Beach, it, too, has mostly mastered its temper. North Beach was originally the Latin Quarter of San Francisco, then Little Italy in the 1880s.

There are still lots of Italians in North Beach—the Italian influence is everywhere—but don't expect a "Little Italy." For better or worse, Italians have long been assimilated into the mainstream of American society.

MUSIC: CHURCH ORGAN IN AND UNDER

Peter and Paul's is a "Romanesque" cathedral with a sculpted, three-dimensional form that seems infused with light. The dark wood of the church's interior, the sturdy confessionals lining both sides of the sanctuary, and the soft flickering glow of votive candles in alcoves-these all serve to calm the overloaded senses. Who knows? Without this church, North Beach might spin totally out of control on a high caffeine day.

From your bench in the park you'll spot other notable "institutions," most offering food and drink. A little walk around the "trapezoid" and the "triangle" and you'll find some of San Francisco's most notable restaurants: Moose's, Little City; the legendary "Wash Bag," the venerable Fior D'italia; and not far away, North Beach Restaurant and Rosa Pistola. The Italian-French Baking Company, offering fresh bread warm from the oven, is only a block away on Grant. You aren't going to go hungry in North Beach; the bounty is enormous and your cup will run over, staining your tie or your blouse. Your car, however, may feel neglected, even unwanted. Guide books suggest a taxi, and that's probably a good idea.

MUSIC: JAZZ SAXOPHONE, IN AND UNDER

There's music in North Beach, like jazz at Pearl's. There's a famous book store there where you will be strip-searched these days for stolen goods and still feel thankful to be among the literati of San Francisco. There's entertainment, including one show that came and never went, a rare babbling on that continues to delight. And of course there are the "girls" if you are into that.

SFX: PARK SOUNDS—CHILDREN AT PLAY, ADULT VOICES SPEAKING ITALIAN AND CHINESE, IN AND UNDER

Unlike other kinds of city space, there's plenty of bench space in the park.

In the middle of the park by some trees you'll spot a statue. Washington? No, Franklin. Why Franklin's there is a little hard to say. Franklin may have been the only statue available for this park. He stands atop a high pedestal, which may be wise. High, of course, means out of reach of vandals and graffiti defacers. Franklin, the man of practical wisdom, would have appreciated that.

You remember, of course, that Franklin was a man of letters, a "writer," if you will. According to the books, he was the only one of the founder fathers to sign all documents that helped create the United States: the Declaration of Independence; the Constitution; the Treaty of Alliance . . . Franklin personally composed parts of the Declaration of Independence and the Constitution.

He also had his own printing company and came up with the idea of Daylight Savings. You know, squeeze a little more fun into a day. You've heard about Franklin's party days in Paris, no doubt. Probably the only thing wrong with this place perhaps, is the name of the square. Or the trapezoid. Or the triangle. But get a grip, drink some grape. In Heaven it doesn't matter.

MUSIC: "I LEFT MY HEART . . .," UP TO CLOSE.

ANALYSIS

Finally a feature report that doesn't bore me . . . Not just saying that because I wrote it. I believe feature reports that grab an audience and pull them in is an art that I have yet to master. This piece deals with the social and entertainment aspect of feature reports. I focused on North Beach, primarily Washington Square (the best kept secret in San Francisco). The themes used in this piece were the non-universal themes of peace, simplicity, order, and perfection. The universal theme of beauty was predominant.

   As you know, I was very sick this semester. I would have my good days and my bad days. However, when I was feeling like the old John, l wouldn't waste the day by staying home and being cooped up in a bedroom all day. So I headed to North Beach. Not to drink (couldn't anyway) or to see the "girl shows," but to experience San Francisco beauty at its best. Washington Park is a very special place for me because it was so peaceful. People watching was a plus, as well. Whenever you get a chance to visit this magical place, who knows—I might be sitting on the bench next to you.

FEATURE REPORT
TITLE: "Music Makes the Memories."
BY: Ariana Deacon

(NOTE: "SB" stands for "sound bite.")

MUSIC: "BEGIN THE BEGUINE" (PLAY 15 SEC.—FADE UNDER)

NARR: Do you remember the Tommy Dorsey stage show, with Frank Sinatra and the Pied Pipers . . . dancing to Artie Shaw's "Begin the Beguine"

. . . the 1939 World's Fair with Benny Goodman, the "King of Swing" . . . the radio announcer saying "And now, from Frank Dailey's Meadowbrook, on scenic Route 22, we bring you Glenn Miller and His Orchestra, featuring Tex Beneke and the Modernaires with their new hit, "Chattanooga Choo Choo?"

MUSIC: "CHATTANOOGA CHOO CHOO" (10 SEC, THEN FADE UNDER)

NARR: You can relive it all and more with the Golden Years of the Big Bands, a live production created by The Walter G. Tolleson Musical Organization nearly three decades ago and filled with fond memories and fabulous music.

MUSIC: "SING , SING, SING"—10 SEC.—FADE UNDER

NARR: Nostalgic music was just one of the many products and services you got when working with a tried and true San Francisco society Band leader like Walt Tolleson. He and his staff created, over the years, countless supper shows, theme productions, musical tributes, and much much more. Some of the most memorable were "The Sights and Sounds of San Francisco," his "Salute to the Big Band Era" featuring Count Basie, Duke Ellington, and Glenn Miller.

SB: (FEMALE) "As always, Walt Tolleson, you're just too good to be true, and too marvelous for words."

MUSIC: TRUMPET PLAYING "BOOGIE WOOGIE BUGLE BOY"

NARR: At the age of eight, Walter Tolleson discovered the trumpet . . . that was the last time he ever put one down. He tooted his way through college, graduating with a Masters degree in music with an emphasis in composition and arrangement. A minor in English just about topped it off . . . Walt Tolleson was ready for the real world, but was the world ready for him?

MUSIC: "IN THE MOOD"—7 SEC—FADE UNDER

NARR: Music is nostalgic, a certain tune or song can take you back to a special occasion or period of time in your life. Walt's favorite thing to do was share the joy of his music with others and most important make them wanna dance.

SB: (FEMALE) "The whole band seemed to have as much fun as the guests, and the guests really picked up on that."

SB: (MALE) "Everyone loved the music; it was hard to get them off the dance floor."

NARR: Once he got his orchestra blowin' and the dance floor kickin' there was no stopping him!

MUSIC: "IT DON'T MEAN A THING, IF IT AIN'T GOT THAT SWING"—
10 SEC—FADE UNDER

NARR: The Walt Tolleson Band has played for many of San Francisco's most prestigious events. Aside from opening almost every major hotel in the City, His orchestra has performed for Senator Diane Feinstein's wedding, the U.S. Conference of Mayors and many more highly social events. Clients include Charlotte Maillard Schultz, Chief of Protocol; Ethel Kennedy and the Robert F. Kennedy Foundation; and The American Bar Association. They play for many of the Bay Area private Country Clubs, and the band has been flown all over the world to play for special occasions of every kind.

SB: (FEMALE) ". . . thank you for having been a key element in a fantasy wedding . . . We look forward to dancing to your tunes in the future."

NARR: Walt had charm, he had charisma, and most of all, he had music in every sense of the word . . . and he loved it.

MUSIC: "SENTIMENTAL JOURNEY"—10 SEC—FADE UNDER

NARR: Walt Tolleson passed away in October of 1997. He was seventy-one years young. But neither Walt, nor his music will ever be forgotten.

SB: (FEMALE) "Your music and dancing made the event; it was a success in every way."

MUSIC: "I GO TO RIO"—10 SEC—FADE UNDER

NARR: The Walt Tolleson Organization was founded in 1956 and is still going strong. Now owned and run by his wife, Diane Tolleson, the company took some new turns in preparation for the new millennium. Without Walt as the feature attraction, the marketing strategy had to be reanalyzed and reformed—and that's just what they did. They wanted to keep the Tolleson Touch that had kept the company going for so long. That is personalized service, great attention to detail, and wonderful dance arrangements. The Organization has brought the Walt Tolleson Legacy into the 21st Century.

MUSIC: "MOONLIGHT COCKTAIL"

NARR: So if you're looking for a great addition for your event to create mood, ambiance, and atmosphere . . . don't forget the music! Whether you want to dance all night—or just enjoy soft background tunes . . . you can find it all in one of San Francisco's oldest and most distinguished music and entertainment companies; The Walt Tolleson Musical Organization.

SB: (FEMALE) "We've been overwhelmed with notes, letters, and comments on what a fine contribution your orchestra made to the festivities."

MUSIC: "DANCE TO THE MUSIC"—LET IT PLAY OUT

ANALYSIS

My target audience with this report was those old enough to remember and relate to the music and era that I discuss. I used the emotion of nostalgia to grab the interest of the listeners, which is why I started it off with such a popular song. Then, the first words are of the scenario that's intended to bring them back to that time and make them remember the way they were. I think, as I mentioned in the report, that much music is often forgotten or placed low in priority—but there's a whole musical world out there that many people may not even think about. Music is truly important in our lives, and I hope that I got that point across while featuring a wonderful native Bandleader. The music I selected was carefully thought out to fit with the copy/script, as well as be recognizable by a large percentage of the target audience.

PUBLIC SERVICE ANNOUNCEMENTS

The PSAs that follow were written by college students for two nonprofit attractions. The first set includes spots for the San Francisco Zoo, and the second set for the Exploratorium. The main thrust of these spots could apply to similar attractions found in any large metropolitan area.

Here is the assignment sheet to which the students were responding:

BECA 370—PUBLIC ART PSA ASSIGNMENT—FACT SHEET

Your client is a nonprofit institution offering programs for a broad audience. Select one of these institutions, conduct research into it, and write both radio and television spots for it. For your research, use the Internet—all of these institutions have home pages with huge amounts of information. Of course, you may also visit your "client" to see what goes on there firsthand, but please don't make unnecessary contact with personnel at the agency—we could wear out our welcome if a number of us were to start phoning for information!

Here are suggested institutions:

1. Legion of Honor
2. San Francisco Zoo
3. Morrison Planetarium

4. Oakland Museum of California

5. Exploratorium

(If you have some similar attraction you'd like to advertise, discuss it with me ASAP.)

Develop an advertising campaign. Invent and use a slogan or phrase that will identify your institution—as in, "it's the water," or "the quality goes in before the name goes on."

Design a logo for your institution (for TV spot).

Use specific attractions for these spots, and highlight different attractions in each script.

Write These Spots:

1. Two :30 radio spots, promoting your institution, aimed at adults, including parents, teachers, and any other adult demographic group you may choose.

2. Two :30 radio spots, promoting your institution, aimed at children.

3. A :30 television spot targeted at a heterogeneous audience

4. DON'T FORGET YOUR ANALYSES! Your analyses of intended audience, appeals used, and universal themes touched on will be of great importance in shaping your approach and successfully reaching and motivating your target audience.

(Note: Not all of the five scripts and analyses submitted by each student are reproduced here.)

THE SAN FRANCISCO ZOO
CLIENT: THE SAN FRANCISCO ZOO
LENGTH: :30 "Kids"
BY: Samantha Wiedmann

ANNCR: Hey kids! What do Rainbow Lorikeets say?

KID 1:   (LAUGHING) Rar-Rar. Rarrrrr!

KID 2:   BRRRRGH!

KID 3:   (GIGGLES)

ANNCR: Okay. Then what do Wallaroos say?

KID 1:   Lala Rooooo Lala Rooooooooo (LAUGHS).

KID 2:   Ruufff— (Laughs).

KID 3:   Peep-Peep. (GIGGLES)

ANNCR: Here's a tricky one. What do furry chinchillas say?

KID 1:   There's no such thing.

KID 2:   A furry what? Let me see it!

KID 3:   Can I have one? (GIGGLES)

ANNCR: What do parents say when their kids want to go to the zoo?

PARENT: Let's Go!

ANNCR: Rediscover your world. The San Francisco Zoo. Children 3 and under are free and children of all ages will have fun. For more information, call the San Francisco Zoo at 555-7165. THE SAN FRANCISCO ZOO.

*   *   *

CLIENT: THE SAN FRANCISCO ZOO
LENGTH: :30 "Aye-Aye"
BY: Samantha Wiedmann

ANNCR: Imagine a creature with the claws of a wolverine, the nose of a rat, and the glowing eyes of a gremlin.

(SPOOKY MUSIC)

What you get is an Aye-Aye (eye-eye). Aye-Ayes are just as wild as they look. They live in trees and chew through wood to get food. There are only about 500 left of these endangered lemurs in the world and two of them are at the San Francisco Zoo in the Primate Discovery Center.

Rediscover your world. For more information on the aye-aye or our other exciting exhibits including our new baby gorilla and rhino, call the San Francisco Zoo at 555-7165.

ANALYSIS

For my San Francisco Zoo spots, I chose the theme of "Rediscover your world." It is clichéd, but most tags that work are. I figured that most people have been to the zoo before, but they haven't gone in a while and they probably don't know about the new attractions. This appeals to the desire for new experiences, to experience the beautiful, and to see an unusually-stimulating physical side of the world.

The children's spot is targeted at kids up to age 12. "Aye-Aye" introduces a rare creature that most people haven't heard of, so it should appeal to everyone's curiosity. Most parents and educators look for different ways to get their children to enjoy learning. This spot should make parents feel like they too can learn if they go to the zoo. Each spot has a tag that offers general information about the zoo.

AGENCY: San Francisco Zoo
LENGTH: :30 Radio "Gorilla World"
BY: Sarah Elizabeth Valdez

SFX: ZOO SOUNDS—MONKEYS, ROARS, ETC., UP AND OUT

ANNCR: What you just heard were sounds from your youth. You have just entered the ZOO ZONE where anything is possible.

SFX: GORILLA NOISES

ANNCR: You can visit Gorilla World and pretend to be an ape—and not that grown-up adult you pretend to be.

SFX: BIRD SOUNDS

ANNCR: Or, try relaxing next to the Bird Conservation Center after a hard and stressful day at the office.

MUSIC: INSTRUMENTAL "IT'S ALL HAPPENING AT THE ZOO" IN AND UNDER

ANNCR: Whatever you may decide to do, do it fast because in 2004 . . . we'll have a new look.

MUSIC: UP AND UNDER

ANNCR: The San Francisco Zoo, Creating a Family for a LifeTime.

*   *   *

AGENCY: San Francisco Zoo
LENGTH: :30 Radio "Prop C"
BY: Sarah Elizabeth Valdez

SFX: BIRDS CHIRPING, GORILLAS BANGING THEIR CHESTS.

ANNCR: Let me take you back

SFX: DREAM "TWILIGHT ZONE" SOUNDS.

ANNCR: Remember when you were voting and you came upon Proposition C?

SFX: TICK TOCK NOISES (CLOCK).

ANNCR: Proposition C passed, and just in time. The 68-year-old zoological institution, known as the San Francisco Zoo, needed a face lift, and you helped make it happen.

SFX: CROWD CHEERING AND CLAPPING

ANNCR: Your Zoo now has new spectacular attractions for the whole family to enjoy, with more scheduled to open this Summer. But why wait?
You helped make it come true, so come out and help us celebrate! General admission for San Francisco adults is only $7. Seniors even less. The San Francisco Zoo, Creating a Family for a Lifetime.

ANALYSIS

First off, I wanted to comment on my overall project. I decided to use the San Francisco Zoo as my non-profit organization because it was the only institution listed in the assignment that I'd visited and I felt that my personal experiences could help play a major role in getting my advertising campaign done. Once I looked at the website for the San Francisco Zoo, my mind started going a thousand seconds per minute and I became very wrapped up in the assignment.

Choosing my target audience was not very difficult because I found some interesting information on the San Francisco Zoo home page. Immediately, I decided my approach would be to aim the spots towards adults. I used our universal attraction to, and fascination with, animals to help support my spots. I feel that both radio spots were well targeted towards my given audience.

I decided to bring the zoo to its audience, so I included SFX of animal and human voices. I wanted to be able to bring some of the most fascinating attractions to our audience so that they'd get excited and want to go to the San Francisco Zoo right away. I decided to include the Admission prices because the San Francisco Zoo is not expensive and I wanted everyone to realize that.

My slogan was developed because I was trying my hardest to come up with something that was catchy but not clichéd. After thinking about it all day, I decided that since the San Francisco Zoo provided learning for the whole family, why not become part of their family for a lifetime? My slogan became friendly and straightforward.

I enjoyed doing this assignment. It did take a lot of time to develop, but I feel I was able to reach my intended audiences and have fun at the same time.

The Exploratorium

The same assignment that produced the zoo spots offered other options for students, including a large science museum, the Exploratorium. This attraction is in a large hall with a myriad of hands-on displays, all centering around science. A major feature is the Tactile Dome, which is pitch-dark inside; the treat is to explore your sense of touch in ways never before imagined. Here are a number of the spots that, cumulatively, tell listeners a great deal about the museum's attractions.

AGENCY: R&L ADS
CLIENT: EXPLORATORIUM
LENGTH: :30
BY: LeRoyn Elizabeth McDaniel

SFX: SOUND OF EXCITED KIDS CHEERING "YAAAAY"

ANNCR: (FEMALE): Isn't that the sound that every science teacher wants to hear? The sound of children having fun while they learn?

MUSIC: SLOW, JAZZ TUNE, FADE IN AND UNDER

ANNCR: If you're a science teacher, the Exploratorium's teacher institute can do that for you. The institute offers summer workshops for teachers of grades six thru twelve. The staff offers a mix of content-based discussions, classroom experiments, and teaching strategies based on the Exploratorium's many exhibits, but you must mail your registration by April 14.

For more information, contact the teacher institute at (415) 555-0313.

MUSIC: UP TO CLOSE

ANALYSIS

For this spot, the target was science teachers. I felt that kids cheering would attract people (especially teachers of school-aged children) and make them wonder what all the excitement is about. It eventually points out who the target audience is. And most teachers want their students to enjoy learning. I chose to have the jazz playing in the background so that it would cater to the contemporary audience. The music might help the somewhat dull information flow better to the listeners. This spot provides pertinent information to those who are interested.

This television spot was a joint effort by two members of the writing class.

AGENCY: R&L ADS
CLIENT: EXPLORATORIUM
LENGTH: :30
BY: LeRoyn Elizabeth McDaniel and Rassheedah Schelbie

VIDEO	AUDIO
1. MS of people walking into the Exploratorium	MUSIC: UP-TEMPO; HAPPY

MALE ANNCR: (ENTHUSIASTIC) The San Francisco Exploratorium is one of the few museums where visitors are encouraged to touch the exhibits!

2. B-Roll of kids and parents touching exhibits and laughing and more shots of hands-on activities. MS of little girl holding red balloon above her hair showing the static effects.

The Exploratorium provides access to and information about

3. B-Roll, scientific demonstration showing light bulb go off

science,

4. Cut to MS of frogs in pond

nature,

5. Cut to CU of a sculpture

art,

6. Cut to side shot of lecturer with kids and elders around a computer.

and technology.

7. Cut to loose MS of Palace of Fine Arts

So come join us at the San Francisco Exploratorium located at the Palace of Fine Arts.

8. Dissolve to white with logo: exploratorium in black

The Museum of Science, Art, and human perception.

9. CG: The Museum of science, art & human perception.
(415) EXP-LORE

ANALYSIS

For this television spot we were told to target a heterogeneous audience, so we developed a spot that we felt would appeal to everyone. This spot was made with shots showing the different activities because we wanted to show how fun the Exploratorium is. And we showed a mixed audience: children, adults, parents and elders, as well as people of various ethnicities. And we wanted the audience to come away with the fact that the Exploratorium isn't just for kids but for anyone who wants to simply learn. So this appealed to that desire to learn found in everyone.

We chose quick cuts and uptempo music because we wanted the audience to actually feel the energy of the Exploratorium. So if the viewers have stepped away from the television, the upbeat music and ohh's and ahh's from the commercial may force them to look. And the intention is to make the audience see what a good time everyone else is having, so of course they're going to want to be part of it too. After all, most people want to be at the most happening place.

So in conclusion, the main point of this spot was to communicate fun and squeeze in as much information and video clips as we could. And we did!

CLIENT: The Exploratorium
AUTHOR: Ben McClintock

MUSIC: (UPBEAT INSTRUMENTAL. UP FULL, AND UNDER THROUGHOUT)

ANNCR: You may think the Exploratorium is just jazzed-up, candy-coated, kid's stuff. Boy, have you got the wrong idea! The Exploratorium has over 650 hands-on exhibits where kids can find out how science is used in real life. There's lots of different activities for kids—in groups large or small. Learn about the science behind hockey games. Learn how vision works by dissecting a Cow's eye. If you're in the mood for a family outing . . . or a field trip that's more than just a tour . . . come to the Exploratorium.

We're open seven days a week, at 3601 Lyon Street in San Francisco.

Explore your world—or you may miss it!

*   *   *

CLIENT: The Exploratorium
AUTHOR: Ben McClintock

MUSIC: (UPBEAT INSTRUMENTAL. UP FULL, AND UNDER THROUGHOUT)

ANNCR: Got the science blues?
Think you're gonna scream if you hear about that Newton guy one more time?
Then come to a place that puts reality . . . and fun . . . back into science.
Here at the Exploratorium.
Become an aircraft designer.
Make your own blimp and learn why it works!
Make model buildings out of gumdrops and toothpicks.
These are just some of the things you can do at the Exploratorium.

Tell your parents. Tell your teachers. Tell them you want to go to the Exploratorium! Come and take a look around. And especially, make learning fun!
The Exploratorium.

ANALYSIS

The first radio spot is for an adult audience. The message of the spot is to get them to take their kids or students to the Exploratorium. This is done by appealing to the parental need to be involved in the positive upbringing of their children. The ad also touches on the yearning for the perceived simplicity of childhood, even though we know it to be complex. Other needs presented are the need to be informed as to how the world works and the need to see order imposed on the world.

The second spot is directed toward children. The goal is to get children to persuade their parents to take them to the Exploratorium. This is done by appealing to the childhood dislike of boredom, in this case the boredom of learning about a potentially dry subject in a traditional classroom environment, and by telling them that it doesn't have to be that way. The need to see order imposed on the world is also present here as well as the need to have fun and be amused.

Other themes seen or heard in the ads include the innocence of youth, familial love, truth, and order.

MUSIC: (UP TO CLOSE)
CLIENT: Exploratorium
BY: Melea Martinez
LENGTH: :30 seconds

ANNCR: (MAD SCIENTIST VOICE) Hey kids, what are you doing this weekend? Are you ready to go to a place where you can play all day? This is a place that your parents will be happy to take you to. You have to come see my latest exhibits and creations. Like there's an exhibit where you stand against this wall, you pose, there's a flash and your shadow appears on the wall behind you. Another exhibit that is amazing to see is the wind exhibit. There's wind whirling around in this tube and it looks like a tornado. See you this weekend! Explore your imagination at the Exploratorium.

NO ANALYSIS WAS SUBMITTED.

CLIENT: EXPLORATORIUM
AGENCY: Melea Martinez
Length: 30 seconds

VIDEO	AUDIO
GRADE SCHOOL LUNCHROOM. MCU OF JOE AND JOHN SITTING IN BACKGROUND AT TABLE, EATING.	(SFX: NOISES OF PEOPLE TALKING)

CU OF JOHN	JOHN: Whadya do over the weekend?
	JOE: My Mom took me and my sister Megan to the Exploratorium.
MS OF THE OUTSIDE OF EXPLORATORIUM.	
	JOHN: The what? Never heard of it.
CU OF JOHN	
	JOE: It's kinda like a museum but not your usual, boring museum.
DISSOLVE TO SHOT OF ALIEN VOICES EXHIBIT	It's filled with cool stuff to do and look at. There's this one exhibit that you sit in phone booths and you can hear alien voices.
CU OF JOHN	JOHN: And your Mom went with you? What did she do?
MS OF JOE'S MOM AND SISTER LAUGHING/SMILING AT ONE OF THE EXHIBITS.	JOE: My Mom had just as much fun as my Sis and I did. Ask your Mom to take you there.
SUPER LOGO OVER PREVIOUS SHOT.	ANNCR: Explore your imagination at the Exploratorium.

NO ANALYSIS WAS SUBMITTED.

CLIENT: The Exploratorium
AGENCY: Sky Line Entertainment
TITLE: "Ex . . . Plor . . . Er"
LENGTH: :30 Radio
BY: Jedediah Gildersleeve

SFX: CRICKETS CHIRPING AND SUBTLE SPLASHES OF WATER

FROG 1:   Ex . . .

FROG 2:   Plor . . .

FROG 3:   Uh . . .

LIZARD 1:   Hey, did they change jobs or something?

LIZARD 2:   Nope, they're just talking about their home.

LIZARD 1:   Home?

LIZARD 2:   Yea the Exploratorium. In fact all their relatives are staying there as well through September.

LIZARD 1:   Pretty big home, huh?

LIZARD 2:   Yea, it's awesome and the best part is that they love having guests. Adults and kids can have a great time under the same roof.

LIZARD 1:   Well, let's go!

ANNCR: Don't miss out on the excitement and fun this Summer at the Exploratorium, the museum of science, art, and human perception. For more information call 555-EXP-LORE. That's 555-EXP-LORE.

ANALYSIS

This radio spot should be a big hit with adults (especially beer drinkers) because the spot mimics and in a way makes fun of the Budweiser frog commercials. This spot would air early in the morning (during rush hour periods) and at night during sporting events. Adults will think this spot is cute and will be more inclined to take their kids to a place where they can learn as well as have fun.

CLIENT: The Exploratorium
AGENCY: Sky Line Entertainment
TITLE: "The Simpson's go to the Exploratorium"
LENGTH: :30 Television
BY: John Sidhom

VIDEO	AUDIO
OPEN ON LONG SHOT OF HOMER AND BART IN THE CAR DRIVING	(SFX: TRAFFIC NOISES, HORNS, ETC.)
CU OF HOMER	HOMER: Ooh, we're never gonna get there.
CU OF BART	BART: Chill out, Homer . . . What's the hurry?
CU OF HOMER	HOMER: We have to get to the Exploratorium before the frogs leave!
CU OF BART	BART: Wow! Man, they got frogs?

CU OF HOMER	HOMER: Yep, and Crusty the Clown says it's the greatest place on earth!
CU OF BART	BART: Wow, Homer.
CU OF HOMER	HOMER: Okay boy, now hold on!
MS CAR ACCELERATING	(SFX: NOISE OF CAR RACING AHEAD)
LONG SHOT OF HOMER AND BART IN FRONT OF THE EXPLORATORIUM	
CU OF HOMER	HOMER: We finally made it!
CU OF BART	BART: They're closed, man!
CU OF HOMER	HOMER: DOPE!
EXPLORATORIUM LOGO	ANNCR (VO): Don't miss out like Bart and Homer. Head to the Exploratorium to discover the wonders of the frogs. Call 555-EXP-LORE.

ANALYSIS

This television script is intended for both adults and children. "The Simpson's" is a very popular TV program and is a major hit with all ages. The adults love it for the different levels of comedy and the kids love it for the cartoon based (non-reality) humor. The universal themes used are the sense of curiosity and the need to have fun. All in all, I enjoyed writing the scripts.

AGENCY: AD ART
CLIENT: EXPLORATORIUM
LENGTH: :30 TELEVISION
AUTHOR: FAWN LUU

VIDEO	AUDIO
THREE FROGS SITTING ON A LOG IN THE SWAMP.	SFX: SWAMP SOUNDS
	FROG #1: Ribbit, ribbit. FROG #2: Ribbit, ribbit. FROG #3: Ribbit, ribbit. Quick, hide.
ALL THREE FROGS JUMP INTO WATER AND UNDER A LILY PAD	They're coming this way.

LITTLE BOY HOLDING HIS MOTHER'S HAND, WALKING THROUGH SWAMP. MOM LOOKS AROUND, PEERS RIGHT INTO THE CAMERA	BOY: Mom, this isn't fun, you promised I'd get to see some frogs. MOM: Don't worry honey there are plenty of frogs here.
BOY SCRATCHES BACK OF KNEE.	BOY: Ouch, I just got another mosquito bite.
	ANNCR: (VO) Looking for frogs? Save yourself the time, trouble, and money.
BOY AND MOTHER STILL LOOKING, CROUCHED ON KNEES. FROGS UNDERWATER ARE STILL HOLDING THEIR BREATH.	Visit the Exploratorium. See the new frog exhibit,
DISS TO MONTAGE TO SHOW WHAT IS BEING DESCRIBED	observe the stars of our solar system, perform science experiments. For information, call 1-555 EXP-LORE, or visit our web site, www.exploratorium.edu Exploratorium—where the learning never ends.

ANALYSIS

This script is aimed towards both children and adults. Children are always curious about animals. Adults will go out of their way to save money. However, since the adults make the decisions, the children have to go along with the decision and maybe suffer the consequences. The mother in this commercial wanted to bring her son to the swamp to save money because she thought the Exploratorium would cost a lot. The consequence for the little boy is that he gets mosquito bites all over him. The mother doesn't know that the Exploratorium is really quite inexpensive. The frogs shown at the beginning and towards the end are used to get the audience's attention, making them think that this is going to be another Budweiser commercial. In a way they're the comic relief, because towards the end, I have them holding their breath underwater. We all know that they don't need to struggle to hold their breath underwater—they're amphibians. With this commercial I hope to bring more children and adults to the Exploratorium because learning never stops, no matter how old you are.

COMMERCIALS

These commercials for a computer store were written by students in the Writing for the Electronic Media class. The assignment sheet follows, but notice that I changed the name of the store each semester. I wanted to see what students might do with the merchants name.

BECA 370—WRITING FOR THE ELECTRONIC MEDIA

Assignment: Two radio commercials Due March 4th

Fact Sheet

Your agency specializes in creating commercials for local merchants. Your assignment is to meet with the owner and manager of an Apple/Macintosh store to work out details and the "flavor" of a series of radio commercials. You have few restrictions other than those indicated on the fact sheet you prepare following your conferences with store management.

CREATING EFFECTIVE COMMERCIALS FOR THIS CLIENT REQUIRES THE USE OF SELLING POINTS THAT WILL MOTIVATE YOUR LISTENERS.

Write two radio commercials, one :30 and one :60.
Use a different approach for each.
Base scripts on this fact sheet:

KKTD FACT SHEET

CLIENT:	SOLOMON'S APPLE GARDEN
OCCASION:	BACK TO SCHOOL SALE
MERCHANDISE:	Power Macs starting at $999, monitors from $399; iMacs, $1,249; Powerbooks from $1,199; Apple printers below cost; Software close-out: Quicken Books, $99; all games, 50 percent off
NOTE:	CLIENT WANTS HUMOROUS COMMERCIALS— YOU DON'T HAVE TO MENTION EVERY SALE ITEM.
DATES OF SALE:	AUGUST 30TH–SEPTEMBER 15TH
ADDRESS:	CORNER CHAPMAN AND PIXLEY, CORTE MADERA

On a separate sheet, state the motivational devices you've used for each spot. Use concepts from your class text.

AGENCY: KKTD Radio
CLIENT: Solomon's Apple Garden
LENGTH: 30 seconds
BY: Sharon Yamane

SFX: SOUND OF STOMACH GROWLING

ANNCR: Hungry for new computer equipment?

MAN: Yes! I'm starving!

ANNCR: Then Solomon's Apple Garden is the place for you! Dig into the
         luscious back to school sale. You can have a Power Mac for $999,
         smothered with monitors for $399 each, and top that off with Quicken
         Books for $99 a helping. We have many other tantalizing offers, but
         the sale's for a limited time only. It starts on August 30th and ends on
         September 15. Solomon's Apple Garden is located on the corner of
         Chapman and Pixley.

         Hurry on down and satisfy your computer needs!

ANALYSIS

The concept of this commercial is to parody food advertisements. Food is a great
physiological need. It's necessary for survival, so every human can relate to
hunger, and it can cause many different responses in a human. For example, it
can cause a person's stomach to growl, or mouth to water. Because of that, I
think food commercials are more successful at attracting people than any other
kind of appeal.

I had the human's strong reaction to food in mind when I wrote this
commercial. The "Solomon's Apple Garden" sale is presented like a restaurant
ad to entice people into listening. This technique is also used to channel their
desire for food into a desire for computer items. I think that making computer
products sound just as appetizing as food is humorous. However, the association
between food and computers might make consumers hungry for the sale (pun
intended). Therefore, I think this ad could help motivate customers to shop at
"Solomon's Apple Garden."

CLIENT: Chang's Apple Garden
OCCASION: Back to School Sale. "Guys and Dolls" :60
BY: Jedediah Gildersleeve

(NOTE: Guy is a takeoff on Humphrey Bogart. Dame is the stereotypical girlfriend
of a tough detective.)

SFX: (AMBIENT NOISES OF STREETCARS, UNDER ENTIRE SPOT)

SFX: (STREETCAR ROLLS TO A STOP, DOORS OPEN AND BELL
          SOUNDS VOICE TRACK BEGINS)

DAME: Oh Johnny, don't leave me now! Not like this!

GUY: Sorry doll, but when Chang's Apple Garden has a Back to School Sale,
          there's just some things a man's gotta do.

DAME: But Johnny . . . !

GUY: *Try* to under*stand!* They got PowerMac G4s starting at $1,400 (READ:
          FOURTEEN HUNDRED), iMacs from $1,000 (READ: ONE GRAND),
          and PowerBooks below cost.

DAME: Well if ya'd just said somethin' . . .

GUY: Don't go worryin' that pretty little face of yours. After I get back, you'll
          never have to use that miserable computer lab again!

DAME: Gee whiz Johnny, you're the greatest!

GUY: Yea, but I'd be nothin' without Chang's.

SFX: (AUDIO OF STREETCARS FADES OUT)

ANNCR: Don't miss the Back to School Sale going on August 30 to September
          15 at (PAUSE) Chang's Apple Garden. On the corner of Noriega and
          Quintara in San Jose. Chang's.

          NO ANALYSIS WAS SUBMITTED.

AGENCY: KKTP
CLIENT: SOLOMONS APPLE GARDEN
LENGTH: :60 radio
BY: Mari-Ela David

SFX: (DOOR CREAKS OPEN. DOOR SLAMS. FOOTSTEPS WALKING
          ON CREAKY FLOORBOARDS.)

WITCH: All right. This facelift should do the trick now. (EVIL LAUGH)
          (LOUDLY) Mirror, mirror on the wall! NOW who's the fairest of us
          all?

MIRROR: (ECHO CHAMBER) How many times do I gotta tell you?! It's Snow
          White!!! SNOW WHITE!!! And what in the world did you do to your
          face? You gonna gimme a . . . (MIRROR CRACKS) . . . oh now you
          done it.

WITCH:	Darn, and I paid 50 silver pieces for this face, too.
MIRROR:	(ECHO CHAMBER) You gonna have to pay 50 G0LD pieces if you wanna compare to Snow White!
WITCH:	That's it. It's time for Plan B . . . I'm going to kill her with this poisonous apple. Then I'll be the fairest! (EVIL LAUGH).
MIRROR:	(ECHO CHAMBER) You gonna have to poison more girls than that. Shoot, you might as well kill the whole kingdom!
WITCH:	Oh shutup.
SFX:	(3 KNOCKS ON DOOR)
SNOW WHITE:	Who's there?
WITCH:	Just a poor old maiden.
SFX:	(DOOR OPENS)
SNOW WHITE:	Well, hello there. My my, grandma, what a huge nose you have!
WITCH:	No no, wrong story. That's Little Red Riding Hood. Get it straight.
SNOW WHITE:	Oh, sorry. May I help you?
WITCH:	Help this poor old soul and buy an apple from me, would you?
SNOW WHITE:	Oh, I'm sorry. I've already got one. Solomon's beat you to it.
WITCH:	Who?
SNOW WHITE:	Solomon's Apple Garden! They're having a huge Back-To-School Sale . . . with PowerMacs starting at just nine ninety-nine and iMacs for only twelve forty nine!
WITCH:	I meant . . .
SNOW WHITE:	Plus ... they're having a software close out and all games are half-off!
WITCH:	(GRUMBLING) So much for Plan B . . .
ANNCR:	Solomon's Apple Garden Sale . . . located on the corner of Chapman and Pixley in Corte Madera. Sale ends September 15th.

ANALYSIS

This radio commercial attempts to reach an audience that knows enough about computers to recognize what Solomon's Apple Garden is selling. I decided to take a chance with the sixty-second script. I wanted to tell a complete story despite the fact that listeners wouldn't know what was being advertised until almost the very end. My hope is that the story will arouse curiosity, and that people will stay with it to see how it ends. It incorporates themes of good versus evil, villains, the hero (Snow White), and magical transformations. It also shows the needs to see virtue triumph over evil, experience the ugly, and experience the beautiful.

The following commercials were written for a pet store. Here is the assignment sheet:

BECA 370—WRITING FOR THE ELECTRONIC MEDIA

Assignment for October 6th
Two radio commercials

Fact Sheet

You work for a small-market radio station. In the mornings, you sell commercial packages to merchants, and, with the merchants help, work out a "fact sheet." Back at the station, you write commercials, and then produce them. Production backup includes a music library, a sound effects library, and a collection of fanfares, musical intros, bridges, etc. You work with standard audio equipment—console, CD player, cart players, a microphone, and a DAT recorder.

Write two commercials, one :30 and one :60. USE A DIFFERENT APPROACH FOR EACH. BASE SCRIPTS ON THIS FACT SHEET:

KKTD FACT SHEET

CLIENT:	ALLISON'S PET CENTER
OCCASION:	CHRISTMAS SALE
MERCHANDISE:	Guppies and goldfish, 99 cents each; Aquariums, 10 gal., with filter $39.95; White Mice, $10.00 a pair; Squirrel Monkeys, $250.00 each; Leashes, 33 percent off; Dog overcoats, 50 percent off
NOTE:	CLIENT WANTS HUMOROUS COMMERCIALS— YOU DON'T HAVE TO MENTION EVERY SALE ITEM.
DATES OF SALE:	DECEMBER 10 'TIL CHRISTMAS EVE.

ADDRESS: CORNER MAXWELL AND OAK STREETS, MILLBRAE

ON A SEPARATE SHEET, STATE THE MOTIVATIONAL DEVICES YOU'VE
USED FOR EACH SPOT. USE CONCEPTS FROM YOUR CLASS TEXT.

CLIENT: Allison's Pet Center
LENGTH: :30
BY: Staci Smith Johnson

MUSIC: (BELLS PLAYING "JINGLE BELLS")

SFX: (SOUNDS OF A MALL)

SANTA: Ho Ho Ho! And what do you want for Christmas, Mary?

GIRL: (IN A CUTE LITTLE GIRL VOICE) I want some fishies, a kitty, a new
           leash for Spot, a little puppy, and make sure you get a coat for him
           'cause it's real cold and I don't want him to get a doggie cold!

SANTA: (AMUSED AT THE GIRL'S REQUESTS) Well! It's really a good thing
           Allison's Pet Center is having its Holiday Sale.

ANNCR: Allison's Pet Center is where you'll find goldfish and guppies,
           aquariums and filters, dog leashes and overcoats, white mice, and
           even squirrel monkeys! All on sale through Christmas Eve. Allison's
           Pet Center—on the corner of Fulton and North Streets in Millbrae.

ANALYSIS

In this radio commercial, the targeted audience is adults, both men and women,
and focuses more on parents or persons buying Christmas gifts for a child. I'm
attempting to send the message that if animals or miscellaneous items for
animals are on the person's gift list, the best place to go is Allison's Pet Center.
In doing this I'm using the universal theme of the "Innocence of Youth" by
having an innocent young girl recite her wish list (of animal-related items) to
Santa.

AGENCY: KKTD
CLIENT: Allison's Pet Center
LENGTH: :30
BY: Staci Smith Johnson

MUSIC: (LARGE SYMPHONIC CHOIR SINGING)

On the first day of Christmas my true love gave to me,
  a goldfish in an aquarium.
On the second day of Christmas my true love gave to me,
  two mice a squeaking and a goldfish in an aquarium.
On the third day of Christmas my true love gave to me,
  three guppies swimming, two mice a squealing and a goldfish in an
  aquarium.
On the fourth day of Christmas my true love gave to me
  four doggie overcoats, three guppies swimming, two mice
  a-squeaking, and a goldfish in an aquarium.
On the fifth day of Christmas my true love gave to me,
  five Squirrel monkeys! (UNDER FOR:)

ANNCR: Experience the Christmas spirit at Allison's Pet Center, and save big at
           their Christmas Sale going on now through Christmas Eve. Allison's
           Pet Center—on the corner of Fulton and North Streets in Millbrae.

ANALYSIS

In this radio commercial I'm aiming for the Christmas shopping crowd; this
includes all persons getting in the Christmas spirit while attempting to find gifts
for their loved ones. I attempt to set a holiday mood by using a familiar Christmas
song and adding humor by having the ridiculous tune sung by a prestigious,
serious group of vocal artists. The motivational devices I use are two themes:
that of "Peace," which is associated with "The Prince of Peace," and the theme
of having fun.

AGENCY: Anderson Erikson
CLIENT: Allison's Pet Center
LENGTH: :30 seconds radio
BY: Andrew Johnson

MUSIC: (Song, Instrumental—"Lion Sleeps Tonight")

SFX: Jungle Noises

ANNCR: Hey folks, looking for that special gift to give to that special someone
           this Christmas? How about a new pet from Allison's pet center! At
           Allison's, we have all kinds of pets to choose from. Everything from
           Mice and Macaws to Marmots and Monkeys. That's right, we have
           something for everyone—whatever your animal inside desires.
           So come on down and see us and find that perfect pet for that perfect
           someone.

           We're located on the corner of Fulton and North streets in Millbrae.
           Hope to see you soon!

MUSIC
& SFX: Lion music and jungle noises up

ANNCR: Sorry—we don't have lions!

MUSIC & SFX UP TO CLOSE

ANALYSIS

In this assignment I attempt to inform prospective pet owners about Allison's Pet Store and some of the specials going on there this Christmas. The :30 commercial isn't aimed at any particular age group or niche and uses humor to hold the attention of potential customers.

The humorous device used is a funny tune ("Lion Sleeps Tonight") and a tag line that says "we don't have lions." Another device used is the whole idea of releasing the animal instinct inside. People may possibly find this appealing since it's common to lose touch with this in normal modern life.

EIGHTY UNIVERSAL THEMES

Many or even most of these themes may be archetypal. Lack of precise knowledge about the origins and causes of universal themes prevents me from being dogmatic about their nature. The themes listed and described in this section are those culled from years of reading stories from many cultures and ages and from examining stories, works in the plastic and graphic arts, and arts-related rituals and ceremonies. The themes I've labeled "archetypal" include those most often identified as such by Jungian scholars.

There is no intended order of importance to these themes. All are important; all appear over and over again in the public arts. Some reflect our most basic preoccupations—sex and food, for example. Others might be considered more exalted or nobler—love and heroism, for instance. Attempting to arrange them in any kind of hierarchical would be subjective and pointless.

Public arts can be used to uplift people, or they can be used to pull people down, as happened in Germany, Italy, and Japan during the 1930s and 1940s. We must realize that people don't change in any permanent way simply by experiencing universal themes in a single story. The manner in which a work addresses needs and illuminates universal themes determines whether the work is useful, pointless, uplifting, or irrelevant to those who experience it. A violent adventure story replete with danger themes is useful—even enjoyable—when it provides us with excitement, diversion, and a happy ending, but it doesn't automatically lift us up. *Saving Private Ryan* embodies even more danger themes than does *Twister* or *The Perfect Storm,* and all three are equally melodramas. But *Private Ryan* has the added dimension of moral choice, and this makes it a different kind of melodrama—not a better one in the opinion of many moviegoers—but one that causes those seeing it to consider the differences between acts motivated by expediency, and those motivated by a moral code.

While themes themselves can bring about gratification through their dramatization in a story, human growth does not and can not come about simply through exposure to universal themes. That would be too easy. The growth theme of justice, for example, is present in some public arts, but unless individuals make a commitment to justice in their daily lives, it remains only an abstract principle. It's important that significant concepts continue to be presented before the public, in hopes that these concepts eventually will motivate people to think, discuss, and perhaps even to act in a positive manner.

A note about some themes that aren't included here. For many years themes have been created by corporations and advertisers to *manufacture* preoccupations. Bad breath, body odor, feminine odor, overweight, underweight, skin blemishes, unwanted hair, baldness, constipation, short stature, and a great many other preoccupations would not be as important as they are if they weren't constantly pushed by those who want to sell a remedy. Few of these themes were important in the public arts of the past. Even today they appear only occasionally in satires or parodies and although they appear regularly in commercials, they're not eternal or universal. They would make a fascinating study in themselves, but are not within our considerations here.

The themes roughly follow Maslow's hierarchy of human needs, with some differences. As mentioned earlier, needs and themes aren't the same things. For this reason, some categories not mentioned by Maslow have been added: animal themes; archetypal themes; imaginary creatures themes; and wish-fulfillment themes. Also, a number of Maslow's growth needs have been omitted or placed in other categories. Simplicity doesn't suggest itself as a universal theme, even though it's an important aspect of beauty. Playfulness may be a need, but in the public arts it manifests itself, not as a theme, but as a mood. To avoid possible confusion between Maslow's categorization of human needs, and the list that follows, I've avoided Maslow's terminology. For example, instead of calling a category "safety themes" to parallel Maslow's "safety needs," I call the category "danger themes."

That which follows is in a constant state of change. Themes are frequently added, subtracted, or modified.[1] They're presented here in skeletal form, with a few words about each, followed by some examples.

PHYSIOLOGICAL THEMES

1. Air (oxygen).   We have a need to breathe. Air, being invisible and odorless, was not a specific concern of early people. They were not particularly concerned about the air, probably because they were only aware of it when it was poisonous—as with sulfurous fumes from a volcano—or when air was denied a person through strangling, drowning, or live burial. At the same time, air was one of the ancient four elements, the others being earth, fire, and water. The Mesopotamians had an air god, Enlil, and the Greeks had Zeus, the sky god, but it cannot be claimed that the theme of air was important as such in the public arts of the ancient past. The theme of devastating winds was prominent, but that is not quite the same thing as air. But breath is another matter. Many ancient societies believed that the soul was somehow represented by breath, and various rituals were developed to prevent the "soul" from escaping the body at the moment of death, as breathing ceased. In Genesis 2:7, we are told that ". . . the Lord God formed man from the dust of the ground, and breathed into his nostrils the breath of life; and man became a living being." An ancient means of execution was to prevent a person from breathing through strangulation, live burial, crucifixion, or hanging.

In more modern times, submarine movies, mine cave-in stories, and tales of space travelers often have used the deprivation of oxygen as a theme. As the planet earth becomes more and more polluted, we can expect to see more concern with contaminated air in the public arts—as in *Soylent Green.*

2. Food—Its Absence or Abundance.   Food has played a part in many kinds of stories and celebrations throughout human history. Cave dwellers painted on cave walls pictures of the animals they hunted and ate, and nearly all societies developed some sort of harvest festival. There is holy food (the Christian sacrament of the Eucharist) and tabooed food (the banning of pork and shellfish in the Hebrew and Muslim religions). The themes of famine and hunger are found in stories from the Old Testament (Genesis 41), to news documentaries about ongoing famines in Africa. Today, cooking programs are very popular on PBS, and commercials for foods are seen on every commercial station several times a day. And, explain if you will, our fascination with watermelon and pie-eating contests!

3. Water.   Life as we know it would be impossible without water. Water makes up seventy-five percent of the Earth's surface, and all living creatures are constituted of an even greater percentage of water. It's not surprising that the life-giving rivers of Mesopotamia and Egypt were worshipped by the inhabitants of those regions, while many societies worshipped river gods and goddesses. Aquarius, the bearer of water, is a sign of the zodiac. Many societies use water for purification purposes, as in baptism. Flood was one of the Four Horsemen of the Apocalypse, and water was one of the original "four elements," along with earth, fire, and air. Odysseus battled the sea for years, while the successful escape of the Hebrews from Egypt depended on the parting of the Red Sea. Leander drowned swimming the Hellespont, the god, Poseidon, flooded the land to help the men of Athens bring an end to women suffrage, Hercules diverted a river to cleanse the Augean stables, and Pilate washed his hands to symbolize his innocence when sentencing Christ to death. In many societies, including the Greek and Roman, the way to the underworld was down or across a river. Water in the form of storms at sea (*The Perfect Storm*) or flooding rivers are part of danger themes. Today, with a growing concern over water pollution, we can expect to see water as a more frequent theme in the public arts than it has been in recent times.

4. Sleep.   Sleep is not an important theme in today's public arts, but it was of great importance in the past. Sleep—so deathlike in appearance—fascinated early people. A great many societies worshipped a god or goddess of sleep. To the Greeks, Hypnos, the god of sleep, was brother to Thanatos, the god of death. (It is of interest that the word *hypnotism* derives from Hypnos, while the Roman version of this god, Somnos, gave his name to the opium poppy, papaver somniferum. The word *morphine* comes from Morpheus, the Grecian god of dreams. So, sleep, dreams, narcotics, and hypnotism were connected in the Greek and Roman minds.) In Genesis 2, God causes Adam to fall into a deep sleep, during which He creates Eve. Many fairy tales involve sleep, including *Sleeping Beauty* and *Snow White.* While not a popular theme in later times, *Rip Van Winkle, Treasure of the Sierra Madre,* and *Invasion of the Body Snatchers* treat this theme. Many manufacturers promote one product to help us sleep, and another to help us stay awake.

5. Bodily Wastes.   The regular elimination of bodily wastes is as important for survival as the consumption of food and drink, so it's no surprise to find this need expressed as a theme in the public arts. For the most part, the theme is found in tabooed arenas and in coarse humor.
        Joseph Campbell tells us that ". . . among many advanced as well as primitive peoples the sacred clowns—who in religious ceremonies are permitted to break taboos and always enact obscene pantomimes—are initiated into their orders by way of a ritual eating of filth."[2]

Campbell finds a relationship between the sacred clown of ancient times and the circus clown of today.

The Aztecs and the Romans had a "god of ordure"; the surviving comedies of Aristophanes make hilarious scatological jokes and puns; the Bible speaks frankly of defecation (although the King James version of the Bible translates ". . . Saul went in to relieve himself," as "Saul went in to cover his feet"!); medieval rites called "the Black Mass" or the "Mass of the Ass," featured the burning of manure in a censer; and Elizabethan playwrights used four-letter words for feces, urine, and flatus.

Until fairly recent times, scatology was mostly underground, and existed mainly as graffiti and as one type of "dirty joke." During the late 1980s and early 1990s, there began to be exceptions to this in popular films: *Blazing Saddles, History of the World, Part I,* and *Murder by Death,* are examples. Several comedians, including Richard Pryor, Steve Martin, Eddie Murphy, and George Carlin brought scatological language to stage performances, and these were taped and distributed on cable television with much audience success. Commercials for laxatives, diapers, and products to protect against incontinence had been a part of broadcast advertising for some time, but scatology as a source of comedy was almost totally absent from broadcast television and radio until government, network, and local station regulation broke down. Cable television, which is unregulated, introduced so-called "adult" entertainment and, in an effort to compete, broadcast standards on networks became so loose as to be insignificant.

6. Maintenance of Bodily Temperature.   (This appears as "Exposure to the Elements," under "Danger Themes.")

ANIMAL THEMES

7. Wild Animals.   Wild animals themes include human versus animal and hunting themes. People have always been fascinated by animals. Many, if not most, primitive societies identified with a particular animal (a totem), and totems almost invariably were wild, rather than domesticated, animals. In ancient times, people painted pictures of wild animals on cave walls, and the shaman, wearing an animal skin and mask, danced in honor of the totem. Many of Hercules' labors dealt with wild animals, including the Nemean Lion, the Great Boar, the Bull of Crete, the Man-Eating Mares, and Cerberus, the three-headed dog. Other stories of wild animals include the Tarzan books and movies; "killer" movies, including *Killer Bees, Killer Fish, Killer Grizzly, Killer Leopard, Killer Shark,* and *The Killer Shrews;* also, *Jaws, Cujo, Elephant Walk, Attack of the Crab Monsters,* and *Attack of the Giant Leeches.* The wild animal theme is seen in bull fights, cock fights, pit-bull fights, as well as in lion-taming acts. Marine World, Africa USA centers around wild animals that have been "tamed." Many circus acts feature once-wild animals.

8. Animals Acting Like Humans.   We seem always to have found amusement in depicting animals as acting like humans, or in training animals to imitate humans. Think of Aesop's Fables, Elsie the Borden Cow, Smoky the Bear, Morris the Cat, Garfield, Fred Basset, Mr. Ed, Lassie, Mickey Mouse, Daffy Duck, Goofy, Road Runner, Pepe Le Pew, Sylvester the

Cat, and Tweetie Bird. We also take pleasure in watching chimps dressed as humans and acting like humans.

9. Humans Pretending to be Animals.   Humans mimic animals in ritual hunting dances, totemistic rites, and in puberty initiation rites. Today, we sometimes see people wearing animal suits—a gorilla suit, for example—or a pair of people dressed in a cow or a horse costume. We often see people wearing animal masks at costume parties. Gary Larson's *Far Side* frequently has humans acting like animals, as well as the reverse of this. Despite these few examples, the theme of humans pretending to be animals is not a prominent one in today's public arts, but was quite prominent in earlier societies.

10. Serpents.   Serpents are listed separately from wild animals because they seem to occupy a special, probably archetypal, niche. Examples abound: The myth of Laocoön; Medusa, with her coiffure of snakes; the Israelites' identification of Satan with the serpent; the serpent tempting Eve; the death of Cleopatra by the bite of a snake; fundamentalist snake handlers; snake charmers; the snake pit in *Raiders of the Lost Ark;* stories of rattlesnakes in the desert, boa constrictors in the jungle, and cobras in India. The Aztecs were but one of several meso-American societies that held snakes in special reverence. (See the many references to snakes in Campbell's *The Masks of God,* and in Frazer's *The Golden Bough.*)

11. Hybrid and Imaginary Animals.   Fantastic animals have appeared in folklore since ancient times: the unicorn; the Phoenix; dragons; mermaids; gargoyles; King Kong; the Golem; Godzilla; the Cyclops; the Minotaur; Cerberus (the three-headed dog); satyrs; the Yeti; Bigfoot; in recent public arts, *The Thing; The Creature from the Black Lagoon;* many creatures in *The Far Side.*

12. Animal-Gods.   Animal-gods, while not important in today's public arts, were very important in most primitive societies. Both Campbell and Frazer treat the prevalence of animal-gods in these societies (see their sections on "totems").

DANGER THEMES

13. Pestilence.   Public arts dealing with the theme of pestilence include *The Decameron; The Mask of the Red Death* (Poe); Joseph's plagues in Egypt; one of the Four Horsemen of the Apocalypse; Typhoid Mary; the 1978 movie *Plague; The Omega Man; The Andromeda Strain;* and *Panic in the Streets.*

Plague was a present but not prominent theme in the public arts of recent times until the identification of AIDS in 1980. After the nature of this disease became known, several plays, movies, and television programs addressed our growing preoccupation with the theme of plague. In 2001, following terrorists attacks on the World Trade Center, anthrax spores were mailed to several prominent figures in news and politics. The fact that discussions of anthrax dominated the news for weeks underscores our vulnerability to fears of pestilence that lurk within us, like spores, patiently waiting to be activated by new developments.

14. Flood.   Examples of floods occur in Noah and the Deluge; celebrations of the annual inundation of the Nile; the 1976 disaster movie *Flood!;* the movies *Earthquake, The River;* and many others about rivers where floods are common occurrences. Today, however, because most rivers have been dammed, which prevents most flooding, the theme of flood has lost some of its impact.

15. Famine.   Examples of famines throughout history include: one of the Four Horsemen of the Apocalypse; the famine that brought Joseph's brother to Egypt; the film *Soylent Green* and *Shoes of the Fisherman.* Today, famine is treated on news and in documentaries (Somalia, Bosnia, Sudan, Afghanistan, etc.), but in this society occurs infrequently as a theme in the storytelling arts.

16. Fire.   Fire, as one of the four elements, has long been a theme in public arts: ancient fire festivals; Prometheus, the bringer of fire; Loki; hell scenes; Moses and the burning bush; burnings at the stake; Hephestus; walking on burning coals; fire eaters; burnt offerings; films, including *The Towering Inferno; Quest for Fire.* Today, buildings on fire and forest fires are very big on television newscasts. See the lengthy discussion of fire in Frazer's *The Golden Bough.*

17. Exposure to the Elements.   This is one important element in many stories that feature other themes, including being marooned or lost in the wilderness: *Robinson Crusoe; Swiss Family Robinson; Avalanche!; The Odyssey; Lawrence of Arabia; Snowbound; Outcasts of Poker Flat; Lifeboat; Bridge on the River Kwai; Lost Horizon.* In past ages, exposure was a form of execution.

18. Darkness.   Darkness continues to be an important theme today as it was in ancient times: Moses' plague of darkness (Exodus 10:21); darkness on Calvary (Matthew 27:45); eclipses; black clothing as the mark of a villain; darkness in stories of werewolves, Dracula, or Frankenstein's monster; *Wait Until Dark; Gaslight; Blackout; The Dark.* Fear of darkness is used in commercials, such as flashlight ads.

19. Earthquakes.   As a natural phenomenon that cannot be controlled, earthquake themes remain universal. Many stories of earthquakes appear in the Bible, including Zechariah 14.5; movies about San Francisco; *Earthquake;* the buffalo as the cause of earthquakes (folk explanations from Bali, Flores, Borneo, Bulgaria); in other parts of the world earthquakes occur because of a restless hog, turtle, serpent, crab, fish, or frog; both the Hebrew and Christian religions have explained earthquakes as God's wrath.

20. Physical Traps and Fear of Being Buried Alive.   Being trapped or buried alive is related to claustrophobia. It's often associated with the themes of earthquakes, avalanches, ship sinkings, submarines, underground mining; darkness, and drowning; many space, submarine, and scuba-diving stories; Poe's *The Premature Burial;* mazes; houses of mirrors; *Aida;* quicksand as an element in stories; *The Poseidon Adventure; Marooned; Raiders of the Lost Ark; The Deep; Murder by Death; Man in the Iron Mask; Whatever Happened to Baby Jane?*

21. Physically Deformed Persons.   In past ages, and down to rather recent times, people who showed a physical deviation from the norm were often seen as evil or magical. Dwarfs, giants, people with misshapen limbs, and even such "deviants" as red-haired persons, twins, or left-handed persons were discriminated against. Many villains have been depicted as physical deviants from the norm. Examples include Medusa; Goliath; the Niebelungen; Shakespeare's Richard III; the Phantom of the Opera; Captain Hook in *Peter Pan;* Hephaestus (Vulcan); Frankenstein's monster, and Igor; *The Face Behind the Mask* (Peter Lorre); Mr. Hyde, in *Dr. Jekyll and Mr. Hyde* (no relation); *The House of Wax; The Hunchback of Notre Dame; Pyro;* and *Dracula.* Note that several of these physical "deviations" were the result of an injury, often caused by a fire.

"Physical deviation" is a helpful tool in assessing the level of development of a given society: at the lowest level, physical deviants are exiled or put to death; at a higher level, physical deviants are tolerated, but are seen as comical; at a still higher level, physical deviants are accepted, but often pitied; at the highest level, physical deviants are not only accepted, but are seen as one or more of the infinite variations of the human condition. (See also No. 53, Ridicule of Societal Deviants.)

22. Mental Derangement.   As with physical deviations from the norm, mental derangement and the way it is treated in the public arts tells us much about the culture that portrays it. Some societies killed mentally deranged persons; some laughed at them; while others have tried to understand and treat mentally deranged persons. In a few cultures, mentally deranged persons were seen as being in touch with God; more commonly, however, mentally ill persons were seen either as being possessed by the Devil or as being punished by God for a committed sin. There are two aspects to this fear: the fear of mentally deranged persons; and the fear of becoming mentally deranged. Examples in the public arts of mentally deranged antagonists include *The Cabinet of Dr. Caligari;* stories of Jack the Ripper and Bluebeard; Caligula; *Sweeny Todd; House of Wax; Rasputin;* and several Hitchcock films. Examples of the fear of going insane include *Gaslight* and *One Flew Over the Cuckoo's Nest.* (See also No. 53, Ridicule of Societal Deviants.)

23. Spells.   Spells appear in voodoo, hypnotism, and black magic, in *Sleeping Beauty, Snow White, The Frog Prince, Beauty and the Beast* (and endless variations), *The Spell, The Witch, The Dunwich Horror, The Brotherhood of Satan,* and *Curse of the Voodoo.* In addition to evil spells, there are spells associated with love potions: *Paolo and Francesca, Tristan und Isolde, Elixir of Love,* and the song, "Love Potion Number Nine."

24. Mutilation.   The theme of mutilation has a long and popular history. Examples include the dismemberment of Osiris; the self-mutilation of Bata in the *Tale of Two Brothers;* much Elizabethan drama, including Shakespeare's *Titus Andronicus,* Marlowe's *Tamerlane,* and Kyd's *The Spanish Tragedie;* many paintings of the martyrdom of saints (John the Baptist was beheaded, as was Holofernes; one saint was sawed in half, and another had his intestines pulled out and rolled up on a capstan); religious reliquaries (the mummified tongue of St. Anthony is on display in Padua); for many years, the pickled head of Joaquin Murietta and the hand of Three-Fingered Jack were displayed at carnivals. Many movies have shown us mutilation, including *Spartacus, Psycho, Dressed to Kill,* and dozens of horror films. The

Parisian theatre, The Grand Guignol, for many years featured mutilations on stage. Recent films, including *Indiana Jones and the Temple of Doom,* and *Raiders of the Lost Ark,* as well as several films by Sam Peckinpaugh (*The Killer Elite*) and Brian DePalma (for example, *Dressed to Kill*) have reveled in mutilation scenes.

25. Cannibalism.   People have practiced cannibalism at various times and some societies viewed it as a natural or spiritual act. For the most part, though, societies have viewed cannibalism as a revolting and subhuman practice. It most likely isn't a universal theme, but it does appear in the public arts. In most so-called "primitive" societies, the eating of human flesh usually was an intergral part of a public ritual—coming of age, preparing for battle, or celebrating a victory. A few works in the public arts that show us cannibalism include The Cyclops in *The Odyssey;* Shakespeare's *Titus Andronicus;* the book and movie *Alive!;* stories of the Donner Party; and the movies *Eating Raoul, I Was a Teenage Werewolf, Quest for Fire, C.H.U.M.* (Cannibalistic Humanoid Underground Dwellers), *The Corpse Grinders; The Beast Must Die!; The Texas Chainsaw Massacre,* and *Sweeney Todd.*

26. War.   War stories are apparently eternal and universal, ranging from *The Iliad* to *Saving Private Ryan.* Viewers of cable television could view the following war stories during a single month: *Across the Pacific, Air America, Bataan, The Blue and the Gray, Casablanca Express, Command Decision, Commando, Delta Force* and *Delta Force 3: The Killing Game, Flight of the Intruder, Hamburger Hill, The Last Train from Madrid, Passport to Suez, Counter-Espionage, The Mortal Storm, Off Limits, O.S.S., Pork Chop Hill, Run Silent, Run Deep, Sergeant York,* and *Vera Cruz.* (This list does not include stories of "Indian Wars," or stories of pre- and postwar adventures.) Additionally, viewers of cable channels such as Arts and Entertainment (A&E), The History Channel, and Discovery generally have war documentaries available on a weekly basis.

    War stories include many themes—heroism, deprivation, courage, mutilation, fear, death, etc, yet there is also the theme of war as a preoccupation. Stories that take place on the battlefield sometimes provide us with antiwar messages, even as we covertly enjoy the danger, the suspense, and the inevitable carnage. America's preoccupation with Operation Desert Storm and later with the Afghanistan campaign is illustrative of the public's fascination with war.

27. Executions.   Executions of various kinds have long held the public's attention. Beheadings include stories of the Gorgon, Medusa, Perseus and Andromeda, Judith and Holofernes, Salome and John the Baptist. Death by hanging is found in stories of all ages, including several in the Old and New Testaments of the Bible (Judas hanged himself), the song "Tom Dooley," the poem "Danny Deaver," and the film, *The Ox-Bow Incident. The Execution of Private Slovik* and *The Death of a Princess* are two made-for-television films involving executions. Executions in the electric chair or the gas chamber have been featured in many films. The burning of Joan of Arc at the stake has been told many times in books and films.

    Christian painters and sculptors through the Middle Ages and the Renaissance delighted in depicting the executions of saints and martyrs: there are many versions of the death of St. Sebastian, killed by arrows; the stoning of St. Stephen, the beheading of St. Paul, the crucifixion of St. Peter, the stoning and clubbing of St. James, and the death by the sword of St. Cyprian.

28. Drowning. The universal fear of drowning is associated with physical traps and floods. Unlike themes such as mutilation or executions, drowning usually involves an accident rather than an act by an enemy; because it lacks an antagonist, it's not compatible with a "good versus evil" melodrama. While it appears in many stories and is a universal fear, drowning is not a major theme in the public arts.

29. Being Marooned. There are many stories in the public arts of being marooned, including *The Odyssey, Robinson Crusoe, Swiss Family Robinson, Lord of the Flies, Lost in Space, Gilligan's Island, Swept Away, Donner Pass, The Road to Survival, Marooned, The Admirable Crichton, Shipwreck Island, The Blue Lagoon, The Green Goddess, Greystoke, Lost Flight, Lost Horizon,* and, in a somewhat different sense, *Lifeboat.*

30. Fear of Heights (Fear of Falling). Trapeze and tightrope performances, ferris wheels, amusement park parachute jumps, skydiving, hang gliding, and roller coasters tantalize our universal fear of falling (have you ever dreamed you were falling?). Fear of heights pops up in many adventure films as one of several danger themes.

31. Perilous Journey. The perilous journey is a big theme. The perilous-journey format provides the opportunity for the introduction of a great variety of danger or fear themes, including fear of heights, fear of serpents, fear of drowning, and so forth. The relationship between the perilous journey theme and rite-of-passage rituals, particularly in tribal initiation, is obvious.

Some perilous journey stories are characterized by extreme and continuous peril, such as *Raiders of the Lost Ark* and *Journey to the Center of the Earth*. In other stories, such as *Huckleberry Finn*, the danger is less frightening, and often gives way to incidents of humor or human interest. There are several categories of "perilous journey" stories:

I. *The Quest*—searching for something or someone, or seeking a specific goal. Moses and the Promised Land; Brigham Young and the Mormons; the Holy Grail; Inanna's Descent into the Underworld; Jason and the Golden Fleece; *Journey to the Center of the Earth; The African Queen; Raiders of the Lost Ark; Romancing the Stone; Parsifal; Wagon Train; Gilgamesh* (Mesopotamian); *Knights of the Round Table; Aliens; Don Quixote; Lawrence of Arabia; The Overlanders; Moby Dick.*

II. *The Flight—Three Days of the Condor; The Informer; The Tale of Two Brothers* (Egyptian); *Gwion Bach* (Wales); *Odd Man Out; The Lost Patrol; The Most Dangerous Game; Huckleberry Finn.*

III. *The Long Journey Home—The Odyssey; The Wizard of Oz; Aeneas; Lost in Space; Lassie Come Home; Honey, I Shrunk the Kids; Hansel and Gretel.*

IV. *The Wanderer—*The Wandering Jew; *The Flying Dutchman; Candide; Easy Rider.*

IMAGINARY CREATURES THEMES

32. Ghosts.   Ghosts have been an important part of rituals and public arts since prehistory. Ghosts are sometimes friendly (departed ancestors who return for food and homage), but more often than not, they're malevolent and to be feared. Ghosts appear in stories as dissimilar as *Hamlet* and *Ghostbusters*. There are ghost stories from ancient Mesopotamia and Egypt. Ghosts appear in the public arts and ceremonies of people from all parts of the world. Some stories in which ghosts appear: *Topper; Caspar, the Friendly Ghost; The Ghost and Mrs. Muir; Ghost in the Invisible Bikini; The Invisible Creature; Ghost Breakers; Ghost Chasers; Ghost Catchers; The Ghost of Frankenstein;* and *The Ghost Goes West*. Ghosts will always be with us (better lock that door!).

33. Witches.   Witches appear in stories from many lands. A few examples include *Macbeth, Hansel and Gretel, The Wizard of Oz, Rosemary's Baby, The Omen, The Other, The Brotherhood of Satan, Burn, Witch, Burn, The Dunwich Horror, The Witch, Witchcraft '70, I Married a Witch, I Dream of Jeannie, The Addams Family, Bewitched,* and *Witches of Salem*.

34. Vampires.   We know about vampires chiefly through the story by Bram Stoker, but tales and poems of vampires go back thousands of years, to Mesopotamian times—perhaps as far back as 5,000 B.C. Blood has long been recognized as the fluid of life, and the drinking of human blood has enjoyed the same ups and downs as has cannibalism: in some cultures, it is an important part of solemn rituals. For most societies, though, the drinking of blood is repugnant. A few examples of vampires in the public arts are *Dracula, The Bat, Queen of Blood, Nosferatu, Track of the Vampire, The Last Man on Earth, Count Yorga, Vampire, The Vampire Lovers, Love at First Bite, Interview with a Vampire, Dracula Saga,* and *Buffy The Vampire Slayer*.

35. Werewolves.   A werewolf is a person who changes or transforms him- or herself into a wolf. This is but one variation of transformations into carnivorous animals, the particular animal being determined by the region of the world in which the legend is told. The man/beast is a bear-man in Scandinavia; a jaguar-man in South America; a tiger- or leopard-man in Asia and Africa; and a wolf-man in Central Europe. Sometimes called "lycanthropes," werewolves were known to the ancient Greeks and Romans and appear in early stories of Armenia, Scandinavia, India, Africa, Japan, Bulgaria, Romania, and South America. We know this transformed person best as a wolf-man, or werewolf. He appears in such stories as Michael Jackson's *Thriller, Werewolf of London, The Wolf Man, I Was a Teenage Werewolf, Frankenstein Meets the Wolf Man, The Werewolf, Moon of the Wolf, Werewolves on Wheels, The Howling,* and *Dr. Jekyll and the Wolf Man*.

36. Ghouls.   Ghouls eat human corpses. Although they're related to vampires and cannibals, they're a distinct species. Unlike cannibals, ghouls are imaginary creatures, even though from time to time history records demented persons eating corpses. The ghoul has appeared in the public arts since prehistory. The earliest written record of ghouls comes from

Mesopotamia. Ghouls appear in the folk literature of the Hindu culture, and they appear as jinns in the Koran. Ghouls are mentioned in *The Arabian Nights,* and they appear in the folklore of Japan and the Philippines. Ghouls have played a role in some American movies, including *Donovan's Brain, Isle of the Dead, The Mad Ghoul, Dawn of the Dead, Night of the Living Dead,* and *The Walking Dead.* These few examples would seem to indicate that ghoulish activities, while present in our public arts, are too horrible to be depicted on a widespread scale.

37. Mermaids.   (Finally, a pleasant imaginary creature!) Mermaids have been a part of folklore since at least Phoenician times. They're found in the legends and tales of Ireland, England, Scandinavia, Germany, and Denmark. The movies have given us a few mermaids in such films as *Mr. Peabody and the Mermaid, The Mermaids of Tiburon,* and *Splash!* A mermaid is used as a logo for Chicken of the Sea tuna. P. T. Barnum displayed a mummified mermaid. Mermaids are featured in many children's stories. Mermaids are depicted more often in the graphic and plastic arts, than in the storytelling arts, perhaps because of their visual power.

38. Dragons.   The dragon is an ill-defined creature that varies from the contemporary version (four legs, scales, wings, breathing fire) to giant snakes. Because of this, it is sometimes impossible to determine the physical appearance of dragons in ancient myths and legends. It's clear that large, dangerous reptiles called dragons are of widespread, if not universal, concern. The dragon is the national symbol of China, and both the Chinese and the Japanese depict dragons in visual arts and legends. Dragonlike creatures are mentioned in the *Iliad,* in *Beowulf,* and in both the Old and the New testaments. Dragons are also found in Wagner's *Siegfried,* in stories of St. George, and in tales of King Arthur. Dragons have fallen on bad times in today's public arts, and have generally given way to prehistoric creatures or newly invented creatures, including those in *Godzilla, The Beast from 20,000 Fathoms, Destroy All Monsters, Valley of the Gwangi, Twenty Million Miles to Earth, Track of the Moonbeast, Return of the Giant Monster, Reptilicus,* and *Monster from the Prehistoric Planet.*

39. Half-Human, Half-Beast.   Satyrs, mermaids, Caliban, Enkidu, Pan, centaurs, and similar imaginary creatures aren't very popular in the public arts of America, but they enjoyed a lengthy reign in the stories and statues of the ancient world.

40. Giants.   Again, not very popular today. Giants include the Titans, Goliath, the Cyclops, Gog and Magog, Fafner and Fasolt in Wagner's *Das Rheingold,* and *Jack and the Beanstalk.*

SEX THEMES

41. Heterosexual Erotic Sex Themes.   Heterosexual sex themes have been part of the public arts forever. Prehistoric Venuses, Enkidu and the prostitute, Song of Songs, pinups, magazines such as *Playboy, Playgirl, Oui,* and *Penthouse;* belly dancing; strip-tease shows;

most pornographic movies; some movies that also feature romantic love, adventure, and so forth.

42. Taboo Sex Themes. Taboos vary from culture to culture and from time to time. Because of this, specific themes may not be universal; what is universal is the notion that some sex practices are unacceptable. Incest, orgies, homosexuality, sodomy, and bestiality (sex with animals) are often considered taboo by various societies, but remember: in Egypt, marriage (and therefore sex) between brother and sister was approved of; in Greece, homosexuality and sodomy were widespread and were accepted as normal; and orgies were an accepted part of Roman life. In many, but not all, societies, sex with prepubescent children has been seen as unacceptable, but only in recent times has this subject been dealt with openly in the public arts as child abuse.

43. Rape and Abduction. Until fairly recently, rape and abduction were not viewed as repugnant by those who created the public arts. Examples of rape seen as either natural or acceptable include The Rape of Europa, *The Sheik, Swept Away,* and many pornographic films in which a woman resists rape for a time, and then succumbs with delight. (For some, this may be a wish-fulfillment theme.) Because rape is now seen for what it truly is—a violent crime—we can expect to see it portrayed as unacceptable and repugnant in more and more stories, movies, and television shows.

44. Sex as Humor. Many scenes in the comedies of Aristophanes; dirty jokes, songs, and stories; underground paintings by major artists, including Rowlandson and Picasso; Groucho Marx; many situation comedies on television; and many movies.

WISH-FULFILLMENT THEMES

45. Utopia. Utopias include the Golden Age, Paradise, the Good Old Days, the Garden of Eden, Platonic and Aristotelian Utopias, Shangri-La in *Lost Horizon, The Green Pastures,* and *2001.* Examples of the good old days include Camelot, Robin Hood, the Gay Nineties, the '50s (*American Graffiti* and *Happy Days*) and many westerns and stories of the South Pacific.

46. Romantic Love. Romantic love is a feature of many fairy tales, melodramas and comedies, medieval romances, soap operas, *Romeo and Juliet,* tin pan alley songs, Barbara Cartland and Harlequin romances, *Love Story, The Way We Were, West Side Story, Love Is Forever, Love Letters, Love Me Tender, Love with the Proper Stranger, Lovesick, Love Crazy, Love from Paris,* and *Sleepless in Seattle.* Historically, this is one of the most important universal themes, and was so even during the days of arranged marriages.

47. Magic and Miracles. Miraculous occurrences in the epics of *Gilgamesh, the Odyssey, Beowulf, Chanson de Roland,* and the *Niebelungenied;* miracles in both the Old and New Testaments; miracles of saints; Merlin; *1,001 Arabian Nights; Miracle on 34th Street; I Dream of Jeannie;* and *Bewitched.*

48. Get-Rich-Quick.   Getting rich quick has been a preoccupation of more modern times: Any rags-to-riches story; stories of lost mines, buried treasure, or the discovery of sunken treasure; television game shows, such as *Wheel of Fortune, Jeopardy, Who Wants to be a Millionaire?* Many adventure movies, such as *Harrowhouse 11, Money to Burn,* or *Treasure of the Sierra Madre;* winning big at the gambling table.

49. Eternal Youth.   The quest for eternal youth is not a prominent theme in the public arts, but very important in advertising for hair restorers, wrinkle removers, age-spot removers, plastic surgery, etc. In the public arts, this theme is to be found in the story of Ponce de Leon, *Lost Horizon, Dr. Faustus,* and stories of Hebe, the Greek Goddess of youth.

50. Magical Transformations.   Magical transformation is a major theme in the public arts. In the earliest stories, transformations take place as a matter of course, and are not seen as unusual (the Egyptian *Tale of Two Brothers* and Mesopotamian *Gilgamesh*). In later times, magical transformations are seen as miraculous; for example, in *Cinderella; The Ugly Duckling; Superman, Batman; Spiderman;* many Disney movies, including *Beauty and the Beast;* and *The Frog Prince.* Some transformations are physical, some psychological, and some are both, as in *Dr. Jekyll and Mr. Hyde* and *The Picture of Dorian Gray.* Some are good, and some are evil. Many products promise a magical transformation: bust developers, diets, wigs, hair dyes (Blondes have more fun!), and certain types of wearing apparel (The pants that turn a dude into a stud!).

51. Innocence of Youth.   The innocence of youth was not a very prominent theme in early times, but it can be found in Andy Hardy movies, Eugene O'Neill's *Ah, Wilderness, Leave It to Beaver, My Three Sons, Father Knows Best, The Partridge Family, Mayberry R.F.D.,* and *The Waltons.* This is an important aspect of comedy of the naive.

52. Ridicule of Authority Figures.   One of the major themes in the public arts of any free society, or ancient society that allowed a period of license is ridicule of authority. This theme relates to unmasking, caricature, and hostile wit. This is the ridicule of choice for many stand-up comics today. Many television sitcoms ridicule authority figures for laughs: *M*A*S*H, Hogan's Heroes, Sergeant Bilko,* and *Beverly Hillbillies.* Political cartoonists use exaggerated features to ridicule politicians.

53. Ridicule of Societal Deviants.   Societal deviants vary from culture to culture and change from time to time, but all societies regard some actions and physical appearances as being unacceptable. (Today most Americans view both the actions and the appearance of skinheads as unacceptable deviations from the norm.) The ridicule of societal deviants illustrates a low level of hostility. With high-level hostility, direct action is taken, including punishment, exile, or extermination. With a lower level of hostility (or where laws protect deviants), people handle their aggressive instincts through hostile wit.[3]

Until recently, hostile witticisms were directed toward alcoholics; people with mental disabilities, speech impediments, or severe physical disabilities; gays and lesbians; and people from nondominant races or religions. All of these depictions may yet be seen in old movies still shown on television. For the most part, however, laughter directed at societal deviants has disappeared from our public arts—except in the work of a few comedians, such as Don Rickles.

Sympathetic portrayals of people who possess physical or mental disabilities became vogue in the public arts in the 1980s and 1990s, and included films such as *Elephant Man, Mask, The Rain Man, Being There, Bill, Children of a Lesser God,* and *Tell Me That You Love Me, Junie Moon.*

Ridicule of societal deviants can be useful when directed against hypocritical politicians, superpatriotic militarists, racists, and others whose actions are seen as unacceptable. We see examples of hostile wit directed against such persons chiefly in political cartoons, and comic strips such as Doonesbury.

54. Evil Punished. From the very beginning of public arts, audiences have taken delight in seeing evil people punished. Most epics, myths, legends, melodramas, and fairy tales involve the punishment of evildoers. We've seen this theme in James Bond movies, *Superman, Hawaii Five-O, Hill Street Blues, Charlie's Angels, Kojak, Miami Vice, Perry Mason, Cannon, Starsky and Hutch, Cagney and Lacey,* and *Dirty Harry.* Many daytime serials (soap operas) involve bad people who eventually are punished.

55. Virtue Rewarded. Rewarding virtue is the flip side of evil punished. Nearly every story that shows evil people includes virtuous people to oppose them. Most melodramas, myths, legends, epics, and fairy tales present us with heroes (male and female), and most end with the good agents triumphing over the evil agents. The theme of virtue rewarded is found in nearly every cowboy movie, in detective and cop stories, and in many Disney films.

56. The Worm Turns. The theme of the weak becoming strong has been very popular for centuries. Any story in which the protagonist is kicked around during most of the actions, and in the end manages to overcome the antagonist, is an example of this theme. Popeye combines this theme with that of evil punished, and we nearly always find these two themes working together in certain types of melodramas. We also see this theme in professional wrestling matches, where the hero takes a terrible beating from a cheating villain, only to finally give up being Mr. Nice Guy, and in turn beating up on the cheating bully. Several movies have been made in which a reformed outlaw allows himself to be pushed around for most of the film, only to eventually strap on his guns and bring about justice.

LOVE THEMES

57. Heterosexual Love. Despite the fact that homosexuality goes back to prehistory, only recently has it been portrayed with any frequency in the public arts. For the most part, love in the public arts has been love between men and women. The "boy meets girl, boy loses girl, boy gets girl" formula goes back as far as we can see in antiquity. We find it in such Greek tales as *Pyramus and Thisbe, Orpheus and Eurydice,* and *Pygmalion and Galatea.* Shakespeare used this theme in such plays as *As You Like It* and *Romeo and Juliet.* We see heterosexual love portrayed on both day and nighttime soap operas, and in many, many movies and television dramas. This theme is also the basis of the lyrics of tens of thousands of songs and is the focus of popular romance novels, such as Harlequin Romances.

58. Homosexual Love.   This is not truly a universal theme in the public arts, undoubtedly because it's been a tabooed practice in many cultures and ages. However, the theme can be traced back to Homeric times (ninth century B.C.). Sappho, who flourished in the seventh century B.C. and hailed from the isle of Lesbos, wrote exquisite poems celebrating lesbianism.[4] The Greek poet Anacreon (sixth century B.C.) celebrated "wine, women, and boys." In modern times, the Gay Liberation movement brought homosexual love back into the public arts. It was championed in autobiographies by Tennessee Williams and Christopher Isherwood, and was a featured aspect of the movies *Death Trap, Down and Out in Beverly Hills, Victor/Victoria,* and *La Cage aux Folles.* Homosexuality was a prominent feature of the cable television series *Brothers. In Living Color* often featured two gay men in comic sketches. There are many pornographic films that feature homosexuality, some with and some without love. We can expect to see more works in the public arts dealing with this theme.

59. Forbidden Love.   Homosexual love was represented as forbidden just prior to the present period. *The Children's Hour* by Lillian Hellman dealt with this tabooed subject, as did a few other plays and stories. For the most part, though, forbidden love has focused on parental objections—*Romeo and Juliet;* religious differences—*Abie's Irish Rose;* incest—*Oedipus Rex, Phaedra, Coyote Marries His Daughter* (Native American tale); interracial love—*Guess Who's Coming to Dinner;* or great age difference—*South Pacific, Knickerbocker Holiday.* Several popular songs of a few years ago dealt with this latter problem ("Young Girl" by The Union Gap, and "Come up the Years.")

60. Familial Love.   Familial love is a universal theme: the Prodigal Son; parent-child love; clan loyalty; sibling love; husband-wife love. Some examples: *My Son, My Son; Heidi; Hansel and Gretel; The Sound of Music* (the von Trapp family); *My Three Sons; Leave It to Beaver; Father Knows Best; The Partridge Family;* and *The Thin Man.* The Bundy family in *Married . . . With Children,* is a rare exception to the romanticizing of family relationships, as is *The Simpsons.* There often is conflict between family members (or there would be little drama), but the family love-bond is present in most stories of families—the exceptions being those stories that center around parent-child conflict or sibling rivalry.

61. Romantic Love.   (see Wish-Fulfillment themes).

62. Lost or Unrequited Love.   Lost or unrequited love has long been a theme in the public arts. Examples include: from Greek times—*Orpheus and Eurydice* and *Pyramus and Thisbe;* Elizabethan—*Romeo and Juliet;* nineteenth-century—*Cyrano de Bergerac;* more modern times—Chaplin's *City Lights.* Variations of this theme appear in *Madame Butterfly, The Blue Angel,* and *Porgy and Bess.*

ARCHETYPAL THEMES

63. God.   God appears as an archetypal theme chiefly, but not exclusively, in religious tales and rites. God appears as an agent in medieval Miracle and Mystery plays, but was not depicted in Christian graphic arts until the Italian Renaissance. Earlier theology forbade the depiction of the likeness of God, so God usually appeared as a hand coming out of a cloud. God (or gods) is a universal theme, but the specifics of appearance, nature, etc., are not universal. God is not a prominent theme in today's public arts, but the play *The Green Pastures* and the movie *Oh, God* give us two rare examples. In the days of the Mesopotamians, Egyptians, Greeks, and Romans, various gods appeared frequently in the stories, drawings, and plays of the public arts.

64. Satan.   Satan is seen in the public arts far more often than is God. A few examples: *Dr. Faustus* and *Faust, Der Freischutz, The Flying Dutchman, The Devil and Daniel Webster, Rosemary's Baby, The Exorcist,* and *The Omen.* Why is Satan more popular than God in our present day public arts?

65. Earth Mother.   Mother Earth is also known as Great Mother. This archetypal theme represents both sex and virginity! "The Queen of heaven, the daughter of god, goddess of the morning and evening star . . . who, as the morning star, is ever virgin, but, as the evening star, is the 'divine harlot.'"[5] This complex concept is difficult for the modern mind to grasp, but it centers around the maternal figure, the mother who succors and helps, and who also bestows fertility. Some manifestations in the ancient worlds are Astarte (Phoenicia); Cybele (Phrygia); Ishtar (Babylonia); Rhea (Crete); Atargatis (Canaan); Isis (Egypt); Anaitis (Persia); Inanna (Sumer); Aphrodite (Greece); and Venus (Rome).[6]

Who represents Earth Mother today? In some ways, we see her in modern movie queens, although most are long on sex and short on the maternal aspects of this archetype. Perhaps we have lost this concept for our time, even though we can enjoy experiencing it in the public arts of the ancient past.

66. Wise Old Man.   Throughout history, the theme of the wise old man has been important: tribal elders, village priests, Solomon, Moses, Ben Franklin, gurus, Zen masters, Charlie Chan, Ben-Gurion, Gandhi, Albert Schweitzer, Albert Einstein, Walter Cronkite. In American society today, where the elderly are not universally held in great respect, we've lost some of our veneration for the Wise Old Man, and therefore he does not often appear as a theme in our popular arts.

67. Wise Old Woman.   The wise old woman, or crone, has also traditionally held much power: Queen Elizabeth I, Queen Victoria, Eleanor Roosevelt, Golda Meir, Mother Teresa, Jane Pittman. As with the Wise Old Man, and for the same reason, this theme isn't prominent in the public arts of our society today.

68. The Hero.   The hero has always been with us: Hercules, Achilles, Odysseus, El Cid, Robin Hood, the Knights of the Round Table, Simon Bolivar, Tarzan, Matt Dillon (*Gunsmoke*), Superman, Indiana Jones, Elliot Ness, Mr. T., John Wayne, Kunte Kinte (*Roots*), the Cisco Kid, Davy Crockett, the marshal in *High Noon,* The Lone Ranger, Zorro, Sgt. York, James Bond, Dirty Harry, many movie cowboys (including Tom Mix, Gene Autry, Hoot Gibson, and Roy Rogers), many movie detectives (including those played by Humphrey Bogart, Paul Newman, Robert Blake, and Clint Eastwood), Rambo, and Captain Kirk. Non-European heroes include Gilgamesh (Mesopotamia), Samson and David (Israel), Marduk (Babylonia), Osiris (Egypt), Quetzalcoatl (Aztecs and Toltecs), Onkonkwo (Igbo people of Africa), and Connla (the Celts).

69. The Heroine.[7]   Most of the women heroes I know are from the Western world, so I'm not certain that the heroine is a universal theme. Some examples: Isis, Ruth and Esther in the Old Testament, Electra, Antigone, Boadacea, Joan of Arc, Anne Frank, Wonder Woman, Sigourney Weaver in *Aliens,* Xena, Buffy.

70. Death.   The theme of death is not about the topic of death, but about its personification. We know Death today through depictions of the Grim Reaper, a figure with an hourglass and a scythe. Mexicans know Death as a skeleton, and Death is celebrated each year on the Dia de las Muertos. Medieval Europeans knew Death through depictions of the Dance of Death. In Africa, the Basumbwa see Death as a Chief; the Tenne see Death as a young man; and the Gagu see Death as the Demon of the Woods. The Hindus see Death as Yama, while the Japanese see Death as Emma O. In ancient Greece, Thanatos was the personification of Death, and he was seen as a winged youth. Death is seen as an undertaker in a top hat by Haitians, and the Central American Indians saw Death as a skeleton named Mitlantecuhtli. Despite his popularity in the past, as well as in some modern cultures, Death is seldom seen as an agent in today's public arts of the United States, but representations of the Grim Reaper abound on Hallowe'en.

71. Hell.   There are two main Hell themes: the first, a descent into Hell and a return to earth (*Orpheus and Eurydice; Inanna's Descent to the Underworld*); the second, the punishment of evil persons in Hell. The concept of some final resting place for the spirits of the dead seems universal. As far back as Neanderthal times, people were buried with food and tools for use in the afterlife. Ancient Mesopotamians went to The Palace of the Queen of Darkness; Native Americans went to the Happy Hunting Ground; to the Hebrews, the resting place was Sheol, a terrible pit; Hell or Hades (by whatever name) was accepted by Buddhists, Hindus, Moslems, Chinese, Greeks, Tibetans, Zoroastrians, and Christians. Hell is not a prominent theme in today's public arts.

72. Rebirth and Resurrection.   Rebirth and resurrection are related to the cycling of the seasons, the death and rebirth of vegetation. Osiris, Tammuz, Christ, and many others died and were reborn. Some aspects of this theme appear from time to time in science fiction movies, but the motivation is far different. While no longer popular, it does exist here and there, for example the theme of *Frosty, the Snowman.*

73. Fertility and Infertility. Fertility rites developed in most, if not all, early societies for two purposes: to guarantee a bountiful crop; and to guarantee the reproduction of the human species. Infertility is a theme in some soap operas, and there are many mentions of it in both the Old and New Testaments (Genesis 11:30, and Luke 23:29, for example). Medea, in the play of that name by Euripides, was rescued by a king searching for a cure for his wife's infertility. Infertility has lost much of its power as a theme in the Western world because: (1) Children are no longer seen as an economic necessity to work the fields; (2) overpopulation as a fear has caused many people to not want children; and, (3) various scientific advances have made infertility less common than in the past. This is, most likely, no longer a universal preoccupation in industrialized nations.

74. Parent versus Child. The counterpart to familial love is the theme of parent versus child, although both themes may be present in the same story. Examples of this theme occur in *Oedipus Rex;* Noah and his sons; Clytemnestra-Electra; Lear-Cordelia; Hamlet and his mother; *East of Eden;* the Prodigal Son; Homer Simpson; the children in *Married . . . With Children.*

75. Sibling Rivalry. Sibling rivalry, also known as the hostile brethren, dates back to our origins, at least in western cultures: Cain and Abel; Jacob and Esau; Joseph and his jealous brothers; Romulus and Remus; Polyneices and Eteocles; Lear's daughters; Cinderella; Ishtar and Ereshkigal; *Whatever Happened to Baby Jane?; East of Eden.*

76. War between the Sexes. Strife between male and female has always been a popular theme: Noah and his wife; Rip Van Winkle and his wife; Maggie and Jiggs; *The Honeymooners; Lysistrata; The Taming of the Shrew;* Thurber's *War Between Men and Women; Secret Life of Walter Mitty; Nine to Five; Kramer vs. Kramer; I Love Lucy; Married . . . With Children.*

77. The Outlaw Hero. People have long loved (and identified with?) the outlaw hero: Robin Hood; Jesse James; The Cisco Kid; Bonnie and Clyde; D. B. Cooper; *Butch Cassidy and the Sundance Kid.*

78. Loyal Companion. The theme of the loyal companion has always been prominent in the public arts: Enkidu (*Gilgamesh*); Little John (*Robin Hood*); Mercutio (*Romeo and Juliet*); Tonto (*The Lone Ranger*); Sancho Panza (*Don Quixote*); Leporello (*Don Juan*); Punjab (*Little Orphan Annie*); Robin (*Batman*); Gabrielle (*Xena*).

79. Braggart Warrior. Braggart warriors were more popular in earlier times: Miles Gloriosus; Falstaff; Colonel Blimp. Saddam Hussein? This is an interesting theme, but it may not be universal.

80. The Trickster or Mischief Maker. The trickster has been an important theme in almost all societies: Brer Rabbit; Loki; Til Eulenspiegel; North American Indian tricksters;

Hermes; Maui; Harpo Marx; Donald Duck's nephews; Katzenjammer Kids; the Roadrunner (cartoon); Eloise; Prometheus; John Belushi.

NONUNIVERSAL THEMES OF HUMAN ACTUALIZATION

Most of the themes in this appendix have appeared in the public arts of many different societies over a span of several millennia and may be considered universal. The eleven themes that follow probably are not universal, but most are listed by Abraham Maslow as growth needs. They're themes that would only appear in the arts of a culture that had evolved beyond a deficiency-need stage. As you examine Maslow's list of growth needs, and relate them to themes in the public arts, you'll note that they don't appear regularly in the public arts of the United States, but can be found in some movies, including *The Verdict, Gandhi, A Passage to India, Chariots of Fire,* and *All the President's Men,* that concern themselves with justice, truth, individuality, simplicity, meaningfulness, and other growth themes.

At the same time, you'll not find such themes in typical situation comedies or police stories on television. This reality supports the concept that the human drive to meet deficiency needs comes before the drive to meet growth needs. Perhaps this explains why comedies and melodramas have been more popular with audiences over the centuries than have tragedies that deal with moral choices. The importance of growth themes is that they point us in the direction of enhanced humanness. Anyone responsible for creating or programming works in the public arts should be aware of the potential for human growth inherent in these themes. Properly developed in works of art, they may be of some value in helping people grow toward self-actualization. The themes are listed here with little amplification.

1. **Freedom.** The Jews in Babylon and Egypt; Spartacus; John Brown; Nat Turner.
2. **Justice.** Solomon; Themis; The Furies. This is much more profound than the apprehension and punishment of lawbreakers. It deals with the concept of justice, not with the concept of law. It deals with fairness and orderliness.
3. **Truth.** Pure, clean, and unadulterated truth; Oedipus; Phoebus (Apollo).
4. **Order.** Battle between the forces of darkness and the forces of light, and of chaos versus order; Manichaeonism.
5. **Beauty.** Concepts of form; rightness; perfection; completion.
6. **Perfection.** Garden of Eden; Utopia; *The Republic, Nichomachaean Ethics.*
7. **Morality.** Rightness; Moses; Christ; stories of moral choice; codes of ethics.
8. **Spirituality.** The need or desire to believe that spiritual or moral values are more important than is mere physical existence, and that spiritual or moral values are more important than material goods. Where do these topics appear in our public arts?
9. **Individuality.** Self-sufficiency; separateness; independence; self-determination; autonomy.
10. **Commitment to others.** Goodness; transcendence of the self.
11. **Peace.** An absence of war; a state of security; People respecting the rights of others.

NOTES

1. To emphasize the fact that this list, while not arbitrary, is incomplete I want to mention something that happened to me recently. As I listened to NPR, film critic John Powers was analyzing the film *Spy Game*. In describing the relationship between the old spy master and his protege, he mentioned the theme of "passing the torch," and added references to Obi Wan Kenobi (*Star Wars*) and *Harry Potter and the Sorcerer's Stone*. The three films Powers mentioned represent one of two ways in which the old gives way to the new: in the first, a tutor or mentor prepares a younger person for a nearly insurmountable task; the second sees a younger, stronger person taking control from one whose power is waning. How could I have overlooked this important theme with its two variants? My mind went into high gear as I thought of examples: Orderly passing of knowledge (power), Merlin–King Arthur; Master Po–Kwai Chang Caine (the television series *Kung Fu*); Curly and the city dudes in *City Slickers;* and Dr. Gillespie–Dr. Kildare (*Dr. Kildare,* a popular television series from 1961–1966.) The second variant is seen in *Blood and Sand, All About Eve, The Godfather*—the list goes on and on. So accept the themes described in this Appendix, because all appear over and over again in stories from all ages and places, but remember that the list will never be complete. What themes can you add?

2. Joseph Campbell, *The Masks of God: Primitive Mythology* (New York: The Viking Press, 1969), 72.

3. See the discussion of Niko Tinbergen's thoughts on this subject in Chapter 8, "The Anatomy of Comedy."

4. See a love poem by Sappho in Chapter 9.

5. Campbell, *The Masks of God,* 412.

6. For more information on this topic, see Chapter 10, "Mythological Thresholds of the Neolithic," in Campbell's *The Masks of God: Primitive Mythology.* A more complete study of women gods may be found in Merlin Stone's, *When God Was a Woman,* San Diego, CA: Harcourt Brace & Company, 1976.

7. I use this term with reluctance because both women and men can be heroes. Its use here is forced on me because the term is still widely used and is generally recognized.

ARTHUR MILLER'S ESSAY ON TRAGIC DRAMA IN THE MODERN WORLD

Arthur Miller, perhaps the most honored playwright of his time, is convinced that tragedy does not require a noble or otherwise exalted person as the tragic figure. His 1949 drama, *Death of a Salesman,* was both praised and panned by critics, some of whom felt that his central character, Willie Loman, was too common to be a fit subject for tragedy. Miller answered his critics in a now-famous essay, *Tragedy and the Common Man.* I feel that Miller needs no interpreters to make his case; his statement is here just as he wrote it.

TRAGEDY AND THE COMMON MAN
by Arthur Miller[1]

In this age few tragedies are written. It has often been held that the lack is due to a paucity of heroes among us, or else that modern man has had the blood drawn out of his organs of belief by the skepticism of science, and the heroic attack on life cannot feed on an attitude of reserve and circumspection. For one reason or another, we are often held to be below tragedy—or tragedy above us. The inevitable conclusion is, of course, that the tragic mode is archaic, fit only for the very highly placed, the kings or the kingly, and where this admission is not made in so many words it is most often implied.

I believe that the common man is as apt a subject for tragedy in its highest sense as kings were. On the face of it this ought to be obvious in the light of modern psychiatry, which bases its analysis upon classic formulations, such as the Oedipus and Orestes complexes, for instance, which were enacted by royal beings, but which apply to everyone in similar emotional situations.

More simply, when the question of tragedy in art is not at issue, we never hesitate to attribute to the well-placed and the exalted the very same mental processes as the lowly. And finally, if the exaltation of the tragic action were truly a property of the high-bred character alone, it is inconceivable that the mass of mankind should cherish tragedy above all other forms, let alone be capable of understanding it.

As a general rule, to which there may be exceptions unknown to me, I think the tragic feeling is invoked in us when we are in the presence of a character who is ready to lay down his life, if need be, to secure one thing—his sense of personal dignity. From Orestes to Hamlet,

Medea to Macbeth, the underlying struggle is that of the individual attempting to gain his "rightful" position in his society.

Sometimes, he is the one who has been displaced from it, sometimes one who seeks to attain it for the first time, but the fateful wound from which the inevitable events spiral is the wound of indignity, and its dominant force is indignation. Tragedy, then, is the consequence of a Man's total compulsion to evaluate himself Justly.

In the sense of having been initiated by the hero himself, the tale always reveals what has been called his " tragic flaw," a failing that is not peculiar to grand or elevated characters. Nor is it necessarily a weakness. The flaw, or crack in the character, is really nothing—and need be nothing—but his inherent unwillingness to remain passive in the face of what he conceives to be a challenge to his dignity, his image of his rightful status. Only the passive, only those who accept their lot without active retaliation, are "flawless." Most of us are in that category.

But there are among us today, as there always have been, those who act against the scheme of things that degrades them, and in the process of action everything we have accepted out of fear or insensitivity or ignorance is shaken before us and examined, and from this total onslaught by an individual against the seemingly stable cosmos surrounding us—from this total examination of the "unchangeable" environment—comes the terror and the fear that is classically associated with tragedy.

More important, from this total questioning of what has been previously unquestioned, we learn. And such a process is not beyond the common man. In revolutions around the world these past thirty years, he has demonstrated again and again this inner dynamic of all tragedy.

Insistence upon the rank of the tragic hero, or the so-called nobility of his character, is really but a clinging to the outward forms of tragedy. If rank or nobility of character was indispensable, then it would follow that the problems of those with rank were the particular problems of tragedy. But surely the right of one monarch to capture the domain from another no longer raises our passions, nor are our concepts of justice what they were to the mind of an Elizabethan king.

The quality in such plays that does shake us, however, derives from the underlying fear of being displaced, the disaster inherent in being torn away from our chosen image of what and who we are in this world. Among us today this fear is as strong, and perhaps stronger, than it ever was. In fact, it is the common man who knows this fear best.

Now, if it is true that tragedy is the consequence of a man's total compulsion to evaluate himself justly, his destruction in the attempt posits a wrong or an evil in his environment. And this is precisely the morality of tragedy and its lesson. The discovery of the moral law, which is what the enlightenment of tragedy consists of, is not the discovery of some abstract or metaphysical quantity.

The tragic right is a condition of life, a condition in which the human personality is able to flower and realize itself. The wrong is the condition which suppresses man, perverts the flowing out of his love and creative instinct. Tragedy enlightens—and it must, in that it points the heroic finger at the enemy of man's freedom. The thrust for freedom is the quality in tragedy which exalts. The revolutionary questioning of the stable environment is what terrifies. In no way is the common man debarred from such thoughts or such actions.

Seen in this light, our lack of tragedy may be partially accounted for by the turn which modern literature has taken toward the purely psychiatric view of life, or the purely socio-logical. If all our miseries, our indignities, are born and bred within our minds, then all action, let alone the heroic action, is obviously impossible.

And if society alone is responsible for the cramping of our lives, then the protagonist must needs be so pure and faultless as to force us to deny his validity as a character. From neither of these views can tragedy derive, simply because neither represents a balanced concept of life. Above all else, tragedy requires the finest appreciation by the writer of cause and effect.

No tragedy can therefore come about when its author fears to question absolutely everything, when he regards any institution, habit or custom immutable or inevitable. In the tragic view the need of man to wholly realize himself is the only fixed star, and whatever it is that hedges his nature and lowers it is ripe for attack and examination. Which is not to say that tragedy must preach revolution.

The Greeks could probe the very heavenly origin of their ways and return to confirm the rightness of laws. And Job could face God in anger, demanding his right, and end in submission. But for a moment everything is in suspension, nothing is accepted, and in this stretching and tearing apart of the cosmos, in the very action of so doing, the character gains "size," the tragic stature which is spuriously attached to the royal or the high born in our minds. The commonest of men may take on that stature to the extent of his willingness to throw all he has into the contest, the battle to secure his rightful place in his world.

There is a misconception of tragedy with which I have been struck in review after review, and in many conversations with writers and readers alike. It is the idea that tragedy is of necessity allied to pessimism. Even the dictionary says nothing more about the word than that it means a story with a sad or unhappy ending. This impression is so firmly fixed that I almost hesitate to claim that in truth tragedy implies more optimism than does comedy, and that its final result ought to be the reinforcement of the onlooker's brightest opinions of the human animal.

For, if it is true to say that in essence the tragic hero is intent on claiming his whole due as a personality, and if this struggle must be total and without reservation, then it automatically demonstrates the indestructible will of man to achieve his humanity.

The possibility of victory must be there in tragedy. Where pathos rules, where pathos is finally derived, a character has fought a battle he could not possibly have won. The pathetic is achieved when the protagonist is, by virtue of his witlessness, his insensitivity or the very air he gives off, incapable of grappling with a much superior force.

Pathos truly is the mode for the pessimist. But tragedy requires a nicer balance between what is possible and what is impossible. And it is curious, although edifying, that the plays we revere, century after century, are the tragedies. In them, and, in them alone, lies the belief—optimistic, if you will, in the perfectibility of man.

It is time, I think, that we who are without kings, took up this bright thread of our history and followed it to the only place it can possibly lead in our time—the heart and spirit of the average man.

This is Arthur Miller's view of tragedy in our time. His essay, like his play, was both praised and condemned. If you're stimulated by this clash of ideas, I urge you to search for more information and, if you want to join the debate, you couldn't start at a better place than by reading the tragedies of Arthur Miller.

NOTE

1. Arthur Miller, *The Theater Essays of Arthur Miller,*
   ed. by Robert A. Martin and Steven R. Centola.
   (New York: Da Capo Press, 1996).

INDEX